# ACROSS THE
# SOUTH PACIFIC

# ACROSS THE SOUTH PACIFIC

## Island-hopping from Santiago to Sydney

**Iain Finlay**
**and**
**Trish Sheppard**

Angus & Robertson Publishers

ANGUS & ROBERTSON PUBLISHERS
London • Sydney • Melbourne • Singapore • Manila

This book is copyright. Apart from any fair dealing for the
purposes of private study, research, criticism or review, as
permitted under the Copyright Act, no part may be reproduced
by any process without written permission. Inquiries should
be addressed to the publisher.

First published by Angus & Robertson Publishers, Australia, 1981

© Iain Finlay and Trish Sheppard, 1981

National Library of Australia
Cataloguing-in-publication data.

Finlay, Iain, 1935— .
    Across the South Pacific.

    ISBN 0 207 14824 4.

    1. Voyages and travels.   2. Pacific Ocean.
    I. Sheppard, Trish, 1942— .   II. Title.

910'.091648

Typeset in 9 pt Helios Medium & 9 pt English Times by
Setrite, Hong Kong

Printed in Hong Kong

*For Jan, who house-sat
and Brenda, who dog-sat*

# Authors' Note

Following the style we set in *Africa Overland*
and *South America Overland,* readers will once again
find that we have interspersed our points of view,
Iain's comments being in the bolder type

# CONTENTS

# PHOTOGRAPHS

Between pages 106 and 107

# MAPS

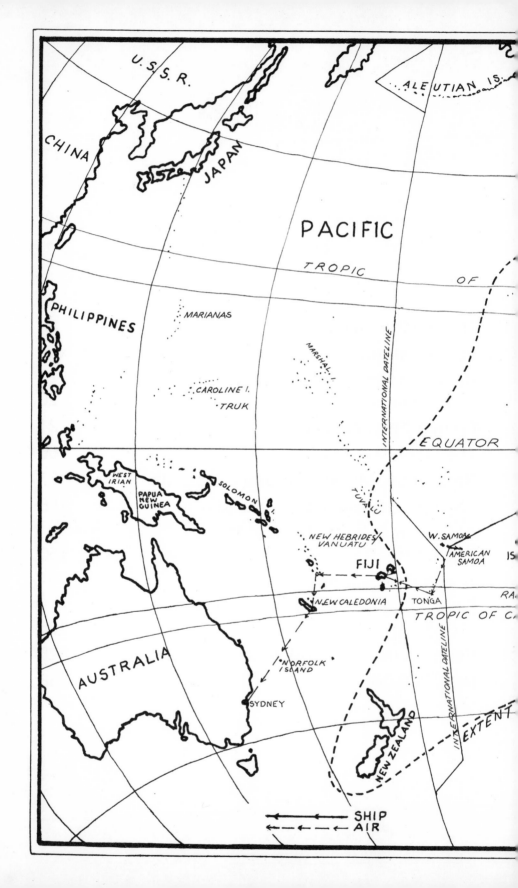

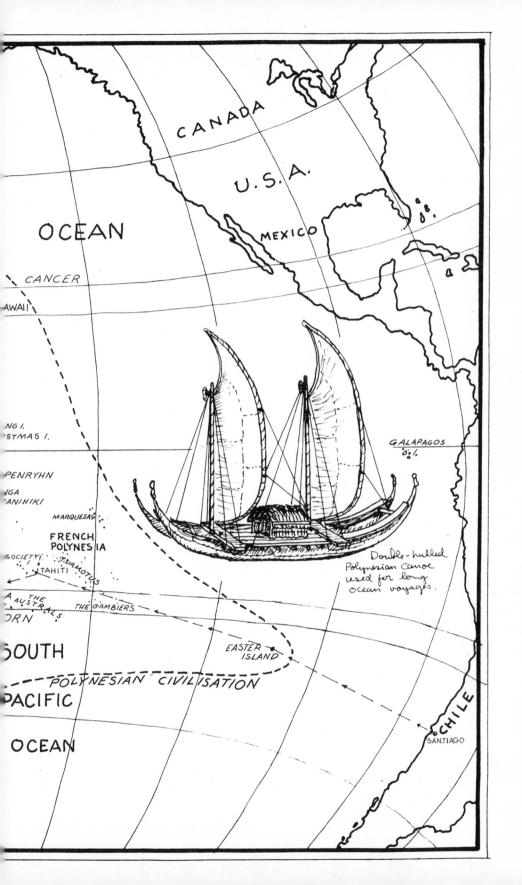

CANADA

U.S.A.

OCEAN

MEXICO

CANCER

AWAII

NG I.
'STMAS I.

GALAPAGOS
°.°.'

PENRYHN

NGA
'ANIHIKI

MARQUESAS

FRENCH
POLYNESIA

SOCIETY I.
TAHITI

TUAMOTUS

A THE
AUSTRALS

ORN

THE GAMBIERS

EASTER
ISLAND

SOUTH

POLYNESIAN CIVILISATION

PACIFIC

CHILE

SANTIAGO

OCEAN

Double-hulled
Polynesian canoe
used for long
ocean voyages.

# PREFACE

When the first European explorers sailed into the Pacific Ocean, they met with something of a shock. Nearly all of the tiny specks of land they found sparsely dotted over the vast ocean (over 160 million square kilometres), were inhabited! And, what was even more astounding to these pale newcomers from the other side of the world, was the fact that the language and culture of all the tall, handsome, brown-skinned people they met, wherever they went, seemed to have common roots. Even people living on islands that were separated by thousands of kilometres of open sea spoke similar languages and used similar artifacts in their everyday life, for their religious ceremonies, for boat-building and for warfare. They were in fact the same people...the Polynesians.

But how had these pleasant and graceful people managed to sail such enormous distances to establish themselves in the Pacific? The first Western navigators quickly noted that the native sailors of the islands they visited had no compasses, no charts of a conventional nature and nothing remotely resembling a sextant. Europe's great ocean voyages of exploration were, by contrast, only undertaken *after* these aids to navigation were developed. When the Polynesians told those first European visitors that they navigated long distances with only the wind, the waves, the stars and the sea-birds to tell them their course, they were not believed.

Perhaps to an island group just over the horizon, the visitors thought, or even a journey of a couple of days, with luck, but a 4000 kilometre voyage from Tahiti to Hawaii, from the Southern Hemisphere to the Northern Hemisphere, *across* the prevailing winds and currents and then back again...on a quite frequent basis? There was no way Europeans could accept that. It was impossible, they said, without 'modern' instruments. And yet the evidence of solid, long-term contact was there; racial, cultural and linguistic.

How and when the Polynesians had populated the Pacific remained a mystery for centuries. The answers were all there, but it wasn't until the early part of this century that a really concerted effort was made to study them and to chart the progress of the great migratory expansion of Polynesian society. And only in the last decade have we achieved a reasonable understanding of the complex methods they used to accurately traverse such vast distances of open water.

To put the thing into context, Polynesia, which, as we've mentioned, includes people of the same race, culture and similar linguistic roots, sprawls over a huge triangle with Hawaii at its most northerly point, Easter Island in the southeastern corner and New Zealand in the southwestern corner. An area of some 56 million square kilometres, large enough to include all of the USSR, China, Canada, the United States and Australia combined!

We now know that the first human steps into the Pacific were taken by black-skinned people from New Guinea into the outlying islands of the Solomons, the New Hebrides and Fiji (what we know now as Melanesia), about 25 000 years ago.

Then, about 4500 years ago, the brown-skinned people of island Asia— the Philippines, Indonesia and Taiwan—reached out into Melanesia and beyond to uninhabited Tonga and Samoa. It's believed that these forebears of the Polynesians were isolated there, in the islands of Tonga and Samoa sufficiently long enough (about 2000 years or more), for them to develop the physical characteristics, the language and culture that Polynesians now have in common, before their first big expansion eastward across the Pacific.

This major step came about the time of Christ, when Tahiti, the Society Islands and the Marquesas were reached and colonised by the Polynesians. This was a 2500-kilometre spread which only seemed to whet their appetites. From the Island of Raiatea, which they called Havai'i and which became the spiritual home, a sacred centre for all Polynesians, they then launched into the truly epic ocean voyages which established the outer limits of their far-flung domain. The voyage to Easter Island, some 3800 kilometres to the southeast, a lonely, empty dot, just 20 kilometres long and the most isolated island in the South Pacific, which was reached in the face of prevailing winds and currents, must be one of the most remarkable feats of navigation in history, if not an extremely lucky accident.

By 500 AD, they had also pushed 4000 kilometres westward and south to New Zealand and 4000 kilometres north to Hawaii, the limits of their expansion. From then, for over a thousand years until the coming of the white man the Polynesian people ruled the Pacific, not as a unified society, a single empire or kingdom controlled from one centre or by one person, but as separate groups of people who, although living under different rulers, kings and chiefs, were nevertheless bound to each other by this extraordinary common heritage and the universality of their culture, customs and traditions.

Surprisingly and happily, we were to discover that this same bond is still there, still remarkably strong, despite the imposition, over the past two centuries, of foreign (European) rule and the Christian religion. A Maori from Rotorua, for instance, is technically a New Zealander, but put him down in the Cook Islands, Samoa, Tahiti, or even Hawaii and he is welcomed as a brother, a compatriot. Shuffle them all around, and the same thing applies. They all feel, even now in the 1980s, after all the years of being part of *French*

Polynesia, *American* Samoa, *American* Hawaii, *German* Samoa, *New Zealand* Cook Islands and so on, that they are 'island people', Polynesians first and whatever the overlaid nationality is, second. They sing the same songs, dance the same (or very similar) dances, and tell the same legends of their great past.

I think this was the most pleasing discovery for us on our own journey across the South Pacific, to 'discover' the Polynesian people and to a lesser extent (only through lack of time), the Melanesians of the western Pacific.

The islands themselves are, of course, beautiful, but it was the people who really made them for us. They are big, attractive and friendly people, the sort of people you feel really deserve to live in what is probably the closest thing to paradise on earth.

# INTRODUCTION

When we first began to think seriously about making a long, island-hopping journey across the South Pacific, we were living in a small stone cottage on a dairy farm in Somerset. We had just been through England's worst winter in two decades and the concept of sitting on a white, sandy beach beneath waving palm trees, sipping from a freshly-opened coconut while gazing across a blue lagoon, seemed so remote and fantastic as to be almost unbelievable.

This sense of the remoteness of the South Pacific was obviously shared by a large number of people, as I discovered through three phone calls I made in London prior to our eventual departure. The first was to the London office of the Banque National de Paris. I told the man in the Foreign Department that I wanted to find out about having some money transferred to me in Tahiti.

'Tahiti?'...(pause)...'now, is that getting out towards the Far East... Singapore...that sort of thing, or would that be in the Pacific?'

Next I put the same question to an equivalent officer of the Standard Chartered Bank.

'Tahiti?' he said, '...that's not Fiji, is it?'

And then, thinking that perhaps the Americans might be a little more 'with it', I called the London Head Office of the Citibank Corporation to see if it might not be easier to have the money sent ahead to Pago Pago, in American Samoa.

'Samoa...?' the man's voice was cautious. 'Where's that?'

'In the South Pacific.'

'Oh, I thought Samoa was in Indonesia, or the Philippines...out that way somewhere.'

Those are real comments. I was so surprised at the time that I wrote them down. But, although I include them here to illustrate what I feel is a widespread ignorance of the Pacific in most people, particularly people from Europe, it would be wrong for me to patronise or imply any real criticism, because we too were ignorant of many things about the Pacific before this trip and, while we learnt a great deal during the course of our travels from one side of the Pacific to the other, each new discovery only revealed how much more there was to know about this vast ocean which occupies *one-third* of the entire surface of the earth.

When I was 18 I performed in my one and only stage role as one of Bloody Mary's girls in an amateur production of *South Pacific*. Wrapped in a chaste version of a Tahitian *pareu,* the English whiteness of my goosefleshed skin disguised with lashings of instant suntan cream, I sang, 'I'm gonna wash that man right outa my hair' and promptly fell in love with the leading man, who was called Jeremy! Perhaps it was his bold-patterned Hawaiian shirt, the like of which I had never seen before and which was excitingly out of place in that grey part of the world.

The love affair died, as such exotic blooms will in the coldness of reality (when last heard of, Jeremy was managing a family store in Birmingham), but the allure of the South Pacific lingered. And now here I was, with Iain and the children, in Santiago and about to zig-zag our way across 20 000 kilometres of ocean to Sydney.

On the wall maps of my youth the Pacific Ocean was dismissed almost contemptuously as the seam in the world's surface: the point at which, with the one-eyed xenophobia of Europeans, we pushed the world off the map. In this manner the Pacific was invariably split into two manageable halves and appeared as merely a blue border lapping down the west coast of South America and surfing up the east coast of Australia.

It was only when the map was taken off the wall and rolled around so that the seam was joined that the truly majestic proportions of this body of water were perceived. In one gulp the Pacific Ocean could swallow up Europe, Africa, Asia, Australia and North and South America, plus etceteras like Antarctica, and then go on to breakfast.

And yet the thousands of islands and tiny atolls which manage to poke their heads above the surface of this enormous watery mass add up to a land area of only 100 000 square kilometres. The whole lot could be contained almost twice over in the British Isles, or in the State of Victoria!

To make this island-hopping journey we decided that, as with our two previous journeys (which we have described in our two previous books, *Africa Overland* and *South America Overland*), we would all carry backpacks. That way the children could carry their own gear and all of us would have our hands free to hang on, or push off, according to the demands of the situation!

Buying the few pieces of lightweight casual clothing we would need posed a few problems in England in September. But we managed to get what we wanted. Then we decided that this time we would also take along a couple of two-person tents. They had to be as light, but also as strong as possible and, on their trial run, Iain gave them a heavy going-over with extra waterproofing. . .the seams in particular.

As it turned out, our dreams of sleeping under the coconut trees on fine white-sand beaches were fulfilled very rarely because camping is heavily frowned on by the powers that be in most of the island groupings we visited. Camping and backpacks are for them synonymous with hippies and drugs. Naturally enough they are wary of being 'discovered' by the international drifters set.

Along with the few clothes and the two tents, we took our tried and trusty 'Primus' camp stove and our 'just-in-case' small medical kit. Iain was in charge of the cameras and film. All up, the kids' packs weighed in at about 10 kilos each, mine at around 16 and Iain's at a spine-bending 25 kilos.

Feeling conspicuously like new chums, our hearts a-flutter with a mixture of anticipation, excitement and anxiety, we shouldered our way through the commuters along the Upper Richmond Road to East Putney tube station. The Pacific then seemed infinitely remote.

From Heathrow we embarked on the cheapest route possible with that real friend of all travellers, Sir Freddie Laker, to Miami. A few days of sunshine to acclimatise ourselves and then the long hop down to Chile.

We had decided on Chile as the starting point for our journey across the Pacific for the simple reason that there was no other way to get to our first stop, Easter Island, unless we'd been coming from the opposite direction. We'd set our minds on getting to Easter Island, I suppose just because it *is* such a remote and unique place, even though to include it was going to make the trip considerably more expensive.

We'd already accepted the fact that, unlike the previous surface transport journeys we'd made through Africa and South America, much of the Pacific trip would of necessity be by air. The Easter Island sector was a case in point. It is served by only one Chilean supply ship a year and everything else goes in by air. The Chilean National airline is the only carrier flying the 3800-kilometre leg from Santiago to the Island and they charge pretty exorbitant fares (around $400). Sean was at this stage not quite 12 so he still qualified for a child fare, but Zara, at 13, was required to pay full price.

Our sense of comparative displeasure over having to make such a large outlay right at the beginning of the trip was compensated somewhat by a fortunate meeting with Gustavo Gutierrez of Sernatur, the National Tourist Office in Santiago where we went seeking information about accommodation on Easter Island and the possibility of camping there. Gustavo was a small man in his mid-30s with an Abraham Lincoln beard. He was a bundle of energy, yet at the same time urbane and gracious. He invited us to have dinner at his home in Oriente, one of the suburbs of Santiago and to meet his wife Paula, who was eight months pregnant with their first child, but still lecturing daily on tourism at a government training centre. We talked about Easter Island and Gustavo gave us the names of several people to contact there.

'I wish we were going with you', he said as we ate an excellent pizza and drank Chilean 'Cristal' beer. 'You know, I once sailed on a yacht across the Pacific to Samoa...and then lived there for a year!'

He spoke perfect English with a slight American accent—he had lived in the United States for some time. He had apparently also hitch-hiked twice from the States overland to Chile...and had once camped in the mountains around Machu Picchu, the 'Lost City of the Incas', in Peru for a month...all of which had Zara and Sean listening in rapt attention.

'I like him', Zara said later as we lay in bed in our small residencia, talking softly as we dropped off to sleep, '...he's so adventurous.'

It was the night before our flight to Easter Island and the beginning of what was to be for us, too, a real adventure. As it happened, the adventure started a little earlier than expected. Shortly before 4.00 a.m. we were awoken by the sound of rattling and rumbling. The whole room and all the furniture was shaking. In a second I was wide awake and sitting bolt upright in bed.

'What is it?' Trish whispered.

'An earthquake', I said, throwing off the covers as the shaking quietened and stopped.

The tremors didn't return, but we lay uneasily awake for some time wondering if perhaps we might *not* be aboard a plane bound for Easter Island in the morning, but lying under a heap of rubble.

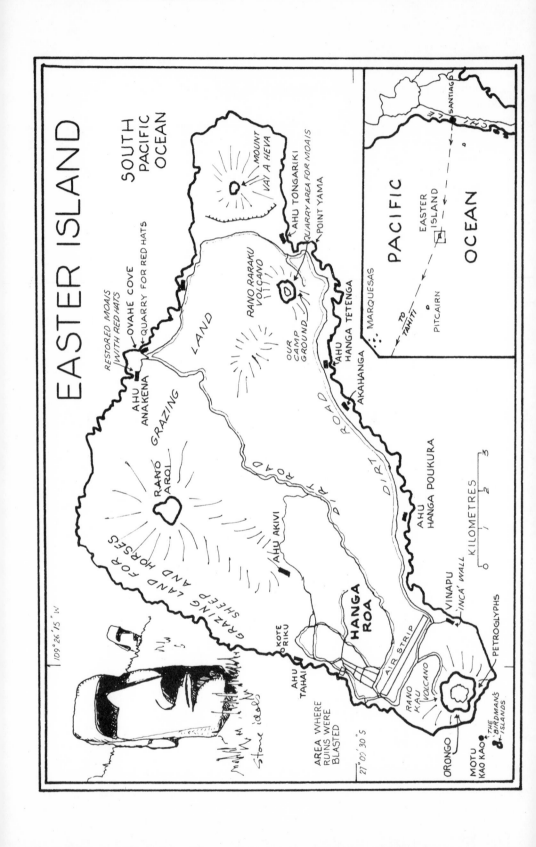

# EASTER ISLAND

SOUTH PACIFIC OCEAN

MOUNT VAI A HEVA

RESTORED MOAIS WITH RED HATS
OVAHE COVE
QUARRY FOR RED HATS

AHU TONGARIKI
QUARRY AREA FOR MOAIS
POINT YAMA

AHU ANAKENA

GRAZING LAND

RANO RARAKU VOLCANO

OUR CAMP GROUND

AHU HANGA TETENGA

AHU AKAHANGA

RANO AROI

DIRT ROAD

DIRT ROAD

GRAZING LAND FOR SHEEP AND HORSES

AHU AKIVI

AHU HANGA POUKURA

KOTE RIKU

HANGA ROA

AHU TAHAI

AREA WHERE RUINS WERE BLASTED

27° 05' 30" S

AIR STRIP

VINAPU 'INCA' WALL

PETROGLYPHS

RANO KAU VOLCANO

ORONGO

MOTU KAO KAO

THE BIRDMAN'S ISLANDS

109° 26' 15" W

Stone idols

KILOMETRES
0    1    2    3

PACIFIC

SANTIAGO

MARQUESAS

TO TAHITI

PITCAIRN

EASTER ISLAND

OCEAN

# 1 RAPA NUI
## 'One of the world's greatest mysteries'

'If it is too rough to land we must turn around and go back.' I gave up anxiously scanning the vast trackless expanse of ocean far below for sight of land and turned my attention to Hernan Rodrigues, the man sitting in the aisle seat of the plane next to Iain and me.

'Almost 4000 kilometres back to Santiago.' He rolled his eyes. 'And instead of landing they sometimes decide to overfly and go straight on another 4000 kilometres to Tahiti.'

I rolled *my* eyes and, misreading their message, he assured me 'It is alright. They carry enough fuel for such events.'

I tried explaining in my halting Spanish that I was less worried about the fuel than the prospect of bad weather forcing us to overfly Easter Island. We had been warned that this was a not unusual occurrence and that due to the difficulties of trying to accurately forecast what the weather conditions would be at a particular tiny spot in the middle of a vast body of water, it was impossible to be certain of being able to land until the plane was more or less flying over the strip. The disappointment of not landing, after making the considerable detour from the usual routes in order to start our Pacific journey on this remote island, would be so intense that we would have preferred to turn back to Santiago and have another chance at it. After all it's not the sort of spot about which you can feel, 'well never mind, we'll include it the next time through.'

'I too shall be very disappointed if we cannot land.' Hernan loosened his tie. 'I have, well, I have people to see and things to do.' He took off his tie and rolling it up put it in the pocket of his dark jacket which he had discarded some little time before.

When Hernan had introduced himself five hours before as we left Santiago he had looked what he said he was: a married man (perhaps in his late 40s) with three teenage children and on a business trip to Easter Island to check the underwater piping installation his company was constructing at the small port facility. Now, with his jacket and tie off, he began to take on a different air. He unbuttoned the cuffs of his cream silk shirt and turned back the sleeves a little. Aware that I noticed all this, he smiled engagingly, looking now 10 years younger and positively handsome. 'The islanders are very friendly,' he said. It sounded like an explanation.

'There it is! There!' He leaned across us and with obvious excitement began to point out various landmarks. We made a wide sweep over the island and headed back toward the minute strip. 'The wind is from the west. See the chop on the waves. It will be a rough one, but we will be able to land.'

Hernan was right. It was a very rough, nasty landing, but we had hardly stopped bouncing over the runway when he was on his feet, shirt unbuttoned two extra stops, jacket swung casually over his shoulder. 'Get in touch with me if you need anything,' he offered and then grinning broadly, his eyes sparkling, he was off down the aircraft steps. By the time we had struggled out after him, he had run across the little airfield to the small crowd of waiting people from which a truly beautiful young woman stepped forward. Smiling, she hung round his neck several garlands of flowers which were promptly crushed in his enthusiastic embrace. The girl was at least eight months pregnant.

Mataveri Airport is of the tiny snap-it-together-yourself variety. Outside the one all-purpose room at the edge of the strip are a number of stalls selling wooden carvings of mythological creatures and of course, the familiar Easter Island statues. We began to ask around among the stall holders if they knew of any inexpensive places to stay. It takes a little while, when we first get on the road again, to get back into the swing of all this and it was not an auspicious start. There seemed to be only one hotel which was run by the Chilean government and charged $120 a double! Shock. Horror. What about residencias? Private homes which took in paying guests? Yes, there were a couple but they charged 50 to 60 dollars a double. Food was on top of that and, as we were to discover, it was also astronomically expensive.

We had just started to ask about where the best place would be for us to put up our tents when we were approached by a woman who garlanded us with bead necklaces, gave us the Chilean embrazo (the quick touching of cheek to cheek) and introduced herself as Maria de Rapu, a friend of Gustavo Guttierez. Gustavo had phoned ahead from Santiago to say we were coming and we were invited to stay in Maria's residencia, Apina Nui. Already we were beginning to feel the hospitality and generosity which was to be so much a part of our island experiences.

From the window of our room in Maria's simple house we looked down over Hanga Roa, a straggling township where almost all the 2000 people on the island live. Their stone and wood homes are very simple with fairly basic facilities. None of it has any of the look or feel of a South Pacific island, but rather of an isolated and rather neglected outpost of a South American community. The few roads are not sealed, not even in the township and there are no street lights. But there are about 40 cars, none of which have licence plates because everyone knows to whom each one belongs and anyway, there are no traffic regulations to infringe.

Late in the afternoon, excited at the prospect of our first view of the ancient and gigantic stone figures of Easter Island, or moais, as they are called, we walked down through Hanga Roa across what looked like recent excavations (more of that later) and through the tiny churchyard where the cows chewed the cud between the lopsided headstones.

A kilometre or so on the other side of the village we could see a group of the *moai* outlined against the lowering sky. This site is called Ahu Tahai and is the result of years of work by the American archaeologist William Mulloy, who originally accompanied Thor Heyerdahl on his first visits to the island in the 1950s and who stayed on to devote the rest of his life to this work. He died in 1978 and is buried under a simple mark overlooking his work.

Even from this distance the moais exude great presence. They are imbued with much *mana,* a word used here, as well as in the other islands of the South Pacific, to signify as nearly as possible the inexpressible idea of strength and power above the normal.

The seven moais at Ahu Tahai, the tallest of them 9.8 metres high, stand with their backs to the seas as if determined to ignore this constant reminder of their isolation. It's been suggested that at the peak of its civilisation the island's entire coastline was ringed with groups of moais, spaced at intervals of a kilometre or so. If this was the case, then the claustrophobic effect of being under inescapable scrutiny must have been all pervasive.

It was while we were standing there, almost as if having to summon up the courage to go closer, that we spotted a little fat-tyred, three-wheel motorcycle wheeling towards us. It was driven by Hernan and clinging on behind him was his pregnant lady whom he later introduced as his wife, Christine Paula. He won Sean's undying gratitude by offering him a spin on the grown-up tricycle. While Sean, with whoops of delight, careened around over the broken, stony ground, Hernan kept his arm protectively around his madonna-beautiful Christine Paula. She smiled enigmatically as he smoothed her swollen belly and talked with boyish enthusiasm of the baby which was expected any day.

'She is a real islander,' Hernan explained with pride, while Christine Paula remained silent, seemingly content to let him do all the talking. 'She can trace her family back six generations. She is heir to all this.' His wide gesture embraced the whole visible coastline and the parade of moais. 'And he will be too,' he patted the baby-to-be, proprietorially certain of its maleness.

When they left, jolting away on their very twentieth-century vehicle, we went down to the cliff edge in a walk back through time to come face-to-face with the ancient statues. They are just as impressive close up. Their vacant, expressionless faces give them an aura of sneering, uncaring contempt for mere mortals which only those beyond the reach of untidy human emotions can attain.

As we sat at their feet and watched the horizon roll on around out of reach of the sun's warmth and light, I was very glad to have been born with a void where my soul should be. . .to be untrammeled by the taboos and demands of such omnivorous gods. Even so, they still gave me the shivers!

Easter Island remains one of the world's great mysteries. Even now, more than two and a half centuries since its discovery by Europeans and after decades of scientific and archaeological research, no definite answer has emerged as to how or why a civilisation and culture of such astonishing complexity emerged on an island so totally isolated from the rest of the world. No other inhabited place on the earth's surface is more remote from other areas of human habitation than is Easter Island.

It is the tip of an ancient undersea volcano. . .or rather, three big volcanoes and a series of little ones which rose from the sea millions of years ago to break the surface of the water in the vast reaches of the eastern Pacific, leaving a small, lonely dot, 160 square kilometres in area, in 2.5

million square kilometres of otherwise empty ocean. That primitive man should have landed on this isolated speck of real estate is incredible enough in itself, but the fact that over the centuries, these people went on to develop the most advanced and complex society in the Pacific, with unequalled technological and artistic skills, is a source of unending fascination and puzzlement to all who visit the island.

The puzzlement, the mystery of Easter Island, comes from the fact that although it was inhabited by between two and three thousand natives at the time of first European contact (on Easter Sunday, 1722, when the Dutch nagivator Admiral Jacob Roggeveen arrived to spend three or four days there), none of the islanders could explain the origins of the huge stone figures which were spread in hundreds all over their island. Yet it was clear to Roggeveen and his sailors and to the string of other Pacific navigators (including Captain Cook) who followed, that these massive monoliths were the work of master stonemasons from a highly-developed civilisation. The degree of organisation required in any society to have allowed for the diversion away from agriculture of large numbers of people to such mammoth public works projects; the quarrying and sculpting of stone figures up to 10 metres high and 80 tonnes in weight and then their transportation for distances of up to 10 kilometres to the sites where they were erected, would have been considerable. These were feats comparable to those of the ancient Egyptians or, more significantly, of the Incas.

But this amazing civilisation had risen and fallen hundreds of years before the arrival of Western explorers, leaving only these colossal stone sentinels as its legacy. Some researchers believe that in its heyday, the inhabitants of Easter Island numbered between 40 and 50 thousand, yet those descendants who were there when Roggeveen arrived knew practically nothing of their own history. A few traditions that were pointers to a way of life, a few tales passed down from generation to generation by word of mouth, but nothing significant. They had even completely forgotten how to read their own 'Rongo-Rongo' writing, which was discovered on numerous stone tablets on the island and is now famous (though still as yet undeciphered) as the only written language of the Pacific.

They had several names for their island home. Most common was 'Rapa Nui', the name still used by the inhabitants today. It means 'Big Paddle' and is possibly some reference to the long sea voyage which brought the first arrivals to the island. It was also known as 'Tei-Pito-Te-Huena', meaning 'The Navel of the World' and there are references in early books to it being called 'The Island of Great Silence'.

Archaeological research has done a great deal to make the story of the first Easter Islanders more clear, but there are still many unanswered questions. One of the major areas of disagreement amongst anthropologists is over the question, 'where did they come from?' Most scientists believe that the first Easter Islanders came from the West...Polynesia. But in the 1950s Thor Heyerdahl presented convincing arguments to support his theories that Easter Island and indeed other parts of Polynesia and the Pacific were populated from the East, that is from South America—notably Peru and Ecuador. But the weight of evidence is in favour of Polynesian origin. Their language and what remains of their traditions are unmistakably similar to those of the people of the Marquesas, some 3500 kilometres to the northwest, whose own origins are definitely from other parts of Polynesia even further westward.

Yet much of the Easter Islanders' pottery and their small idols and carvings bore the stamp of pre-Columbian South America and their stone work in some parts of the island is almost classic Inca; magnificent walls of beautifully-worked stones, keyed together perfectly. Even during our visit to Easter Island, significant new evidence of Peruvian influence was unearthed by archaeologists. So the consensus now seems to be that the original people of Easter Island came from both directions. The main source was probably Polynesia with South America providing a secondary, but technologically and artistically important stimulus. There is no way of knowing who was first, but it's a safe bet that, whichever direction they came from, their arrival (around 300 or 400 A.D.) on that lonely speck of land was extremely fortuitous.

It probably presented a more welcoming picture then that it does now. Now it appears desolate and barren. Shaped roughly like a triangle with extinct volcanoes in each corner, the island is virtually treeless. It is covered instead by grass, ideal grazing land for some 10 000 sheep, bred originally from Australian stock, and roughly 4000 wild horses.

You can hire horses to get around, but to cover the distance over which the hundreds of statues are spread would take weeks so, on the morning after our arrival, we joined with three other people to share in the hire of a small mini-bus. We'd been told that to see the most important of the sites, even by car, would take at least a couple of days. Maria de Rapu, our hostess at the residencia, organised it all. Her cousin, Juan Atan, would drive us and her brother-in-law, Victor Briones, could be guide.

The three other passengers were guests at the government-run Hotel Hanga Roa. They wanted to cover roughly the same ground. They were two Australians, Tom and Jenny Moxon and an elderly Frenchman, André Herbert. Tom ran a timber business in Brisbane and he and his wife had just completed a business trip to Brazil where they had bought timber. Herbert, as he preferred to be called, was a retired doctor from Rouen, who had been just about everywhere in the world. Patagonia?...'But of course.' Antarctica?...'Certainment.' India, Africa, Alaska, China, Siberia...even Ayres Rock and the Olgas: 'I have also been...how you call it...up a gum-tree!' He was short, with a steel-grey crew cut—quiet for most of the time, but given, as we soon discovered, to sudden verbal outbursts of enthusiasm.

Our travels together began with a drive up the sloping sides of Rano Kau, the volcano which sits at the southwestern corner of the island only a couple of kilometres from the township. Leaving the vehicle, we climbed to the rim where we stood and gazed into the crater. It is filled with swampy water and reeds which are apparently of the same genus as those which grow profusely in Lake Titicaca, which borders Peru and Bolivia.

Turning outwards the view is spectacular, for here the volcano's outer rim plunges almost vertically hundreds of metres into the sea. And in this dramatic setting early Easter Islanders built into the rocky hillside a string of strange, low, stone houses which could only be entered on hands and knees. Nearby, they carved numerous intricate symbolic pictures, or petroglyphs, into the rocks on the edges of the vertical cliffs. Orongo, as the site is called, was evidently a sacred centre at a time when the islanders worshipped a birdman, a figure with the body of a man and the head of a bird.

Legend has it that the leadership of this birdman cult could only be won by an extraordinary annual feat of physical prowess—a race between the strongest men in the tribe. The race began on the top of the cliffs by the rim of the volcano and all who competed had to descend the sheer, 200-metre-high cliff face, hurl themselves into the ocean, swim out to a craggy pinnacle of rock, a nesting place for thousands of birds, which juts from the waves about a kilometre off shore, take an egg from one of the nests, swim back to the cliffs, re-climb them and arrive at the top with the egg still intact. The winner became king for a year.

'Plenty die,' Victor said with a smile. 'Fall off cliffs...sharks...and sometimes they get back to the top, but egg is cracked.'

We didn't bother to ask how he spoke with such authority, but leaning over the cliff edge to look down, one could well imagine that there would have been quite a few casualties.

Following the volcano rim back to our vehicle, we took off next to a place called Vinapu, a few kilometres to the east. All of the sites on the island which have any archaeological significance or importance have names, even though they may appear to be nothing but a jumble of stones. The terrain at most of the sites is just rolling brown grassland running down to a foreshore of black, broken volcanic rocks. But at Vinapu as you walk across the fields towards what looks like a ruined wall, you begin to feel a sense of awe, for you are suddenly confronted with a piece of stonework of consumate artistry.

It is an *Ahu*, the base for half a dozen or so of the great statues, the moais like those we had seen the previous evening. But here, as at most of the Ahu sites around the island, the giant figures have been toppled facefirst into the ground...the result of a legendary war long ago, between two tribes, the 'Long Ears' and the 'Short Ears', which researchers believe precipitated the decline and fall of Easter Island's advanced civilisation. But even though the statues of Ahu Tahiri at Vinapu are toppled over, it is the broad base on which they stood that excites the most interest. The huge stone blocks have been cut with such precision and fitted together without mortar, but with such accuracy that they can only be compared to the magnificent stonework of the Incas in Peru.

Later in the afternoon, after a lunch of fish and egg soup back at our residencia, we headed off again in the bus, this time towards the centre of the island to explore a number of caves. Driving across open grassland, following rough, dusty tracks, we came to a bunch of greenery; shrubs and small trees growing from a depression in the ground. Clambering down through the bushes and stunted fig and banana trees, we entered a hole which led into a vast network of caves.

'This island is like honeycomb,' Victor said, shining his flashlight around the walls. 'Hundreds of caves...many never explored.'

We moved through from chamber to chamber following easily defined paths. There were no cave paintings or constructions, but ample other evidence of habitation in several of the caves in the form of human bones and skulls.

'There are still secret caves,' Victor stopped and turned around in the darkness, flashing the light from side to side, '...secrets which only the islanders know and will not tell.'

I remembered reading that in the early days of European occupation and control of the island, the local inhabitants had taken and hidden great collections of artefacts, carvings in wood and stone and hundreds, maybe thousands of pieces of rongo-rongo writing. Only a fraction of this archaeological treasure has ever emerged from its secret repositories.

Back above ground again we felt the impact of the mid-afternoon heat but the air was fresh and clean and as we walked to the vehicle, there was a great sense of space—of openness and isolation. From where we stood, the ground rolled down and away from us presenting clear views of the dark, blue sea in the distance to the west, the south and to the east, a great sweep of unbroken horizon.

'Why do the islanders still keep these secrets?' I asked Victor as we walked. 'Surely these things represent a part of their history they could be proud of...that should be known and understood.'

He shrugged his shoulders. 'Who knows...perhaps they feel it is all they have that ties them to their ancestors. A secret is a much greater bond than something in the open, you know.'

'My great-great-grandfather bought Easter Island for £2000.' Edmundo Edwards, taking a long draw on yet another cigarette, which he had lit from the butt of the last one, looked pleased with our exclamations of surprise and interest.

When we had arrived back at Maria's, physically tired by the hours of severe jolting over stony, dirt tracks, there was an invitation from Edmundo to spend the evening at his place. We had heard about Edmundo from Maria, from Victor, from Juan...from just about everyone, once we started asking questions about the island's history. 'You should meet Edmundo,' they all said. But it seemed that once more it was the thoughtfulness of Gustavo, our friend in Santiago, which had made it happen.

'Gustavo tells me that you are writing a book,' Edmundo had said when we arrived at his modest, comfortable home on the edge of the township. 'He phoned to say that I would enjoy meeting you.'

Edmundo's darkly attractive 27-year-old wife, Gloria, an architectural student who was writing a thesis on the history of housing on the island and the type of accommodation most suitable for the present day, excused herself and went off to work in a further part of the house. Edmundo settled in to his favourite pastime, talking about Easter Island. For him the rest of the world hardly exists. He has about him that slightly other-worldly air which surrounds anyone who is deeply in love. His passion has lasted for far longer than many who are devoted to merely another human being!

Edmundo, who was 36, first came to the island when he was 13 and, apart from a brief return to Santiago to finish his education and then to lose all his worldly possessions in the 1973 coup which toppled President Allende, he has spent almost the whole of his adult life on the island.

As he says, 'It's in my blood. From a very early age I used to hear about how my great-great-grandfather had bought the island, or anyway lent the money to the bankrupt Chilean government to buy it. The money was never returned so I suppose that, technically, the family still owns it! Chile only wanted to buy it to stop the French from moving in. They were expanding out from Tahiti.

'In those days,' Edmundo went on, 'there was a scheme for it to become an important naval base and fuelling station on the then important routes between Sydney and Valparaiso and also on through Panama to the vast marketplace of Europe. But as we all know the Indian Ocean and Suez proved a more profitable way to go, so the Chileans were stuck with their remote island, which proved to be, and still is, a tremendous financial burden.'

Edmundo took us through into a small back room crammed with the paraphernalia of writing. Opening one drawer of a sizeable metal filing cabinet, he played his fingers across the densely packed cards covered in neat typing, much as a card sharp might flamboyantly display his dexterity. 'These are the basis for my book.' He pushed shut the drawer and motioned to the rows of others. 'These all contain the personal stories of nearly all the islanders and the oral histories they have told me.

'When I first came here, I worked with William Mulloy on his excavations. I would spend months camping at the various sites and living with the people. Because of my family's connection with the island, they accepted me. They have been so badly treated by the Chileans over hundreds of years, that they dislike and distrust them. But for me it is different. I speak Rapa Nui better than I speak Spanish. They accept me as one of them.'

He took down a large clip-ring file and opened it to reveal pages of well-typed manuscript. 'This is their story. There has been a great deal written about the island's ancient history; where the original inhabitants came from, European discovery, the wars between the "Big" and "Small Ears", the Peruvian Blackbirders who stole the islanders and took them back to work as slaves on the mainland, so diminishing the population that all the present islanders are descended from a mere 15 couples.' He paused. 'There is also the competition between the French and Spanish, the British and even the Americans for control... but there it stops. And that's where I pick it up. A history from the 1880s to the 1940s. All of it told by people alive today. Fascinating stuff.'

'But why not go right up to the present day?' Iain asked. Edmundo closed the file. 'I can't. I've been warned off. The junta in Santiago have said that if I tell anything about what has happened here in the last 40 years... out.'

'Out?'

'Back to Chile. And then who knows where.'

'But they can't do that,' I insisted naively. 'Easter Island is Chilean territory and you are a Chileno... so...'

Edmundo smiled at my notions of Chilean democracy. 'The junta,' he said, 'can do anything it wants. Anything. There are no channels of dissension or even complaint. Right now that is how Chilenos want it. Their brief flirtation with Marxism was enough to persuade them that this is preferable.'

'But what happened here that is so bad that it needs this cover-up?'

Edmundo lit another cigarette. 'Well, for a start, as recently as the '60s, the place was run like a military naval station and for any slight infringement of rules, or merely at the whim of the mainland-appointed governor, the people were publicly lashed and beaten.

'Just to give you an idea about the calibre of the men sent as governors, we have recently had a new one appointed, Marine Commander Governor Gonzalez Ariel. He, of course, had to leave his mark, like all his predecessors. This one decided that his would take the form of a football ground down by the cliffs, almost in the middle of town. Fine. The kids need a playing field. There's little enough for them to do here, except of course watch TV, which is flown in on video tape from Santiago and serves only to disorientate them still further. Ariel wants the job done, but fast, so when they come across a few big rocks which are in the way, he has them dynamited. The blast reveals a couple of deeply buried moais and part of a complex system of walls which seem to be those of an ancient temple. So what does he do? Carries on blasting away! That is, until I phoned the minister of the interior in Santiago and told him that unless he ordered an immediate halt to this desecration, I would tell the world's press what was happening. Our leaders are very sensitive to world opinion, which couldn't sink much lower.'

'So it was stopped?'

'Oh yes. But of course it doesn't improve my popularity with the governor or the junta.'

Back in the living room, Edmundo told stories about his childhood in Santiago which would make a good book in themselves. Raised by an English nanny in an all English-speaking family, he did not discover that he was Chilean and that Chilenos speak Spanish until he was 12! 'It took me years to get over the fact that I was not English. My father and my grandfather before him had gone to Oxford. It was assumed that I would go too. But then I discovered that, not only were we not English, we were not rich either. My great-great-grandfather, the one who bought this island, owned banks and insurance companies and railways and was very, very rich. My great-grandfather, grandfather and father simply spent it all for him, so that by the time it got to me there was nothing left.'

And yet more stories followed about his beloved island in the course of which we discovered that Hernan's beautiful pregnant lady, Christine Paula, was the great-granddaughter of a woman, who in the 1850s, was declared the queen of Easter Island. A French adventurer, called Dutrou Bornier, lured to Tahiti by traveller's tales of easy love and power, found that he was 50 years at least too late. All the princesses were spoken for and all the kingdoms occupied. Undismayed he moved on to Easter Island and married an island girl, called her his queen and set up his realm here. It was shortlived.

Two hours and 20 cigarettes later, we were still listening rapt to Edmundo's love story when Gloria came in to say that she was off to bed. It was a hint for us to leave and, as we stood up, she smiled gratefully. 'He would talk all night but he has to work tomorrow. He must take around a group of American amateur archaeologists. They may be amateurs but they have studied the island for a long time from a distance and they will ask very searching questions.'

Hardly an onerous task for Edmundo, I thought. It seemed he couldn't talk enough about his island!

Edmundo apologised for not being able to show us around the place himself and asked where we planned to go on the next day.

'Anakena and Ranu Raraku. We want to camp out there.'

'Ah. Wonderful. Wonderful. Now,' he pulled a piece of paper towards him, 'for many months I have camped on that volcano. Here,' he put a cross, 'this is the best spot. The moais will guard you all night and in the morning you must be up and see the sun rise across the crater.'

During the night there was heavy rain, but when I awoke at about 5.45 the next morning, the sky was clear and there was a freshness in the air. I too felt unusually fresh and wide awake. The window and curtains of our small room were wide open so that, without moving, I could see the sky outside gradually turning pink. Trish was still asleep and I could hear no sound from Zara and Sean in the room next to us, so I slipped out of bed and, after pulling on a pair of shorts and a shirt, climbed through the window and walked quickly across the damp patio, and down the track towards the shore.

For some minutes the sky grew brilliant red, then, as the sun began to rise over the hills, it faded slowly back to grey then blue. Sitting on the rocky beach, I could see the houses of the little settlement spread around the small bay in front of me. There was absolute silence, except for the sound of the waves on the rocks. I saw no movement. I felt alone. I tried to imagine what it must have been like for those islanders who lived here hundreds of years ago to have know that they *were* so totally alone...so completely isolated, by thousands of kilometres of sea, from any other humans...or did they even know for sure that there *were* other humans out there? Did they even consider it? Maybe they just felt that they were the only human beings on earth and that, as their name for it implied, their little island really was the centre...the Navel of the World.

And yet, as small and alone as the island was (and still is) in the surrounding ocean, those few inhabitants could still fight desperately destructive wars between themselves, killing each other by the hundreds and destroying their own environment on a terrifying scale. One can't help thinking that, in this respect, Easter Island is like a tiny microcosm of earth itself.

'They were all quite young,' Herbert muttered, turning one of the skulls over in his hands, examining the teeth. We were in another series of caves, only this time along the southern shore of the island at a place called Hanga Poukura. Victor had picked us up after breakfast and, with our companions of the previous day, we had begun the morning by viewing some gruesome relics of a past massacre.

'...and yes, they certainly died violently,' Herbert continued, poking his finger into the large hole in the skull he was holding. He pointed to others that lay about on the floor of the cave. 'You see, they all have the holes in the head.'

Sean felt his own head and looked at Herbert without saying anything.

'Not very nice, eh?' Herbert smiled.

Everywhere we went that morning, we saw the results of that excessively violent period of the island's past. Along the dusty coastal track we came to site after site; Vaihu, Akahanga, Hanga Tetenga, where rows of huge statues...usually six or seven at a time, had long ago been hurled down, pushed forward off their pedestals to be half-buried, face-down in the ground. These great figures, which in their day had inspired awe and reverence in their beholders were now, in their fallen state, somehow sad and degraded.

I couldn't help being reminded of the even more enormous statue of Rameses II we had seen some years previously in Egypt's Valley of the Kings, where it too lies shattered in the sand as a symbol of lost power and inspiration only for Shelley's 'Ozymandias': '...Look on my works ye Mighty and despair!'

The most widely-held theory about the destruction of the Easter Island monoliths seems also to revolve around despair...not in the sense of fear...but in a loss of faith in the ability of these great stone moais to protect the islanders from the horrors and ravages of the wars they were experiencing. The fighting evidently interrupted all of the most important activities, such as agriculture, fishing, the sculpting of the statues and building. The workers could no longer work in safety. The custom of eating human flesh, which had previously been restricted to religious ritual began to assume a more practical purpose; people were killed and eaten in order to make up deficiencies in the food supply. The high priests rapidly lost their authority and there began a steady decline in the general cultural level and a total disintegration of the existing civilisation.

The phasing out of the ancestor worship, which the moais represented, led to the wholesale desecration of the sites all over the island and to their abandonment in favour of the cult of the 'bird-men' of Orongo who were ascendant by the time of Roggeveen's arrival in 1722. By this time though, all significant knowledge of the great civilisation that had once been, was lost. All that was left was a giant outdoor museum for generations of scientists and archaeologists to puzzle over.

After a picnic lunch, we followed a dirt track towards the northern shore of the island, passing all the while large herds of wild horses grazing quietly in the long, dry grass. These were imported during the earlier days of European occupation of the island. The only sign of humans we saw was a lone man on horseback riding along the crest of a distant hill. At a small cove called Ovahe, Victor pointed out an entire cliff of dark-red volcanic rock.

'This is the quarry for the hats,' he explained.

'Which hats?' Zara asked.

'The hats for the moais...soon I will show you...come.' He bundled us all back into the Kombi and we drove a short distance around the headland to another small cove, which we were suprised to see full of coconut palms.

'Look at the trees!' Trish said as we stopped in the little valley and parked the van. 'I didn't think they had coconuts here.'

'No, that is right,' Victor laughed. 'These are the first. They were brought from Tahiti. But they are beautiful...no? And look...,' he pointed towards the beach. 'You see the hats?'

Standing in line just back from the beach were seven huge moais. The bodies of two of them were broken, but five were complete and of them, four were wearing what looked like giant hats made from the red volcanic stone we had seen earlier. Opinion is divided over whether the ancients intended these to be hats or representations of elaborate hairdos. Whichever it was, the effect is startling. Each 'top-knot' weighs at least eight or nine tonnes and to get them to stay up on top of the statue's head required a balancing feat of extraordinary precision. These particular moais, however, were fallen ones that had been re-erected and restored with present-day techniques under the direction of local archaeologist and museum curator Sergio Rapu, whom we were to meet later.

The statues, the coconut palms and the beach at Ahu Anakena, as the site is called, make a setting of considerable beauty so, after inspecting and photographing the moais, we spent half an hour sitting on the beach and going for a brief swim in the surf, our first surf for over two years. But it was only a brief entry because the water was decidedly untropical... decidedly cold in fact.

From Ahu Anakena we left, heading back towards the centre of the southern part of the island to what is, without question, the *pièce de resistance* of Easter Island... Rano Raraku, the great extinct volcano from where the ancient inhabitants quarried all of the massive statues on the island. They were hand-carved out of the mountainsides... using only stone tools and then transported, somehow, over long distances to various sacred sites around the island.

It was here at Rano Raraku that Edmundo Edwards had suggested I try for a series of photographs of the sunrise. We had brought our packs and tents in the van and after we had looked around with Victor and the others in the group, we intended to find a campsite, where they would leave us to spend the night.

As we approached the volcano's cone, bumping along the dusty dirt track that winds across the grasslands, the first thing we saw on Rano Raraku's slopes were scores of dark stone monoliths standing upright in the soil, many of them at drunken angles, still waiting for their last journeys to their appointed sites... journeys that were never made. With the long wars and the collapse of Easter Island's civilisation, the moais at Rano Raraku were left to stand... forever waiting.

'This is the only kneeling moai to yet be excavated on the island.' Victor patted the large belly of the statue which was embedded half-way up the outer slope of the volcano.

'Why is it so different from all the rest?' Sean asked.

Victor shrugged his shoulders.

'I like it best of them all,' Zara said and I agreed with her. Its softer body contours and features made it appear more companionable, less contemptuous and autocratic. Unearthed by Thor Heyerdahl on his 1957 expedition, it poses many unanswered questions and suggests an even more complex history than has yet been ascribed to the island.

Climbing on up through the knee-high coarse grass, we moved among dozens of the regular moais, some of them buried up to their shoulders and others up to their chins in the volcanic soil. Abandoned like a spoilt child's discarded toys.

A short steep climb above them and we came to the quarry and one of the most amazing sights I have ever seen anywhere. Huge moais, the longest about 20 metres, lying face up, almost completely hewn away from the surrounding rock. A couple still joined along the back by only a slender rock-sliver umbilicus to mother earth.

This was the birthplace of these strange, gaunt, unfriendly figures. We moved among them, carefully avoiding standing or even leaning on them, all the while under the jealously protective eye of Victor, who behaved as though they were his own family's personal precious heirlooms.

Whatever happened to halt this work, it happened suddenly. It was as if the workers had suddenly downed tools one afternoon and gone out on the longest strike in history. Frozen at the moment of parturition, the moais would require very little midwifery to send them on their way.

A further climb brought us to the rim of the volcano. From here we could see another huge moai nursery spread around the inside curve, with dozens more of the dark statues, which are conspicuous enough against the yellowy grass to appear from any distance like large grazing animals. Below us was the crater lake, filled, as at Rano Kau, with the hardy totora reed of the type which grows in Lake Titicaca in southern Peru. Another connection.

The sky was very blue, the air still and strangely silent, because bird life, if not completely absent was surely very sparse. As we sat on the rim, I could fully understand how Edmundo could fall so wholeheartedly under the spell of the very compelling atmosphere the island exudes.

Back down at the base of the volcano we said goodnight to Victor and Juan, Dr Herbert and the Moxons. Jenny Moxon, who has three almost adult children and to whom Zara and Sean had immediately responded with affection, because she is very confidence-inspiring, warm and motherly, was anxious about our safety. We assured her that the moais would take care of us. 'But do you have enough food?' she asked, still not happy at leaving us out for the night.

We all laughed because the Moxons had been with us when on the previous evening we stopped off at the island's only supermercado, a more than grandiose name for what was nothing more than a shop. In preparation for our overnight camping we bought a half kilo of sausages for $5, a can of green beans, $3, a can of tomato paste, some pickles, a few bread rolls and a can of apricots, which alone cost $4. The grand total was $25! We decided against a bottle of lemonade for $6 and a pack of butter, $3. The Moxons also decided they'd drink their own brandy straight and forego the $6 bottle of dry ginger!

Now we can go down to our local supermarket to do the week's shopping and feel grateful that we are not an Easter Islander earning one-fifth of what we earn and paying those prices because all their requirements are air freighted in at enormous cost.

'Yes, yes, we have enough to eat. We're dieting till we get to Tahiti' (little did we know!). But Jenny insisted on leaving with us the remains of the picnic lunch.

It took us an hour to make camp. Just two two-person tents. An inordinate amount of time for the procedure, but as this was the first time since a dry-run in a back garden in Putney, shouting above the roar of the traffic as the Southern Express shook the foundations and Concorde rattled the windows...all of it light years away, ...we felt sure we would improve.

The slope of Ranu Raraku gently shadowed and, in the failing light, the moais seemed to move closer together, perhaps whispering the secrets of their history.

We cooked up our decidedly non-gourmet meal and consoled ourselves that no restaurant, even if it had the best cuisine in the world, could provide the view we had from our eating place. We crawled into our separate tents and listened to the silence.

We had been worried about wind. I felt reasonably sure that our tents would be waterproof, but they were such lightweight affairs that a high wind would play havoc with them and Victor had warned us that there were often strong winds that swept across the open grasslands from the sea. But the night was calm and quiet and we were all warm and comfortable, sleeping peacefully, until I heard the first patter of rain on the fly-sheet and on the plastic cover on our packs. As there was no room inside the tents for our packs, we'd stacked them outside and covered them with plastic groundsheets. Just as well, because the pitter-patter turned into rain, then heavy rain, then a downpour.

Trish and I were now both wide awake and we lay listening for the tell-tale sound of drips coming through the fabric of the tent, but there were none. We called to Zara and Sean, who were also awake, and they confirmed that their tent seemed to be watertight. Great! We began to relax slightly and to revel in the idea that we were snug and dry in our little tents while it continued to bucket down outside. Things didn't look too hopeful for my sunrise photographs, but I remember feeling that perhaps it would be a repeat performance of the previous night. . .that by dawn all the rain would have gone. In any case, once the immediate fears of getting drenched had been allayed, the sound of the rain became soporific and we soon drifted off to sleep again.

During the next few hours, I awoke a couple of times and, on each occasion registered that the rain seemed to have stopped—maybe there would still be a chance to catch the sunrise. At 5.00 a.m. a dim light began to suffuse the tent. Opening the flap I peered out into a grey mist, then curled back up in my sleeping bag again, cursing. At 5.30 I had another look. The mist had gone, but the sky was still overcast. There were patches of clear sky, but the photo prospects were not bright. Still, I thought, if it was going to be done at all, it would have to be now.

'Are you coming?' I said to Trish as I slipped out of the tent and into some clothes.

She examined the grey morning and smiled. 'No,' she replied knowingly.

Sean called from the other tent. 'Are you going now Dad?'

'Yep,' I said, trying to sound positive. 'Want to come?'

'Okay. . .hang on.'

'What about Zara? Is she coming too?'

A pause while Zara pushed the flap back and looked about. She smiled also and shook her head. Women's intuition.

I grabbed my camera gear and Sean and I took off through the long wet grass, soaking our jeans to above the knees immediately. We were heading for the slope that led to the lowest part of the volcano's rim. From there we could retrace the path we had followed the previous day to the top of the rim for the best view of the sun coming up (if it did come up) over Pau Katiki, the main volcano cone which occupies the eastern corner of the island.

As we walked, we passed through a large herd of wild horses which was moving slowly across our path. They were soaking wet from the night's rain, but showed little concern for us. A couple of frisky foals shied and ran away, but the others just moved apart and stared a little disinterestedly at us as we made our way up the hillside amongst the standing moais. It took us roughly 20 minutes to reach the high point of the rim...arriving there at 6.00 a.m., some 10 minutes before the sun was due to rise. The air had a misty chill to it, but we were both wearing rain jackets and were warm from the steady walk up the sloping rim. We sat down to rest and wait, but it was clear from the moment we arrived that there weren't going to be any sunrise photos. It was as grey and dreary a morning as you could wish for...or *not* wish for. And yet there was an eerie quality about the place. Several hawks wheeled silently below us near the sheer cliffs of one portion of the volcano's outer rim and from our vantage point we could take in a vast sweep of the landscape around us. It was grey, still and empty...and beyond it there was only the unbroken horizon of the surrounding sea.

A light wind sprung up and we began to feel a chill. Sean and I clambered down into the crater and began to make our way back along the inner slope, inspecting the various figures that were sprinkled across it. At the far end of the crater, a small canyon...natural or manmade, we didn't know...cut through the crater rim providing an avenue, in those long-gone days when the great works were still in progress, for the moais inside the crater to be moved to the outside.

It was difficult to avoid the sensation, as we trekked past these great, grey stone faces, that we were being watched. It sounds corny, I know, but in that sort of setting—with everything damp and dull, and a slight wind whistling about—all those horrible fairytale stories of inanimate objects coming to life seem to be really possible. Sean started it off by saying, 'What would you do if one of them moved, Dad?' I laughed, but looked a little more closely at the figures as we passed them and felt reassured to find their sunken eyes still staring vacantly out over the reed-filled crater as they had done for centuries.

Back at the camp we found Trish and Zara up making ready for breakfast. Extracting our little portable benzine stove from the packs, we cooked up a great meal of scrambled eggs with cheese sandwiches, bananas and coffee. A short while later we began to pack up the camp...a slow process, firstly because the tents and their fly-sheets had to dry off and secondly because none of us really wanted to leave. It was an ideal site with a great feeling of space and serenity about it. We could easily have stayed there for several days. By about nine o'clock however, the sun had broken through the thin cloud cover and with the help of the light breeze, our tents had dried off completely.

Victor and Juan arrived in the Kombi at about 10.30 to pick us up and drive us back into town to Maria Rapu's little residencia, where we did some washing and wrote some letters before lunch. This was to be our last afternoon on the island and both Zara and Sean were desperately keen to go horse-riding, having been told by Victor that almost anyone in the town would hire their horse out for a very small fee. The fee *was* small enough, I suppose...$5 for the afternoon, but, as it always is with us, we had to multiply by four. In any event, it seemed a pretty good way to spend our last day and, as Tom and Jenny Moxon had also expressed an interest in going riding, by about 2.30 we were all setting off together on horseback to visit some of the Ahu sites that were close to the town.

There was only one thing wrong. Our horses had been obtained from several different residents around the town and somehow mine was the last one to be arranged.

'There ees horse, Señor,' I was told by the owner, 'but...so sorry, no saddle.' Nor were there any reins.

The man kindly offered me a hessian sack to throw on the horse's back, then he looped a piece of nylon rope through the animal's mouth and handed the ends to me. I think my jaw must have dropped open because he seemed to register the fact that I was a little nonplussed. He held his hand up. 'Momentito,' he said and dashed inside his small wooden house, emerging a moment later waving a thin, battered cushion in his hand.

'Muchas gracias,' I muttered between clenched teeth, having finally mounted the horse after three embarrassing attempts and the same number of failures.

I don't know how many kilometres we rode that afternoon, but the way the base of my spine felt, it could have been three hundred. Looking back on it, I suppose I can take some pride in the fact that I only fell off once, but even though I managed to stay on the rest of the time, it was hell. What really terrified me was when everyone else galloped on ahead and I had to try desperately to prevent my steed from racing off too. On the couple of occasions when he did take off like a rocket, I was just bounced about like a cork. The cushion slipped sideways, my feet flew out in the air and my coccyx fought it out with the horse's backbone (the backbone won). It was a miracle I stayed on at all. I came away from it wondering how the hell they do it in the movies. All those bareback Indian riders I'd seen in countless cowboy sagas over the years had suddenly earnt my belated and retrospective admiration.

The actual afternoon was something of a blur for me. I know we returned to Ahu Tahai, the site we visited on our first day on the island, and I know we also reached the great lone statue Ko-te Riku a little further up the coast. He was the first one that William Mulloy was able to restore with his red 'top-knot' hat in place...a giant in every respect. He stands almost 10 metres tall, weighs about 82 tonnes, plus about 10 tonnes for his hat. I know we saw him and Ahu Tahai, because somehow I managed to take photographs of them. But sadly, my most vivid memories of that journey are of my aching thighs and my bruised rear end.

We had so far resisted buying any of the wooden carvings which had been offered to us because they were so outrageously expensive. Local artisans produce miniature moais, birdmen and rongo-rongo writing in relief, which varied in workmanship but only marginally in price. They started at $60 and the people selling them thought poorly of my natural tendencies to haggle.

But on the last morning it somehow seemed stupid and mean not to invest in a couple of pieces, because after all, Easter Island is Easter Island and we don't expect to make frequent stopovers! The craftsmen seemed to sense this weakening of the resolve and, by contrast with similar stall-holders in other parts of the world, who, when they know you are very shortly on your way, lower their prices dramatically just to get a sale, these ones hiked their charges even higher.

'Jeans,' one of the women pointed at Zara's denim'd legs. 'I want. This,' she gestured at her carvings, 'you want?' It seemed that children's clothing was at a premium, because very little of it is brought in due to the mammoth expense of freight.

In the middle of the bargaining Sean appeared, flushed with excitement, to inform us that he too had been offered a moai for his extremely well-worn-in jeans and yet another for his watch for which he had carefully saved up his pocket money. They were both in their element. It's always been my observation that it is natural for the human animal to barter in preference to paying over little pieces of dirty paper and lumps of foul-smelling metal. They undid their packs and began offering various other items of clothing.

At this point I could see that unless I was firm, we would all be leaving Easter Island wearing only our bathers and carrying empty rucksacks! But no, that wouldn't do, because it's not at all easy when we are travelling in odd corners, with the minimum of specially suitable clothing, to replace even simple articles.

In the end they each decided on parting only with their jeans because from now on it was most likely that the weather would be too warm to wear them anyway. I also extracted an undertaking that they would not moan about being unable to get new ones until they were home. In return, they received a small wooden moai each. Iain and I coughed up hard cash for a birdman and a piece of rongo-rongo writing...as if we didn't already have a houseful of this type of stuff!

Victor seemed rather down in the mouth about us going. 'I have never been to Tahiti,' he said. 'Beautiful girls,' his hands sketched the outline.

'But there are beautiful ones here too,' I said, which was feeble, because I knew what he meant.

'Here it is just a village,' he said. 'You cannot do one thing...and everyone knows immediately about it. Sometimes I feel like I am in prison. It is so far from anywhere and it is impossible for me to leave. Now the government has made it that we Easter Islanders must pay full airfare to and from the island. Before, we pay only $150 to go and come back. Now we must pay the same as you, $700, and how can I ever afford to do that?'

'Why did they change the rules?'

'Because now we must start to be no longer a money drain on them. This is of course not possible. They know it. But we must try. During Allende it was not necessary. We were supported. But the new junta says everyone must take care for themselves.'

'So Allende was a good man?' I probed.

'No. No. Disaster. Because of him no more tourists come and also the Americanos go away from here. Before him they have a base, a how do you call?...communications base, here. Plenty work, plenty money, plenty everything. Allende comes, they go. Take away the lot.'

'So the Americans were good?' I was confused.

'No. No. Terrible. Before them *no-one* has money. So no-one *need* money anyway. Nothing to buy. Everyone grow their own food. I have a pig, you have taro. I want taro, you want pig. We swap. OK? Then the Americanos come, employ men, pay money. Now I have a pig and want taro, but you work for Americanos and no more grow taro. Instead pay money and buy canned fish. No good.'

Victor looked sad but then he began to smile. 'I remember one time, the Americanos call the Thanksgiving. They bring a big boat offshore. Too big to land. A navy boat. They send off helicopters to drop parcels. The things in the PX they come like that. From the sky like gifts from God. And on this day you know what they drop?' He laughed. 'Chicken! It's true. Big chicken called turkey. I not believe it, if I not see with these own eyes. The chicken drop out and fall to earth. Big, dead, frozen chicken. Everyone else see it too and after that they won't eat their own chicken. It must be frozen and in a plastic bag from America. Only trouble is, then Allende comes and Americanos go. They take the PX and jobs and money and no-one wants to go back to hard work like planting taro or growing pigs anymore.'

On the tiny airfield we met Sergio Rapu, a very tall, broad-shouldered man in his 30s who is the first Easter Islander to qualify as an archaeologist and return to work on unravelling the mystery of his own island. He is married to an American woman who helps run the small museum and he was delighted to learn that we had gone across to the seldom-visited site at Anakena where he had been personally responsible for the restorations of the Ahu and the moias with their red top-knots.

Presently he was working on the site in town where the governor had dynamited his way into Edmundo's affections! Sergio was rather surprised to hear that we knew the story and he tried to skip over the nastier bits.

'What I am most excited about is that we have uncovered a moai which, unlike any other so far seen, has eyes!' He widened his own in pleasure. 'Eyes of white coral with pupils of black obsidian. I know of no other similar style anywhere in the Pacific Islands...only in the artwork from Peru. This would seem to substantiate Heyerdahl's theories that there was a definite input from the South American continent. It's very interesting and we are tremendously excited.'

As we were leaving, Maria de Rapu embraced us and again draped us with shell leis. 'Please return,' she smiled.

We were almost at the plane when we heard the shout. 'Hey Australianos!... Australianos!', and turned back to see Hernan waving madly from the edge of the field. 'My baby is born!' He laughed. 'Is a boy. Yippee!'

# FRENCH POLYNESIA

## 2 TAHITI
'Ia Ora Na'

In 1946, when I was little more than 10 years old, I crossed the Pacific in a former troop-ship called the *Marine Falcon*. It was a liberty ship which had been hastily converted to carry civilian passengers, but it wasn't much of a conversion. My father and I slept in a huge dormitory for men while my mother slept in an equally vast one for women. We were heading for San Francisco and then Canada, where my father, who was in the Australian Army, was being posted. After the long leg from Fiji, I recall the sense of eager anticipation with which everyone on board, including my parents and I, awaited our arrival in Tahiti.

Thirty-four years is quite a gap between visits, but some of the feelings I had about Papeete, the bustling little capital of French Polynesia, remained in my consciousness over all that time. What I remembered most was the atmosphere—that is, the colour, the smells, the warmth and the beautiful, all-embracing tropical 'feel' of the place. I even remember the infamous Quinn's Bar...not as a patron, although in retrospect, I'd have loved to have been one...at least once. 'What goes on behind those doors,' a crewman on the ship had told me in advance, with a knowing smile, 'is nobody's business.' When my parents pointed out the shabby, wooden-fronted building as we passed it on the waterfront, I viewed it with a feeling of awe and wonder.

So, while I approached Tahiti this time with a sense of expectation not unlike that experienced on my first visit, it was tempered by a degree of trepidation. It couldn't possibly be the same, and of course it wasn't. It had changed enormously. Quinn's was long gone...replaced now by a modern office building, and the waterfront shone with the light reflected from the windows of new boutiques, multi-level shopping plazas and department stores. Modern cars sped by along the tree-lined waterfront boulevard and there was an air of prosperity and sophistication about the town.

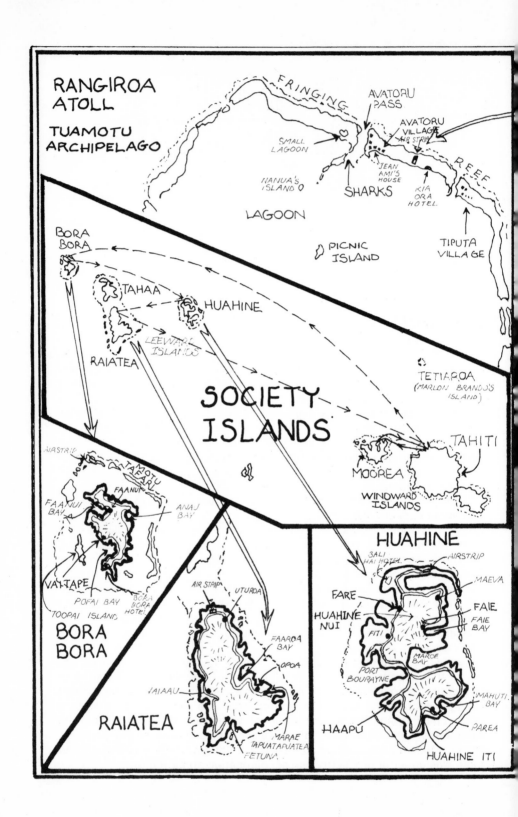

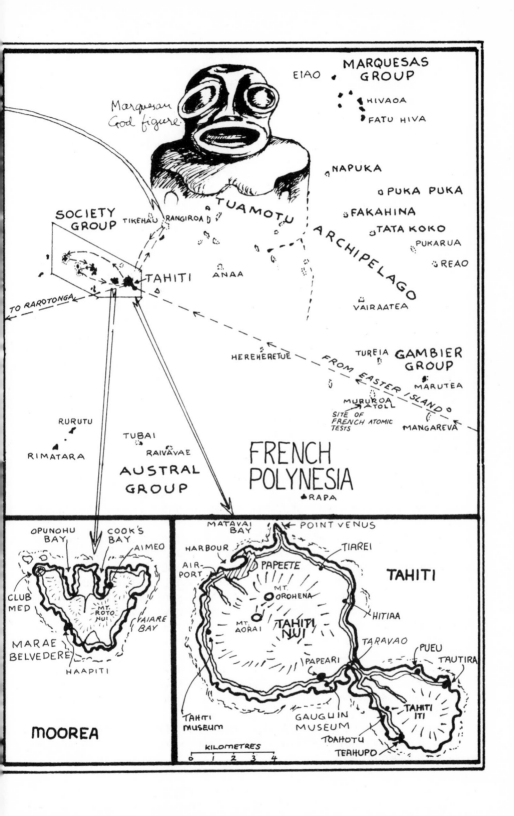

Marquesan God figure

MARQUESAS GROUP

EIAO

HIVAOA

FATU HIVA

NAPUKA

PUKA PUKA

FAKAHINA

TATA KOKO

PUKARUA

REAO

SOCIETY GROUP

TIKEHAU   RANGIROA

TUAMOTU ARCHIPELAGO

TAHITI

ANAA

VAIRAATEA

TO RAROTONGA

HEREHERETUE

TUREIA   GAMBIER GROUP

FROM EASTER ISLAND

MARUTEA

MURUROA ATOLL

SITE OF FRENCH ATOMIC TESTS

MANGAREVA

RURUTU

TUBAI

RAIVĀVAE

RIMATARA

AUSTRAL GROUP

FRENCH POLYNESIA

RAPA

MOOREA

OPUNOHU BAY

COOK'S BAY

AIMEO

CLUB MED

MT. ROTO NUI

VAIARE BAY

MARAE BELVEDERE

HAAPITI

MATAVAI BAY   POINT VENUS

HARBOUR

AIRPORT

PAPEETE

TIAREI

MT. OROHENA

TAHITI

MT. AORAI

TAHITI NUI

HITIAA

TARAVAO

PUEU

TAUTIRA

PAPEARI

TAHITI MUSEUM

GAUGUIN MUSEUM

TAHITI ITI

TOAHOTU

TEAHUPO

KILOMETRES

0 1 2 3 4

And yet, it wasn't just another Waikiki, because somehow none of those things I remembered about Papeete from the past was missing. There was still riotous colour; in the easy-going clothes of the men and women, in the brilliant red hibiscus, white tiare tahiti or pink frangipani flowers they all wore in their hair, in the multi-hued green of the dense foliage that lines the roads and climbs the hills behind the town, in the turquoise of the lagoon and in the garishly painted buses. The smells of the sea air, the waterfront, and the marketplace were still there and, despite the modernity of the Boulevarde Pomare and the Quai de Commerce, just a few streets back from the waterfront we were able to find small shops, cafes, bakeries, bars, the markets, churches and old tin-roofed, verandahed buildings which exuded that comforting aura of gradual decay, without which tropical towns don't seem quite right.

Papeete now seems to have a bit of it all. It's quite a town; big, small...a sophisticated town, a simple town and one filled with amazingly beautiful people. Even the Tahitian matrons who tend to become rather rotund after many years of good living, are somehow fine-looking people, as are their husbands and/or lovers (some of whom are as big as Sumo wrestlers). Yet, as huge and fat as many of them become, they seem to be always smiling or laughing. A sense of humour always makes a person look more beautiful.

And the younger women...the vahines! A mixture of almost everything you can think of, but with that mainstream of Polynesian blood that makes them amongst the most attractive women in the world.

The only drawback to it all—it seems there always has to be a drawback—is that the whole of French Polynesia is ridiculously expensive. It's crazy—out of all proportion. And it isn't only because of rich tourists, even though there are quite a few who are able and willing to part with their pennies at the rate of over $200 a night just for twin hotel accommodation! The high prices apply everywhere, including the grocery stores and markets, though these are really the only places to buy food if you are on a budget, as we were. Restaurants are prohibitively expensive and it's all but impossible to find a cheap place to stay.

On our arrival, we tried a few phone calls from the airport (public phones charge 50¢ a call) and reeled back when we discovered that 'moderately'-priced hotels were charging 3300 to 3600 francs ($44 to $48) a night. After $5 or $6 worth of fruitless calls we went into town and found a couple of hotels at one end, not far from the Naval yard, at which the tariff for the four of us would have been $26 a night, but they were rather seedy and it was pretty obvious that they were brothels. We then tried the Mahina Tea Guest House in town. It was clean and respectable and about the same price, but unfortunately booked out for a week.

We shrugged our shoulders and settled for the Hotel Tahiti, about a couple of kilometres along the waterfront from the town centre, where for $33 a night we had a self-contained, thatched roof bungalow facing right onto the water.

'Marlon Brando stayed here when they made *Mutiny on the Bounty* in 1963,' we were told by an elderly maid, who spoke excellent English, almost as soon as we arrived.

'Not this actual bungalow?' Trish asked as if it had been Mary Queen of Scots.

'Oh no. These bungalows were not here then...he stayed in the main building. This was the best hotel in Tahiti then.'

A lot had happened since then. It had long since been surpassed by numerous larger and more glamorous hotels but the Tahiti was still a very pleasant place with a profusion of tropical greenery in its grounds.

It was more than our budget allowed, but after some pretty exhaustive research, we figured it represented the best value for money. At the same time we were becoming resigned to the fact that we'd be spending a good deal more money in French Polynesia than we'd anticipated. We could only hope to make it up somewhere else, later on.

The official reason for what's generally called Tahiti's 'over-heated' economy is that there are no income or property taxes. To get the income they need to run the territory, which is designated as an overseas department of France, the government slaps a heavy tax on all imported goods, and just about everything except fruit, vegetables, fish and pork is imported. That's the official reason, and obviously it's a factor which contributes to higher prices, but the real reason—the most important reason—is that the French government's nuclear testing programme on the remote Muraroa Atoll has brought in thousands of military and technical personnel (who also pay no income tax). The situation has injected billions of francs into French Polynesia's economy and pushed wages and prices through the roof. It's believed that 60 per cent of all the money in circulation throughout the region at the moment is directly or indirectly attributable to the French nuclear programme and the resulting military presence.

But all of this fades into the background as Papeete grows on you. Just walking along the waterfront gazing at the incredible line-up of international yachts moored stern-first to the sea wall is exciting. Schooners, ketches, yawls. Glamorous ones, workaday ones, home-built ones even...big, small and in-between. You read the names on the transoms: Courser, Los Angeles, Aeolus, Pireaus, Don Quixote, Jersey and you look at the people on the deck or sitting in the cockpit in their shorts and suntans and realise they've all had a hell of an adventure just getting here. There are yachts from Mexico, Germany, England, Australia, Japan and several from the east and west coasts of the United States, all pausing for a few moments, or several months in Tahiti before moving on. A percentage perhaps will never leave.

Back at our hotel on that first evening we swam in the pool and watched light planes coming in to land at the nearby airstrip against a background of stunning beauty; the sun sinking lower and lower over the magnificent and omnipresent island of Moorea, some 17 kilometres to the west. On the little wharf that runs from the hotel grounds out to the edge of the coral reef, we sat silently in the soft, warm evening air—entranced. In situations like that, who needs money.

'Ia Ora Na', health to you. And welcome to Tahiti.

Yes it's expensive, outrageously so. And yes the French abroad are, *zut alors!* unbelievably arrogant. But it's...well it's Tahiti. And I love it!

Even now as I write this in smell-less Sydney I can conjure up the sensuous thick fragrance of the tiare tahiti which blooms profusely everywhere and the rich, warm-earth smell of coconut.

I tend to go off my brain a bit when let loose in the tropics. My movements slow, my limbs loosen, yet I also feel super-charged, exuberant, larger than life and in love with everything and everyone.

It was also good to be back in a society which is up early and gets going because that's how my own body clock works. In Latin countries, including those in South America and even on Easter Island, nothing happens until 10 a.m., by which time I am exhausted with impatience. And at 9.30 p.m., which is the time dinner is served, I am too tired to eat.

So by 7.30 on our first day in Tahiti we'd done our laps in the hotel pool and were catching 'le truck' into Papeete. 'Le truck' is a truly Tahitian form of transport and not recommended to anyone with sensitive ears. For if you don't see it coming, and that would be difficult, as they are all painted a startling combination of bright red and yellow, it is definitely impossible not to hear the approaching blare of pop music, which is blasted out at such volume over the speakers, that the whole bus and its occupants fairly vibrate.

We clambered up the steps at the back, bending almost double to avoid cracking our heads on the low ceiling and sat on the hard wooden slat benches which ran along either side. The windows have no glass and above the empty frames, every square inch of available space was adorned with a collection of personal memorabilia belonging to the owner/driver. Family photographs, post cards from friends, pin-ups of Tahitian beauties and highly coloured portraits of Christ and the Virgin Mary.

All routes start and end outside the central market and take in the 50 or so communities all around the 115 kilometres of the island's circumference. Beyond the centre of Papeete there are no designated stops and schedules depend entirely on the whim of the driver, who may pull over to chat to a friend for a while or buy some mangos and breadfruit.

The single fare to anywhere is the equivalent of 50¢ which is a bit pricey if you are just going the couple of kilometres in from the main hotel area to the town centre, but it's cheap for the locals, most of whom ride long distances and carry baskets of produce, a couple of live chickens and a baby, not to mention the upwards of a 100 kilos of their own bulk, for the majority of the people verge on the gargantuan.

In town we headed immediately for the market where we went bananas and bought bananas. And papaya and pineapple and mango and avocado! All in a delirium of joy. It was two years since we had tasted such tropical fruit. Two years of controlled atmosphere apples and limp lettuce and oh boy, were we now going to make up for it...in an orgy of fabulous fruit.

Up and down the aisles, between the scores of stalls we went, picking up and smelling the biggest and most tasteful mangos we've ever had anywhere; gently squeezing the large firm-fleshed papaya and laughing like kids with the excitement of it all.

I don't think of myself as particularly interested in food until I find myself, as I was then, actually salivating with anticipation. Reeling, as much with excitement as from the bulk of our parcels, we headed back across the street and into *un petit boulangerie* where we bought metre-long sticks of real French bread. Fresh, yeasty-smelling, crisp loaves.

Already the streets were crowded with people wearing bright tropical colours. But it wasn't so much what they had on, as how little they had on, which caught my eye. There seemed to be acres of bare brown flesh. Again it was over two years since we had been in a place hot enough, and more importantly relaxed enough, for people to unselfconsciously expose large areas of their body. The combined effect of all this left me in need of a sit down and a cup of coffee.

Up some stairs over the bread shop we found a small café run by a short, fat, friendly Chinese fellow who trusted his customers to the extent that he left kilo bags of sugar on each table from which they could add however much they wanted to their coffee.

When we were all more of a piece again we braved the excitements of the street once more, stopping for Zara to drool over some yellow satin shorts and for Sean to ravel through the rows of bead necklaces displayed at the line of roadside stalls.

We were delighted to find at one of these that Easter Island carvings similar to ours were selling for over twice what we had paid for them. On the strength of that I bought a really quite beautiful necklace in which butter yellow, cream and coffee coloured tiny shells were strewn together so as to look like a stem of spring flowers. Sounds awful but it's really very pretty...and it was only $5.

Although Tahiti is in the *South* Pacific, if you look at it in terms of its relationship to the land masses surrounding the Ocean, it's near enough to being in the *middle* of the Pacific. It's about equidistant from California and Australia and also half-way between Tokyo and Santiago.

Most people who have never been there tend to think of Tahiti as a group of islands in the same way that Fiji and Hawaii collectively describe whole groups. But Tahiti is only one of some 130 islands that are scattered over an area as large as Europe to make up French Polynesia. The actual land area of all the islands put together though is little more than one and a half times the area of greater London or greater Sydney—about 4000 square kilometres.

Tahiti, with a quarter of that area, is the largest in the group and also holds almost two-thirds of the territory's 150 000 inhabitants—close to 40 000 living in Papeete alone. The other islands are divided amongst five separate and quite different groups: the Tuamotus, the Gambiers, the Australs, the Marquesas and the Society Islands. The Society group is also broken into two sub-groups; the Windward and the Leeward Islands (see map). Some are volcanic (or high), while others are coral (or low) islands.

The Society group contains the high islands you tend to hear about more often; Moorea, Bora Bora, Huahine and Raiatea, whilst those in the Marquesas, the Tuamotus, the Gambiers and the Australs have names most people have never heard of: Raivavae, Hereheretue, Vairaatea, Fakahina, Eiao; islands which are even now, this late in the twentieth century, still remote from civilization and rarely, if ever, visited by tourists, something which tended to make them more attractive to us. We had to decide which of the islands we would try to see. Obviously it was going to be impossible to get to them all.

At the Tourist office in town it was suggested that, if we wanted to see what life was all about on an atoll—'very different from here in Tahiti'—we should go to the Tuamotu group, and in particular to the big atoll of Rangiroa, some 350 kilometres from Tahiti. We talked it over and decided that, if we went to the Tuamotus for a week and then returned to Tahiti, we'd be able to meet up with an old friend, Peggy McCarr, who had written to us in England to say that she would be coming through Tahiti from Australia about the same time as we were. We thought that maybe she could join us to go out to some of the high islands in the Society group. At least that was the way we *thought* it would work out.

Our first problem was in getting to Rangiroa. Checking the flights we found them fully booked for a couple of days (the Marquesas group was booked five *weeks* ahead!), so we opted to explore the rest of Tahiti in the meantime.

We had decided to hire a car to go around the island, rather than take 'le truck' because we wanted to be able to control our own deviations, so to speak, and to explore Tahiti Iti and Tahiti Nui at our own pace.

Driving anti-clockwise around the island we went out past Fa'aa airport and made our first stop the Musée de Tahiti et des Îles which is inconveniently tucked away down a narrow, rutted track, 15 kilometres out of town. For all that, it's a superb little museum and a very helpful introduction to the history and culture of the Pacific people. We'd done a certain amount of preliminary reading prior to leaving the UK but at that stage it all had an aura of unreality. The travel brochures and tourist information sent to us in envelopes decorated with exotic stamps and showing white sun-drenched beaches ringed with swaying palms were the final dreamlike touch.

We'd even gone to a very comprehensive exhibition held at London's Museum of Mankind to bone up on Captain Cook's Pacific voyages and now that we were actually in the South Pacific. I was amused to see that the museum in Tahiti tried valiantly to dismiss the great English seadog as somewhat of an also-ran to the 'brilliant French navigator explorer Louis Antoine de Bougainville'.

Prior to this, the Spaniards had called the South Pacific 'our sea' since the early 1500s. A century later, the Dutch, too, were on the scene. So that Captain Samuel Wallis was somewhat of a late entry by the time he arrived in 1767 and claimed Tahiti for the British. With astounding pedantry he named it 'King George IIIs Island'! Then, as if that wasn't as frightening a display of unoriginal thought as anyone could wish for, he went on to name the beautiful island of Moorea, 'Duke of York Island'!

The French entry, Bougainville, did only marginally better when less than a year later he arrived, claimed Tahiti for France and named it New Cythera, after the goddess of love, Venus.

Wallis's glowing reports of friendly, very friendly, natives and plentiful food and water must have influenced the Royal Society which, at the time of Wallis's return to England, was putting together an expedition to the south seas under the leadership of a Captain James Cook to map the transit of Venus. Cook was ordered to Tahiti, landed at Matavai Bay in 1769 and stayed three months.

The Spaniards, realising that what had been until then their part of the world, even if only by default, tried to establish a mission at the far end of the island. But it was too late. Nineteen years later, in 1788, William Bligh of *Bounty* fame, turned up to collect his breadfruit seedlings which he planned to take on to the West Indies to see how they would go as a staple food for the slaves in the sugar plantations. (No worries about quarantine restrictions then. No large men in shorts and long socks charging aboard your craft waving spray cans of stuff which, according to the ads, *kills* unwanted intruders, *dead*.)

Everyone now knows how, after being forced to leave behind the charms of willing Tahitian maidens, the crew of the *Bounty* mutinied. (The British still blanch with horror that this could have happened on board a ship of the Royal Navy.) The much maligned Bligh was cast adrift in a rowboat and HMS *Bounty* returned to Tahiti under the command of Fletcher Christian (or was it Marlon Brando?). An attempt to establish an idyllic south sea paradise colony on Tubai, in the Australs, 460 kilometres south of Tahiti, failed and when the mutineers came back through Tahiti, they off-loaded a few fellows before sailing on to their self-imposed exile on Pitcairn. The ones who stayed behind helped the local chief, Pomare, to conquer most of Tahiti. (Bligh of course survived his ordeal and came back the following year looking for the mutineers and more seedlings!)

Next came the London Missionary Society, an outfit we were to hear plenty about in almost all the islands during our crossing of the Pacific. A Protestant group of very dedicated, courageous men and women, they soon persuaded the locals that their own brand of moral puritanism was the way to everlasting life and thus smoothed the path for a growing stream of English merchants and entrepreneurs.

The French, worried about the influence of the British (and through them, the Protestant church) tried a few polite diplomatic moves of their own. But, so the saying goes, when all else fails, force wins the day. In 1842 a French admiral arbitrarily established a protectorate over Tahiti and Moorea. A year later they annexed the islands by the simple expedient of naval force.

The British being otherwise occupied in various parts of the world, and seeing this area as rather small beer, retired from the scene in a gentlemanly manner, leaving the Tahitians to wage a three year guerilla war, which, naturally, they lost. So by 1880 the protectorate of Tahiti and Moorea was formed into French Oceania, a formal French colony, and gradually, by 1909, all the other islands had been grabbed in the same manner.

For almost 50 years this was the status quo, until in 1958, in a referendum vote, the population voted to remain with the French government and French Oceania became French Polynesia with a more autonomous form of government than previously but still as a colony of France.

The Musée de Tahiti et des Îsles makes all this history come alive, and more beside. Being a Rupert Brooke fan, I was delighted to find there a verse, handwritten by the man himself, during his stay on the island in 1914.

> And the whispering scents that stray
> Above the idle warm lagoon
> Hasten, hand in human hand
> Down the dark, the flowered way.
> Along the whiteness of the sand
> And in the water's soft caress
> Wash the mind of foolishness
> Mamua, until the day.

For me the most poignant exhibit in the museum was a photograph of King

Pomare V, the last King of Tahiti, laid out for his funeral in 1891. Poor bugger died at the age of 52, reputedly of the booze, but seeing him lying there on his bier, all done up like a dog's dinner in a be-medalled French military uniform, I think that a mixture of shame and bewilderment at what had happened to his people might have been a sizeable contributing factor.

Tahiti is shaped like a turtle: Tahiti Nui is the body and Tahiti Iti the head. The road clings to the coast and we very soon decided that perhaps it might have been better to go the other way around the island. That way we would have had the inside lane; not that there is much traffic, because, as Iain has pointed out, with almost half of the island's population living in Papeete, that leaves the rest of the island pleasantly under-populated.

Tahiti's scenery takes some beating. Its highest mountain, Orohena, the dwelling place of the old gods of Tahiti, is 2257 metres. It was not successfully climbed until 1953 and the climbers found a Tahitian shrine on the top. Less high, but still as dramatic, peaks crowd the centre of the island, making it impossible for the road to do anything other than cling to the coast. Lush, dark-green jungled hills sweep down to the aquamarine sea. By the time you get to the end of this book you are going to be sick of phrases like that. But it's difficult to be subtle about scenery so unsubtle that it assaults your every sense.

Later we drove into the settlement of Mataiea which shows no sign of having been a home, at different times, to a trio of famous men. Gauguin lived in his private hell here, and Rupert Brooke fell in love with a local girl, while Somerset Maugham chose this same spot to research *The Moon and Sixpence*.

Another couple of hours of travelling, slowed by wanting to absorb every view, each more spectacular than the last, brought us across the thin isthmus and onto Tahiti Iti. Along the southern coast of this almost separate island the road goes slowly beside the flat, sandy beach and calm lagoon of Toahutu, the site of Zane Grey's fishing camp, 'Flower Point' which is described so vividly in his *Tales of Tahitian Waters.*

At the very end of the road along the northern coast is Tautira, where Robert Louis Stevenson spent a month on board his yacht *Casco* in 1888. After a while you get the feeling that anyone who's anyone has been to Tahiti! It probably has changed hardly at all since then. This is also the spot the Spaniards chose to make their abortive attempt at a settlement and where Cook, in what I found to be an unexpected gesture, carved the dates of English visits on the reverse side of a cross left by the Spanish.

Back across the isthmus and on along the northern edge of the main island we left the road to gawp at the splendid Cascade de Faarumui (you might even get to be sick of waterfalls too by the end of this crossing). Almost next door is Papenoo where we stopped to enjoy the spectacle of young men on surfboards crashing in towards nasty looking rocks. All the while, Sean gave a knowledgeable running commentary about the mistakes they were making. (Australians are as contemptuous of other nationals' surfing techniques as the English are about any lesser person's attempts to make tea.)

Dusk was coming up like the opposite of thunder when we sped by the closed gates of the Commissariat a l'Energie Atomique (CEA), the French Atomic Energy Commission which is the civilian arm of the nuclear tests in the Tuamotus. In 1975 adverse world opinion made them decide that it would be better to lock up here and move to Muraroa.

By dint of some spontaneous driving on Iain's part, we managed to make it to our day's final port of call, Point Venus, in time to watch the sun slip behind the cut out of Moorea pasted against the western sky. Point Venus is where the unimaginative Captain Samuel Wallis, in retaliation to Tahitians who hurled stones at his crew from their canoes, blasted hundreds of them out of the water with cannon fire. It's also where Captain James Cook built a fort with moats, spiked pallisades and mounted cannon, not to keep the Tahitians out, but to keep his own men in! So that they wouldn't all be out and about in the bushes with the vahines when it came time to map the transit of Venus. The celestial, not the earthly one.

The idea was that if an astronomer could successfully triangulate a body of a known distance, that is Venus passing before the sun, then the astonomer could successfully compute the distance to the sun, which in 1769 was unknown. This particular Venus transit was important because a previous attempt in 1761 had failed and the next transit of Venus would not take place for a further hundred years.

Cook, always a man for meticulous detail, as can be seen from his superb maps of the entire coast of New Zealand and of the east coast of Australia, made the observation, but it wasn't until he returned to England that scientists realised the measurements, made by the only instruments available at the time, were not precise enough to be of value.

Even so the Tahitian trip was a great success. Joseph Banks, the wealthy young botanist who helped finance the trip, collected a myriad plant specimens, wildlife and fish, all new to the scientists of Europe.

But perhaps even more importantly, this journey was the starting block from which Captain Cook took off and never looked back.

During the following day we noticed half a dozen or so young men fooling around in the hotel swimming pool with three or four glamorous vahines. Trish commented on the shortness of the fellows' hair, almost all of them had crewcuts.

'They're soldiers,' an American sitting nearby commented. 'French soldiers.'

Later, while talking to Bill Wong, the Chinese manager of the hotel, we asked about the young soldiers and learnt that the French military organisation in Tahiti maintains a permanent block booking for a certain number of hotel rooms, not only at his hotel, but at others also. The servicemen who use them are constantly changing, as they reboard their ships or aircraft or move off to Mururoa or other islands which the government uses in the nuclear test programme—the Centre d'Experimentations du Pacifique, or CEP as it's more widely known in the region.

The atom test programme is extremely unpopular with most people in French Polynesia, as it is, in fact, throughout the Pacific. The concept of idyllic atolls and the waters for kilometres around them being polluted by radioactivity is anathema for nearly all islanders. The first nuclear device was exploded in the atmosphere over Mururoa Atoll in July 1966. The programme continued, in the face of mounting international protest, until 1975, when the French government changed to underground tests on Fangataufa atoll in the Tuamotu group. But it still goes on.

'My wife's brother is Charlie Ching,' Bill Wong confided. 'He's in jail because of his involvement in the anti-nuclear protests.'

Charlie Ching? The name rang a bell, but it took a few minutes for the pieces to fit together.

'Charlie Ching?' I said. 'Wasn't he the leader of the Tahitian Independence Party?'

'That's right,' Bill said. 'But he was also mixed up with a splinter group called the "Toto Tupuna"... which means "Blood of Our Ancestors". It was actually a guerilla outfit which was planning to attack French military targets here, such as aircraft and ships, to try to get the French to stop testing and go home.'

We had been sitting in Bill's office, off the lobby. The telephone rang, interrupting our conversation. He was preoccupied for a few minutes on the line and from what he was saying it was clear that he was going to have to leave us.

'Look,' he said after he'd put down the phone. 'I'm sorry, but I have to go into town now. But would you like to join my wife and me for dinner?'

We were dying to hear the rest of the story about Charlie Ching, but there was nothing we could do about it. Anyway, the prospect of dinner with Bill and his wife was a pleasant one. He was a charming man, probably in his late 30s, very Chinese in appearance, but fluent in French and English, which he spoke with just a trace of an American accent.

Later in the day there was a message delivered to our room saying that Bill and his wife Therese would pick us up at 7.30 that evening. They were on time and, having organised a meal for Zara and Sean, we left them at the hotel to drive downtown with the Wongs to the relatively new Kon Tiki Hotel on the waterfront.

'Surely this is helping the opposition, coming here?' I asked as we went up to the top floor in the elevator.

'That's right,' Therese laughed, 'but it's Chinese food here, that's why we like it.'

Both Bill and Therese were Hakka-speaking Chinese, as are the great majority of Chinese in French Polynesia. Both their families had been in the islands for several generations and presumably were descended from the original Chinese coolies, about a thousand of them, who were imported to labour on Tahitian cotton plantations during the American Civil War, when the northern American states couldn't get cotton from the Confederates. Only about a hundred of the coolies stayed in Tahiti when the operation folded up, but they formed the nucleus of what has become a powerful society of middlemen and merchants who now comprise about 10 per cent of the population.

Therese was in her mid-30s, attractive and elegantly groomed. We wanted to ask her about her brother, but the opportunity wasn't presenting itself. The food was beautiful, if outrageously expensive and the view, from the sweeping, circular rooftop restaurant, across Papeete harbour, was spectacular.

'Your brother...?' I said a trifle hesitantly, '...is he...all right? Do you hear from him at all?'

She too hesitated a moment, as if it was something she didn't really want to discuss. Bill looked at his wife, but said nothing. 'No,' she said. 'He is in France. I think in the Baumettes Prison in Marseilles.'

Since talking to Bill in the morning, we had boned up a little on Charlie Ching, his Independence Party and the trial that shocked French Polynesia. Five members of the Toto Tupuna guerilla group had planted a bomb against the walls of the Tahiti Telephone Exchange. No-one was hurt and little damage was done when it went off, but two weeks later one of the group, a Marcel Tahutini had murdered a French businessman in cold blood in his own home, leaving a message saying, 'We do not want any more Frenchmen in our country.'

It was proven during the trial that Charlie Ching was not implicated in either incident, but he admitted having been involved in the actual establishment and organisation of the guerilla group. He got 10 years, the others 18 and 20. The uproar and publicity surrounding the trial has long since died down, at least on the surface, but the situation that sparked those events remains, and the issue is bound to bubble to the surface again. It's not only the bomb, but the French presence as a colonial power. The radicals like Charlie Ching and the Toto Tupuna who want total independence are only a small minority, but that's usually all there is in most independence movements.

The French managed to take a good deal of heat out of the situation in July 1977 when they introduced constitutional changes giving the territory an almost autonomous system of government. Its Territorial Assembly, which has wide legislative powers, consists of 30 members who are elected every five years by popular vote. These members then elect seven people to form the Government Council (Conseil de Gouvernement). The remaining bones of contention are firstly, that the Council is presided over by a high commissioner who is a French civil servant appointed by Paris. He is the chief executive of the whole territory and wields considerable power. Secondly, France still runs French Polynesia's foreign affairs, citizenship, defence, police and justice departments as well as secondary education.

Nevertheless, the territory has been controlling its own budget, and in all other aspects running its own internal affairs, using its own language and flying its own flag since July '77. 'That is enough for now,' the vice president of the Governing Council, Francis Sandford, has said. 'The rest will come.'

And that's more or less the view of most of the middle class, or white-collar workers in French Polynesia to whom the concept of violent change, as prescribed by Charlie Ching and the Toto Tupuna is worse than the French presence. Therese, I think, shares that view. 'I'm not really interested in politics,' she told us after my question about Charlie.

After we finished our meal at the Kon Tiki we sat and talked over a drink before Bill and Therese drove us in their big air-conditioned limousine back to the hotel where Trish and I sat on the sea wall for a while in the warm night air, watching the moonlight reflect in the lapping shallows of the coral pools.

It was ridiculous to think of terrorists in a place like Tahiti. 'Problems in Paradise'...the ubiquitous catch-phrase headline kept coming to mind... and yet it was true. The twentieth century was catching up fast with places that for generations had somehow remained immune from it. I couldn't help thinking that in the days of Quinn's Bar, there'd have been no post office explosions—too many more important things to do.

In the morning, our friend Peggy McCarr phoned. We'd left messages for her at the American Express office in Papeete but hadn't expected her to arrive for another week or so, after our return from the Tuamotus. She had arrived early. We explained that we were due to leave for Rangiroa the next day.

'I'll come with you,' she said.

I told her of the difficulties we'd experienced in getting seats on the plane and said that she might have some trouble too. But apparently our own seats had become available because a group had cancelled their flight, so there was still a seat left for Peg.

# 3  **RANGIROA**
'Shark!'

A beautiful atoll seen from the air is, I think, one of the world's greatest spectacles. It has somehow an air of unbelievability about it. The colours; the wonderful azure and turquoise of the lagoons seem unreal, particularly to those, like ourselves, who don't live in the islands.

Rangiroa certainly had this effect on us as we flew in over it after a 350-kilometre flight, lasting just on an hour, from Tahiti. This particular atoll, though, *does* have a few other things going for it apart from just beauty. For a start it is huge! Its lagoon is well over 1000 square kilometres in area, amongst the largest in the world. The entire island of Tahiti, which as we've mentioned, is the largest in all of French Polynesia, could be enclosed within Rangiroa's lagoon. And yet, on this immense ring of coral reef, tiny islets and slightly larger islands that are covered with coconut palms, there are only two small villages which contain between them, less than 1500 people.

In retrospect, it's strange that such a small place (small I mean in population and in the actual area that is lived on and used) should have impressed us so much. At first glance, the small island on which we stayed would seem to have little to offer. About 10 kilometres long by about half a kilometre wide it is flat (no ground higher than about three or four metres above sea level), hot and dry, and really nothing much on it except coconut trees. But Rangiroa presented us with such a kaleidoscope of colours, people and events, that it sits in our memories as a fascinating place of great beauty.

It began with our landing on the tiny airstrip which had been bulldozed out of the coral. The 'terminal' was a thatched-roofed, open-sided building in which a group of people waited with flowers in their hair and dressed in colourful clothes (or a lack of them) to greet friends and relatives coming off the plane with leis of frangipani or tiare tahiti.

Unfortunately, we had no-one to meet us and we weren't sure where we were going to stay. There was only one hotel on the island, the Kia Ora, a sprinkling of attractive, Polynesian-style bungalows set back from the beach in a coconut plantation. But it was way too expensive for us so we picked at random from a list we had been given of local inhabitants who offer simple accommodation in their homes. Chez Jean Ami looked okay; about the cheapest on the island, although still a good deal more pricey than we would have liked.

'Connaissez-vous Jean Ami?' I tried my basic French on a bystander.

He turned, 'Oui, il est ici,' and gestured to a moustachioed man in his 40s standing nearby.

A few words of greeting and enquiry to Jean Ami and, yes, he had a small hut he could spare. Then, within a few minutes, we were off in the back of his Landrover for the five- or six-kilometre drive to the little township of Avatoru. A friendly kelpie bitch which had evidently just whelped, had taken a liking to us during the short time we were at the airfield and leaped into the back of the vehicle just as we were leaving to accompany us into the town.

The sky was an absolutely clear, dark blue, not a cloud to be seen. It was hot and dry, it felt almost arid, although there was plenty of greenery about. Twelve or 13 years ago, when Zara was only a couple of months old, we spent an idyllic six weeks in a tiny, primitive house on one of the out-islands of the Bahamas, Cat Island. This place had something of the same ambience. It was a nice feeling.

We met Jean Ami's wife, Marie. She was fat and smiling; a comfortable person. She showed us to our accommodation: a two-bedroom, thatched-roof fare on stilts over the water. Very basic, but it was fine for us. Zara and Peg would share one room, Trish and I the other, while Sean would sleep on a divan in the small hallway between the doorway and the verandah which looked straight out onto the coral and the crystal-blue lagoon. Fantastic!

Sean and I went for a swim almost immediately while the others rested and settled in. The water on the reef was very shallow for 50 metres or so from the hut, but we eventually reached a deeper channel, seven or eight metres deep, parallel to the shoreline where the water was running by very quickly. It was spectacularly beautiful; coral heads, small fish of every description and colour. As we drifted along in the current, looking at everything, our eye balls rolling from left to right behind our masks, the only sound we heard was the soft hhhhsss...sssshhhh of our breathing through the snorkels and the hardly-definable scratching and crackling background noise of the sea washing on the sand and coral floor.

The water had very soon carried us a 100 metres or so down the channel and along the beach, so we began to make our way back through the shallower water over the reef, gliding along in probably only half a metre of water, pulling ourselves by hand from one coral formation to the next. Suddenly a large, greeny-grey head emerged from a hole in the coral. We stopped in our tracks. Beady eyes examined us venomously. The head emerged further. It was a moray eel! The first we had seen. We back-pedalled fast and detoured around him to make our way back towards the hut.

Then we went back out again with Trish to repeat the whole process of drifting down the channel. Trish hasn't really been, as they say, 'into' snorkelling in the past, but this was an eye-opener for her. She was ecstatic. The water was so clear and warm, the colours so wonderful and the coral and fish so fascinating, that it would be difficult *not* to be impressed. (We hadn't told her about the moray eel!)

Next we were strolling down the one street in the town to explore. Two young men sat on a wall strumming a guitar and banjo. They smiled, said hello and kept playing. Everybody on the road smiled. Everybody said hello. So friendly, and they all seemed so huge, the women too. Big straw hats, brilliant floral dresses—happy.

The road had only one curve in it and was lined with small houses, some made of coral stones, some of concrete blocks and cement, some with thatched roofs, some with tin. But they were all surrounded with plenty of shrubs and plants and trees; coconut, mango and papaya. The light seemed incredibly bright. A group of women were sitting cross-legged on the verandah of one house weaving mats. They waved as we walked by, but the dogs sleeping under the house and on the steps didn't move. We passed another house bearing a sign saying 'Bank of Tahiti' and three different churches all painted brilliant white. Shortly we arrived at the end of the road, having walked from one end of the town to the other in not more than seven or eight minutes.

After a siesta in the afternoon, Jean Ami gave us a lift to the Kia Ora Hotel, which was back past the airport, about eight or nine kilometres away, at the far end of our little island. The hotel whose name means 'welcome' in the Tuamotan dialect, has a small bar which opens onto a wooden deck over-looking a fenced-off pool in which several sharks swam continually back and forth, back and forth, a source of endless fascination for the bar patrons sitting on the deck. At the far end of the pier that runs out from the beach, a half dozen or so young men and three or four women were swimming and we were reminded that this was definitely *French* Polynesia. The women were all topless.

Then, gazing across the lagoon, there was the incongruous sight of a warship at anchor near a small island. The young men next to us on the pier were apparently sailors from the vessel. There was a two-way radio beside them which crackled every so often with communications from the ship, which was, one of them told us, the French navy's destroyer escort *Bleny*. It had just sailed out from France via the Cape of Good Hope, the Indian Ocean and Australia. One of the others who had been on the same ship for a few years, said that the previous year they had also come out to French Polynesia but via the Atlantic and Panama. Not a bad life.

'Are you out here in connection with the nuclear testing programme?' I asked.

A cautious raising of eyebrows and a reluctant nod.

'And *this* is what you call duty?' Trish said, smiling.

Laughter...relaxing...'But of course...c'est formidable...eh?'

Before we left the hotel (we had arranged to meet up with Jean Ami again at about 5.30), we browsed through the little shop attached to the hotel office. I picked up an illustrated book which was written in English and called *Sharks of Polynesia.* As I flicked through it, something about Rangiroa caught my eye. Trish, Peggy, Zara and Sean were looking at other things. I read quickly on. I can't remember the actual phrasing, but it gave details of how a French scientific team had captured a number of black and white tipped reef sharks of various sizes, up to about two metres long. They fitted several of them with a form of radio transmitter by which they could plot their movements in and out of the lagoon. There was a map. It showed how these sharks cruised at specific times of the day, depending on the tides and currents, up and down the deep pass which runs by the town of Avatoru to the open sea, and also in the channel in which Sean and I and then Trish had been swimming. Gulp. I was on the point of showing it to the others but then hesitated. It might only scare them off snorkelling completely. I shut the book and put it down.

Back at the hut, we cooked up our first meal; tinned sausages in tomato paste with green beans (also tinned) and bread and butter. Jean Ami said that his wife could provide us with meals if we wished, but at an extra $40 for us all, we opted to take only breakfast, which was cheap ($1.00) and to cook our own food for the other meals.

After dinner we relaxed on the verandah, then went to bed. During the night there was torrential rain. It sounded great on our thatched roof.

My notes for the next day read:
*Today is Iain's birthday. He is 44 and looking good on it. What's more important, he's feeling great on it. Packed a lot into those 44 years and there's more than twice as much to pack into the next 44!*

It was a Sunday and, as it was obvious that everybody else was going to church, we decided that our best plan was to do likewise. The question arose: which church.

'Are you Catholic or Protestant?' Jean Ami asked.

On such deceptively simple questions have depended the fates of whole nations, let alone the lives of individuals. A sixth sense told me that whichever I plumped for would be better than pleading the fifth amendment or disclaiming membership of either half of the same whole. The odds were 50 per cent on, but there again, they were 50 per cent against.

'Protestant,' I spoke up boldly, determined that, as I was to lie, I would lie unashamedly. Jean Ami's face was wreathed in smiles and we all smiled back with nervous relief. But the relief was short-lived for we soon discovered that the Protestant church to which Jean Ami belonged and to which we therefore felt obliged to go, was not at all the Protestant church of our long-past youth but instead took the form of personal witness.

The service began at 8 a.m. and, dressed in the best gear we could muster, which included straw hats for Peg, Zara and myself, we were shown to the very front pews, where we sat, conspicuous in the extreme, while one after another members of the 30 or so strong congregation sprang to their feet behind us and bared their souls. In Tahitian.

The minister, who started off the proceedings, was a very handsome man, perhaps in his early 40s, with only one arm. Speculation about how he lost his other one kept Sean occupied for some little while, but after that he began to fidget. (We were told later that a shark took it.) The only decorations on the bare walls of the plain room were ropes of shells. So there was little distraction to occupy an alert mind. Zara is fine on occasions such as these; she either puts her mind into alpha or plans what she is going to do with her life for the next 20 years. Sean, however, has not developed these inner resources and Iain, in the already heady heat, was in danger of falling asleep. Tahitian is a very soporific language if you don't understand a word of it!

It was a full hour before they paused for breath and all moved outdoors to stand about in the shade of the building and gossip with friends. All the men wore dark, sombre, old-fashioned suits. All the women were adorned with large straw hats decorated with bands of shells or flowers. They all smiled in a warm welcoming way and it was obvious that they were only taking a break before going back for more. But Sean, his limbs twitching with the constraints of confinement, had already begun to run home and we decided to follow suit, though rather more sedately.

Along the track, four or five hundred metres out of the village, we found a white, sandy beach. Just us and the second biggest lagoon in the world. Sean and Iain donned masks and flippers and James Bonded away into the depths.

Peg, Zara and I sat on a large slice of barely submerged coral and talked. Peg is one of our longest-standing friends. She's known the children since they were in nappies and me through the various multi-faceted aspects of motherhood. For Peg there have been marriages, children and heartbreak. She's one of those rare people who are kind and unselfish, yet seem to have a monumentally unfair share of bad luck. Although she never complains, her situation is enough to make you wonder if life is indeed a bad joke perpetrated by some mad fiend.

Two months earlier, after she had been through major surgery and told that future prognostications were uncertain, she decided that it was now-or-never time and threw in her high-powered, well-paid job. Leaving a few things in store with friends and selling up the rest, she bade farewell to family, friends and colleagues (the majority of whom were full of doom and pessimism at such a move) and bought a one-way ticket out of Sydney to points east: Tahiti, Hawaii, Alaska, Mexico, Peru and wherever the whim and events led her. It's called courage, it's also called living.

A very few people are certain of the limitations put on their alloted time. The rest of us mostly manage to pretend that it won't ever happen...that the end is an unimaginably long time away. It isn't. Today is gone and is not coming back. There are only 365 todays and bang, there goes a year. And if you're lucky...you've got 75-80 of those 365 gone-todays and then the really *big* adventure. That was the sort of thing we talked about, sitting out there on a slice of coral surrounded by the warm, blue water. It was conducive to considering such weighty matters!

'Hey, Peg, come and have a look at this,' Iain shouted and waved and when Peg joined him, helped her into flippers, mask and snorkel for her first such watery excursion. For half an hour I could see the tips of their snorkels off the edge of the reef and hear Peg's exclamations of delight and surprise. Then they swam up to the beach, to which I had retreated in search of the minute amount of shade, and Peg was in a paroxysm of joy. Couldn't get the words out fast enough. 'A new world...Wonderful. Fantastic...Going to take scuba lessons...Been there all this time and I've never seen it...What a waste...Fabulous...Let's go back in...Come on, Trish.'

I offer no excuse over the fact that I am slow to undertake new physical ventures. There is none. It's just fear of the unknown I suppose; of being in an alien environment over which I have no control. I need to be encouraged. Slowly. Then once I get the bit between my teeth there's no stopping me and quite often people are sorry they started it!

So it was with snorkelling. I loved seeing the fish, the coral, the colours, the foreignness, having the new experience. But only in very short bursts, because I would suddenly be overcome with irrational fear. It was very strange. I wanted to go in so very badly and yet I had to force myself to push off over the edge of the reef, to watch the solid world drop away beneath me. I suffer a clutch of fear just writing about it! I did manage several little forays but the day really belonged to Peg who leapt in, boots and all.

The next morning we were awoken at six by the sound of motors and engines roaring. Looking out of our window we saw that just along the waterfront two huge yellow dredges were hard at work digging a miniature harbour out of the coral. A big, fuzzy-haired Tahitian we had seen on a couple of occasions sitting around at Jean Ami's playing a guitar and shooting pool was driving one of the machines.

The noise was distracting...not what we really wanted on a tropical paradise, but then, when we thought of it, one could hardly deny Rangiroa islanders a decent, protected place to moor their boats just because a few visitors don't like the sound of dredging.

The sky for a change that morning was dark. Heavy with rain clouds. So, not being in a hurry to rush out and swim or sunbake, we sat for two hours over our breakfast of French bread and coffee from a thermos and talked to another of Jean Ami's few guests, an Italian girl called Leda.

Leda was minute. She stood little more than 1.6 metres tall and could not have weighed more than 40 kilos. She went everywhere in just her bikini and she was burnt almost black. I would have said she was about 35, although it could have been a little less. She was on holiday for a month, she told us, from her job as a hostess with Ethiopian Airlines.

'Ethiopian Airlines?' We were all equally surprised. It seemed a long way from Addis Ababa to Rangiroa, but then, Rangiroa was a long way from anywhere. She'd been on the island for about 10 days or so and knew a great deal more about it and the people on it than we did. She'd been diving, she said, with the fisherman, Nanua, in the deep pass next to the town.

'The Avatoru Pass?' I asked, thinking immediately of the book I'd seen in the small shop at the Kia Ora Hotel.

'Yes, that's right. It is absolutely fantastic. The water is 20 to 30 metres deep and you can see clearly right to the bottom. Nanua dives almost all the way—at least 20 metres.'

'And...I, er...don't suppose you see any sharks?'

'Sharks?' She blinked and pursed her lips in what seemed a peculiarly Italian expression. 'Ha!' she laughed. 'Of course. There are plenty of sharks.'

'Plenty? But surely they're dangerous!'

'Oh no...I'm sure they're not. They are too well fed to worry about humans. There are too many fish to eat.'

'What sort are they?'

'I think they are reef sharks. They have black tips or white tips on their fins. There are bigger kinds...I think. How do you call it "hammerhead"? But they mostly stay out in the open sea. Would you like to come out to dive with Nanua?'

There was a pause. 'Well...er...you see,' I began.

'Terrific!' Peggy put in. 'I'd love to see a shark in the flesh.'

I turned with a little alarm to glance at Peggy, but she was looking at Leda.

'Good,' Leda said. 'Later in the week. I'm going again. It's great!'

I gave a weak smile. Peggy's new-found enthusiasm for sub-aquatic delights was one thing, but swimming with sharks...? Anyway, at least it looked like resolving one issue for us. We had been intending to only stay three or four days on Rangiroa and then shuffle on to another atoll or two, but really we'd hardly had a chance to scrape the surface here. It would be foolish to leave too soon.

As the weather was still overcast and gloomy, we sat around in our little fare and read.

Also during the morning I carved a coconut. More than twenty years previously, when I was in northern Queensland, I managed to make quite a reasonable living for a short while carving faces in coconuts and selling them to tourists for £1 each. This was the first time I'd tried to do it again for many years. The children were mightily impressed. It seemed I hadn't lost the touch. I thought maybe we should set up shop on Rangiroa.

About this time we met Herold, the big Tahitian dredge operator who had woken us up so noisily that morning. He came back for a tea-break to Chez Ami and we talked for a while before he went back to the job. He was 24 years old, we learnt, and had been trained to drive heavy earth-moving equipment in the French Army.

'Was that National Service?' I asked. 'The draft?'

His English was surprisingly good as he had apparently only recently spent some time in Hawaii, where he had played guitar in a pop group. 'Yes,' he said. 'Everybody in French Polynesia must spend one year of military service.'

'Tahitians...Polynesians also? Not just Frenchmen?'

'Correct. Tahitians...everybody—all young men. They go to France also.'

'You were in France?'

'Of course, many do their army training there. Some stay. But I am not liking France. Finished with Army now. I am working.' He raised his eyebrows and smiled. 'Very good money.'

Not being one for great delicacy in these matters, I asked him, 'How much?'

'120 000,' the answer came, without hesitation or embarrassment.

'120 000 francs?'

'Right.'

'Per month?'

'Yes.'

Which translates to US$1 600 per month, or roughly $400 a week. Not bad for a 24-year-old, but also an indication that although prices are high in French Polynesia, wages are too.

Herold went back to his work and almost at the same time, the sun came out so, collecting our costumes, masks and snorkels, we set off to follow a small path across the island, about a kilometre, I suppose, to the ocean beach, just to see what it was like. The track was absolutely deserted; no houses or people. It was scorchingly hot and when we got to the shore it was disappointing. Very jagged coral which was covered for almost 200 metres out from the beach by only 10 centimetres or so of water right to where the surf was pounding heavily on the reef. Nowhere to swim.

We turned and walked back to the white sandy lagoon beach from which we'd swum the day before, to spend a lazy afternoon snorkelling, getting up a good sun-tan, reading, talking and then walking back to our little fare to sit on the verandah sipping at my birthday Chivas Regal and watching the sun go down in a blaze of glory.

We'd bought some tinned Chinese food at the local store during the day—duck and pork—so I cooked that up with some tinned vegetables for dinner, followed by a big papaya Madame Ami had given us. Strangely there were very few mangos on the island. Nothing like the huge beauties we'd had in Tahiti. We didn't know it at the time, but right across the Pacific we would not once be able to find mangos like those from the market in Papeete.

After dinner we played backgammon on Peg's portable set and also pontoon, which Sean won handily.

Then, at 9.30 Jean Ami's generator which generally hummed away as a sort of background noise, slowly died and the lights with it, glimmering softly out to blackness.

By our fourth day on Rangiroa we had caught the disease which is inescapable for anyone who spends more than a few weeks in the islands of the South Pacific. The symptoms are feeling slow and easy and like there's nothing which can't be done tomorrow, probably better than it can be done today. 'Aita a pe'a pe'a' (It's no big thing), is roughly the equivalent of, 'She'll be right, mate', in Australia. Having caught this malady we missed hitching a lift in the butcher's van which was taking bread down to the Kia Ora Hotel. So? So we walked.

It was hot. Iain with a sarong wrapped round his head and wearing sunglasses looked like a happier version of Yasser Arafat. We walked slowly along the narrow strip of tarmac; on one side the still lagoon and on the other the surf. The vegetation looked hardy, rather than lush. It *has* to be in order to wrest enough nutrient from the bleached dead coral to live.

At the eight kilometre point, opposite the tiny aerodrome, we fell into the lagoon to cool off and Sean took gruesome delight in finding a metre-long dead shark on the sand where it had probably been left after being caught by a fisherman. It was tan with a black tip to its fin, skin like tough sandpaper, fearsome even when dead. It didn't make me any more relaxed about snorkelling or even simply swimming.

Refreshed, we started off again and after only a couple of hundred metres, heard the approach of the only vehicle we had seen so far that morning. We smiled, looked exhausted and stuck out our thumbs. The little van, a hotel runabout which was driven by a Tahitian woman who had a small child beside her, stopped and we all thankyoued and clambered in the back. She was going to the hotel and travelled the remaining few kilometres in short order, letting us off before the turn-in to the hotel grounds so that the owners wouldn't know of her act of charity.

A short cut through a coconut plantation brought us out to the pass which we wanted to cross for no other reason than just because it was there and Tiputa was on the other side. It was some little while before we sighted anybody nearby and then a fisherman appeared a short distance up the bank and Iain asked him for a lift across the 200 metre gap.

Tiputa is startlingly different from Avatoru. In addition to the coconut trees, which grow most other places on the atoll, Tiputa also has frangipani, hibiscus, tiare tahiti and my favourite, plumeria. There are also fruit trees, papaya, banana, limes, avocado. And most unusual of all there's grass. The homes are more substantial. They have gardens and small lawns and the one little street is bordered by low, coral walls which are white-washed and very attractive. There's more a feeling of communal pride.

The reason is that Tiputa, at the turn of the century, was a relatively affluent little place, a centre for the mother-of-pearl industry in the Tuamotus. Affluent enough to ship in soil from Tahiti and trees from Singapore, Samoa and Sri Lanka. With the advent of plastics, the bottom dropped out of the mother-of-pearl button market and Tiputa stood still. 1885 is the date above the door of one abandoned house. There are a number of empty houses, many of them stylish, in the little village whose population is now 500. One of the most impressive of these is a Chinese-style place, very similar to the old places in Singapore or in Malacca, which are fast disappearing.

Not all these people have gone for good, some have only gone walkabout to one of the deserted motus in the lagoon where they can live on fish and coconut milk in solitary communion with the sea and the sky, just for the change, to have a break from 'city' life in downtown Tiputa.

Alongside a small grocery store we found a very old lady who sold us a large beer and a large soft drink and who was pleased to sit stringing beads and talk to us in English. She was a Cook Islander. 'I came here 27 years ago,' she told us. She still doesn't speak French. How's that for Anglophilia.

After crossing the Pass back to the Kia Ora we found that the van, the same one we'd hitched a lift in on the morning journey in, was available to give us a lift back: $9 for the five of us for fourteen kilometres, almost as much as a New York taxi!

After dinner back at our fare, we talked some more with Herold, the dredge operator, who was complaining of boredom. Apparently his machine had broken down early that afternoon, though a message had been sent to his employers in Papeete and a mechanic would be flying up to see what was needed to fix it. He was unhappy at the idea of just sitting about in the sun, playing his guitar and having an occasional dip in the lagoon. Boring!

Instead he had happily agreed to drive our neighbour's bulldozer on the same project for a day so that this man could spend time with his girlfriend whom he had brought up from Papette and who was going off her brain sitting around all day with nothing to do while he worked.

'Good for him,' Herold smiled his broad, warm smile, 'and good for me too. 3000 francs ($40) he pays me. On top of my own money.' He didn't sound like the projected image of a Polynesian.

'Are you saving up for something in particular?' I asked.

'Yes. I want to go back to Hawaii in a couple of months time. I have a girl there. I show you photos.'

He brought out half a dozen or so which showed him with a bunch of friends fooling about on the beach. Herold, a large strong, muscular young man, had his arm around an attractive blonde and, in the crook of the other, held a handsome boy of about seven.

'Who's this?'

'My son. He lives with my girl. She is a popa'a.'

'Popa'a?'

'Yes. Popa'a means European. But he is not her son. He is from a Chinese girl in Papeete. His name is Moana.' He held the photo carefully and his voice softened. 'It is difficult to explain exactly, but it means something like the edge of the reef...the place where the water becomes suddenly deep. Moana. I miss him.'

It was at this moment that I became aware of the 'one-ness' of Polynesia. A young man of 24 with a son of seven. So he had become a father at 17. No marriage. No big deal. And now the boy was cared for by an American girl in Hawaii, an island which technically is part of a different nation from Tahiti, but for this man is simply another South Pacific island and therefore part of his heritage. And his son is called Moana... 'edge of the reef, where the water is suddenly deep.' And he missed him. I smiled in an inadequate expression of understanding.

The home of Nanua the fisherman consisted of a strange ramshackle collection of huts and a couple of broken-down cars set in amongst some big trees on a piece of land that fronts straight onto the Avatoru Pass. Nanua was a very large man...fat, as only Polynesians can be. His wife, who, like Madame Ami was also called Marie, was however considerably smaller, positively slim in fact, which is unusual for Tahitians over 30. Her straight, dark hair, showing a few streaks of grey, was cut in a fringe and there was a gentle smile always on her face. Her maiden name was Pomare...the name of the Tahitian Royal family. She was a descendant of the last line of kings of Tahiti before it was ceded to France.

At 8.00 o'clock in the morning, when Sean and I called on them, Nanua was working on the outboard motor of his small open launch while Marie was cleaning a rough-hewn wooden table which stood in the centre of their white sandy back yard. There were two large benches beside it and it served very adequately as a permanent outdoor dining table. We had come to ask if the four of us and Peggy could join our Italian friend Leda when she went out with Nanua later in the morning. A boyfriend of Leda's who was staying with Nanua was also apparently coming along. We had met him the previous day. He was a tall, well-built Dutchman named Guy who was aged about 24 or 25, I guess. We wanted to check whether the extra five people would be too much for his boat.

Nanua as I mentioned, was a giant of a man, fat, either as a result of eating too much over the years, or of a genetic strain in the race...or both. In fact, since meeting Nanua we have read that there is a theory which holds that, of the ancient Polynesian ocean voyagers, those most fitted to survive the incredible privations of such epic journeys were those with a more than ample supply of body fat which could tide them over for longer periods without food or water. If these *were* the ones who survived more readily, it would explain the huge size of their descendants. Anyway, whatever the reason, Nanua was certainly fat. He had a huge stomach, which hung over his shorts, a couple of broken teeth and was unshaven. He could hardly be described as 'attractive' and yet he had almost perfect skin, a wonderful smile and was probably one of the happiest people one could expect to meet. He came across to talk to us and we asked if the boat was big enough to take all of us.

'Of course it is,' he insisted, with a wave of his hand towards the little orange and white boat which looked less than five metres long. 'We leave at 10.00 o'clock.'

On the way back to Jean Ami's place, Sean and I stopped on the large concrete pier which juts from the shore, a short distance from Nanua's house, out into the Pass a short way. A group of half a dozen people and several children were on the pier, fishing. Sean and I stood there for a while watching what for me was one of the most amazing displays of fishing I have ever seen. They were all simply casting weighted handlines as far out into the Pass as possible and pulling them slowly back in from the deep, swiftly flowing water. And, almost as fast as they could bait the hooks with squid and throw them, they were pulling in five and six-kilo fish, over half a metre long. We stood open-mouthed as a large woman just kept hauling them in, one after the other; snapper, parrot-fish, some sort of mullet, another that looked like tailor and dropped them into a large, open basket she had suspended in the water from one of the bollards on the pier. A fisherman's fantasy. Something they dream of in other parts of the world. On Rangiroa, it was just a normal morning's fishing.

When we all left, at shortly after 10.00, crammed into Nanua's boat, there was some disappointment and some relief. The disappointment was over the fact that we weren't immediately going to swim with the sharks which was also why *we* were relieved.

'I want to show you my island first,' Nanua said. He pointed ahead to a tiny motu about a half a kilometre out into the main lagoon.

We had seen the island before from our hut at Jean Ami's and had fantasised about owning a little paradise like it. It was delightful...a miniature Robinson Crusoe island, only 100 metres long by about 20 metres wide with white sandy beaches and a small coral reef that extended out for 10 or 20 metres around it before the water became deeper. Lush vegetation covered the whole island; coconuts, pandanus and shrubbery, almost completely hiding two tiny thatched huts at one end. Just the place to get away from it all...not that Nanua wanted to get away from anything. Apparently the island had always belonged to his family and he was now thinking of making it into a little honeymoon retreat for tourists who *really* wanted to be alone.

We walked around it for 10 or 15 minutes admiring it and dreaming of what we'd do to make it livable...put in a water tank to collect rainwater, plant a few little vegetables etc. etc. And then suddenly Nanua waved his arm. 'Okay,' he shouted, 'we go and see the sharks now.'

We piled into the boat, rather silently I thought, and Sean asked, 'How far away will the sharks be?'

'I don't really know,' I said, swallowing slightly more than usual. 'Not very far, I suppose.'

What is it, I wondered, that motivates people to do things they're actually scared of doing?

Nanua started the outboard motor and headed the boat out over the coral heads towards the pass. Cruuunnch!! Bang! The motor bounced up and almost came off the transom.

'Merde!' Nanua swore.

We had hit a coral head and broken off a sheer-pin (which locks the propellor in place) on the motor. Nanua was quickly over the side and on to the coral in waist-deep water to pull the boat back towards his little island. He didn't have a spare sheer-pin on board, so with hardly credible ingenuity, he set about fashioning one from a piece of metal he found on the island, hammering it into shape with a piece of coral.

People have various ways of signposting their lives. Many women will say, 'That must have been before Charlie was born', or 'When I was pregnant with Jennifer.' Men tend more towards, 'When I was working for,' or 'While I was playing football for.' That's not sexist...it's fact. In our family, but only when we are alone (because we are aware that it sounds a bit much to other people) we shorthand conversations with prefixes like, 'before Singapore,' 'after Africa,' 'until South America.' Now I have another way to recall and measure time: 'Before and after *the shark.*'

Within minutes of Nanua fixing the broken pin, we had motored to a spot on the far side of the pass and thrown out an anchor onto the edge of the coral wall. It had all happened so quickly, I hadn't time to work myself up into a frenzy of fear before everyone was holding their noses and falling off the boat backwards in a very professional manner. There was much spitting into masks and adjustment of snorkels and then...there it was below me...the edge of the reef. Crikey! It was deep. Fifteen, 20, 25 metres. So deep and yet clear to the bottom. And thick with fish. Parrot-fish, grouper, puffer fish, angel fish, bone-thin trumpet fish and dozens more varieties, in schools and alone. And then there was coral, great lumps of it all down the edge of the reef, green, pink, blue.

We hovered on the surface, close to the edge of the reef, watching Nanua dive. It was quite amazing; in the water, all of his huge bulk and fat seemed miraculously to disappear. He became at once a swift, svelte creature, completely in tune with his environment. A big lungful of air, a few flips with his fins and he was dropping, head-first towards the bottom, his speargun held downwards in front of him, compensating all the way for the rapidly increasing depths by squeezing his nose and blowing hard to pop his ears and equalise the pressure.

I tried to follow, but could get no deeper than six or seven metres and then only stay for a few moments before returning to the surface to watch Nanua. Down, down he went to more than 20 metres where he held on to a piece of coral to steady himself against the current, then waited and watched as hoards of fish came inquisitively closer. The seconds ticked by. High above, on the surface, breathing easily through our snorkels, we watched as Nanua just stayed there. A minute, a minute and a half. Then *snap!* you could hear it through the water as the speargun went off and Nanua was immediately coming up fast to the surface, the speared fish trailing behind.

It was on his third catch, which had lasted more than two minutes, that I first saw the sharks. Two of them coming slowly from the darker blue of one end of the channel. They were small, not much more than a metre-and-a-half long, with black-tipped fins. Reef sharks . . . the 'friendly' ones we'd been told about. But a tingle of fear went through me, particularly as, when Nanua was bringing his catch to the surface, they began to follow him and come towards us.

Oh lord, is it? Yes. Yes. Help. Help. Don't panic. SHARK! Panic. Two of them. Different from every other fish. Moving without moving. Like torpedoes, only oozing persuasive confidence. Other fish move aside to leave a clear path for them. Fifteen metres down and coming my way. Fast. Panic. I grunted. Loudly. Pointed. Flailed my legs and arms and began to lunge my way back to the safety of the boat which seemed a hell of a long way off. Next thing I knew, Iain had grabbed me, ripped off his mask and was quietly but with great emphasis insisting that I should stop flapping about, endangering everyone else. I felt tears of fear and rage behind my mask and it's just as well he let go, because I might have bitten him, which I have been known to do from sheer terror.

I made it back to the boat, going as slowly and quietly as I dared and Nanua's son helped me scrabble up so I could flop over the gunwale. There I lay trying to take slower, smaller breaths, for I was in danger of choking, and also attempting to get some strength back into my muscles which had quite suddenly lost all power.

Iain swam back to rejoin the others. The next time Nanua came back to drop off some fish, he smiled kindly at me. 'Don't worry about the sharks,' he said. 'They will not attack without plenty of warning. They begin to come closer and to circle if they feel aggressive. These ones are OK.' I smiled weakly back and declined his suggestion that I should venture forth again. Zara came aboard looking unhappy. 'Did you see . . .?' I nodded. Zara and I suffer from the same excess of imagination.

There was quite a chop on the water and after I had recovered sufficiently from my fear to notice it, I started to feel a little queasy sitting in the boat which was moored only 10 metres or so off a small motu in the pass. I thought about it for a while and then persuaded Nanua's son to accompany me through the very shallow water to the little beach. The decision was a tussel between fear and imminent sea-sickness, but having reasoned that if the young boy came with me, this would decrease the risk of personal attack by 50 per cent, we left Zara in the dinghy, where she said she preferred to stay, and half-swam, half-crawled our way across the coral. The young boy left me there to wait for a further half hour or so, while the rest of them played out their dice with death.

Nanua caught more fish and gradually, one by one, the rest of them swam back to the boat. Iain, who doesn't have a nasty bone in his body, swam over to accompany me back. 'Come on. Hold my hand. You'll be all right. Sorry I shouted at you.'

He had taken my hand and with his other was feeling his way as we floated back toward the boat, when suddenly he let out the most almighty yell. Loud enough, I thought nastily, to attract every shark within 20 kilometres. 'Stone fish!' he yelled, putting his hand above the water. 'I put my hand on it.' The horrendously ugly thing moved slightly and it was only then that I realised it was a fish and not just another lump of coral. From a crevice in my consciousness where I store away, under lock and key, all nasty thoughts, burst forth the information that the spines on a stone fish are so poisonous that anyone touching them dies in dreadful agony within minutes. So he had grappled with me and shouted at me, but that didn't mean I wanted him to die in terrible pain!

Nanua came across, spear in hand, and thrust it through the fish which hardly registered its terrible impaling. Then he examined Iain's hand and forearm. He looked very serious. 'You are lucky,' he smiled, 'very lucky. You touched it this way,' He indicated, carefully moving his finger above the fish's back, 'so that the spines were lying down. If you had come from the other direction, the spines would stand up and stick into you. You would die.'

Iain was very pale beneath his tan and I was secretly reassured to know that he could register real fear. Back on board everyone examined the dying fish and Iain, much recovered, posed for a photograph. Quite a trip. Sean talked non-stop all the way back about what he had seen, especially the sharks.

At Nanua's, Maria, who had an open fire ready, was dextrously plaiting coconut leaves to use as roofing. With a big red hibiscus behind her ear, she stood beside the fire and cooked up her husband's morning catch, which we all helped devour along with generous amounts of hot Tahitian-style doughy bread. The fat rippled up and down Nanua's even more gigantic brother who arrived on the scene and was told of the morning's experiences. Nanua's imitation of my fear of the sharks *was* very funny.

Before we left, Iain gave Maria the coconut which he had carved and she was delighted. Immediately, without us saying a word, she could see its potential! 'If I carve more like these,' she said, 'and paint "Nanua's house" or "Rangiroa" or "Kia Ora" on them, I can sell to visitors. Yes?'

'Please tell your friends about us,' Nanua said. 'They would be most welcome. I am going to build a few more fares on another motu which I own on the other side of the lagoon. Very simple fares. We want a place, a real South Pacific paradise where you can go right back to nature. Fish for your food and we will make sure you have water and shelter. I think it will be wonderful. I know that many of your people want to get away from it all and this will be just the place.'

Back at Jean Ami's we reluctantly packed our bags. Herold came to the airport to wave us off and to put the large malfunctioning part of his dredger on the plane back to Papeete, where it would be repaired or replaced and sent up on the next week's flight.

Leaving was a wrench. I wasn't prepared to feel so sad at leaving Rangiroa. I'm usually OK at partings. But there were to be many more across the Pacific and they did not become easier.

# 4  MOOREA
## A night attack

The mountainous profile of Moorea quickly becomes a familiar backdrop for any visitor to Tahiti. Only 25 kilometres across The Sea of Moons, the dramatic, jagged peaks of Tohirea, Mouaputa and Rotui are constantly etched against the tropical sky. Unlike many things in life, on closer inspection they became even better.

A flight to Moorea from Fa'aa airport takes only 10 minutes but we enjoyed a gentler introduction from the decks of *Keke II* on an early morning hour-and-a-half-long voyage from Papeete harbour. The sea was calm, the air hot and the 14-metre, twin-diesel, modern vessel was filled with an international assortment of visitors because Moorea, which is named after a beautiful yellow lizard, is a tourist mecca.

Approaching the break in the necklace of the lagoon on the northeastern tip of the island, the view was of dense green jungle entirely smothering the mountainsides, which plunged down into the flat blue water, only rarely leaving space for more than a sliver of white beach.

We stopped briefly first at the little pier belonging to the Bali Hai hotel, which looks like everyone's dream of a South Pacific paradise. A select number of wooden, thatched roof fares built out on stilts above the lagoon. One problem; prices go to $340 a double and $315 a single for bed and breakfast.

Impossible not to feel envious of the few people who disembarked, but the envy was short-lived because no sooner had we pulled away than we rounded the tip of the island and entered what surely must be the most beautiful bay in the Pacific. Cook's Bay is named after the great navigator, despite the fact that he never moored there. Even the crew were still and silent as if in homage. Friendly banter among the passengers ceased, nobody even 'oohed' or 'aahed'. Such beauty demands silent appreciation. The bay is a narrow finger probing into the jungled mountains which rear up to tower above in awesome gothic splendour.

The Hotel Aimeo, whose private pier we moored alongside at the far end of Cook's Bay, is the oldest hotel on Moorea. Overnight in a five-bed fare would have cost us $224. The Dutch woman owner, on seeing our packs, suggested we try Chez Jacqueline, a guest house a couple of hundred metres back along the bay. At $26 a night it would have been OK, but it was full, whereas both the hotels were more than half empty. That should tell the tourist people something!

Half-covered in a faded *pareau,* Jacqueline, a large, part-Tahitian woman whose black hair dye had crept down her forehead, appeared genuinely sorry she hadn't room for us and suggested we try Chez Albert, a family pension up behind and overlooking the bay.

'$40 a night. But you must stay for at least two nights and pay in advance,' insisted Albert, when we got there. He was a German-Swiss, who, on hearing where we were from, told us that he had two grown daughters living in Sydney. Nevertheless, business came first. 'A shorter stay is not worth the price of washing the sheets,' he said.

We had disturbed him working on his mountainside garden and we made polite remarks about how well kept his place was and how beautiful the island was and what a great place to live. 'You think so,' he grimaced. 'Once upon a time I thought that too. Now I know better. I came here 43 years ago and all I have done is work. I don't have time to admire the view. Forty-three years in a fools' paradise.'

Some people are just born negative!

On the spur of the moment, we decided on a completely different approach. For about $40, including gas and mileage, we could hire a little white-painted Suzuki jeep in which we'd be able to tootle around the island at our leisure, looking at all the beauty spots and at the same time probably find a place to camp overnight. We weren't exactly prepared, as we'd left our tents back at the hotel in Papeete. We knew we'd only be a day or so on Moorea and didn't think we'd need them. As it happened, it was just the place we *did* need them. We had some groundsheets though, so at least we'd be able to rig some sort of shelter next to the car. This way we'd save the expense of a hotel and see Moorea to boot.

We'd hesitated over doing it this way, or rather, were almost completely put off, when we saw that Avis Rentacar were charging 800 Francs ($10.60) *an hour*! For a Mini Moke! On a normal 24-hour basis, the rental would come to a staggering $254! Talk about a rip off, that beat everything. But then we found Elise Rentacar, a little family-run organisation in the village of Pao Pao whose rates were much closer to reality.

It's only about 60 kilometres around Moorea and if you wanted to hurry, you could probably do it in little more than an hour. But we weren't in any great rush. Things were a little cramped, perhaps, in the back of the Suzuki, but everybody was in fine spirits as we took off, leaving Pao Pao and the sealed coastal road at the head of Cook's Bay to drive up into the mountains of the Valley of Opunohu.

Within a kilometre or so, as we followed the road up through hills thickly wooded with mape, or Tahitian chestnut trees, we came to our first *marae*, one of the ancient shrines at which the early Polynesians prayed to their ancestors. Although the site is marked on the local tourist guide map and is visited by many people, there was no-one else there when we arrived. We wandered in silence and some awe amongst the great trees that have wound their roots over and through the thousands of stones that make up the shrine. Here, the supreme god, Ta'aroa, and a whole panoply of lesser deities held sway. Although the sun was shining brightly on the mountain road where we had left the car, at the *marae* under the trees, we were in dense shade and there was an air of mystery and magic about the place.

A little farther up the valley we found a place with a different kind of magic, a lookout called Roto Nui, from which there is a view of breathtaking beauty. From this vantage point it is possible to look down the whole of both Cook's Bay and Opunohu Bay. These two spectacular, fjord-like, deep-water harbours, less than a kilometre apart are separated by the majestic, almost-vertical peaks of Mount Rotui, which itself rises almost a kilometre above the water.

It was the small village of Papetoai, at the western entrance to Opunohu Bay which became the headquarters of the London Missionary Society in 1811, the centre from which Christianity spread throughout the Society Islands and to the rest of the Pacific. The old octagonal church, built there in 1829, still stands, the oldest European building in use in the South Pacific.

As you continue around the coastal road from Papetoai you feel that Moorea has almost a surfeit of beauty. Cook's Bay and Opunohu Bay provide probably the most spectacular scenery, but wherever you go, you are presented with some magnificent new vista, some wonderful panorama which includes the 1200-metre-high Mount Tohivea or perhaps the incredible, needle-like spire of Mount Muaputa, which has a hole through its summit.

With all this beauty, Moorea is understandably one of French Polynesia's greatest tourist attractions. Consequently, there are a dozen or so luxurious (and extremely expensive) hotels spread out at various intervals around the island. Amongst them, Eric Taberly's Club Mediterranée on the northwest corner where the occupants of a guardhouse prevent any but the Club's guests from entering the grounds. Patrons of the Club Med can and do spend their entire Moorea holiday without leaving the area of the Club itself, probably without ever seeing a Polynesian who was not a hostess or employee of some sort of the Club.

Farther on around the island near the village of Haapiti we saw an enormous mango tree by the side of the road, so laden with fruit, we had to stop. As a great many had already fallen onto the ground where they had been left to rot, we thought it all right to ask in the small house on the property if we could pick some. A jovial elderly woman answered the door and then came out with a long pole and two children to help us collect a dozen or so beautiful mangos from the tree. We ate one each on the spot, and then, after thanking her profusely, drove on to continue our tour of the island. But the mangos were so delicious we didn't get more than a couple of kilometres before we had to stop at a little beach to eat some more and then drive on again.

Moorea is actually the remnants of a huge volcano. It is about 160 square kilometres in area and most of the soil on the mountain slopes and in the valleys is very rich, you can grow almost anything on Moorea. A considerable number of the island's 6000 people still follow the traditional agricultural way of life: raising pigs, doing some general farming and fishing. There are no big industries on Moorea, although there is a pineapple juice factory being built and the government is experimenting with freshwater shrimps and cattle.

In the old days, around the turn of the century, Moorea was a very big producer of vanilla. On our way, we passed several of the gracious old vanilla plantation homes built in colonial style with wide, elaborately-decorated wooden verandahs; most of them were set well back from the road. Today they are only relics of a more glorious past, because when the vanilla market faltered between the wars, the industry on Moorea died.

The only salaried jobs on the island now are in the tourist industry, which handles about 3000 visitors a month, or in government administration, or in the military.

It was late afternoon by the time we returned to Cook's Bay. We'd thought that we might find a camping spot on our way around the island, but some vacant beachfront land we'd seen earlier, near Chez Jacqueline's just outside the village of Pao Pao, was as good as anything we'd seen elsewhere. We asked Jacqueline and she said she was sure it would be all right for us to camp there. She knew the owners of the land and as they were away in France there should be no problems! We found a good position, under the widespread bows of a huge tree, which was secluded and quiet. We began setting up camp by tying the groundsheets from the car to one of the large branches of the tree. We were right on the water and the view across Cook's Bay was worth a million dollars.

After a campfire meal, eaten as the light faded behind Muaputa, we each chose our sleeping spots. Sean clambered into the back seat of the jeep and hung his legs through the side flaps. Iain and I sandwiched Zara between us and lay out on our sarongs beside the jeep, under the tarpaulin. Peg, who always manages to do things with a bit of style, spread her classy Harrods raincoat out under an upturned canoe which was blocked up a metre or so off the ground.

The pounding of the sea on the reef beyond the bay, combining with the regular hiss and suck of the water on the pebbles of our beach, was so soporific that even though I wanted to lie awake and watch the stars, I soon fell into a dreamless sleep. I awoke with a terrific start sometime later when I was given a hard hit on the head. Instantly fully awake, I turned my head and came eyeball to eyeball with a big crab who had his large pincer poised for another impatient rap. I jumped to my feet, hitting my head on the branch to which the tarpaulin was attached. My yell brought Iain to his feet. Whack! He too cracked his head and reeled back. It would have been good on film. No doubt the crab was highly amused by all this chaos he had caused, until Iain began shooing him off down to the sea. Apparently I was lying right over the crab's 'house-hole', and although Iain assured me that the crab would not return, I slept only fitfully, coming fully awake at any isolated noise, until the morning. We dozed in the incredibly soft, still, dawn air until about 7.30 am, when a young Tahitian man arrived with a bunch of sweet pineapples as a gift from Jacqueline, who hoped we had slept well. Then we packed up and returned the jeep. The owner of the small car and bike-hire outfit offered us the use of his lean-to kitchen on the side of his small wooden home. Here we heated up water for coffee and spread our fruit on the table for breakfast. He insisted that we use the family's tablecloth and their cups and plates and repeatedly asked if we needed anything else.

We found this again and again across the Pacific (and everywhere else in the world). If you stay in regular hotels you are treated as a regular tourist: no Tahitian fellow wakes you with a bunch of sweet pineapples or asks you to breakfast in his home.

We were intending to take the *Keke II* back to Tahiti in the afternoon, so, with plenty of time to spare, we went down onto the little wharf next to the Aimeo Hotel to swim and sit in the sun. The water in Cook's Bay was nothing like as clear as that on Rangiroa and the sandy bottom shelved quickly away to deep, dark water, but it was warm and pleasant to swim in, so we stayed there.

Later in the morning we met two young Americans, Bob Rhodos and Tom Kunz. They were in their early 20s, I guess, and were making their way across the Pacific in a manner something similar to ours; with backpacks, taking their time but keeping an eye on costs so as to make it all last longer. They'd been travelling together for quite some time and, while it was clear that they were the best of friends, they were a bit touchy with each other; they seemed to argue or disagree over everything. They did it in a friendly way, but it reminded me of a period I spent in my early 20s, travelling in Africa for months on end with a friend. He was my best friend, and still is, but by the end of that journey, we were coming to blows. We could see the same signs in Tom and Bob.

'I bet'cha you can't swim across the bay,' Bob said to Tom.

We all looked across to the far side. The steep jungled wall of Mount Rotui rose sharply out of the waters of the bay. It was easily 800 metres or a kilometre across to the far shore.

'Yeah?' Tom said. 'How much?'

'Coupla bucks.'

'Double if I swim back again?'

'Ha!' Bob laughed derisively. 'Sure.'

Tom stood up, looked out across the water, then turned and smiled at us. 'See ya,' he said and dived in to begin swimming out amongst the yachts moored in the bay.

'He won't do it,' Bob said. 'You wait. He'll turn back.'

But Tom didn't turn back...he just kept on going until, about half an hour later, we saw the tiny black dot of his head in the water, right over at the far side of the bay, where he just turned around and started back again. It was the sort of thing you wouldn't get an Australian to do...at least not *this* Australian. Deep water, a harbour, splashing feet on the surface. No way!

Tom made it back to the wharf and triumphantly collected his four dollars from Bob.

They were heading back to the beach area a short distance down the bay where they'd been camping, so, as we said goodbye, we exchanged addresses in the hope that we'd meet up again at some stage in the future.

The sky darkened and heavy rain clouds began to roll in along the valley and over the bay. We stayed out on the wharf watching the spectacle. The air was still and warm and you could almost smell the rain coming. For a while the light played tricks with the needle-hole on Mt Muaputa, outlining it sharply against jet-black clouds in the background. Under conditions like these it was easy to see how superstitious people would readily accept legends as fact: the legend of Mt Muaputa has it that the hole in the peak was made during a spear-throwing contest between the gods. The winner's spear not only pierced the mountain, but went on for another 150 kilometres to almost split the island of Huahine in two when it finally landed!

The rain began to spatter on us in big, fat, warm blobs. We shifted our gear under cover and sat beneath a little thatched-roof shelter to watch it all happen. There is something tremendously exciting about a real tropical downpour—at least I find it exciting. One minute the air is heavy and dark with expectancy, the next, the rain is just bucketing down, pounding on everything, bouncing and running in instant rivulets everywhere. Looking out into the bay was like looking out through a silver sheet, from behind a waterfall. The water of Cook's Bay was covered with countless millions of tiny silver splashes and the people out there on the cruising yachts at anchor sat looking back at us from under their canvas tarpaulins. We waved. They waved. Zara and Sean went for a swim in the rain and we sat and watched it all. Better than any TV show or going to the movies.

The rain stopped and not long after, *Keke II* arrived to take us back to Tahiti. Unfortunately it was a very rough passage during which several of the passengers, including Zara and Trish, felt decidedly ill. The only memorable thing about the one-hour voyage was the sight, for most of the last part of the trip, of hundreds and hundreds of beautiful flying fish breaking the surface ahead of the boat and streaking, with their wings (or fins) flapping madly, like little silver aeroplanes, across the waves.

# 5  BORA BORA
## The effects of a 'hurricane'

Coming in to Bora Bora, you expect a lot. It's been written about so often as one of the most beautiful islands in the South Pacific, your sights are already high, but when you come almost directly from Moorea, as we did, it's got to be really something, because Moorea is a tough act to follow. Nevertheless, Bora Bora proved it can be done, even in the less than ideal circumstances under which we saw it.

We'd said goodbye to Peggy in Papeete that morning. She was flying on to Pago Pago in American Samoa and then on to Hawaii and the States, planning to take lessons in scuba diving on the way. It was a sad goodbye for us all really, because we didn't really know where or when we'd meet again.

Tahiti was being drenched in torrential rain when our plane took off and we flew the whole 260 kilometres to Bora Bora in dense cloud to land on the island's narrow airstrip. The strip was built by the US Air Force during World War II on one of the small coral islets on the rim of the fringing reef and the connection with the main island is by small ferry. It was drizzling when we landed, but as we crossed the lagoon, startlingly blue even under overcast conditions, the cloud lifted considerably and we were treated to the spectacular profile of Bora Bora. The island is dominated by the brooding, flat-topped bulk of Mt Otemanu which looms 730-metres high, cathedral-like, over the township of Vaitape.

A group of Americans who had come in on the same plane were also on the small launch which was chugging across the lagoon. One of them, a tall man in his 50s, was wearing a big white Stetson. While his wife remained inside under cover, he stood outside with a companion, looking intently at the shore.

'Goddam,' he said, 'that's the same church that was there before. And that house...no, the town's changed a bit, but not much. Hell, I can still recognise it all.' He turned and beamed at his friend, myself and some others who were also standing on deck watching the shoreline.

He was a rancher from Idaho, but 35 years ago he'd been in the US Navy. 'Sailed on an LST for 31 days...non-stop...from Panama to here,' he said proudly. 'This is the first time I've been back.' He shook his head as if mentally trying to span the years, then gave a wide grin. 'Jeeze, you know this was a helluva place back in '44. There were 5000 Americans here.'

The concept of 5000 American servicemen on this little dot in the South Pacific was a little difficult to picture, but it was this American naval base on Bora Bora which served as the inspiration for James Michener's *Tales from the South Pacific*. 'Bloody Mary' of *South Pacific* musical fame was apparently a real woman living on Bora Bora at the time and the drink of the same name originated here during those hectic World War II years on Bora Bora.

For the 2000 inhabitants of Bora Bora the American 'occupation' was a cultural shock of major proportions, the effects of which have never really disappeared. For four years the economy was dominated by Coca Cola,

Hershey bars, and Lucky Strike cigarettes, not to mention the effects of motion pictures, baseball, ice-cream and apple pie.

The little ferry launch pulled in to the pier at Vaitape and we were once again faced with the difficult job of finding somewhere to stay. Difficult only because our budget forced us to look for the most reasonably-priced places and these were few and far between. The Americans on the launch were being met by the bus from the Hotel Bora Bora, but there was no way we could contemplate staying there. The cheapest bungalow for four was $125 a day.

Fortunately, as we'd found on Rangiroa, there were several local residents who provided accommodation. Amongst them, one of Bora Bora's real characters—Alfredo Doom.

Alfredo was the antithesis of his name. He was a small, rollypolly man with a big smile. He wore shorts, a battered straw hat and was into just about everything that was happening on Bora Bora. He ran a bus line, hired bicycles, motor scooters, fishing launches, outrigger canoes and had two very comfortable, thatched-roof A-frame cottages for rent: $26 a day each. 'Dino de Laurentis stayed here for six months,' Alfredo informed us as he showed us into one of them.

We had already heard about the second 'invasion' of Bora Bora, which took place in 1977 and 1978 when the Italian film director de Laurentis and some 500 actors, technicians, extras and hangers-on descended on Bora Bora to make the film *Hurricane.* de Laurentis, who regularly vacationed on Bora Bora, chose it as the site for what was supposed to be American Samoa in the 1920s. They built three complete sets on the island; a Samoan waterfront town, a native village and the governor's mansion, all of which was to be blown down during a mammoth hurricane.

'I am the judge in *Hurricane,*' Alfredo informed us with a smile that looked either cynical or supercilious, I couldn't determine which.

'The judge? You mean you were acting in the film?' Trish asked.

'Oui,' the smile broadened. 'I am sentencing the hero to prison.'

We made up our minds there and then to see the film. Alfredo would make a good judge, I thought. He had the right eyebrows, very bushy. But if the position of judge was beyond Alfredo in real life, it seems he'd come pretty close to being mayor of Bora Bora on a couple of occasions.

'I would like to be mayor here', he told us as we unpacked some of our gear. 'I think I could do a lot for the people of this island. But in the last elections Toro Teruere won. He has a very big family on Bora Bora, at least 30 or 40 members. Of course they all vote for him and work for him, you see...'

At that point a tremendous clap of thunder and the spattering of rain sent Alfredo hurrying off to his own house across the road. We were left to settle in by ourselves and to sit by the open doorway, gazing out on to the lagoon at the rain which became steadily heavier.

By morning the rain had stopped and we thought we'd better take advantage of the lull to get out and about on some of Alfredo's bikes. Sean chose the ritziest looking one from among the careless heap behind the Doom's house, but it blew a tyre as he cycled it across the roadway back to our place.

He swopped his racer for another bike which was about as scruffy and ill-fitted to the human frame as ours were and, undeterred either by the ropey transport or the weather, which was still grey and blustery, we set off to cycle the 30 or so kilometres of road which goes around the island.

Leaving Alfredo's and heading clockwise, we went back into Vaitape, the only settlement of any size on the island. Centred on the small wharf are the mayor's office, the police station, the bank, the infirmary and the inter-island airline office which doubled as a craft shop. And that was it, apart from Chin Lee's, the Chinese store which sold all one could possibly need on a tropic island and more besides. We stopped there and purchased a small perforated metal ball, hinged into two halves, which we could fill with tea-leaves so as to be able to brew up a refreshing cuppa. Chin Lee's was much more than just a shop, it was the hub of village life. People drifted in to meet friends and pass the time of day and drifted out again to pass around the news.

Once past Chin Lee's, the road lost its tarmac which made biking rather tough, especially as we were riding into quite a wind. The scenery was magnificent—those densely-jungled mountain sides plummeting down to almost push us into the lagoon which was grey today, reflecting the leaden skies.

The eastern side of the island has almost no population, because there's no organised water supply. We occasionally passed small, shabby, wooden huts occupied by people who were noticeably poorer than any we had seen before in French Polynesia. These people lived off what their own land and the sea produced, and they harvested a small cash crop of copra. A couple had set up stalls to sell tired-looking necklaces, but they didn't seem particularly anxious to do any business.

Large black sows waddled off into the undergrowth at our approach, followed by their litters and, quite often, a flock of baby chicks. The soil along both sides of the road was a mass of holes made by crabs. I had developed quite a dislike for these since the night 'attack' on Moorea, so I didn't chastise the kids too heartily when they began tossing loose soil at the crabs trying to score a hit before they scuttled sideways down their burrows. There must have been scores of them per metre and perhaps it was their large number which encouraged my distaste for them.

The cycling became increasingly difficult, even though we only had to manage one slight incline on the whole circumnavigation. One of the pedals on my bike was twisted to such a degree that it dragged my whole leg around at an awkward and finally painful angle. Iain, always the gentleman, swopped bikes with me, and after a kilometre or so of putting up with it, stopped and tried to straighten out the pedal. It snapped off and he was left with a nasty-looking piece of pointed metal which he could only push around by turning his foot to an angle for which it was not designed and pressing hard on the metal shaft with the ball of his foot. Very fortunately he was wearing thick-soled sandals but even so the metal quickly gouged a hole in the sole of the sandal.

Added to this the high wind continued to buffet us, so that it was more than two hours before we rounded the far side of the island to begin the homeward stretch.

That evening we went with Alfredo Doom in his bus to the Hotel Bora Bora. He had told us about the Tahitian dancing that was put on there two nights a week as a free show for guests at the hotel. Alfredo provided the transport for the dancers and suggested that, if we came with him, we could slip into the bar and watch the show. On this particular night there was more singing than dancing. The group consisted of mainly older men and women dressed in beautiful floral-patterned, loose-fitting gowns and leis of frangipani around their heads and over their shoulders. They swayed to the rhythm of guitars and drums and sang a series of Tahitian, Hawaiian and island songs. We were surprised to find here in French Polynesia and during the rest of our trip, that the music of the Pacific seemed to cross all national barriers within the region. The people of the Cook Islands, for instance, sing the songs of Tahiti, Samoa, Hawaii and Maori New Zealand, while the inhabitants of all those islands can invariably sing songs from any or all of the other groups. Polynesian songs are known and sung right across the South Pacific. The lead singer in this group at the Hotel Bora Bora was a fat, jovial man with a round face. He was apparently also the hotel's head gardener. With a combination of talents like that, he must enjoy life.

We'd been given this snippet of information by an Australian couple who had been sitting at a table next to us, watching the performance. They introduced themselves as Laurie and Maxine Stewart. They were on their way back to Sydney after a short business trip to Los Angeles. Laurie, we discovered was a new car dealer and had been to a marketing conference in the US. Even though they were travelling in considerably better style than us, staying at the hotel, they also commented on the high costs of French Polynesia.

'Everything is ridiculously expensive,' Laurie said. 'The only consolation, of course, is that it's such a fantastic place. And the diving! Have you been diving here by the hotel?'

We shook our heads. Sean's ears pricked up.

'There's a trench. . . a long channel through the coral out there. . . about 100 metres off the beach, which is unbelievable. . . incredibly beautiful coral and fish. You'll have to come and swim here tomorrow.'

We said that we'd like to do that and began to lay plans to come back to the hotel the following day to either bluff our way in or sneak through to the beach. As it happened, neither was necessary. A short while later, while having a drink in the bar, we met Monty Brown, the hotel's manager. We talked for a while and he questioned us about what we were doing in the South Pacific. When he learnt that we were hoping to write a book, he immediately suggested we stay a while at the hotel. (If only there were more people like Monty Brown!!)

'But we are only on Bora Bora for one more night,' I said, my surprise and eager willingness to accept his offer perhaps a trifle too obvious. 'We've been staying with Alfredo. . .' I began, '. . .and. . .'

'Never mind,' he interrupted. 'Come here for tomorrow and tomorrow night. Alfredo will not mind. We have more dancing tomorrow evening. . .the real dancing.' His eyebrows lifted suggestively. 'The young girls tomorrow. . . The real Tahitian hula.'

We didn't want to leave Alfredo's because it was so clean and comfy, just the sort of place we'd like to make a home in for a long while, compact and simple without any of the un-necessities with which we all seem to burden ourselves in more materially affluent circumstances. But he had another couple waiting to move in and we reasoned that, as we wouldn't have another opportunity to stay in such a swish place as the Hotel Bora Bora, we should take advantage of it.

The fare they gave us at the Bora Bora Hotel was set back in the well-maintained, attractive garden. It was built in tropical style with a thatched roof and plaited pandanus leaf walls. Inside however it had all 'mod-cons'; a couple of springy double beds, a smart bathroom—a coffee-maker, cane furniture, bright curtains—very comfortable. The whole complex was an attractive blend of local and imported materials and ideas. We didn't know then, but the design and materials used in hotels in French Polynesia were to be the best we would see anywhere in the South Pacific. After dumping our packs, we went off to inspect the facilities. The large bar and restaurant opened up onto a patio over the beach. A quick glance at prices made certain that *we* would be having cook-ups in our room. Even simple hamburgers served outside were an outrageous price.

The day was grey and blustery and a number of guests sat about looking fairly dejected. If I had saved hard for ages in order to blow it all on a two-week vacation-to-remember on Bora Bora I'd be cheesed off too if it rained all the time, but even more so if I was paying such insupportable prices. In all the conversations we had with visitors to French Polynesia the high prices were an inevitable topic: even if you could afford them, it's still awful to feel that you're being ripped off.

We decided that again the only thing to do was to ignore reality and pretend that it was hot and sunny. We borrowed flippers and masks and snorkels from the reception desk and, thus equipped, walked along the little beach to the tip of Point Raititi and then swam out a short distance before letting the current carry us back down to the fares. The four of us, holding hands like those photographs of sky-divers, floating across the top of the most magnificent coral garden. Enormous free-standing trees of coloured coral, with trunks which spread out into big flat tops like African thornbush trees, as if offering shade, but instead of sheltering rhinos and wildebeeste, they were protection for a collection of flash-dazzling fishes. The world really is an exciting, endlessly fascinating place.

All four of us were so excited that, when we found we had been propelled all the way down to the fares, we scrambled out onto the pier and ran back to do it again. Each time it was more spectacular because we became more at ease and could notice the detail of the scene. Only the chill forced us out and back to our fare, where we all had hot showers.

Leaving the kids to play gnip-gnop, or if you must, ping-pong, in the hotel's recreation fare, Iain and I started off to walk the six kilometres to Chin Lee's for some supplies. We were only halfway there when it started to bucket down with rain and despite our rain-gear, we were drenched by the time we got there. After doing our bit of shopping, it was still tipping down so we joined the small number of people who were chatting animatedly as they waited under the shop's awning for the weather to ease. The Dooms' youngest child, Dominique, a very attractive girl, drove up in one of the island's few cars and, having bought some groceries, offered us a lift back to her home.

'I'm glad you came by,' Mama Doom said when we arrived, producing Sean's reflector sunnies (mirrored sun glasses) in which he fancies himself a cool cat. 'We found them under a bed and would have had to post them on to you.' She invited us to have a cup of tea and while we sipped, she showed us with pride her collection of shells and of key-rings, given to her by visitors from all over the world. (Funny the things people keep; string, newspapers, plastic flowerpots. When they carry us out, they'll have to wade through maps. Everything from street plans of Addis Ababa to three dimensional projections of our solar system.)

The rain which had eased slightly, started up again, heavy, tropical, drawing the smells from the earth and vegetation. Mama's garden started where Papa's garage spilled its contents. Rusty springs, stripped pistons, coagulated engine parts mingled with papaya, banana and mango trees. There was a taro patch and caged chickens, silently sullen in their wet feathers. The rain fell off the corrugated metal roof in sheets, landing on the coral chip pathway, jumping back up again from the force of its fall. As the rain was obviously not going to ease, Dominique offered to give us a lift back to the hotel, where the few guests who had not taken to their beds for the afternoon sat around drowning their rainful sorrows.

That evening, despite the still-falling rain, young men and women from Vaitape came up to the Bora Bora to dance. A number of the fellows pranced about, obviously enjoying the opportunity to get dressed up and perform in public. Overt homosexuality, male or female (the local term is *rei rei*), is as acceptable in French Polynesia as heterosexuality. With hibiscus in their hair and thick leis of tiare tahiti and frangipani, they accompanied the girls, also flower-decked and in tiny half-coconut bra tops and grass skirts. They danced the fast, hip-swivelling tamure, a travesty of which I had attempted to perform all those years ago as one of Bloody Mary's girls in that amateur production of *South Pacific*. It's a really quite amazing dance to watch once you get past the immediately rivetting effects of all that pulsating bare brown flesh. Only the hips move. The feet, lower legs and torso stay completely still while the arms undulate slowly. An odd and very effective combination. You can see why the first Europeans to see it were so struck, coming as they did from socially-frigid, cold climes.

Alfredo, who had brought the villagers in his bus, told us that they were paid 500 francs ($6.50) a night and that usually two members of the same family danced or sang. As they performed twice a week, this added a welcome 2000 francs ($26) to the family kitty which would soon be swallowed up by the expense of living. Jokingly, I think, he also told us that for a mere $4216.85 we could hire the entire population of Vaitape, plus 80 canoes to stage a native fishing party! That's what Dino de Laurentis has done for Bora Bora.

# 6  HUAHINE
## 'Flowers...for you'

Huahine is my favourite among the Society Islands. It's always difficult to explain precisely what it is that makes one place more appealing than another, especially when, superficially, they are as alike as the volcanic high islands of French Polynesia; mountains, lush tropical greenery, blue, blue water.

The waterfront of the main town, Fare-nui-atea, sums up all that has ever been expressed about the South Seas. Pure Michener: two blocks long, it has six stores, (four of them Chinese owned) and an open-sided copra shed...that's Fare-nui-atea or, more simply, Fare. And everything about Fare and Huahine is simple.

About 130 kilometres northwest of Tahiti, it seems barely touched by the pre-packaged outside world. One fellow to whom we mentioned this, along with the fact that the people seemed more genuinely friendly than on Tahiti, Moorea and even Bora Bora, explained, 'We have only a few visitors so only a small number of our population, which is only 3000, are involved in the tourist industry. The rest of us keep to the old ways.'

Asking around for a moderately-priced place to stay, we were directed to Madame Maramu Vaihu's place, a family home set back off the road at the end of the water-front. A couple of bedrooms, a bathroom and even a covered patio where we could sit and watch the world go by. This patio area was cluttered with a strange collection of chrome and shiny veneer furniture and adorned with stuffed nylon fur dogs of the sort given as prizes at fun fairs.

The majority of visitors stay at another Bali Hai Hotel. It was built on reclaimed, swampy land and when work began, the first dredger load of muck brought to the surface a treasure trove of ancient artefacts. The Bishop Museum of Honolulu was informed and Dr Yosihiko Sinoto, an expert on the pre-history of French Polynesia who has been responsible for many digs and restoration projects, came to supervise the work. The lobby of the hotel is an on-the-spot, living museum; wooden adze handles, pearl shell coconut graters and fish hooks, canoe anchors, shell pestles, chisels and grindstones and photographs taken during the excavation. It was to see this exhibition that we went to the hotel during our first day on Huahine. It is about a half a kilometre from the township.

At the site they found remnants of an ancient, 25-metre, ocean-going canoe, which has been left where it was found because if it was excavated and exposed to the air, it would immediately deteriorate. But perhaps the most dramatic finds were some wooden, hand-held *patus,* or warclubs of the same size and shape as those made out of greenstone by the Maoris of New Zealand. The *patu* provided a definite link between the two countries and, as the wooden *patu* could be carbondated, it established as fact something which previously could only be educated speculation; that the natives from Huahine, or its neighbouring islands, voyaged to New Zealand.

The *maraes* on Huahine are generally regarded as the most important in French Polynesia. Almost 70 of these fascinating prehistoric sites have been discovered and many of them restored. In most cases the sites are believed to have been used as family ancestral temples, but a few, and one in particular at the village of Maeva on Huahine, have quite clearly functioned as communal temples. At least, that's what we were told but it was difficult for us, as uninformed laymen, to see how this sort of conclusion could be reached as most of the *maraes* we saw were...well, just a jumble of large stones! They usually appeared to be a large courtyard area laid with rough, unfinished black volcanic rock, with a wall of much larger stones standing at one end.

Archaeologists, however, can see considerably more in these things than most people, fortunately, and they say that the collection of *maraes* at Maeva village are remarkable because they represent a facet of early Polynesian society not seen elsewhere—centralised government. Apparently at Maeva, a total of eight chiefs, their families and associated tribes coexisted reasonably peacefully, side-by-side instead of living in their separate territories and constantly fighting with each other for supremacy.

To get to Maeva we took 'le truck' at 7.30 in the morning. When we reached the village we decided to continue on to Faie at the end of the road, just to see what was there and then stop off at Maeva on the way back. At Faie we helped an old man unload a couple of 20-kilo bags of Australian-grown rice and then prepared to have a look around. There wasn't a great deal to see—a school . . . no children in evidence though. It was a holiday, All Saints Day, when, so we were told, all Polynesian families swept, cleaned and decorated the graves of their parents and grandparents.

On the way back we left the bus about half a kilometre outside of Maeva so that we could walk in and examine a series of *maraes* that were spread out along the roadside on the approaches to the village. We noticed that one or two of the larger stones at a couple of the *maraes* were carved with small figures of turtles, which were supposed to be a favourite food of the gods throughout most of the South Pacific. Aparently only the chiefs were allowed to eat turtle. It was definitely *tapu* (forbidden) for all lesser mortals.

After exploring a few of these strange, ancient sites we walked in to the township. The sun was hot and the crushed coral roadway brilliantly white. Several of the houses in Maeva had large family graves in their front yards. This is a practice followed almost universally in Polynesia where land generally remains the property of one family for generation after generation. We were to see it in virtually every island grouping we visited until we reached Fiji. Here on Huahine it was obvious, too, that the practice of cleaning and decorating the graves was a tradition that was alive and well. Several families were working on their ancestors' graves as we walked by. Nearly all of the graves had been built with a miniature roof over them and were being brushed down, scrubbed and then strung with lines of frangipani and tiare tahiti flowers. From aging grandparents to little children, everybody was hard at work doing something, sweeping, tidying, even painting the tombs. Flowers and various other offerings were placed in glass bottles at the foot of each grave. It was very much a family affair.

Back at Madame Vaihu's guest house we rested for a while, cooled ourselves down and then, suckers for punishment that we seem to be, went out again to take another bus, this time down the other side of the island across the narrow isthmus to Hauhini Iti and on to its southern tip and a small town called Parea. It would be a one-hour ride.

'When are you coming back?' we asked the driver . . . (again in our fractured French).

'Demain.'

'Tomorrow? But are there no other buses?'

He shook his head. 'No other buses.'

A few moments indecision and then . . . 'What the hell,' I said, 'let's go anyway. We must be able to get back somehow.'

It was a beautiful ride; winding roads, little bays and inlets, spectacular views of small islands, mountains, brightly painted houses and entertaining company . . . a slightly sloshed, but very pleasant old man on the bus who spoke continuously to us in passable English, until we reached the half-way mark where he stepped off the bus clutching a half-empty litre bottle of wine which he waved in the air with a smile as the bus drew away.

Shortly afterwards we crossed the narrow causeway that separates Huahine Nui from Huahine Iti. This is where the legendary spear that pierced the hole in Mt Muaputa on Moorea is said to have finally landed, splitting Huahine in two!

There were several Tahitian children on board the bus and as we drove along, they clambered up the ladder on the back of the bus to the top. Before we knew it, Sean had joined them to help them grab mangos from the trees as the bus trundled along underneath them. We were naturally concerned that they might fall, or to be more accurate, that Sean might fall off. I climbed out to check what was happening and saw that there was a large roof rack for them to hang on to, but even so, I was about to tell Sean to come down, when the driver shouted back to me from the cabin. I didn't hear what he said, but he smiled and waved his hand and gave a typical Gallic shrug which I interpreted as, 'Leave them be...boys will be boys.' So we left them be...and won ourselves some more mangos as a result.

The town of Parea was a string of relatively modern wooden houses along the edge of the lagoon with hardly anybody to be seen about the place. We walked through the settlement, which seemed to have no centre to it, out onto the beach which also fronted the lagoon. We ate some of our mangos then went for a swim, a brief one, as the water was brown and unattractive from all the rain and there were mosquitoes everywhere. So, after drying off and walking back to the road, we decided to try to head back to Fare.

Nothing doing. No vehicles coming or going. Well, not for an hour or so anyway, but we passed the time, pleasantly relaxed, in the shade of a large tree by the side of the road.

Eventually a pickup truck drove up from the direction we wanted to go. It stopped, turned around and prepared to return the way it had come. We rushed over to see if they could give us a lift. It was driven by a young man of mixed French-Polynesian extraction seated beside two beautiful young Tahitian girls with leis of flowers threaded through their hair. Everybody wears flowers...it's such an attractive habit, I wonder why we in the West don't do it more ourselves.

Anyway, he readily agreed to take us with them back to Fare. We sat in the back of the small truck listening to the strains of Abba songs coming back from the cassette player in the cabin. They seemed to be relatively affluent kids. He was a student, we learnt later, home on holiday from college in Papeete for a week or so. It was probably his father's truck and he was showing off a little, taking his girlfriends for a joyride. But they were extremely pleasant and friendly kids. Half-way back, the truck stopped suddenly and the three of them leapt out and began collecting bunches of wild orchids and tiare tahiti from the side of the road. We watched with a smile and some puzzlement, thinking how nice it was that they should do it, but when they came back to the truck and handed them to us...'Flowers...' they laughed, 'for you.' We were bowled over.

# 7   RAIATEA
## The heart of Polynesia

The island of Raiatea is the legendary starting point for the great westward and northward migrations of the Polynesian navigators who discovered and colonised the Cook Islands and eventually New Zealand and Hawaii. Raiatea was the ancient religious and cultural capital of that part of Polynesia which we now lump together under the name of one island, Tahiti, but which is more correctly, the Society Islands. In those days, the period between 500 and 1000 AD, Raiatea was called Havai'i. The name derives from Western Samoa's big island of Savai'i, from where it is believed the Society Islands themselves were originally colonised by Polynesian navigators around the time of Christ. Hawaii, some 3500 kilometres to the north, also echoes the ancient name which was an important one to early Polynesians as the name of their ancestral homeland, the place to which their spirits would return after death.

The stories of several of those great migrations from Raiatea are entrenched in Polynesian lore. Among them, the tale of Ru, the chief navigator of Raiatea, who led a courageous group of islanders on a 1000-kilometre voyage across the trackless ocean to find a new home. It was at a time when Raiatea's population had outstripped its food supply (a situation hard to imagine even these days on such a lush tropical island).

'I have selected a star,' Ru told his followers, 'and beneath it is a land which will be our new home.' With his family and relatives and 20 maidens, chosen for their beauty, strength and virtue, to help populate the new land, Ru set off in a double-hulled sailing canoe called *Te Pua Ariki,* The Chiefly Flower. During their voyage westward they ran into a terrible storm which pounded them mercilessly for three days and three nights, at the end of which everybody except Ru was prepared to abandon all hope. At this point Ru called on the great sea god, Tangaroa (remember the name of the little town on Easter Island? Hangaroa) to show him once again his guiding star. The clouds parted, so legend has it, and revealed the star low above the horizon. Following the star, Ru and his company eventually landed three days later on the beautiful island of Aitutaki, in what are now the Cook Islands. As we were to discover some days hence when we too landed on Aitutaki, the people there still celebrate the discovery of their island by the great navigator Ru of Raiatea.

In the Polynesian language, Raiatea means 'clear blue sky', but unfortunately when we arrived on Raiatea, at 7.30 in the morning, after a 10-minute flight from Huahine, the skies were heavily overcast and within half an hour it was pouring with rain.

With some 7000 inhabitants, Raiatea is the second most populous island in French Polynesia, after Tahiti. It is also the second largest in size, being about 50 kilometres in circumference. It's a little unusual, too, in that its lagoon encloses not only Raiatea, but another island, Tahaa, which has a population of about 4000. Once inside the reef, it is possible to sail right around both islands without leaving the lagoon. We took a cab into the middle of Uta Roa, the main town, where we settled for a couple of rooms in the Hotel Hinano. Hinano is the name of the local beer and presumably the brewery had a share in the hotel. It wasn't much to write home about, but at $23 for the four of us it was the best thing going. The hotel was run by a Chinese man in his mid-30s, who could have been just the manager, but was more than likely the owner, or part owner. Most of Uta Roa seems to be run by Chinese. Certainly the grocery stores and general merchant shops are all Chinese-owned and operated.

The ground floor of the hotel was a large pool hall which looked as though it could be either lively or rowdy, depending on your point of view, but at 8.30 in the morning, there was nobody playing and all was reasonably quiet. After checking in, we lugged our packs up a slightly dilapidated staircase at the back of the hotel and dumped them into our two big, bare rooms and then just stood by the open window for several minutes staring out at the rain coming down in absolute torrents.

Then, once again deciding that the only thing to do was to ignore the rain, we donned our wet weather gear, left our shoes in the room and went out into the streets to ask about buses. We wanted to get to the southeastern side of the island to a place called Marae Taputapuatea, which is regarded as the most sacred ancient religious site in eastern Polynesia. At the bustling local marketplace we found a bus that was going there but not for almost an hour, so we spent the intervening time wandering through the town, or rather, rushing from shop awning to shop awning to shelter from the rain but getting fairly wet in the process anyway. At least the rain was warm, so we didn't feel in the least uncomfortable, in fact it's quite fun running around in the rain when it's not cold. In the local market, a large Polynesian woman was selling sponge cakes so, as it was Zara's 13th birthday, on the spur of the moment, we bought one to eat then and there.

It was still bucketing down by the time we boarded the bus for our trip to the end of the island. Despite the fact that the rain was warm and bearable, it was hardly the thing for good photographs and I began to wish for some clear blue skies. Our bus was driven by a woman of about 35 and carried on its side a well-executed painting of a flower and the name of the company, Tiare Apetahu, which was also the name of a flower, one of the rarest flowers in the world, we were told by our driver. It is a flower which blooms nowhere else in the whole world except on Raiatea's 1000-metre-high Mt Temehani.

The bus ride was once again wonderful entertainment in itself. Two giant Tahitian women with flashing gold teeth sat opposite us laughing and joking the whole way. Several children, barefoot and dripping wet, sat staring at us *'popa'as'* (foreigners) open-mouthed and fascinated, expecting us, I suppose, to momentarily disappear, or burst into flames, perhaps. When we were almost to the end of the line, we crossed the Faaroa River, the only navigable river in French Polynesia and supposedly the launching site for the long-boats which took off for the Hawaii expeditions so many centuries ago.

Just before the village of Opoa, the woman driver let us out at Marae Taputapuatea, an extraordinary *marae* we could see just a short distance from the roadway. She told us that she would collect us on the way back in about half an hour. The rain had abated slightly but it was still drizzling as we made our way to the imposing *ahu,* or platform, of huge slabs of coral and volcanic rock at one end of the *marae.*

It was a rare occurrence in Polynesia, but on important occasions the offerings to the gods were sometimes 'upgraded' from foodstuffs and animals to *human* sacrifices. These were only performed at the most venerated *maraes,* like Taputapuatea, to mark significant occasions in the life of a chief or events of national importance such as war, or perhaps the departure of the long-boats on their daring voyages of exploration. Captain Cook actually witnessed such a ceremony with human sacrifices during his last visit to the Society Islands.

Strange to think that these dark, imposing rocks, now deserted and drearily wet with rain, were almost certainly the setting for what could only have been rather cruel and tragic proceedings.

It was a Raiatean noble and priest called Tupaia who served as interpreter for Captain Cook's first Pacific voyage. Tupaia interpreted far more than just language though, as Cook 'found him to be a very intelligent person and to know more of the Geography of the Islands situated in these seas, their produce and the religious laws and customs of the inhabitans than anyone we had met with.'

But Tupaia was not so well received by members of the crew who were very put out by the Raiatean's demand that these mere sailors treat him with the sort of respect he felt was automatically due to him as one of Polynesia's upper classes. In the formidable English class system, even the workingest working-class person knows that they are superior to *anyone* not born within the sceptred isle and Cook's sailors, whatever their background, had no intention of bending the knee and tugging the forelock in deference to any *islander,* no matter how noble! Poor Tupaia—having been of great assistance to Cook during the ship's visit to New Zealand, it was the intention to take him all the way on to England but he died in Batavia of some illness.

So it was left to another Raiatean, Omai, who travelled aboard the *Adventure* under the command of Captain Furneaux to have the honour of being the first Polynesian launched into English society.

Omai was introduced to the King, entertained by the eighteenth century equivalent of 'the beautiful people', went grouse shooting and was painted by Sir Joshua Reynolds, who portrayed him as a liquid-eyed, handsome young man. Set up in his own place in London, Omai played the expected role of the Noble Savage to perfection. He was pleasant and likeable and because he was of low rank, and consequently knew little about the workings of his own society, he was no doubt flattered by all the attention. When he left England he was loaded with gifts, including a suit of armour! He himself chose not to return to Raiatea, anticipating, probably correctly, that he would most likely be more able to impress islanders who had not known him before with stories of his exploits. As it turned out Omai wasn't able to slot back into island lifestyle at all and died of natural causes only two and a half years after returning home.

By early evening, as if the heavens had at last run dry, the rain stopped and the sky cleared to a pale pink for a sunset which looked rinsed pure. We wandered down to the quay to watch the full moon come up. There was a battle-grey French destroyer moored at one end, the swarm of sailors looking dapper in their natty, *sportif* uniforms.

It being Zara's coming of teenagerhood we decided to lash out on a Chinese meal.

It wasn't much chop, so it was just as well that we are all accustomed to eating whatever and whenever possible. Iain recalls that we finished up with canned lychees—three each, for $5.

Raiatea was the last of the Society Islands we visited. Our stay in French Polynesia had gone far too quickly, but at the same time, we felt an urgency to move on because we knew how much more there was yet to come. Travel anywhere in the South Pacific is not a simple matter. We now had to return to Papeete hundreds of kilometres to the east in order to fly on westward to the Cook Islands, even though in Raiatea we were closer geographically to the Cooks than many other of the outlying islands of French Polynesia are to Papeete.

# THE COOK ISLANDS

## 8  RAROTONGA
'No drunks after seven p.m.'

For more than 20 years I've wanted to go to the Cook Islands. Ever since I first saw a copy of the *Pacific Islands Monthly* and began to read the occasional article about the Cooks, they've had a special appeal for me. I think it was because from the pictures I saw and the stories I read the Cook Islands seemed to have been less affected by Western civilisation than other parts of the Pacific. To some people that means backwardness, a lack of sophistication and the unavailability of many of the amenities of modern life. Yet those were the very aspects of the Cooks that I found appealing.

Of course 20 years is a long time and I didn't really expect the place to be like it had been in those old magazines. I mean, if we could fly into Rarotonga from Tahiti on an Air New Zealand DC-10 with 250 other passengers, then obviously things had changed. But Air New Zealand is the only international air carrier servicing the islands and two hundred or so passengers once a week from Tahiti is hardly a tourist onslaught...especially when 75 per cent of them fly straight on to Fiji without staying over. The same applies on the reverse flights to Tahiti. There are other flights to and from New Zealand, but there are so many Cook Islanders living in New Zealand that these are regarded almost as domestic flights. In any event, it's safe to say that the Cook Islands haven't really been affected by mass tourism. The rest of the world hasn't woken up to the Cook Islands and they remain relatively unknown and largely unspoilt.

As a nation, the Cook Islands are an artificial creation of the Western powers. Created in 1888 as a protectorate of Britain and then annexed by New Zealand in 1901, they are basically a political arrangement which links 15 inhabited and more than 100 uninhabited islands. The arrangement is hardly a natural one, as the islands fall into two clusters some 1500 kilometres apart. The northern group consists of flat coral islets and atolls with blue lagoons, brilliant white beaches and fringing reefs. The southern islands, in which the bulk of the small population is centred, are volcanic

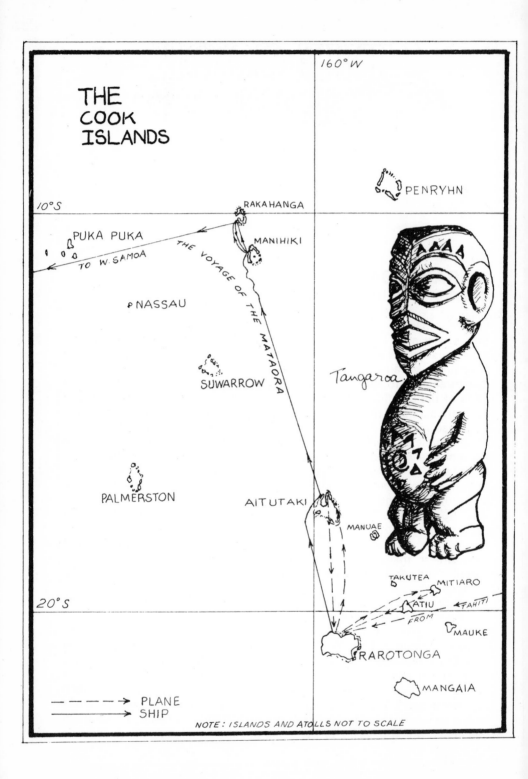

THE
COOK
ISLANDS

160°W

PENRYHN

10°S

RAKAHANGA

PUKA PUKA

TO W. SAMOA

THE VOYAGE OF THE MATAORA

MANIHIKI

NASSAU

SUWARROW

Tangaroa

PALMERSTON

AITUTAKI

MANUAE

TAKUTEA

MITIARO

ATIU

FAHITI

FROM

MAUKE

20°S

RAROTONGA

MANGAIA

- - - ► PLANE
———► SHIP

NOTE: ISLANDS AND ATOLLS NOT TO SCALE

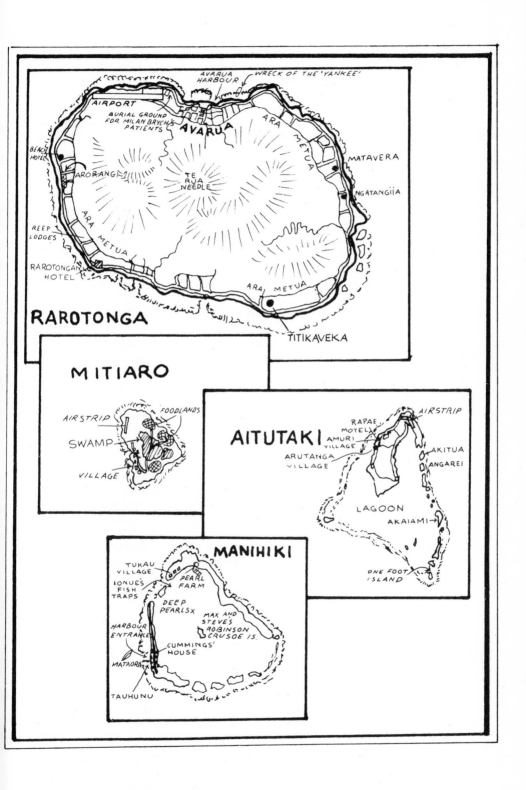

RAROTONGA

AIRPORT
BURIAL GROUND
FOR MILAN BRYCH'S
PATIENTS
AVARUA HARBOUR
WRECK OF THE 'YANKEE'
AVARUA
ARA METUA
BEACH HOTEL
ARORANGI
TE RUA NEEDLE
MATAVERA
NGATANGIIA
ARA METUA
REEF LODGES
RAROTONGAN HOTEL
ARA METUA
TITIKAVEKA

MITIARO

AIRSTRIP
FOODLANDS
SWAMP
VILLAGE

AITUTAKI

RAPAE MOTEL
AMURI VILLAGE
ARUTANGA VILLAGE
AIRSTRIP
AKITUA
ANGAREI
LAGOON
AKAIAMI
ONE FOOT ISLAND

MANIHIKI

TUKAU VILLAGE
IONUE'S FISH TRAPS
PEARL FARM
DEEP PEARLS X
MAX AND STEVE'S ROBINSON CRUSOE IS.
HARBOUR ENTRANCE
CUMMINGS' HOUSE
MATAORA
TAUHUNU

land masses which rise from the seabed, mountainous and fertile. The total land area of all the islands is less than 250 square kilometres and the population is less than 25 000, half of which live on the main island Rarotonga.

Rarotonga is one of the most beautiful islands in the South Seas. Although it is roughly circular in shape with no deep-water harbour, its profile is dramatic. A number of steep, rugged mountains, covered thickly with jungle-like vegetation rise in the centre to sharp pinnacles and peaks.

As we've mentioned, the first humans to settle the Cook Islands were the Polynesian voyagers who set out from Raiatea and the legend has it that they landed on Aitutaki, some 225 kilometres to the north of Rarotonga. There's nothing that indicates the actual date of their arrival on Rarotonga, but scientific evidence produced by anthropologists indicates that the southern Cook Islands have been inhabited for well over 1000 years. A local legend tells of how Polynesians from Tahiti, under Chief Tangua and others from Samoa, under Chief Kariki met on Rarotonga about seven or eight hundred years ago to plan a war against the Polynesian settlers in New Zealand, some 3000 kilometres away!

The first Europeans to discover Rarotonga were Fletcher Christian and his crew of *Bounty* mutineers. In 1789, after he had taken over the *Bounty* and set Lieutenant Bligh and his companions adrift in a long-boat, Christian made landfall at Rarotonga to replenish water and supplies while on his way from Tonga to Tahiti.

The Spanish navigator Alvaro de Mendana had actually sailed through the northern islands of the Cook group some 200 years previously, stopping at Puka Puka, and Captain James Cook, after whom the islands are named, sailed back and forth through the area on his first, second and third voyages (between 1768 and 1779) but he never called at Rarotonga.

After Christian's stopover, there was a very long break in the visits of Europeans to the region until the arrival of another Christian, one by calling, if not by name, the Reverend John Williams of the London Missionary Society, who arrived at Rarotonga on July 25, 1823. From that moment on, the influence of the missionaries on Rarotonga and in the Cook Islands generally was all-pervasive. They spread quickly throughout the islands, converting the inhabitants to Christianity, re-organising their widespread housing arrangements so that villages were clustered around the early churches and church schools. They controlled the native chiefs and, through them, virtually governed the islands. They imposed a strict moral code on the islanders and attempted to change the easy-going lifestyle to which Polynesians were accustomed.

Fortunately they don't seem to have had much success in that area because nearly all of the people we saw and met in the Cooks were amongst the most relaxed, friendly and happy people you could expect to find anywhere. Temu Okatai, our introduction to the Cook Islands was no exception: a terrific guy in his early 30s; round, brown, open face, fuzzy hair, a big smile, engaging personality...say no more, except perhaps...strong New Zealand accent. Temu was in charge of the Cook Islands Tourist Authority, a position he took up after returning to the Cooks a few years previously, having spent the five years prior to that in New Zealand at university.

Temu's office is in the centre of Avarua, the main township on the island. The town is very small, although it is spread haphazardly along about a kilometre of waterfront with a slightly increased density at what is known as 'the Roundabout'. Close by the Roundabout are the post office, the central government offices and the police station. (There are less than 100 police officers in the whole of the Cook Islands.)

We had come to Temu's office for advice. With so many islands in the Cooks, how would we choose which ones to try to visit? As it turned out, our decisions were not too difficult. 'In the southern part of the Cooks,' Temu told us, 'you must first see Aitutaki...it is probably the most beautiful atoll in the South Pacific.'

There seem to be quite a few of these 'most beautiful island' claims in the South Pacific, not that it really matters, I suppose, because if they're appealing enough to warrant the claim in the first place, they must be pretty good and that's really all that matters.

'Also, it has some accommodation,' Temu went on. 'The others have not.'

We examined the map in his office, a cluster of dots to the east and northeast of Rarotonga: Takutea, Atiu, Manuae, Mitiaro, Mauke and Mangaia. Temu swept his hand over them. 'Except for Mitiaro, there is nowhere to stay on these islands and we don't encourage visitors to stay there. It is sometimes possible to stay with local families, but they are simple villagers and it must be arranged through the local Ariki, the chief.'

'You mentioned Mitiaro,' I asked. 'Could we stay there?'

'Yes, I think so,' he replied. 'The local administrative officer there has some rooms in his house he sometimes rents.'

'And what about in the rest of the group?' Trish asked, gazing at the more widely scattered atolls away to the north.

'I think that is impossible,' Temu said slowly. 'There are no planes that fly to them and there is only one boat which goes to them every few months.'

'And they take passengers?'

'Yes. Deck passage. I'm not sure when the next one is going north. You'd have to check with the shipping company, there's only one company that sails to the northern islands. Silk and Boyd.'

We found Silk and Boyd's two-room office by the waterfront at the far end of the town and met Don Silk, a slim, balding man in his mid-40s who is co-owner of the shipping line. The company runs two ships, the *Mataora* and the *Manuvai,* both of about 400 to 500 tonnes, and 50 metres in length, which provide the only links between the capital Rarotonga and the northern islands, some of which are well over 1000 kilometres away.

'We've got the *Mataora* going north,' Don Silk told us, 'but not until the 16th.' It was now the 6th.

'What islands does it call at?' Trish asked.

He picked up a schedule from the desk. 'Well, on this trip she'll be passing through Aitutaki, in the southern group, and then going on to Manihiki, Rakahanga and Puka Puka, before making for Apia in Western Samoa and then Pago Pago in American Samoa.'

Except for Pago Pago and Apia, the other names meant practically nothing to us, but we were immediately excited by his words. It sounded like a great trip, even though it meant a 10-day wait. We told Don that we'd like to travel on the *Mataora* and asked him to put our names down for it.

'No need to book,' he said. 'There's no cabin space left anyway. There's only 20 bunks for cabin passengers and they're all gone.'

We were both crestfallen. 'You mean...you mean we can't go?' Trish asked.

'Oh no, you can go all right. It's just that there's no cabin. You can go deck passage...we can carry a hundred or more people on deck.'

We left Silk and Boyd in good spirits with an assurance from Don Silk that we'd definitely be able to sail on the *Mataora* when the time came. We hardly gave a second thought to just what 'deck passage' implied.

The 10-day delay now meant that we would have time to try to see Rarotonga and possibly a couple of the other islands in the southern group of the Cooks. Perhaps Mitiaro, which Temu Okatai had mentioned to us. Leaving town, we headed around to the south western side of the island, approximately nine or 10 kilometres out, to the Puaikura Reef Lodges, a group of small, self-contained flats we'd heard of which were run by a New Zealander Geoff Porter and his Cook Islands wife. The flat we moved into was as clean and comfortable as any luxury hotel room. It was very modern and well equipped: two bedrooms, a bathroom, a dining-sitting room, a complete kitchenette with refrigerator, stove, crockery and cutlery, a laundry, even a clock radio by the bed. $25 complete, for the four of us.

We bought some food to cook up from the little shop next door, then went for a stroll along the beach which was no more than 30 metres from our door. The sun was low in the western sky and groups of women and children, collecting shellfish from the reef, were silhouetted against the background of the lagoon as if it were a sea of silver. We sat on the beach watching them until some children came and showed us their catch, a mess of curly pink eggs they'd squeezed from long black sea slugs! Would we like to taste some? They motioned the bucket towards us and to their mouths. No thanks! We grimaced and the children laughed.

Back at our little apartment we cooked up instead a meal of grilled sausages, onions, eggs and a tomato salad. It was nice, but we felt terribly conventional.

In the morning Exham Wichman called to collect us in his horse-drawn buggy. Exham's tour was the only one in the Cook Islands and was advertised in the daily *Cook Island News*. Exham's talk, said the ad., 'will cover the way of life, income, land, homes, plant life and history and will end up with Maria's refreshments.' Tours are not usually our bag. In fact I think the last one I went on was as a gawping, teenage country bumpkin on a school outing for my first visit to London! But Exham was something different. Many people had told us this and they were right. For a start the transport was literally three horse power and Exham, who was perhaps 50, talked to his guests as though he was a friend explaining how he lived. 'See that shack on the beach?' Exham pointed to a tumbledown wooden structure with a patch of garden right on the water's edge among the casuarinas. 'Well, don't you go away feeling sorry for those people who live there, thinking they're poor and can't afford any place better. That's just their beach house! They spend a couple of months a year down here to have a break from their farm back up in the hills and also to show the young ones how to adapt to new surroundings, how to care for the trees and plants which grow down here and are so different from those up at their other place, and also how to grow enough food for themselves even in this poor sandy soil. It's important that the children don't get soft through life being too easy [oh, how much I agree with him] so even though they don't need to live down here with such bare facilities, Mum and Dad do it to harden up their children. Mama and I did just the same when our family were young. Now they're all grown and on their own, we can take things a bit easy. Back up in the hills, this family have a place big enough to feed an army.

'And now I'm going to show you how you can tell how a family make their living, just by seeing what they have planted.' He reined the horses in and pointed again. 'See the paw paw and mango trees? They're pig food, so you know they keep pigs.'

'Pig food?' we exclaimed in horror.

Exham smiled. 'I know. You *papa'a* eat them.' He grimaced. 'But we prefer to feed them to the pigs and eat the pigs! And coconut.' He pointed again. 'That's for the chickens. Hibiscus,' he plucked a flower and gave it to Zara, 'that's grown not for the flowers but for its straight, thin branches to tie up the beans, so you know they have beans and probably tomatoes too. And there's a kapok tree.' He gestured to a dead-looking, skeletal, leafless tree with large, hanging pods from which spilled white, fluffy kapok. 'So you know they have kapok mattresses and pillows. Except that nowadays most of us have gone soft and have innerspring mattresses and are just too lazy to chop down the tree! And there's breadfruit, the lazy man's tree. Plant that and it will grow forever and you'll have enough food to never need work again.'

Farther on Exham took us off the main, surfaced road which ran the 32 kilometres around the island, to another road a couple of hundred metres behind it. This unsurfaced track ran roughly parallel to the main one and also went almost right around the island.

'This is the Ara Metua,' Exham told us. 'It was built by a chief called Toi around a thousand years ago. At that time it was paved with coral and lava rock. Archaeologists say that the Cook Islands were first inhabited by Polynesians between 500 and 1000 AD. Tradition has it that three men built the Ara Metua in two seconds, which is not unacceptable when you remember that God created the world in six days.' This remark was made with a dead-straight face and as we knew that Exham was a fervent Christian, it was a little hard to be sure what to make of it.

Beside the Ara Metua we stopped again for an inspection of a group of taro patches. Like the potato or rice, there's more to taro than meets the eye. Swamp taro, giant taro, sweet taro...all have their particular uses and flavours. We had already had taro chips, baked taro and taro-tops done with coconut milk and chillies, all of them yummy. We were to find that, across the Pacific, the names and uses changed slightly but that taro is so much a part of the Pacific diet that islanders living in New Zealand or Australia find out by bush telegraph when a shipment is due and will buy it all up, paying exorbitant prices, as soon as it arrives.

'This tree is a passionfruit tree,' Exham said. He had driven on a little and stopped once more, this time under the shade of an enormous tree. We looked at one another in disbelief.

'Passionfruit?' we asked sceptically.

Exham laughed and nodded his head. 'Passionfruit, yes. You don't believe me but I'll show you. Come.'

We all clambered down and standing by the huge trunk craned our necks to see the fruit which Exham pointed out.

'I'll get one. I'll get one,' Sean said, ever eager to climb a tree. We watched him disappear into the thick overhead foliage, following Exham's directions to the fruit. 'Catch!' he yelled and down through the canopy fell a fruit the size of a large papaya, with a hard green, outer skin.

Exham wielded his machete with the admirable ease displayed by all Pacific islanders and chopped open the fruit. Immediately there was the familiar tangy smell of passionfruit which we hadn't enjoyed for two years. Too long. We fell on the fruit like the ravaging hordes, scooping the slippery little pips and their mucus-like bed out in handfuls! The size of the fruit did nothing to diminish the distinctive flavour. Incredible! Brobdingnagian passionfruit! The stuff of dreams! Exham laughed indulgently at our excitement and climbed the tree himself with Iain to find more for us!

We stopped just one more time on our morning jaunt. 'This is my mother's grave,' Exham called to the horses to slow up. It was a simple concrete slab and headstone set in a neat lawn in front of his mother's home, which, since his mother died two years previously, had been lived in by various members of the family. 'When a person dies here, all the family and friends come round to help. The men dig a hole two metres deep, line it with concrete and make a wooden coffin. The body is then wrapped in a tivaivai, which is a bright cotton handmade reverse appliqué quilt, before going into the coffin for burial. If there is no shroud, everyone in the village will know and talk. The women make the food for the workers and after the burial everyone eats. Before going, they each put in between two and ten dollars to help pay for the wood and cement and food.'

I liked it. For many years I let it be known that when I died I wished to be burnt up and the resultant ashes scattered anyoldwhere. No marker. Nothing. Dead and gone and best forgotten. But I've changed my mind. Perhaps it's partly age, although I don't think that is the strongest influence. Mostly it's because of seeing so many graves over the past few years. In Lima; Pizarro. In London; Nelson. In my home village in Somerset; the humble headstones of peasants and serfs. Then last year we scattered my father's ashes on the waters of the harbour where he had loved to sail and doing so crystallised my growing feeling that it's important to leave a marker, no matter how insignificant. George Allan Clark, Born Midsommer Norton Somerset 20 July 1897. Died Oakville, Ontario 9 February 1979. Otherwise there's nothing. No sign that you ever trod this earth. Not that I expect anyone to be laying flowers or even keeping it tidy. But you see, if everyone from way back had been burnt up and scattered, our knowledge of human history would be tremendously lessened wouldn't it? And it has something to do with being part of the flow. So I've let it be known that, ideally, I would like to be dug in under a frangipani tree in my own garden. But as that's not legal, as we, unlike Cook Islanders, buy and sell land as if it were ours to buy and sell, which of course it isn't, I wish instead to lie rotting away in a hillside overlooking the sea.

Back at his home, a simple attractive place, set in a garden of tropical shrubs, flowers and trees, Exham told us of his own history. He is descended from Papehia, the first missionary to the Cooks who was set ashore by the Rev. John Williams of the

London Missionary Society in 1823. Also in the line was the first British consul, Richard Exham. While he talked, Exham's wife, Maria, was plying us with fruit and with hot scones thickly smeared with avocado.

The other people we had travelled with in the buggy were a middle-aged American couple who had sold up everything and were floating with the tide, and a retired headmistress from Cardiff, South Wales. She was intelligent, bright-eyed and sprightly and had travelled a great deal in Europe. She told many amusing stories of her escapades.

'Quite a number of people ask me if I'm not frightened of travelling alone,' she said, 'but I tell them, "what would anyone want to be doing to an old woman like me!" Mind you I did have my handbag snatched from my arm once in Spain. But the police found it and returned it to me.' Undeterred she now carried a shoulder bag.

'I have been saving for some time for my Pacific islands adventure and I am enjoying it immensely. But this is only the prelude, so to speak. I have planned the whole trip so as to take a flight at the end of December out from New Zealand over the frozen wastes of Antarctica. I have already bought my ticket. Won't that be exciting?'

It was, she told us, something she had always wanted to do. As it turned out it was to be her last adventure. The Air New Zealand plane ploughed into the side of Mt Erubis in Antarctica and everybody on board was killed. We didn't know her name, but this is a memorial to her—someone who had the courage to take the risks necessary to make dreams come true.

Generally, when we're travelling like this, from place to place over an extended period of time, we try to hang on to a few coins and banknotes as well as a few postage stamps from each country, never more than a few dollars worth and just for souvenirs rather than for serious collecting. The Cook Islands, we knew, was an interesting place as far as stamps were concerned because a special philatelic bureau had been set up in Rarotonga during the late 60s with the specific aim of making foreign revenue from stamp sales for the government, and also, as it turned out, for the American entrepreneur and financier Finbar Kenney, who set it up.

In 1965 Kenney happened to meet the then prime minister of the Cook Islands, Sir Albert Henry, in New York. Kenney entered into a contract to become a technical adviser on stamps to the Cook Islands and to establish an organisation called the Cook Islands Development Company, which in turn set up the Philatelic Bureau.

The project was a roaring success. The stamps were designed abroad and found a wide appeal amongst collectors around the world. Many of the recent issues have been extraordinarily beautiful and have covered such subjects as the US space programme, the voyages of Captain Cook and religious painting. The Bureau has also brought in profits of over $2 million a year, one-third of the country's annual budget.

The fact that Mr Finbar Kenney was also clearly making a good deal of money out of the arrangement raised a few eyebrows, but it was generally accepted that it had been his expertise in the business that had got the project going in the first place and, as it was bringing lots of new revenue in for the government, nobody made too many waves. But then the American entrepreneur began playing politics. He became involved in attempts to keep

Sir Albert Henry in power at a time when it looked as if he might lose office in upcoming elections.

The Cook Islands' close relationship with New Zealand, which still looks after the islands' defence and foreign affairs, had produced a difficult electoral situation. Although the population of the Cooks was not much more than 20 000, there are almost the same number (18 000) of Cook Islanders living permanently in New Zealand. In the 1978 elections Sir Albert reasoned that if he could bring as many as possible of these expatriate islanders home to vote, they'd be grateful enough for the free flight, holiday and chance to see their relatives, that they'd cast their ballots in his favour.

The prime minister flew to New Zealand with suitcases full of banknotes provided by Mr Kenney's Cook Islands Development Company and began enticing Cook Islanders home on chartered jet flights which he, Sir Albert, had arranged. Hundreds of voters from key electorates were flown in and, in a close ballot, Sir Albert retained power.

However, in a High Court case, brought almost immediately by the opposition, evidence was presented that Sir Albert had subverted justice and, in effect, rigged the elections in his own favour. He was sacked by the Chief Justice and replaced by the leader of the Cook Islands opposition Democratic Party, Dr Tom Davis, a Cook Islander who had won international acclaim as a medical specialist working with NASA on the US space programme. Sir Albert Henry was subsequently convicted on a number of charges and, in 1980, he was stripped of his knighthood by the Queen. He died in January, 1981.

Finbar Kenney also came to the islands from his home in the US to appear before the Supreme Court to answer charges of conspiracy and defrauding the government. He was convicted and had to pay some $80 000 in fines and costs. Outside the court, he said the whole affair had been an 'error of judgement' which had cost him just on a million dollars!

From all accounts though, Mr Kenney still calls the tune as far as Cook Islands stamps are concerned. The new premier, Tom Davis, was apparently determined to sever the relationship between the Cook Islands government and the American stamp dealer, but it proved impossible. Kenney's contract had enabled him to stockpile, over the years, vast quantities of Cancelled to Order stamps which he had been allowed to buy at little more than their printing cost—$1, $2, $5 and $10 stamps, for instance, at not much more than a cent or two each. If these were released onto the market in large numbers, they would not only wipe out the value of used Cook Islands stamps overnight, but they would seriously affect the mint, or unused, stamps and have a disastrous impact on sales of all future Cook Islands stamps on which the economy of the country now leans so heavily. On the advice of the treasury, the government renewed Mr Kenney's contract, and the situation remains pretty much as it was. The Cooks are still producing their attractive stamps and Finbar Kenney is still making a lot of money from them, as well as some from us, because we bought $20 worth of stamps.

One of the other issues that brought some heavy flak for Sir Albert during his term of office that is perhaps worth mentioning here was his support for the controversial self-proclaimed cancer specialist Dr Milan Brych (pronounced brick).

Brych turned up in the Cook Islands not long after he had been denied the right to practise his particular brand of cancer therapy in Australia. But in Rarotonga the then Sir Albert gave him virtual carte blanche, as well as approval to establish a cancer clinic. Within practically no time, patients suffering from terminal cancer conditions began to flood in from all over the world. Accommodation at the clinic and treatment by Brych came out at around $200 a day and most patients were permanently staying there. Despite widespread medical criticism, even condemnation of Brych's methods, Sir Albert allowed him to continue practising. When Tom Davis took over the government, Milan Brych headed off for three-weeks' holiday and never returned. Davis had previously indicated that he considered Brych a charlatan and would not allow him to continue practising in the Cook Islands. Brych turned up in California where he attempted once again to carry on his controversial cancer therapy. At the time of this writing, he had been banned from practising and was in jail facing charges of medical malpractice and was trying to raise $250 000 bail.

On the coast road a few kilometres west of Avarua township near the airport is a small cemetery in ground Sir Albert Henry's government set aside for the burial of Brych's cancer patients who did not respond to his treatment. The locals call it the 'Brych Yard'. We wandered through it one day and were saddened by the inscriptions on the headstones erected by relatives many thousands of kilometres away in various countries around the world, one in particular from a husband to his wife: 'We shall speak again together and you shall sing to me a deeper song.'

We had come to the graveyard, not out of morbid curiosity, but to see a particular grave, that of a man called Tom Neale who had died two years previously while a patient of Brych. Tom Neale was someone who had excited my imagination almost 15 years earlier when I read a book he had written called *An Island to Oneself.* It was the story of how he had spent six years alone, in two periods of three years each, on an uninhabited coral atoll, less than a kilometre long and only 300 metres wide, in the South Pacific. I recalled it as an extraordinary tale of courage, determination, triumph over adversity and individual self-fulfilment. I remembered, too, that Suwarrow, the atoll on which Tom Neale lived, was part of the northern group of the Cook Islands and when we had first spoken to Temu Okatai at the Tourist Authority office, I had asked him if he knew Tom Neale.

'Of course,' he replied. 'Everybody in the Cooks knows of Tom Neale.' But then he had told us that he had died of cancer.

'Did he ever go back to Suwarrow?' Trish asked, knowing that the two periods described in his book were in the late 50s and early 60s.

'Yes,' Temu said. 'He went back there again to live permanently. In fact he lived most of the 70s there until he became too sick. He came back here to die.'

The world has too few Banana Court bars and they are rapidly dwindling in number, but it is not possible to pass a law for their preservation. Nothing would kill them off faster. For the essence of the Banana Court bar, in downtown Avarua, and its equivalents in other parts of the world, is their free-wheeling spontaneity.

Next door to the Banana Court bar is the Tourist Authority, which owns it, but its well-intentioned anxiety to maintain it as a source of much-needed revenue may kill it off. Good intentions are fatal to the rowdy, not to say rough-house, atmosphere of a place where the crowd-drawing female patrons are called *tarameas*. Taramea is the Maori name for the poisonous 'Crown of Thorns' starfish which destroys coral reefs!! The noise of the band in the Banana Court all but drowns the colourful language of the drinkers, many of whom, because of the shortage of young, available members of the opposite sex, dance around the floor clutching only a can of Leopard beer.

The old wooden building, for which the kindest description could only be 'dilapidated', has in its time been a hospital, a dental clinic, the government legal department office, a courtroom and finally the first hotel in the Cook Islands. This last function made it also the first place to serve alcoholic beverages to Cook Islanders, for under the missionary influence and up until independence in 1965, it was illegal to sell alcohol to Cook Islanders except on a doctor's prescription! There are some people who would say that, if the law hadn't been changed, you wouldn't have to step over flying bodies on a Friday and Saturday (until midnight only when the heavy hand of Sunday descends) in the Banana Court bar. I would humbly suggest that they miss the point.

As we were leaving the Banana Court, we stopped to read a message written in official-looking capitals and stuck to the highly vulnerable glass doors of the bar. It read:

*AFTER 7 PM*
**NO:** SLIPPERS
SHORTS
TEE-SHIRTS
SPORTSWEAR
OR
DRUNKS
**ALLOWED**

It was 9.30 p.m. and the men at the bar in rubber flip-flops, shorts and tee-shirts were anything but sober!

Almost within sight of the Banana Court bar is the rusting hulk of the once-magnificent, 30-metre clipper ship *Yankee,* which sits high on the reef at the edge of Avarua township. Readers of *National Geographic* will remember the *Yankee* skippered by Irving Johnson and his wife appearing regularly in stories of adventure. The one I remember best was the trip they made up the Nile; the immaculate white sails, white hull, varnished woodwork and gleaming brass of the *Yankee* beside the towering statues of Abu Simbel.

Eventually the Johnsons sold the clipper ship and bought a vessel better suited to exploring the inland waterways of Europe. *Yankee* probably changed hands several times before ending up with Windjammer Cruises sailing out of Miami under skipper Derek Lumbers. By the time she reached Raro, the hull was grey and her engines belched black smoke. A crowd of girls went aboard for a party and when the wind got up they were all enjoying themselves too much to notice. The *Yankee* went up on the reef.

On one of our visits to Avarua, we walked out of the township to look at her. A very sad sight. High enough on the reef for it to be possible to walk across to her at low tide. There she sits; reduced to a bare, rusting hull, like a once beautiful, but now ravaged woman, still defiantly displaying her beautiful bones.

# 9  MITIARO
## One hundred ducks and ten Vietnamese refugees

It was Trish's birthday. We hadn't planned anything special to celebrate it, but at least it was a beautiful day for flying. Elliot Cochrane was in a hurry but thankfully not in too much of a rush to ignore the standard checklist of his instruments as he revved the engines of the little Britten-Norman Islander and taxied it out onto the runway.

'Gotta be back here by two o'clock this afternoon to get my bets on at the T.A.B.,' he shouted over the noise of the engine.

'Horse races?' I queried back with another shout. I was sitting beside him in the co-pilot's seat, with Trish, Zara and Sean behind. We were taking off for Mitiaro, some 230 kilometres to the northeast. Our pilot was a slim young man, about 28 or 30 years old, with a shock of thick, wavy blond hair.

'That's right,' he replied, adjusting himself in the seat and gunning the aircraft down the runway. 'I always follow the races in New Zealand . . . they run a tote on 'em here in Raro.'

We climbed quickly, wheeling back along the coast, passing Avarua and heading out over the open ocean. The roar of the engines made conversation difficult and anyway Elliott was preoccupied. When we reached about 2000 metres, he set the plane on auto pilot, opened up the lift-out racing section of a New Zealand newspaper and settled down to study the form of the horses that were going to take his hard-earned cash that afternoon.

Cook Islands Airways fly the small 8 to 9 passenger aircraft to 5 of the southern islands that have rough airstrips. They are always full with either passengers or cargo, although the traffic isn't huge because the population of these out islands is very small. Mitiaro, for instance, had a total of only 300 people living on it.

We had decided to spend a few days on Mitiaro and later on Aitutaki before taking Silk and Boyd's copra boat to the northern islands. We have to admit to knowing practically nothing about Mitiaro before landing there—except the size of the population. The details that we read in the *Pacific Islands Handbook* (an indispensable companion if you're travelling in the Pacific) were not particularly encouraging: 'It is low-lying and much of the surface is taken up with a cliff of old coral, up to about six metres in height. The interior of the island is largely swampy.'

But then, guide books and handbooks don't usually take account of people, and it was the people we met on Mitiaro that made our visit there eminently worthwhile. Firstly, there was Papa Raui, a diminutive 70-year-old dynamo without whom Mitiaro would be much the poorer, both figuratively and literally. We were on our way into the one small village on the island, having landed safely on a rather wavy 900-metre airstrip of crushed coral, when we met Papa Raui coming the other way. He was driving the only car on the whole island, a little yellow Honda Civic, while we were travelling in the 'Airport Bus'. . . an open trailer which was being towed along by one of the island's two tractors. Papa Raui's car skidded to a halt and he waved at the tractor to stop.

'I am sorry,' he exclaimed as he walked across to us, 'I was coming to pick you up. I have been arranging some things for my two other guests.'

Papa Raui runs the only guest house on Mitiaro. It consists of two double bedrooms and a curtained-off verandah in his own home. A cable from Temu Okatai had confirmed there was some space for us and that we would be arriving on the morning flight.

Papa Raui (his real name is Raui Pokoati) is one of the Cook Islands' better-known characters. When he was young, he left Mitiaro for Rarotonga and studied religion. For 20 years he was a minister of the Cook Islands Christian Church, a body descended from the London Missionary Society. He resigned his ministry at the age of 44 because, he says, 'I didn't want to be able to blame God for me not being successful in the outside world.' He immediately launched himself into politics and won a seat in the legislative assembly which he held for 13 years. Then he became undersecretary and assistant minister for agriculture, a position he held for a further nine years.

In his earlier days he was a big man, weighing about 100 kilos, but a heart attack forced him to take off weight so that now he appears small and bent. But his leathery face, hawkish nose and gleaming eyes presented an air of almost grim determination. On his retirement, he returned to Mitiaro bursting with energy and ideas on how to improve the lot of the people of his island, and he has been working non-stop towards that end ever since. During the 70s he was appointed chief administrative officer (CAO) for Mitiaro, a post which gives him considerable influence on the island as well as in Rarotonga.

The two other guests he had referred to were a good example of Papa Raui's success in his efforts to get things done on Mitiaro. We met them as soon as we arrived at his house, a small conventional weatherboard structure with a tin roof and large verandahs at both the front and back. They were introduced as Michel Lambert and Ram Naidu, both members of the South Pacific Commission (SPC).

Michel was a tall, well-built Frenchman in his early 50s; an agricultural expert based in Noumea. Ram was a slim, dark Fiji-Indian who was an expert on tropical livestock. They had both been sent to Mitiaro to find ways to improve the island's productive capacity in the areas they specialised in. Just getting such senior members of the Commission to visit an island as small as Mitiaro, with so small a population, was something of a coup for Papa Raui.

'I spoke to the premier, Tom Davis, a few weeks ago,' Papa explained to us as we all sat on the front verandah drinking tea and eating delicious cakes made by his plump and constantly-smiling wife, whom we knew only as 'Mama'. 'I told him we needed someone to explore the potential of this island. To tell us what to do to make our swamplands productive.'

I raised my eyebrows in surprise. I had seen from a large-scale map of the island that Mitiaro was in fact an atoll in which the central part had not yet completely sunk. In a million years or so the swamp would probably be a beautiful lagoon. But for the moment it was a large expanse of water (which ranged from relatively fresh to brackish), mangrove trees, reeds and mud.

Without actually asking or trying, we four found ourselves swept up into the South Pacific Commission-Mitiaro project, at least for a few days. Within an hour of arriving, we were all off with Papa, Ram and Michel for a tour of the island and a 'survey' of its agricultural capabilities and prospects. Papa hooked a flat-bed trailer to the back of his little yellow Honda and while he, Ram, Michel and Trish travelled in the car, Sean, Zara and I sat in the trailer behind.

First we saw the pigs. Most of the pigs on Mitiaro, as on the majority of the islands in the South Pacific, run free, to forage for themselves. But they don't grow very quickly and consequently take a long time to get to marketable size. 'My pigs are different,' Papa Raui proclaimed proudly as we pulled up to a makeshift pen area with a dozen or so pigs inside. 'These pigs are 50 kilos each, but they are only four months old.' Then he pointed to some small, black pigs roaming around in the bush beside us. 'Those ones are my neighbour's pigs. They are only half the size of mine, yet they are all at least six or eight months old. I feed my pigs properly, just with scraps and mangos, papaya and leaves from the trees. A bit of copra—but not too much because it makes the meat too fat.'

Ram and Michel nodded approvingly.

'Why haven't the other islanders done this before?' I asked.

'Because they don't know,' Papa replied. 'First I must show them the results...here. Already they are very surprised.'

'You see,' Ram put in, turning to me, 'there is still a hell of a lot of education necessary throughout the Pacific, to get people to follow the most basic, but sensible agricultural policies.'

It was strange listening to Ram because every time he opened his mouth you expected to hear the soft, rolling sounds of Indian-accented English. Instead, out of this very Indian-looking face came the broadest New Zealand twang. Ram had lived and studied for many years in New Zealand and married a New Zealand girl.

'...look at those chickens, for instance.' He pointed to some scrawny hens scratching around amongst the free-ranging pigs. 'All over the Cooks, in most of the South Pacific in fact, people generally let their chickens run free. When they want to eat chicken, they simply catch one and kill it. But their eggs...? Well, they just let the hens drop their eggs in the bush.'

'So they don't eat eggs?' Trish asked.

'Oh, yes. Of course they eat them, but they buy eggs imported from New Zealand...$1.20 a dozen.'

'But that's crazy.'

'Sure it's crazy. But that's what happens.'

Papa Raui nodded. 'This is what we must change. On Mitiaro maybe it is possible. It is a small island with only a small number of people, but they are all very poor. . .and there are no young men.'

'Why not?' It was Zara this time who asked.

Papa looked down at her, a little surprised, it seemed, that she had been listening to the conversation and was now participating.

'Because they have all gone. They go first to Rarotonga, as soon as they are old enough, and then to New Zealand where there are more opportunities. Here on Mitiaro there is nothing for them.' He tapped his chest, 'I am an example. It is the way I did it when I was young. But I am sorry now to have done so. We only come back to our home islands to die. In most cases it is too late to do anything. I want to try to atone for my absence. I have much to achieve before I die.'

We drove off again on a road, or rather a causeway of crushed coral rock which had been pushed straight out into the Mitiaro swamp and across to the other side. It had been built by the islanders themselves, Papa told us, to reach a large section of fertile 'foodland' on the far side of the island.

When we reached this so-called 'foodland' it seemed at first glance to be no more than dense, tropical undergrowth, or jungle. But on closer examination we could see that it was being used as agricultural land. Nothing had been done in an organised way, but the villagers had planted all manner of fruit and vegetables in small patches which were sprinkled irregularly in the bush. They seemed to be growing quite well. There was taro, kumera, casava, and arrowroot, the staple South Pacific carbohydrates, as well as ginger, turmeric, cardamom, coffee, capsicum, and tomatoes. Also fruits; papaya, mangos, pineapple, avocados, bananas and, of course, coconuts. At least what soil there was available was incredibly rich. It seemed that you could throw almost anything down on the ground and it would grow.

But Papa Raui was not happy. 'They do not know how to care for these gardens. . .to plan them properly, to weed them and harvest correctly. They use them only for subsistence. If this area was farmed properly we could have cash crops. . .crops which could be sent to Raro and sold in the market there, to make money for the people of Mitiaro.'

Michel nodded. He wandered through the area examining the various crops and taking notes. Then he spent about half an hour talking to Papa Raui and making suggestions about ways of improving the area. 'I will put all this down on paper for you,' he said, '. . .make a plan for you to follow.'

Papa Raui was quiet. 'It is not necessary for us to think in millions of dollars,' he said softly. 'This is a small island. We need something small to help a small number of people.'

That evening, after a dinner of fish and taro, Michel produced a half-empty bottle of whisky and we sat around on the verandah drinking it and talking over some of the possibilities for the island and its swamp. Then the conversation turned to more general matters. We talked about our trip across the Pacific; Ram and Michel told us something of their jobs and Papa Raui talked about some of his experiences as a politician in Rarotonga.

Then suddenly Ram snapped his fingers and sat upright in his chair. 'I think I've got the answer for your swamp,' he said to Papa.

'Yes?' Papa said expectantly as we all turned to Ram.

'Ducks.'

'Ducks??'

'Yes, ducks. They'll love the swamp. They'll breed well and they're a perfect cash crop...even an export-earner if they're managed well.'

'But wouldn't they fly away?' I asked.

'Not if they're Muscovi ducks. They're too heavy.'

Papa Raui drew a deep breath and sat back in his chair smiling.

I don't want to give the impresssion that I am obsessed with dying and burials. It's just that how a society reacts to these finalities is an enormous indicator of where that society is at. On all the Pacific Islands we visited death is treated as a part of life. And as I said before, I like that.

That is the reason I remember with pleasure the graveyard on the outskirts of Papa's little village, close by the end of the airstrip, to which we walked on the following morning. The informal graveyard, right on the water's edge, was simply a collection of gravesites marked with slabs, most of them made with crushed coral, which tends to disintegrate rather quickly. A few were constructed with longer-lasting imported concrete. What made the graves special was that on the majority of them there were displays of the most treasured personal possessions of the graves' occupants. One had a small bowl containing a little mirror and a set of imitation pearl earrings with a matching necklace. Another had a tin mug with a pipe and a tooth-brush sticking out. At the foot of a child's grave was a glass jar to store a pair of tiny, black-patent, first walking shoes and a knife, fork and spoon set. On almost all the graves there was at least one bottle of half-finished patent medicine!

On the return walk into the village we met Papa who, even though he was twice our age, had left the house before we were up on some important errand; probably to feed his well-loved pigs. As we walked, we talked.

Ram and Michel were especially interested in the coconuts, which are the staple and only real cash-earning crop. And it's a tough way to earn cash. At the time of writing, copra was selling for $450 a tonne. To produce that tonne it's necessary to harvest, husk and dry well over 500 coconuts. The trouble is that, as with all farming, the price you can get for your produce varies. Copra prices sometimes fall as low as $150 a tonne. The reason for the present boom ($450 a tonne was the highest it had ever reached), was because the ongoing and continually worsening oil crisis in the West meant that coconut oil, which can be used for heating and lighting, was in increasing demand. Good to know that someone is benefitting from the problem.

The trouble is that the economies of small Pacific nation-states like the Cook Islands are so linked to those of Australia, New Zealand, or France that they are certain to suffer our pinch. The other problem with coconuts is that the tree is prone to diseases and the ravages of nasties like the rhinoceros beetle. This is why Pacific islands are generally so paranoid about disease and bugs being brought in by casual travellers. When we arrived in the Cooks, our baggage was unavailable for two hours because, along with everybody else's, it was stacked in a large airtight room and blasted with enough fungicide and pesticide to wipe out any living thing!

One last thing to remember about copra is that it's a very labour-intensive product.

It takes a very long time to produce a tonne, so it's only in a place where labour is cheap that it's a feasible crop.

Ram was very keen to investigate the possibility of harvesting cardamom on a commercial basis. Being an Indian as well as an agriculturist he knew all there was to know about spices.

'Look into it by all means,' Papa said, 'but remember whatever we do, it must be kept simple. It must be something we can get going ourselves with the bare minimum of outside help. We can't expect anything extra from the government in Raro. We get only $2000 a year from them. That's our total budget. $2000. That's why we have to plan on doing things for ourselves.'

He stopped and turned around, pointing back down the road. 'Like the airstrip. I was at the cabinet meeting when the matter of which islands could have air connections with Raro came up for discussion. Albert [Sir Albert Henry, the former prime minister of the Cooks] said that it all came down to which islands could afford to build airstrips and on that basis I knew Mitiaro would miss out. So I said to him, "If I build the airstrip, will you promise to provide the air service?" and he said, "yes." Then I rushed back here and organised every man, woman and child who could walk, into clearing a strip by hand and laying crushed coral on it.'

We had stopped at the edge of the road beside a couple of big metal containers and Papa showed us how these were used as dryers to preserve the yummy pieres, dried bananas, which are later wrapped in banana leaves and sold in Raro as a delicacy.

'Do you dry your copra in the same way?' Michel wanted to know.

Papa nodded.

'Well, I have a new copra drying technique.' Michel said, 'which I think is ideal for your island. I will draw you a picture of how it works.' He opened the pad on which he had been making copious notes ever since arriving on Mitiaro.

'Not here,' Papa stopped him. 'Let us go home for some cool drinks and there you can show me your copra dryer.'

He led the way through the little village which houses 50 or 60 families and the total population of only 300. In the middle he pointed out the small community hall which he'd had built at his own expense in an attempt to give the people, especially the young, who were the ones he wanted to stay, a place to meet, to play pool, table tennis or just to talk.

There's no TV in the Cooks. . . thank heavens. Its effect on the social life would be as catastrophic as we had already seen in French Polynesia and would see again in other island groupings.

The other homes in the village were small, squat and rather ugly—made from concrete with galvanised tin roofs. A few of them went to the unnecessary trouble of filling in the window space with glass louvres. All of this was totally unsuitable for the climatic conditions. But some twit in New Zealand, who no doubt has never been outside Auckland, has decreed that pandanus or coconut palm roofs and walls are a fire hazard. The fact that living conditions in the Cooks are totally different from those in urban New Zealand is irrelevant: regulations are regulations.

Papa's house was the only one with electric light. He had his own generator. He also had indoor scoop-over bathing facilities, but guests had to be mean with the water because the island has a constant shortage due to the porous soil.

Mama had morning-tea waiting for us. Her role seemed to be one of providing the background comforts against which Papa could operate. She never joined in any of our conversations but stayed in the kitchen and out on the back verandah where she was helped by her four-year-old granddaughter whose parents lived in New Zealand, and by two other boys, Moe Tai and Tera Roto, both a little younger than Sean. Papa had taken these two in when their parents had moved off to Raro to find work.

Sean and the boys sloped off down to the beach while we drank our tea as Michel showed us photographs and diagrams of his patent copra dryer and explained how it worked.

'You see, drying copra in the sun has always been possible, but then you have to be ready to rush out and cover it all whenever it rains, as well as turning it during the day, so it gets an equal amount of sunshine on the whole trayful. My machine is completely covered with a film of clear heavy-duty plastic so that the rain cannot get in.' He spread the drawings and photographs in front of us on the table. It was like a long shallow box, divided into partitions and balanced in the middle on a fulcrum, something like a see-saw.

'In the morning you tilt it towards the east so that it gets the maximum sun and in the afternoon to the west.'

'Wouldn't the copra sweat underneath the plastic?' Iain asked.

'Ah!...non...' Michel smiled, '...because we have the convection currents of hot air. At each end of the box it is painted black to absorb the heat and make the warm air, which as you know always rises, pass continuously over the copra and out of the top. Formidable! Eh!'

Simple. Cheap. Ecologically sound. Papa was very enthusiastic and Michel promised to send him the plans. Everywhere else we went in the Pacific Iain told people about Michel's copra dryer. But most of them were sceptical. The old way had worked for generations, so why change now? People the world over are depressingly reluctant to try new ways.

Sean arrived back at the house looking pretty pleased with himself, as he proudly displayed three small fish, the first ones he had ever caught on his own, though Moe and Tera had probably helped considerably.

'The sea is thick with fish,' Papa told us that night after dinner as we sat sipping more of Michel's scotch. 'It's child's play to catch them. Two years ago when I returned home I could see the opportunity to improve the men's methods and their catch and I bought three small boats with outboard engines. I even had a couple of spare engines. Also the big walk-in freezer room down by the water and two other freezers in the kitchen of the house which I ran off my own generator. I paid 15 men 60¢ a kilo for anything they caught. As much as they could catch. Then I sold it to the mainland and made 15¢ a kilo for myself. In one year they caught so much fish that they cleared $40 to $50 a week each. That's very big money here. Before that they had had to rely entirely on copra. And what happened?' Papa asked himself the question and went on to answer it. 'They spent almost all the money on drink and then they became bored with fishing every day, so they stopped and now they only go when they need something to eat. And my boats and freezers sit idle. An $11 000 experiment which failed. That's why, from now on, I'm thinking small, at least starting small and bringing the people along with me that way.'

Ram and Michel agreed that this was best. Hasten slowly. On the surface the two men agreed on many things and were socially amiable, but it was impossible not to sense that underneath there were currents of restraint. Ram's formal Englishness, due to his having grown up in colonial Fiji, clashed with Michel's exuberant Gallic manner. To Michel the English were..(with raised eyebrows) *'merde alors';* the Americans...(a shaking of the right wrist) 'impossible'; while Australians...(a pulling down of the corners of his mouth) were beyond description.

Ram, I think, saw Michel as a representative of white men, foreigners, former colonisers, made only marginally more palatable by being involved in a regional self-help organisation. Difficult to swallow the fact that the SPC is financed heavily by Australia and also by New Zealand and France. Michel was sensitive enough to be aware of these reactions, which he must have come across countless times in the Pacific and which must sadden as well as irritate him because he feels that the Pacific is his home. He intends to stay on in New Caledonia when he retires. 'I have a farm with a house on it in Champagne and I like to go back,' he told us at one stage, 'but only to visit. My brother is a farmer too and all they ever talk about are the rising prices and the impossibility of making a decent living. They inhabit such a small world. Tsk. Alors!'

The whole time he talked, Michel made extravagant gestures with his hands, and with his extremely mobile face. Several times Papa imitated his actions and we all broke up laughing. Despite the undercurrents I have mentioned, we all found each other's company very enjoyable and stimulating, which was the reason why conversation went on non-stop from breakfast till after dinner and ranged over a wide variety of topics.

I get a terrific mental high in situations like these, the cross-fertilisation of ideas from such diverse cultures; Cook Island, Australian, French, Fijian, English. I feel at such times that *anything* is possible; that *everything* is possible; that between us, we can make the world the magic place it ought to be for everyone, not just for the lucky few, to live in. We can enable everyone to fulfil their potential and do it without irreparably damaging our fragile environment. We can. *We can.*

Sunday. Sundays in the South Pacific mean church. Christianity has a tremendously strong hold in the Pacific islands...its influence being directly attributable to the work done by the London Missionary Society (LMS) in the nineteenth century. In the Cook Islands, and on Mitiaro in particular, it was the Reverend John Williams who brought 'The Word'. He arrived on the island aboard the self-built barque *Endeavour* on July 19, 1823.

The LMS was eventually replaced in the Cooks by an offshoot body, the Cook Islands Christian Church (CICC) which is basically Methodist in its approach to Christianity and in the form of its services.

After a breakfast of papaya, toast and tea at Papa Raui's place, we walked with him about 100 metres from his house towards the centre of the village and the CICC church. Michel continued for another 200 metres to attend a separate service in the island's only other place of worship, the Catholic church.

The church Papa Raui led us to was a small, solid-looking building of stone, painted both inside and out a gleaming white. The interior of the church was simple, but quite beautiful. A wooden parquet ceiling done in complicated patterns with black and white stars, and windows of large pieces of coloured glass. The service was taken by the acting pastor, Tiki

Tetava, who, Papa told us with a whisper, was the M.P. for Mitiaro in the legislative assembly.

But it wasn't the service, the sermon, the colour of the walls, ceiling or the stained glass windows that made that morning memorable for us...it was the singing. We had never heard anything like it before. We have since learnt that what we heard there on Mitiaro is peculiar to the Cook Islands—a kind of rhythmic mixture of primitive tribal chant and traditional European Christian hymn singing. The combination is only a little short of electrifying. When they first began to do it, I found the hair on the back of my neck starting to prickle. I turned to Trish and she raised her eyebrows and shook her head in amazement. The sound was absolutely unique. I suppose the simplest way, to begin to describe it is to call it natural harmonising. No books to follow, no conductors to say who takes which part, yet somehow the congregation knows, and just does it. Underneath, or as a base, you have the actual hymn, a traditional Christian hymn, sung in Polynesian, but along with it, you hear the older men providing a backing of what for all the world sounds like grunting in rhythm, a quite sexual sound really, although I suppose it's wrong to make the comparison in the context of hymn singing. Then, in addition, there is a high-pitched wailing on the part of the women, something almost like a primal scream or perhaps, if you're familiar with the Bee Gees...a bit like Robin Gibb wailing in some of their popular songs.

The combined effect is stunning. Of course, to the congregation on Mitiaro, it's just a normal Sunday church service!

Nothing much else happens on Mitiaro on Sundays. Papa let Ram and Michel know that this was a day of rest and although he had other things he wanted to show them and talk about, it would have to wait until the following day, their (and our) last day on the island. He told them that he had scheduled a meeting for nine the next morning with the village elders. 'Most important', he said.

That evening, to enliven our traditional Polynesian meal of fish and taro, Michel produced (with typical flair) a bottle of French wine and a packet of Camembert cheese. Formidable!

After dinner we all sat around again talking with Papa Raui about the swamp, and other plans he had for Mitiaro's future. He was absolutely determined, despite the setback he'd had with the fishing project, to get some major work underway.

'If we could produce, say 12 000 ducks a year here,' Papa said, as if doing some mental arithmetic out loud, 'that would be $36 000...each duck is worth about $3 in the Rarotonga market...that would give about $600 to each family on this island.' He smiled. 'That would be very good.'

Ram leant forward in his chair. 'I think I'll be able, or at least the Commission will be able, to send you some ducks to get the project going.'

'Good. Good,' Papa nodded. 'But the people here will have to work for it.' His voice became more firm. 'That is the main trouble with Cook Islanders...they are lazy. The Cook Islanders way is to climb a coconut tree, get a coconut and eat it, play the ukelele a while, sleep. Wake up, catch a fish, eat it, play the ukelele, sleep....' He sat back with his arms resting straight along the arms of the easy chair. 'In Tahiti it is the same. There it is the Chinese who feed the Tahitians now. If there were no Chinese there, the Tahitians would be dead.' He shook his head slowly for a moment and then continued with what was clearly a favourite theme. 'No...the only way is to mix the blood. I advise my islanders to go out and marry an outsider...English, New Zealander, Australian, Indian, Chinese, it doesn't matter. They come back and have children. The half-castes are better! Smarter, and they work harder.

'My grandfather was an American Jew.' He laughed loudly. 'You see now where I get my energy, my madness, why I cannot sit still. All my grandchildren are half-castes. My daughters married Australian and New Zealand men and my sons married English and New Zealand girls. That's what Mitiaro needs...new blood. If I could get 10 Vietnamese refugees to come to this island to marry Mitiaro people, I would be very happy. Mix the blood—make good workers, instead of lazy people. Do you think you could get me some Vietnamese refugees as well as the ducks?'

There was no doubt that Papa was serious! I could just see the application form filed at the SPC; *required: 100 ducks, 10 Vietnamese refugees (must be strong and healthy).* Although I think that Papa would probably have put the Vietnamese at the top of the list. When Ram and Michel realised that he wasn't altogether joking, it was with some difficulty that they explained they weren't actually in the refugee placement business!

A conversation on the next day made me wonder just how any Vietnamese would be regarded here. 'That black man, where's he from?' a young girl giggled with embarrassment at her own audacity.

'Fiji.'

'But he's not Fijian.'

'He's a Fiji Indian.'

'Not Fijian.'

'He was born there and so were his parents.'

'But he's not Fijian, he's Indian,' and before I could further protest Ram's racial/national combination...'The Indians own all the shops in Fiji. They make all the money. And there are more of them than there are Fijians now.'

Surprised by her simplistic, but accurate knowledge, I changed tack, 'Why don't you come over and join in the meeting?' I nodded towards where the village men sat under a large flamboyant tree and waited for Papa Raui to open the proceedings. I had left the all-male gathering, to cross over to where the women sat about 10 metres away on the verandah of a small home plaiting coconut palm baskets and embroidering big tivaivais.

'Wouldn't it be better if the women also listened to what is said?' I asked. 'You might want to ask questions or have suggestions.'

They giggled again. 'No, no. We can hear from here and the men like to think that only *they* can decide about such important things. Afterwards, on our own, we will talk about it. But not in public. They don't like it that way.'

I left the women to return to the village meeting where, for about an hour, we sat under the flamboyant tree while first Papa and then Michel and Ram, through Papa's translation, told the men what plans they had been discussing for their island. Throughout the proceedings a black and white dog lay asleep in the middle of the circle, occasionally coming awake enough to give itself a listless scratch.

The men listened attentively and, at the end, one of them, who was obviously chosen by the rest, probably because he spoke good English, asked a few questions, not only about the ducks but also about fungus on taro and the use of sprays. 'We must be very careful,' he said, 'because the island is extremely porous and insecticides can easily filter into our water supplies.'

Afterwards I asked Papa who he was and learnt he was the visiting dentist; a Cook Islander who had trained in New Zealand and come back to work with his people. Mitiaro was his home island, but he was employed by the government to visit several of the islands in the southern group. 'He brings his own portable equipment and does the children's teeth for free,' Papa said. 'The adults must pay, but they can't afford to, so I pay for them all.'

I commented that it was good to hear of an islander who had gone away to be trained and instead of staying where the money was much better, had come back home to help his own people.

Papa smiled. 'It is good for him too you know. This way he stays a whole person. We have a saying in the islands: When you are asked to the palace to dine with the queen. . .as you go through the gate, stop for a moment and turn around to look back down the way you've come. You understand?'

Again Mama had morning tea ready and Zara appeared with Papa's granddaughter. Under Zara's attentive tuition, the little girl had started to speak some English, which pleased Papa Raui no end. Zara had also washed, conditioned and brushed the girl's long black hair to a glossy state and then twirled it up in two knots on each side of her head.

'I've given her a toothbrush, she doesn't have one, and some hairclips,' Zara said, 'also a bar of my special soap.'

Zara has the enviable knack of always looking neatly turned-out, no matter what the circumstance. In all our travelling together, she has never been as scruffy as the rest of us sometimes looked. On this journey her wardrobe was replete with a blue silk handkerchief which she had embroidered with a rainbow and a pair of short, black, lace gloves which she had picked up in the Upper Richmond Road market for 10p. Of course she didn't ever wear them, but no doubt they reassured her that better times were to come and that she wouldn't always be living out of a backpack!

'I've been thinking,' Ram said, 'What about your eels? Mitiaro eels are famous in the islands, aren't they? There should be an overseas market for them.'

Papa smiled.

'We export our eels from Fiji to Germany,' Ram went on, 'so why couldn't you do the same?'

Papa shook his head. 'At the moment, there's plenty of reasons. Not that we can't overcome them of course, but for the time being we are still so tied to New Zealand that all our vegetable produce goes there automatically. They have a monopoly. Which means they control the price. We could do much better elsewhere of course. In Tahiti they would pay at least twice what New Zealand pays for our fruit and vegetables. I know one man who sends his rito hats [rito is a Cook Island speciality] to Tahiti and sells them for $100. In New Zealand he'd be lucky to get $15. And I have heard that some of our tomatoes have been air freighted to New Zealand, simply turned round at Auckland airport and air freighted back to Tahiti, to be resold at almost four times what we were paid for them.'

Iain was indignant. 'They can't do that.'

'They can and do. There is a contract binding us to supply New Zealand. We are their cheap market gardeners. And, as their economy runs down, so will ours. It's like being tied to a drowning man.'

'It's twentieth century colonialism,' I said, 'and even less acceptable from New Zealanders who, after all, have suffered from colonialism themselves.'

'Don't worry,' Papa said, 'we'll break their stranglehold and get into free trade arrangements. This new government of ours has already made steps in that direction. The New Zealanders aren't going to like it, but that's too bad. We actually receive more aid from Australia now than we do from New Zealand and so we can almost afford to grow up.'

Ram cleared the final cookie from the plate. It was to be our last taste of Mama's delicious snacks. Papa drained his cup of tea. 'I think that you must be getting soon to the airport or you'll miss your plane,' he said.

He made it sound like an international connection. 'Mama', he called, and through she came with armfuls of the most beautiful leis of pink frangipani which she must have made while we were at the meeting. We all caught our breath with pleasure and gave her big hugs of thankyou.

While we waited for Elliot Cochrane to check over the dials and gadgets on his little Cook Island Airways plane, Papa took Iain and me aside and asked us for some advice. 'This is a secret', he said, 'but it is my favourite grandson's 21st birthday at the beginning of next year and I would like to give him something special. But I want to combine it with something I wish to do also, so I am giving him a round-the-world airticket, on the understanding that he takes me with him! What do you think? Tell me the truth now. Am I too old to do so much travelling? There are so many places I wish to see before I die. I want to look and see how they do things. I may get some new ideas.'

Of course, we assured him that he was quite definitely young enough to go, and that he'd have a ball. (Look out world!)

He stood at the edge of his own airstrip to wave us off back to Raro, a diminutive figure with a big heart and bursting energy. The world could do with a good few more Papa Rauis.


# 10  AITUTAKI
## 'An aphrodisiac in the punch'

'There it is,' pilot Steve Opie shouted above the noise of the little Cook Island Airways plane. The kids and I leaned forward to peer over his shoulder. Beside him Iain began clicking away with his camera. On the horizon of indigo sea we could easily pick out the pale blue patch. It looked like a bleached spot or a hole in the ocean.

Aitutaki. Reputedly the most beautiful lagoon in the South Pacific. Some say the world. Madison-Avenue-style super hype? Or fact?

But as Steve brought the little Britten Norman Islander in lower and flew over the outer rim of the atoll, then on across the huge lagoon, we could easily see that it deserved its high reputation. The remarkable blue of the water, we were told later, is caused by the suspension of minute flecks of white sand in the lagoon. Yet the water is so transparent, that the huge coral heads appeared somewhat larger than life.

Outside the small one-room airport (on the wall, a notice: NO DANCING PLEASE), we hitched a ride in the only vehicle, an ambulance, whose driver told us that he came out to meet every one of the four weekly flights—just in case. Immediately he launched into politics and asked us what we thought of Sir Albert Henry (Aitutaki is the former premier's home island). We managed to be politely non-committal until he dropped us at the Rapae, the only hotel on the island. It's actually called the Rapae *Motel*. Why, I don't know, as no guest is likely to turn up in their own car. There's practically none on the island. Perhaps they thought motel sounded more modern than hotel. Anyway the Rapae is a small collection of modest bungalows set amongst the frangipani and mango trees just off the beach. We took the family room which sleeps at least six and has a cooker and a fridge.

We'd hardly had time to discover all this and to ditch our packs when Harold Brown the manager, a very large, handsome, though solemn-looking man, gave us a hoy to say that the hotel's truck was leaving immediately to take the few guests to a launch which was going across the other side of the lagoon to an islet called Akaiami. Almost before we knew it, we were trundling back along the dirt track, past the airport, to a little wharf at which was tied a rather beaten-up-looking, seven-metre launch which had a decidedly reluctant engine. There were about 10 of us, including we four and the boat owner and his helper, so we all crammed in once the engine was started, to head out, skimming across the coral heads.

Close up, the lagoon loses none of the initial aerial impact of its beauty. If anything, it's more beautiful. And definitely more breathtaking, because, due to the clarity of the water, the coral heads, seen so clearly from the air, appear to be only centimetres below the surface. And the casual manner in which Rio Ngere, the boatman, delivered the boat at high speed from one side of the lagoon to the other made it difficult for me to concentrate on a conversation which I struck up with one of the other people on board, even though I was so interested in what he had to say.

Desmond Kealey had the quiet, self-sufficient glow usually only exuded by people who are in love. An air of barely suppressed whoops of joy. Desmond was a chubby little man in his late 40s of the type who manage to look conservatively dressed even when wearing only a pair of bathers. He stood at the rear of the open cabin of the boat scanning the horizon anxiously. 'There it is,' he breathed, a slow smile illuminating his cherubic features.

His wife, Margaret, stood up beside him, 'Where dear?'

'There,' he pointed. 'That's where we used to land.'

Old eagle-ears Sheppard embarrassed her kids by immediately asking, 'Have you been here before?'

'Oh yes.' Desmond's smile broadened with the memory. 'Many times. I came with the flying boats.'

'Oh, how wonderful,' I enthused, and embarrassed Zara and Sean still further by plying him with more questions. Not that Desmond needed much prompting, because once he discovered that I was interested, he regaled us with funny stories and information about the 10 years he had spent as a radio operator on the Air New Zealand, or as it was then, TEAL Coral Route. By flying boat from Auckland to

Tahiti. What a way to go. Sometimes I wish I'd been born a hundred or two hundred years ago, so as to be a real explorer, the first white woman to cross the Sahara, that sort of thing. Other times I wish that I hadn't been born yet, so that my turn would come round in the mid-21st century, by which time space travel should be available to everyone. Most of the time I just wish that I could live forever.

'I remember the Christmas we came through here,' Desmond beamed, 'refuelled, and went on to Tahiti, only to discover that the lagoon was full of logs and we couldn't land. So we had to turn round and fly back here. Three times we flew up to Tahiti before we were eventually able to land there. In the meantime we slept on the beach here, ate bananas and coconuts and the fish we caught. Some of the locals brought us fresh water to drink and I remember how many of the passengers said it was the best Christmas they ever had!'

Desmond was in his stride now and there was no stopping him. Everyone, including Zara and Sean, were listening rapt. 'Each time we came through we landed here to refuel,' he explained. 'That took about three hours and all the passengers spent the time swimming in the lagoon. The villagers would bring out the fuel the night before. Just an excuse really to sing and dance and carry on all night. The doctor from the hospital came out too. He was supposed to check the health of the passengers. He'd do that just by walking past the open cabin doors. He'd been up all night too and unless someone had their foot actually falling off, I don't think he'd have noticed anything was up.'

'Were there cabins?' Sean asked. 'On the plane?'

'Oh yes,' Desmond smiled, 'the trip could take up to a week. There were 20 seats upstairs and 40 below and the cabins were in between. Food was served by waiters as in a restaurant. We had one stewardess on each flight and they were treated as something very special. There was even a dumbwaiter between the galley down below and the seating cabin.'

'A dumbwaiter?'

We explained to the children who were naturally intrigued by the term.

'It was a sizeable plane,' Desmond went on, 'and we flew at about 1000 metres, though we could come down as low as 100 metres to avoid turbulence. Even so she wallowed a lot.'

'Where are the flying boats now?' Sean asked.

'In a museum in Auckland,' Desmond sighed. 'Time caught up with us. When Tahiti opened Fa'aa airport, that was the end of the flying boats on the Coral Route. The end of a magic time.' He gave a little grimace.

'This is it.' He brightened as we approached the beach of an atoll at breakneck speed. 'This is where we used to land. There used to be a palm-thatched hut among the coconut trees.'

Rio nodded. 'Fallen down. There's a concrete place now.'

And so there was and very plain it was too.

'And the quay,' Desmond murmured, 'it seems to have silted up a bit.'

Again Rio nodded.

'But it's still as beautiful,' Desmond smiled. 'Nothing can change that.'

We let him be the first to scramble out onto the small, slowly-decaying stone quay. We looked around. And...there it was; the clear, azure water, the fine sand white beach, backed by coconut palms and brilliant lush vegetation. Only this time the quality of the beauty defied description.

'First time I've seen it in 15 years.' Desmond Kealey stood transfixed. If he had been a Latin, he would have wept openly with the emotion of the moment. As a New Zealander, he smiled softly and moved off along the sweep of beach. Even his wife left him to go alone into his memories.

Rio took us on a track across to the other side of the island, a mere 500 metres at the most.

On the way back, we collected coconuts, drank the sweet milk and ate the soft flesh, along with the sandwiches which Harold Brown had packed up for us.

From the flying boat quay at Akaiami we motored a little further around the rim of the lagoon and flung out an anchor on the deeply shelving sandy shore of One Foot Island, Motu Kitiu. In my notes, I wrote of this place, 'the beauty makes one swoon.'

Leaving the others near the boat, Iain and I went along the beach a few hundred metres, and then struck out into the pass between One Foot and the next island. Caressed by the water and enchanted by the fish and the sensation of floating in emptiness, we didn't notice the young crewman from the boat swimming nearby until he beckoned us to follow him. Out in mid-channel, he motioned to us to keep a safe distance while he himself swam down and dropped little pieces of broken coral onto what appeared to be a pile of rocks on the sandy bottom.

The pile moved up towards us. At first I was unsure what I was seeing, but then I realised that the greyish coconut-sized head which had emerged had a mass of eight, rubbery, metre-long tentacles attached to it. An octopus. A large octopus. No. Two octopuses! It seemed likely that we had disturbed them in the midst of a private act.

The trouble with swimming is that there's no reverse gear (I think perhaps God made a booboo there) and I don't really feel like turning my back to swim away from a situation like that. Anyway, once they felt that we weren't going to come any closer, they began to settle back down to their conubial bliss, changing colour, as they did so, from grey to brown. With eight arms to cuddle each other that's four times the joy.

The hours passed too quickly. None of us wanted to leave: a feeling which occurred more often in the South Pacific than anywhere else we've travelled. On the boat trip back Desmond Kealey looked like a fulfilled man. Up on the deck, we talked with Peter Cusack, a blond fellow in his early 30s who looked as though he'd just stepped out of a pub in South Yarra, by which I mean that we'd noticed that many of the foreigners, mostly New Zealanders, resident in the Cooks, looked different from those foreigners passing through. Australians call it 'going troppo'. The British call it 'going native'. Well, Peter had done neither, even though he was married to a Cook Islander called Mum (that was her real name). They live in Raro where Peter makes and sells jewellery. He asked us to look him up when we were back there. At the Rapae Zara found a cat so pregnant it must have been about to pop. She called it 'Preggers' and immediately set about making a nesting box and putting food down for it.

Later we walked the 2 km or so along the one, unsurfaced road to the cinema in the town. The kids had heard it was showing the premiere of a film with the non-inspiring title, *Mr. X.*

The man who sold the tickets for the film, from a galvanised iron shed tacked on the back of the little community hall, was incredibly beautiful. With a crown of pink flowers on his head, he sat with his small daughter on his knee until the time came to shut up his cash box. Then he helped us hang tatty sheets of perforated black plastic over the windows in a not very effective attempt to block out the bright sunlight. He then retired to the projectionist's box-like room to show the film. A one-man cinema operator.

The long backless wooden benches were crowded with kids from 10 to 15 years old.

On the floor in front sat the noughts to 10. Just before it started, there was a loud bellow from outside and the three or four women in the audience stood up to go out. We followed to check what was happening and saw a couple of men on a motorbike. The driver, holding a big conch-shell to his mouth was giving another loud blast to attract attention. They were selling fresh bread. It was only the baker doing his rounds, Cook Island style. We each had a go at blowing the conch, to no effect, and we bought some bread.

Then we resumed our seats in the hubbub inside and sat through a one-and-a-half-hour-long, execrable imitation of a James Bond movie.

The first European to 'discover' Aitutaki was Captain William Bligh in His Majesty's ship *Bounty,* on April 11, 1789...just 17 days before the famous mutiny took place. The next European to arrive on the scene was Captain Edward Edwards on HMS *Pandora.* He dropped anchor off Aitutaki two years later, in April, 1791 while searching for Fletcher Christian and the mutineers. But then another 30 years passed before the next white man stepped ashore.

But this one was not just passing by. The Reverend John Williams of the London Missionary Society came to Aitutaki with two Tahitians, Papeiha and Vahapata, from the island of Raiatea, to work as teachers in the conversion of the islanders to Christianity. For the Tahitians, the arrival on Aitutaki was particularly significant. That it should be the first island in the Cooks to receive 'The Word' in what was to be a new 'wave' sweeping through the islands was symbolic of the earlier great westward expansion of Polynesian culture from Raiatea.

Remember the story of Ru, the chief navigator of Raiatea, or Havai'i as it was in ancient times? How he sailed his family, relatives and a handful of chosen maidens to find a new and more prosperous island to the West? Well, Aitutaki was the place where he landed and the present inhabitants of the island are supposed to be descendants of Ru and his companions on that epic voyage.

Our bungalow at the Rapae Motel was the only one with kitchen facilities, so early in the morning we walked a couple of hundred metres down the dirt road from the hotel grounds to a small shop to buy some supplies: bread, butter, eggs, cheese, tomatoes, coffee, etc. and returned to cook up a big breakfast. Then Sean and Zara climbed a large mango tree, which was growing outside our verandah and collected half a dozen or so mangos, which we ate while sitting on the verandah.

About midday, having read for a while, worked on our notes and cleaned up our gear, we walked into town. The brilliantly white crushed coral of the road reflected the heat and light and was very dusty, yet somehow, walking along it was an extremely pleasant experience. The green of the surrounding foliage and coconut palms, the blue of the lagoon along the shore, the islanders who passed by, either walking or riding little red Honda scooters, all friendly and smiling, all with a ready greeting. It had a good feeling about it...a relaxed and happy ambience.

The village of Arutanga is really not much more than a post office, the church, a few small shops and a 250-metre-long avenue which runs down to the main pier. This avenue, which is the only dual carriageway on the island, is divided by a centrestrip of flowers and it is interspersed with street lights. One side of the road is called Sir Albert Henry Drive, after the former prime minister, while the other side is called Lady Elizabeth Drive, after his wife.

The place seemed very quiet...empty. In the local trading store, A.B. Donald's, Trish asked, 'Where is everybody?'

The woman behind the counter laughed. 'Oh,' she said, 'a big tere party... over 100 people get together to go to a neighbouring island...Atiu.'

This was the first time we had heard of tere parties. 'Why did they go?' I asked.

The woman smiled again. 'Oh, just to have a looksee...see how they getting on over there. They come back soon.'

Tere parties, we found out, are a very common and popular pastime in the Cooks. A group of people just get together, pile onto one of Silk and Boyd's trading boats when it comes by and take off for one of the neighbouring islands, where they just descend on relatives and friends and often complete strangers, who put them up until the boat comes back...probably weeks later. In the meantime, they dance, drink, sing and generally make merry.

Walking out into the street again, we came to a small woodcarving centre on the hill behind the post office. We'd heard of it and wanted to see some of the carvers at work, but unfortunately it was closed. A message pinned to the door said it would be open the following morning.

In the morning the pregnant cat was not to be found, so we were convinced that she had gone off into the bush somewhere to give birth. Zara hunted around, giving plaintive mews but the cat remained unenticed.

We walked into the village to the carving shop, and asked if they had any small wooden statues of the Polynesian god of Tangaroa for sale. Tutai Vaireka, the master carver who trained the other young men of the village, brought out a couple which he had carved himself. We looked at them and then at each other, before looking back at the mutilated version of the great Lord of All Creation whose genitals had been removed, or rather, omitted!

'It's beautifully done,' Iain said, with his omnipresent tact, 'but we'd like to have the real Tangaroa. With all the equipment!' Tutai smiled, and said he would carve us one specially and that we could come by the next morning and pick it up. Simple. Or so we thought then!

We took the road up the small hill leading away from the waterfront to explore a little further. Ambling along between plantations of copra and bananas, we came, after a couple of kilometres, to a man standing by the roadside. He leant on his mattock and put out his hand, 'I'm Tiopu Henry.' He was a big man with a friendly face. 'I'm a cousin of Sir Albert. Not that I'm proud of that. He was no good.' He called out to two young men whom we hadn't spotted before, because they were hidden in the top branches of a big mango tree, to throw down some fruit for the papa'a. Tiopu told us about his farm on which he grew bananas for export to New Zealand. 'They don't give us a good price, but Dr Davis [the prime minister] is going to change all that,' he said. We said we hoped his faith in the new leader was well founded and then, after chatting a while longer, headed back towards the township where we thought that we might hire a couple of the small motorbikes we'd seen around the place.

In the centre of the town, opposite the church, its bumpy coral walls newly painted white, we saw a group of young women, their arms up to their elbows in a big tub. They laughed and called out to us and we went across to ask where we could hire motorbikes. An older woman was sitting on the grass beside them and, at a little distance, an extremely good-looking man was chopping away at a big log, obviously hollowing it out to make a canoe. The woman motioned to us to sit down beside her.

For half an hour we talked to her. She asked us all the usual questions and told us that she had come back from New Zealand to Aitutaki a month ago for the opening of the newly-renovated church.

'Oh, that's why it looks so beautiful,' I said. Set in thick green grass, against the bright-blue lagoon, the sun glinting off the blue and red squares of the glass in the windows, it lacked subtlety, but, of the sledge-hammer variety, its beauty was unsurpassable.

'Yes,' she agreed. 'It is indeed very beautiful. It's the first church ever built anywhere in the Cook Islands. It was opened in 1828 and it was full every Sunday until the big tidal wave.'

'Tidal wave?' Sean took immediate interest.

'Yes, it came with the typhoon a year back and almost destroyed it. But now it's as good as new. Better even.'

Zara and Sean had joined the young girls who were pommelling away at a white, soupy mixture which they seemed to be making by sieving powder through a large perforated tray into the water underneath.

'What are you making?' Zara asked.

'Arrowroot. For my aunty.' The girl gestured to the woman beside us.

'I want to take a whole lot back to New Zealand with me,' the aunt explained. 'It's too expensive there and, anyway, you can't buy the good Aitutaki stuff.' (Rather like Australians travelling with their jars of Vegemite, I guess!)

'Want to try?' One of the girls, who told us her name was Tutai Teokotai, asked Sean who was just longing to plunge his arms into the gooey stuff. Nobody suggested it might be just as well if he washed himself first! Tutai giggled and asked Iain to take a photograph of her and her friend making the arrowroot and to send her a copy.

After a further 10 minutes or so we got around to asking what we'd originally wanted to ask them—where to hire motorbikes.

'Oh, that's Dora Harrington,' Tutai said, pointing. 'She lives just down the road there.'

Dora Harrington is a monumental-sized lady. So large that when she showed me how to kick-start the little Honda '90', she said, 'It'll be a bit hard at first for you, till you get used to it, because you're so little.'

Little! Me! She made all 170 cms and 58 kilos of me feel positively petite!

'Faster Mum, faster,' Sean ordered in masculine tones from the back seat as we took off along the road back to the hotel on my inaugural run on a motorbike. Iain and I have plans for when the kids are off on their own at college or whatever to take a run through Europe on big motorbikes in all the leathergear! This was a small scale taste of pleasures to come. At least I won't have Sean on the pillion seat making positively sexist, caustic remarks about my jumpy gear changes!

At the hotel we picked up our bathers and swopped pillion passengers before starting out to circumnavigate the tiny island.

By the time we'd gone half-way around the island and through the little village of

Vaipeka on the other side, I thought I was getting pretty nifty at the gear changing. There was plenty required because of frequent slow-downs to avoid being thrown off by sudden corrugations or soft spots in the road, and instant stops in order to miss pigs or chickens crossing. Thankfully there were no dogs with which to contend, as dogs are prohibited on Aitutaki due to an old belief that they carried leprosy.

'Stop! Stop!' Zara shouted and pointed at a huge tree dripping with mangos. There was a small, neat farmhouse opposite and Iain went over to ask if we could take a few of the fruit. The farmer's wife was obviously surprised that anyone should feel it necessary to ask and she then insisted on not only coming herself, but also calling to her husband to give us a hand in shaking and poking down the best fruit from the high branches. Iain attempted to repay their generosity by telling them about Michel Lambert's copra dryer, but from their reaction I don't think he made a convert.

Further on, past the slightly larger but still small village of Vaipae (a mere cluster of wooden buildings), we rode down a steep incline, with me clutching the handlebars tightly, and out onto a tiny pier. We left the bikes and waded out into the gentle warm water of the lagoon to eat the fruit.

'This is heaven,' Iain smiled. But it was paradise short-lived, because, a kilometre or so further on, my bike's rear tyre gave a tired sigh and collapsed. Leaving Zara and me stranded, and Sean too, so that he had pillion space to spare, Iain headed back to Arutanga, to try to get the equipment to mend the flat.

Fifteen minutes later the kids and I sprang to our feet at the sound of a motorbike which turned out to be ridden not by Iain, but by a young bloke who gave us the bad news that a short distance up the road he'd come across Iain, who'd also had a puncture, and was now pushing his bike the four or five kilometres back to the village!

A further hour passed in which time the mosquitoes came out to feast on Zara and me before Iain returned, having repaired his own flat, to start mending mine.

After that was done and we were all hot and sweaty and bitten to a frenzy, we drove on around, through Arutanga, where we waved at large Dora Harrington and up to the beach near the airport. Here we peeled off our gear and fell into the cooling lagoon to wash off the layer of grime and dust and to soothe our bites.

Refreshed, we returned to the Rapae, made dinner and then set out again on the bikes, this time to go up to the high school to watch a dance rehearsal.

We have photographs of the girls vibrating their hips and the boys leaping into the air, but they are dead unless, like us, you can recall the fast beat on the drums. We were dumbstruck by them. I have never seen people so naturally musical.

Dawson Murray, the headmaster, introduced himself, telling us that the students were practising for an upcoming tour of New Zealand.

'You should see them in their costumes', he enthused proprietorially, and in the curious pidgin English which he had developed over many years in the islands.

He was a New Zealander who had been teaching for 10 years in the Cooks, of which three and a half had been spent on Aitutaki.

Under the attap roof of the open-sided assembly hall ('We built it ourselves and to hell with their fire regulations') the teenage boys sweated and the girls sang in that curiously haunting, rhythmically contrapuntal style unique to the Cooks. Some dances told old legends and some were merely joyful celebrations of life.

'This is what education is all about,' said Dawson, who was obviously in love with the islands. 'Leaving certificates, exam grades, that's all irrelevant. What we have to do is restore their pride in themselves and their islands. Make them feel that those who leave for New Zealand are the quitters and losers and that those who stay are the real winners.'

Not content with doing the dances once, the students decided which ones needed most practice and did those again. The drummers never let the pace drop. About ten o'clock it began to rain lightly and, exhausted by the day's adventures, we left to go home. On the way I got another flat!

In the morning we went through a crazy routine of shuttling back and forth on our one whole motor scooter to get us all into the village where we collected our Tangaroa. It was well made and we were very happy with it, but Tutai Vaireka, the man who had made the little figure for us, seemed quiet and rather subdued. The Tangaroa had apparently caused something of a trauma in the carving workshop. The fact that we had ordered a proper Tangaroa, complete with penis like the ones we'd seen in Rarotonga (and, in fact, the ones which adorn the Cook Islands coinage and postage stamps and the statue in the museum in Munich) had upset a certain Mr Nga Upu, a director of the wood-carving shop. He was a large, plump man of about 50 and, appearing on the scene a couple of minutes after we had arrived to pick up the carving, asked us to step into his small office a few metres from the shed where Tutai and the other carvers worked.

'If I had been here at the time,' he said to us, 'you would not have been able to order a male Tangaroa. I have given instructions that only female ones are to be made.'

'But,' I said, 'I thought Tangaroa was a male god. There is no female Tangaroa.'

He hesitated a moment. 'That is correct. But it is shameful to see these statues like this. It is better that they are female.'

'But the others you make aren't even female either,' Trish put in. 'They have no vaginas. They're just neuters.'

He looked suddenly embarrassed, as if he thought a woman should not say such things. 'Perhaps, but at least they do not offend people...'

'I find the fact that they have been completely *de*-sexed more offensive than anything,' Trish replied.

'And your children,' he asked, 'are you not concerned that your children will see this?

'Good heavens,' I said, 'why?' The thought had not even occurred to me. I turned to Zara and Sean who were standing beside us. 'Does this upset you?'

They smiled and shook their heads... if anything more embarrassed by Mr Upu's performance than by the carving.

'Surely,' I said, 'this figure...Tangaroa is part of your history, your culture...that cannot be denied by just eliminating a piece of him. He's on your coins, your stamps, your government offices in Rarotonga. We saw big statues of him there, complete with all his equipment.'

'That is Raro...not here. We are religious people. I am an elder of the Seventh Day Adventist Church. Half of the people on Aitutaki are SDA and we think it should be taken off, or covered in some way, perhaps with a sort of skirt...'

'My God,' Trish said. 'Surely what Western missionaries have done already to try and change and destroy Polynesian culture is enough. To try to change your best-known statue, to deny your own history, must be wrong. I mean look at Michelangelo's statue of David in Florence. Admittedly he's nowhere nearly as well equipped as Tangaroa, but he's all there, for everyone to see. It's art!'

The conversation went on for a few minutes in similar vein with no-one changing the other's attitudes. It was not heated, but it really didn't get anywhere. We were allowed to take our Tangaroa after paying the $8 but Nga Upu left us with the impression that it was a one-off job. There'd be no more made like that so long as he had anything to do with it.

We felt presumptuous and guilty, to some extent, about arguing with an islander about his own culture on his own island, but we felt considerably vindicated later on several occasions when we told the story to other islanders. Their reaction was invariably the same as ours and they expressed concern that Nga Upu should be trying to control what the island's wood-carvers were making.

At the nearby community welfare office we stopped briefly to talk to a woman who, like everyone else on the island, greeted us with a 'hello' and a smile. Her name was Ruru Carl and she ran the office which was known in full as 'The Old Aged and Destitute Women's Federation'. On the wall we noticed the fading photograph of an American airman in uniform.

'That's Colonel John Harrington,' Ruru said. 'He was a very nice man. He lived here on Aitutaki for many years.'

Beside the photograph was a press clipping of Colonel Harrington's funeral on the island a few years previously. He'd first come out to Aitutaki with the US Army Airforce in 1942 to work on the airbase they operated. There was an American construction battalion stationed here and they built a double-runway airstrip, the first in the South Pacific, while they were on the island. After the war, Harrington just decided to stay on. He did eventually go back to the States, but not for long. He was very soon back on Aitutaki where he married a local girl and they started a small business.

'That's Dora Harrington,' Ruru told us...and then the penny dropped...Of course, the woman who rented us her motorbikes and who has the agency for the sale of all Honda bikes on the island. A little gold mine.

Not long afterwards, when we returned our bikes to Dora Harrington, we met her new man, a wonderfully calm, pleasant-faced fellow called Maeva Kerikava. Dora, who was carrying an eighteen month old child on her hip, introduced Maeva as her 'sort of husband'. He was a man in his mid-50s, an Aitutaki Islander who, we learnt, had only returned three years previously after 22 years away; 18 in New Zealand and four in Tahiti where he managed a nightclub. He apparently has a wife back in Tahiti from whom he has separated. Now that he has returned to Aitutaki, he doesn't want to leave. 'They'll have to take me out in a box,' he smiled.

We asked Dora if she had any old photographs of her own or of John Harrington's that would have been taken during the War. She shook her head sadly. 'No...they've all gone. I think they were either lost or thrown out.'

'It is the same with me,' Maeva said. 'My mother had many photographs that were taken during those days. I remember seeing them before I left the island. But when I came back, my mother was dead and of course the photos were all gone. It is very sad, because we only realise too late that these are part of our history...part of the story of Aitutaki.'

While we stayed and talked to Dora Harrington and Maeva, Zara and Sean had gone on ahead, so when we left to walk back, Trish and I were walking alone.

'Hey!' Someone called from a house at the side of the road. It was Tiopu Henry, the banana planter...the cousin of Sir Albert Henry.

'Come, I want you to meet my wife.' He waved from his backyard. We were surprised to find him living down here by the water. We had assumed his house would have been up on the hill, near his bananas, where we had first met him. He brought us into his yard and sat us down on a couple of homemade chairs, while he sent one of his young sons to collect and cut open two drinking coconuts for us.

'Mama!' he called out at the top of his voice. 'Mama, come here. I want you to meet someone.'

Mama, who was bending over a tub at the far end of the yard, came over to meet us. As usual for Polynesia, she was large, round and smiling. We had begun to think there was no other sort of person in the Cook Islands.

The yard I speak of, the living quarters that surrounded it and the blackened tin shed which served as a kitchen, would have seemed at first glance, to most Western eyes, a scene of squalor and poverty. The one-room wooden shed in which eight people slept, in four double beds, measured about four metres by six. The yard was covered with old junk, while the kitchen was a rusty and smoke-blackened old tin structure hardly more than a couple of metres high. Chickens and pigs wandered around inside the kitchen and out in the yard where they competed with myna birds to scavenge for food scraps. And yet you could tell there was nothing the family was really in need of. They were well fed and without any question they were happy.

We sat in the yard talking for a while. We got onto politics, Sir Albert Henry, the island's economy and tourism. Tiopu would happily have talked for hours. More fruit was brought out in a bowl: papaya, mangos and bananas. While we ate a mango each, Mama disappeared for a few minutes inside the bedroom hut, reappearing with a huge piece of embroidery in her hands, a *tivaivai*. The intricate appliqué designs which made up a *tivaivai* take months of hand stitching to complete. The traditional use of *tivaivais* is as a shroud. It is important for any member of the family that dies to go to his grave 'well covered' and the relative complexity and beauty of a *tivaivai* that is used in this manner is often taken as an indication of the degree of love and affection held for the departed by those still living. Some *tivaivais,* once they are completed, are stored away in mothballs for just that one occasion, while others are put to good use in the meantime as bed covers, tablecloths, or wall hangings. Many of them are, in fact, pieces of art.

A van with a loudspeaker on its roof drove by delivering a message in the Maori language. Tiopu said that it was telling the people of Arutanga that the banana boat was coming on Monday and that tomorrow, Saturday, everybody would have to cut and harvest their bananas so they could be washed and boxed on the wharf ready for the boat. He gave a mischievous grin. 'It's going to upset the SDAs,' he said. 'They can't work on Saturdays.'

We left Tiopu and his wife shortly after and walked back to the hotel for a siesta to prepare ourselves for 'Island Night' which, we had been warned, was a regular Friday night occurrence that was always a 'blast'. It was apparently the biggest event of the week on Aitutaki.

We decided to splurge a little and have the buffet dinner, which was prepared by the hotel for the evening, instead of cooking our own. The dinner started about half an hour before the show began and it was a beautiful meal: shellfish, raw fish, octopus, chicken, curried meat, chow mein, kumera, seaweed, papaya, mango, banana. . . far more than we could possibly eat.

While we were eating, the drummers had been setting up in one corner of the big, open dining area which had been cleared in the centre, leaving only a few tables around the outside. Crowds of locals had been arriving and they sat outside on the grass drinking cans of beer while they waited for the show to begin. The dancing group of about 15 or 16 girls and half a dozen men were fantastic. In a series of Polynesian dances which appeared to us to be Tahitian, but which we were informed were a very different style from Tahitian dances, the group held us spellbound. Sweating profusely in the humid night air, they gyrated, leapt in the air, stamped their feet, shook, and shimmied to the incredibly fast and powerful beat of the wooden drums played by six drummers. There were several costume changes during the show and despite the heat and the tremendous energy they were putting into it, they seemed always to be fresh and ready to go as each new dance began.

These were not professionals, so Harold Brown, the manager, told us. They were just one of several amateur dance groups on the island who took it in turns each week to dance at the Rapae Hotel on Island Night. Amateurs they may have been, but they were certainly of professional standard.

It lasted about an hour, then there was the changeover to normal dancing in which everyone could participate. A rock and roll band switched places with the traditional drummers and the people who had been sitting out on the lawn, drinking, came in and on to the dance floor. And from that moment, the whole place just took off. Everyone suddenly seemed to go wild. . . almost as if someone had fired a starting pistol. It was quite unbelievable.

What was most amazing was that just about everyone was plastered and you had the impression that they'd been sitting around out there on the lawn just waiting for a chance to let themselves go. Both men and women of all ages and sizes were carrying on as if someone had slipped an aphrodisiac in the punch, and, in addition to dancing, they began performing all manner of erotic movements on the dance floor. This apparently is the normal Island Night scene every Friday night on Aitutaki!

We sat fascinated, just watching it all go on. Not for long, because, within minutes a tall, dark, long-haired girl came across and asked me for a dance, and, almost simultaneously a curly-haired Polynesian boy asked to dance with Trish. It was like that all evening, with the locals getting progressively more and more smashed—Trish had to turn down several prospective dance partners because they literally couldn't stand up, let alone dance.

One of them came up to where we were sitting and gyrated around in front of us, swallowing a lighted cigarette and making it reappear again. He'd curl it back on his tongue, blow smoke through his nose and then curl it out again. He staggered away and when we saw him next, about five minutes later, he was sound asleep under one of the tables.

It was about this time that Zara and Sean trundled off to bed. They would have dearly loved to have stayed on to watch the rest of the proceedings, through to the bitter end, but they were both extremely tired. After that the dance/party/riot—whatever it was, continued for another three hours—and was something of a blur for me. The most memorable scene, I suppose, was that presented by an enormous woman with a huge bosom, dressed in skin-tight tights, from which she bulged precariously, dancing with a tiny man . . . although on second thoughts I guess he was really only small by *comparison.* She was in her 40s, I would say, and yet she could shake and hula dance as well as any of the younger, more lithe girls we had seen earlier. But then she went into an extremely erotic routine, moving suggestively towards her small partner, who backed away slightly. Several people laughed and shouted encouraging remarks to them both, and they continued for several minutes to perform, nothing explicit, just suggestion. The crowd cheered and clapped their hands.

It was all good fun. Everybody was laughing and enjoying themselves with no nasty incidents. If there had been, there was always the watchful eye and considerable bulk of Harold Brown, the manager (apart from Trish, probably the only sober person there), to deter them. We lasted until 2.00 a.m. and then staggered off to bed to the sound of the band still blasting away.

I should never stay up past midnight, because whenever I do, the next day I always feel as though I've turned into Cinderella's ugly sister. Uggh! My system, delicately balanced at the best of times, punishes me all day. It's like it must be to have a hangover, only I suffer without even having had the pleasure of the drink! I spent the morning trying to write my notes and letters and falling asleep on the balcony of our bungalow.

Zara, much to her joy, found Preggers, *still* pregnant and hungry. And Sean, who has a cast-iron constitution, undeterred by the previous evening's debauchery, found that Harold Brown had a set of ricketty bicycles which he hired out at a dollar a day. A morning rest is all I ever manage to impose on my family, so by midday they were yammering to cycle into the wharf to watch the bananas being crated.

The big packing shed alongside the wharf was a scene of frenetic activity. All these people had been at Island Night too, and had been boozing on, so how come they looked so much healthier than I felt?!

Flatbed trucks, their trays loaded with green bananas, were backed up to the open side of the shed. From there the bananas were carried by children younger than Zara and Sean to be dumped into big vats of water. There they were given a cursory wash and topped and tailed so as to be neat and easily packed. The packing was an art. The empty, wooden-slatted crates, each stamped with the individual grower's name, were piled high and, one by one, filled with hands of bananas laid inside in a set pattern, so as to get the maximum number in each crate. Lids were then hammered on by a man whose hammer hand flew so fast it was a blur. Then the crates each went into a large tub of water and out again for a final rinse-off before being manhandled into ceiling-high stacks at the end of the warehouse nearest the wharf.

There must have been at least 80 people of all ages working in that shed and they worked on till the job was completed. Everyone helped everyone else. None of this I'll-pack-mine-and-you-pack-yours attitude. And no demarcation disputes or over-time bans.

There was Tiopu and Mama Henry, both of whom waved and grinned broadly, Tutai Vaireka, the Tangaroa carver, who smiled, and there was Dora Harrington's 'sort of husband', Maeva Kerikava. And wasn't that the fellow who 'swallowed' the cigarettes last night? And the fellow with him, didn't I dance with him? Yes, I'm sure I did, and there was the lady with the large embracing bosom...and...they all laughed and waved to us. On our last day on Aitutaki, it was a nice feeling. It was like being part of a large family.

# 11  THE VOYAGE OF THE *MATAORA*
'The engine chugged slowly to a halt...'

*Mataora* means happiness, but there were times during the 4000-kilometre voyage when the name of our vessel seemed something of a joke...one in which it was extremely difficult for me to see the humour.

From the very outset of this voyage to the northern Cook Islands I could see that it was going to be something which could only be notched up to experience and I set about making it as tolerable as possible.

I was thankful for my puritan spirit, which is an aspect of my character I could on many other occasions well do without. I recalled my Latin mistress telling a classroom full of awfully earnest young girls how she had maintained her sanity as a prisoner of war by translating (in her mind only...there being no paper) all the hymns she could remember into Latin and Greek. The voyage of the *Mataora*, which of course pales to insignificance by comparison with that woman's wartime ordeal, demanded that some similar method of blinkering the mind to the surrounding physical horrors should be found. It was all a case of pretending that what was happening wasn't really happening.

During the few days back in Rarotonga from Aitutaki we spent a lot of time stocking up for the trip. There was not a madly exciting variety of suitable food. Sardines, canned corned beef, processed cheese, dried fruit and packets and packets of cabin bread. We'd never heard of cabin bread before but everybody assured us that this was an essential for the trip and how right they were. It's actually not bread but an eight-centimetre-square, hard, dry, thick cracker: a sort of over-sized Sao biscuit, but I think far preferable. I became quite addicted to it and am sorry that I haven't seen it for sale any place other than the Pacific islands.

We looked through our small stock of essential medicines and I spent a considerable time checking the ingredients of various brands of anti-seasick tablets: anti-histamine, which is present in almost all of them, knocks Zara and me about with palpitations and a nasty sense of disorientation. Eventually we located some without this and bought, would you believe, eight packets.

For our last stay in Raro we didn't put up back at Geoff Porter's Puaikura Reef

Lodges, not because we didn't like it (it was spot on) but because our budget was still recovering from our stay in French Polynesia and we thought we could find cheaper. On our horse-drawn carriage journey with Exham Wichman, a couple of weeks earlier, he had pointed out a quartet of small rooms on the Ara Metua, the inland road encircling the island, with the incongruous name of Rose Cottages. In reply to our questions, he had told us that they were for rent to locals who came back from New Zealand to visit their families. We located the owner, Arfo Farui and he was delighted to rent two of them to us for $5 a night each. They both had a double bed, kitchenette and bathroom. The water wasn't on but he quickly brought around two 44-gallon drums full and put them out on the back lawn. His small daughter brought papaya, tomatoes and a big cabbage.

We contacted Peter Cusack, the jeweller, and met his wife, Mum and baby daughter, Teramoana (star of the ocean). In the workroom behind his shop, which was almost opposite the Rarotongan Hotel, Peter showed us some of his exquisite little pipi pearl shells which he had delicately rimmed with gold, set a single pearl in the heart and hung on a chain. He also had rings, earrings and other necklaces, almost all made with pearls and gold. Mum, an attractive, petite, honey-coloured girl, made coral necklaces and brightly-patterned cotton beach clothes for sale. The way all this was displayed and their laid-back, non-hard-sell approach made the little shop so attractive we felt they really deserved to succeed.

We invited them around to Rose Cottages for dinner. Such a pleasant change—we felt like a newly-married couple playing at keeping house! When they arrived, Peter had brought some cans of Foster's lager and Mum a bowl of taro tops which had been minced and sieved, boiled with coconut and spiced with chillies. Delicious. We spent the evening talking about politics and the Cook Islands, about which they knew a great deal, and also about Australia, which, it was obvious, Peter did not miss in the least. We also talked about his jewllery which he sells in Europe, California and Australia and, when we told them we were leaving on the *Mataora* he said, 'If you stop in at Manihiki you must say "Hi" to the Cumming family. They run a pearl farm there. I get some of my pearls from them.'

'I'll bring some things down to the boat for you to take to them,' Mum said.

'Have you made the trip?' I asked Peter.

He nodded and made nasty, heaving motions with his hands. 'Rough,' he said. 'But I tell you what makes all the difference. Hammocks.'

The one thing we didn't have!

'We'll make some,' said Iain.

I should have known better, after all these years, than to doubt him, because he did! He bought some heavy-duty cotton material and some strong cord and took it all to a little shop where we had seen handmade dresses for sale and there he showed the woman owner what he wanted done.

So by 4.30 p.m. the next afternoon there we were on board the *Mataora* with our packs, the food supplies, some fresh fruit and coconuts given to us by Exham and Mama Wichman, plus hammocks and a few additional packets of anti-seasick tablets which I had bought at the very last minute.

Mum and Peter arrived with a couple of boxes of fresh fruit for us to deliver to their friends the Cummings. And Temu Okatai, of the Tourist Authority, also came along to farewell us with frangipani leis.

Despite the seeming chaos on the quay—the last minute parcels being thrown aboard and several members of the crew being decidedly inebriated (one of them, wearing tatty cover-alls and a crown of pink flowers, danced on the pier until the very last minute, then jumped aboard)—the *Mataora* did eventually pull out into the pass to sail through the break in the lagoon. We waved to the diminishing figures and to the receding skyline of Rarotonga, flung our leis into the wake to ensure our return, and Zara promptly threw up.

Within half an hour, before the sun had even set, the kids and I were huddled in our sleeping bags on the hard, unyielding metal of the rear upper deck trying to settle down to a hideous first night at sea.

The *Mataora* pitched and tossed and wallowed while, immediately above our heads, a bicycle, destined for some lucky person on one of the outer islands, swung precariously about, threatening to lose its hold and come crashing down on us.

The stars and the moon lurched sickeningly into view between the rails and the overhead awning and then lurched out again. I fed the kids and myself tablets and tried to sleep but every time the boat made a particularly heavy lunge, Zara came wide awake and made a grab at her pack which was stashed against the funnel between her and the four of us, sardined as we were across the upper rear deck space. I couldn't have cared less if her pack, my pack, all our packs had gone over. In these seas, it was impossible to sling the hammocks and even if we had, we would have been pitched out of them at each dreadful plummet down a mountainous wave.

But those of us who had lain down on the upper deck were considerably better off than the 40 or so other deck passengers who were huddled under the heavy canvas awning tied across the front cargo hatches. Crouched there in the airless dark, with the waves whooshing up over the side, right next to them, must have been an even more horrendous nightmare. The fact that we were only paying $66 each (half for the kids) for the entire voyage, also seemed of little consequence.

By the time the sun rose on our miserable situation, we were within sight of Aitutaki, our first port of call. Why, oh why, hadn't we just stayed there and picked up the *Mataora* as she went by. None of us mentioned this thought to each other, but we each knew that the only thing we wanted to do was get off this damnable boat. Still in the clothes we had boarded in, and slept in, we staggered to the side of the vessel as she anchored outside the reef and gazed longingly at dry, stable land.

'What a night!' Iain managed to say to one of the crew.

The man looked at him in surprise, mixed with superiority as he replied, 'That was nothing.' And to our chorus of groans, added, 'You'll be all right once you get your sea legs.'

Returning to Aitutaki after such a brief period was a pleasant experience. It's a good feeling to know your way around a place when you first arrive and, as we'd liked Aitutaki so much anyway, it was doubly enjoyable, almost as if we hadn't left at all.

We went in on one of the several barges and launches that were hovering around the *Mataora* awaiting their turn to carry ashore the offloaded supplies, a task that began immediately we dropped anchor.

It was already extremely hot although we were only mid-way through the morning. After walking down all 200 metres of Sir Albert Henry Drive, we turned down the main road, to make a call on Tiopu Henry and his wife. Tiopu was away getting clams from the reef, but Mama was sitting in the yard working on one of her *tivaivais.* She was surprised to see us back so soon and offered us a seat beside her. We sat and talked and after a while she offered to show us some of her other *tivaivais.* She led us into the little wooden shack in which the family slept and, opening three or four wooden linen chests, produced an array of appliqué work that could have been hung in an art gallery, it was so beautiful.

Most of the pieces were large, bed-spread-sized sheets which had probably been sitting in the chests for years, never seeing the light of day, waiting for the time when they would eventually go to the grave with one or other members of the family. She was obviously very proud of them, with good reason. She spread them out on the floor of the room and on the beds in the corners, explaining, as she did so, that the technique was traditionally passed on from one generation to the next.

'My father taught me how to do it,' she said. 'What you see me doing now, outside, the sewing, is the easy part, even though it takes months to do. The hard part is the cutting of the material. That is what my father taught me.'

'Do you ever make any for sale, Mama,' I asked.

She wagged her head slowly—it seemed to be neither a positive nor a negative response. 'It takes a very long time to make one, you know, at least six months.'

'Yes,' I said, 'I'm sure it does...so you don't...'

'But occasionally I will make one...for a friend, if they are not in a hurry.'

'Oh, we are not in...' I began.

'They are not cheap you know. The material is quite expensive. There is a lot of it that is required.'

'Yes, I can see that. How much material would you need?'

We discussed for a while the various materials, colours and costs and eventually Mama agreed to make us a *tivaivai* for $90. She accepted the money on the understanding that she would not be able to start work on it for some time, and, even when she began, it would only be a part-time job that would take many months. At the time of this writing, we've just received our *tivaivai.* It's a beauty! Green and orange in a complicated pineapple design and pretty unusual around these parts. But best of all is the thought that Mama made it for us. It's a small link that we've retained with Aitutaki.

Back at the wharf we saw the *Mataora* sitting offshore, beyond the reef, still busily offloading goods from her cargo hold, including a number of large drums of aviation gasoline and some 15 000 litres of diesel fuel, which was being pumped out into a barge. We sat watching the procedure from the pier until it was time to rejoin her. No-one was particularly keen.

'Do we *have* to go, Dad?' Zara asked. 'Couldn't we fly to Samoa from here...or back to Rarotonga...instead of going by boat?'

The prospect of more rolling swells and rough weather was not particularly appealing to any of us and, understandably, I felt a little as if I was forcing the rest into doing something they didn't really want to do.

'You'll be all right,' I said. 'I'm sure it won't be as bad today as it was yesterday. Anyway, you heard what that crewman said earlier...after a while, you start to get your "sea legs" and get used to it.' I don't think I sounded too convincing. Both Zara and Sean gave me rather cynical looks, while Trish just nodded knowingly as if to say, 'Oh yes. . . I've heard that one before.'

As it happened, I was not too far wrong. Once we'd cleared the lee of Aitutaki we did hit quite a stiff easterly wind again but the swells seemed smaller and none of us felt as ill as the night before. Still, this was only the beginning. We were off now on a journey over almost 1500 kilometres of open ocean to our next island, Manihiki, which would be a good two and a half days' travelling under ideal circumstances, but, in the Pacific, so they say, ideal circumstances never last for long.

We made up some food; cabin bread, Vegemite, cheese and tomatoes and set up our 'sleeping quarters' so that they'd be a little more comfortable than before. There was a large tarpaulin folded up on the after deck. We hauled it into a better position and rearranged it so that we could sleep on it. It was several layers thick and a considerable improvement on the hard, steel deck of the previous night.

Once again, as soon as darkness fell, we were ready to sleep. Of course, there were the stars to watch and the wonderful sight and sound of the darkened sea gurgling and rushing by, illuminated and sparkling with the reflected light of the ship. But we were too tired to watch for long and soon fell onto the tarpaulin, where we stretched out side-by-side in our sleeping bags sound asleep by about 7.30 p.m.

In the middle of the night I was awoken by a drop of water on my face. . . then another. There was a second large tarpaulin stretched above the poop deck which we'd thought would protect us from any rain but it was intended mainly as a sunshade and there were several holes in it. In any case, the wind was sufficiently strong to send the rain slanting in under the awning and across the deck. Fortunately, we were on the port side while the wind was on the starboard and we were protected, to some extent, by the ship's funnel. But we were moving in a tropical downpour and, as the rain became more heavy, water started sloshing back and forth across the steel deck and I was sure we'd be drenched. But it just ran underneath the folded-up tarpaulin we were lying on and, even though it continued to fall above us and run underneath us, we managed to remain quite dry in our sleeping bags and after a while we drifted back into a reasonable sleep.

We were awake at about 7.00 a.m. to shower in one of two tiny cubicles that opened onto the deck below. The ship itself was in a filthy condition. . . grease and dirt everywhere. It was impossible to move around or even to sit down without getting dirty. We decided to keep wearing the same outer clothes, so as not to completely mess up more than one set of clothing. By washing ourselves and changing only our underclothes, we found that we were able to at least *feel* reasonably clean.

After a simple breakfast of cabin bread, cheese and fruit, we sat around on the open poop deck reading and watching the sea and the sky. The weather was overcast and dull and the view was hardly interesting but there was nothing much else to do anyway.

There were only two other passengers on board who were not Cook Islanders; a tall, blond, moustachioed New Zealander who, we understood, was an electrician employed by the Cook Islands government to 'wire up' the island of Rakahanga. The one other European on board, apart from the captain and the cook, was an Austrian who had also been desperately seasick on the leg from Rarotonga to Aitutaki and whom we met properly, for the first time, only when he staggered up onto the deck during the morning of our first day out from Aitutaki. He was travelling alone, although we'd seen a woman, who was obviously his wife, and a young girl, presumably his daughter, wave him goodbye when the *Mataora* had pulled out from the harbour at Rarotonga.

'My name is Herman,' he said, reeling to one side with the ship's movements. 'Herman Reidl. I am going to Samoa. . .are you?'

'Yes,' I said, 'to Western Samoa and to American Samoa also. . .and then on to Tonga and Fiji. . .and you?'

'Oh, I am going back to Raro.'

'On this ship?' Zara put in in shocked tones.

'Oh, no,' he laughed. 'Enough will be enough. I will fly from Apia.'

He was a slim, fit-looking man of about 40. He was not very tall, had smooth, suntanned skin, wore rimless spectacles and had several days of stubbly growth on his chin. We guessed it was meant to be the beginning of a beard.

'Do you live in Raro?' Trish asked.

'No. My wife is a Cook Islander. Did you see her on the wharf when we left? This is our first trip back to the Cooks for 14 years. We have been living in Europe all that time. Our home is in Austria, near Innsbruck.' He stopped trying to balance himself against the ship's motion and sat down beside us on a bench seat. 'I have taken three months off from my job. We are visiting friends and relatives.'

'And this trip. . .on the boat?' I said, stating the obvious. 'Your wife did not come?'

He laughed again, although you could see that it was not a happy laugh. He was clearly still not over his seasickness. He waved his hand around. 'And you see why she did not come,' he said. 'She told me, "Herman, if you must go on this boat, then do so, but there is no way that you will get your wife and daughter to come also." I am beginning to understand her.'

We all smiled—in sympathy for ourselves as much as for him. And there was no avoiding the thought that there might be more to come.

'And yet,' Herman continued. 'I have always wanted to do this trip. . .to get to the northern islands. This is the only way you can do it.'

We agreed and told him that we'd been similarly motivated, although not for as long as he had. It didn't really make the discomfort any easier, however. And now we could see the sky darkening ahead. There appeared to be several rain squalls spread around the horizon. We were heading into some rainy weather. We could see it coming across the sea towards us and then suddenly we were in it. . .buckets of it. Blinding rain.

We were forced to leave the poop deck very quickly. The tarpaulin sunshade worked for a while but the rain was being driven horizontally underneath it again. Our packs were already stacked below decks, but our food boxes were still up on deck, so we covered them with another big sheet of canvas and then sought refuge outside the galley on the deck below.

**Right:** Sean stands dwarfed by the huge moais at Ahu Akivi, the first to be restored to standing position by the American archaeologist William Mulloy. EASTER ISLAND

**Centre:** ... yes, they certainly died violently .... Trish examines some gruesome relics of a past massacre at Hanga Poukura. EASTER ISLAND

**Top:** The moais at Ahu Anakena with their red stone 'top knots', each weighing eight or nine tonnes. '... a balancing feat of extraordinary precision.' EASTER ISLAND

Above: Papeete vahines. 'There was ...
riotous colour; in the easy-going clothes of
the men and women, in the brilliant red
hibiscus ... or pink frangipani flowers they
all wore in their hair ...' TAHITI

Below: Sunset over Moorea. '... we sat
silently in the soft, warm evening air — entranced. In situations like that, who needs
money?' TAHITI

**Left:** Iain with the stone fish he leant on. 'You are lucky,' Nanua said. 'If you had come from the other direction . . . you would die.' RANGIROA ATOLL

**Below:** Nanua the fisherman and his family. '. . . in the water, all of his huge bulk and fat seemed to miraculously disappear. He became at once a swift, svelte creature, completely in tune with his environment.' RANGIROA ATOLL, Tuamotu Group, French Polynesia

**Bottom:** The market at Papeete. 'Up and down the aisles, between the scores of stalls we went . . . laughing like kids with the excitement of it all.' TAHITI

**Above:** Tahitian children playing TAHITI

**Below:** The entrance to Cook's Bay. 'Such beauty demands silent appreciation ... jungled mountains ... tower above in awesome gothic splendour.' MOOREA, Windward Group. French Polynesia

**Left:** Island girls dancing the tamure. An 'amazing dance to watch ... all that pulsating bare brown flesh.' BORA BORA, Leeward Group, French Polynesia

**Below:** Maeva, a small, sleepy village on the island of Huahine. HUAHINE, Leeward Group, French Polynesia

**Bottom:** One of the **maraes** near Maeva village. These strange ancient sites were the scenes of early Polynesian religious rituals. HUAHINE

**Above:** Uta Roa harbour. '. . . the rain stopped and the sky cleared to a pale pink for a sunset which looked rinsed pure. RAIATEA. Leeward Group. French Polynesia

**Below:** Islanders bringing fruit and produce to the market in Uta Roa. RAIATEA

**Above:** Villagers collecting sea slugs from the reef. 'Some children came and showed us their catch . . . Would we like to taste some?' RAROTONGA. Cook Islands

**Below:** 'The rusting hulk of the once-magnificent, 30-metre clipper ship **Yankee** . . . high on the reef at the edge of Avarua township.' RAROTONGA

**Right:** Papa Raui, with Ram Naidu and Michel Lambert. 'Do you think you could get me some Vietnamese refugees as well as the ducks?' MITIARO, Cook Islands

**Below:** Village women, in their Sunday best, sit around chatting on the steps of Mitiaro's little church after the morning service. MITIARO

**Bottom:** Washing the banana crop on Aitutaki. '... wasn't that the fellow who "swallowed" the cigarettes last night? And the fellow with him, didn't I dance with him?' AITUTAKI, Cook Islands

**Left:** Mama Tiopu Henry and her **tivaivais**. 'She led us into the little wooden shack . . . and . . . produced an array of applique work that could have been hung in an art gallery . . .' AITUTAKI, Cook Islands

**Above:** A 4,000-kilometre deck-passage voyage on board the **Mataora**. 'On the hard unyielding metal of the rear upper deck . . . a hideous first night at sea.' COOK ISLANDS

**Top:** The M.V. **Mataora**. 'The engine chugged slowly to a halt . . . and that was that.' COOK ISLANDS

**Right:** Max Cumming shows some black-lipped clam shells with their cultured half-pearls. 'The Japanese have kept the technique to themselves ... but from watching them ... I think I've got it taped.' MANIHIKI, Cook Islands

**Above:** Villagers with mangos for the market in Apia. '... only 20 cents for six ... we were in danger of overdosing!' WESTERN SAMOA

**Top:** Mahia Tupou and Mary Amarama 'singing — harmonising wonderfully ... we sat on the little open verandah of the house for half an hour, listening, entranced ...' RAKAHANGA, Cook Islands

**Above:** A tropical rainstorm hits Pago Pago. 'It was as if a giant stalked, whistling down the main street ...' AMERICAN SAMOA

**Below:** : Pago Pago Bay seen from the cable car. '... the cab jolted to a halt, swinging rather wildly in the air some 300 metres above the water. AMERICAN SAMOA

**Right:** Tongan women dancing for the king. '. . . they started slapping banknotes onto her oily skin . . .' TONGA

**Below:** Cricket Samoan style. 'The MCC . . . would most definitely choke with indignation . . .' WESTERN SAMOA

**Bottom:** Women making tapa cloth from beaten bark. '. . . the equivalent, in our society . . . of ladies' tennis mornings, or Tupperware parties.' TONGA

**Left:** In Oscar's cave at Oholei Beach. '. . . a show of spectacular contortions and acrobatics with blazing torches.' TONGA

**Above:** The royal palace in Nuku'alofa, a 'wooden fantasy of cupolas and gingerbread, straight out of a fairytale.' TONGA

**Top:** Indian newlyweds bedecked with gold sovereigns. '. . . But ours is a **love** marriage.' FIJI

**Above:** The road to Buca Bay. A whole morning's bus journey for a dollar. 'Cheap, yes, but very hard on the posterior.' VANUA LEVU ISLAND, Fiji

**Below:** Trish and Zara contemplate a sunken brigantine at Savu Savu. '. . . like a scene from a Joseph Conrad novel.' VANUA LEVU ISLAND

**Above:** Sunset over Taveuni Island.
TAVEUNI ISLAND. Fiji

**Below:** Children at play near the village of
Bouma on Taveuni. TAVEUNI ISLAND

**Left:** Calcott Matas Kelekele, a prominent member of the Vanua'aku party which led the New Hebrides to independence in 1980. '. . . it will be an upsetting time . . .' VANUATU (NEW HEBRIDES)

**Below:** The once-bustling waterfront of Levuka, the former Fijian capital, on Ovalau Island, is now all but asleep. '. . . a little bit of history preserved . . . almost unchanged . . .' OVALAU ISLAND, Fiji

**Bottom:** Children swimming in Anse Vata bay, near Noumea, where a man on the beach was making $700 a day. NEW CALEDONIA

Shortly, a young Cook Island galley hand, George, everybody called him, ushered us inside the small dining saloon to meet 'Arch' the cook. Arch was a little, rolly-polly man with a van Dyke beard who wore nothing but a pair of greasy shorts over which a large beer-gut hung. He was a New Zealander, a former Army sergeant, who'd been working on the *Mataora* for more than a year.

'Why don't you hop down below?' he said, pointing to the stairwell at one side of the saloon. 'There're a few bunks down there. You can have a zizzz.'

We thanked him and descended into the ship's innards. Immediately the throbbing sound of the engine became louder and the heavy smell of diesel fumes more intense. We knew that the *Mataora's* five small passenger cabins were down here, Herman was sharing one with another man, but we had not been below decks to have a good look at them. We were booked to occupy one of the cabins from Manihiki onwards, but in theory we were deck passengers until then. Nevertheless, as one of the four-berth cabins had three empty bunks, (an islander was lying asleep on the fourth), we looked around enquiringly at George, who had followed us down.

He nodded. 'You can sleep there for a while.'

It was still only the latter part of the morning, but, with the rain pouring down and the view through the porthole one of endless grey water, we crawled into the three available bunks—Zara and Sean shared one—and we all promptly fell into a deep, dreamless sleep.

Four hours later I awoke and went up onto the deck again without waking the others. The rain had stopped and the sea was more calm, although there was still a good wind blowing. I sat on the wooden bench at one side and read a *Newsweek* magazine about 'The 80s and what the Future holds in Store': Iran, the Persian Gulf, Salt II . . . it all seemed so incredibly remote.

Trish arrived a little later, brushing the sleep from her eyes, followed by Zara and Sean. We made some lunch then sat around reading some more. The children seemed to have a better 'feel' of the boat by this stage. They took off on their own and, within no time, were in the wheel-house, the dining saloon, playing cards, doing their puzzle books or chasing each other around the decks. The card game in the saloon gave me a slight pause. Sean was playing rummy with the cook, the New Zealand electrician and Lance, a Cook Islander who was the ship's engineer. The illustrations on the back of the cards were of various undressed ladies in assorted cheesecake poses. I was about to say something to Sean about it, but hesitated and didn't say anything. They were all so engrossed in the game, and what was on the front of the cards, that my comments would have been out of place.

That evening, after eating dinner, we slipped down into the vacant cabin again to sleep on the three empty bunks. But during the night the ship's engine started playing up. It had hiccoughed and spluttered a few times during the day, but now it began to really sound sick, slowing to a halt, and then, after a few minutes, starting up slowly again. The engineer, Lance, whose cabin was next to the one we were in, was up and down all night, in and out of the engine room tending to the ailing monster. A door next to his cabin led directly into the engine room and, with this open for his continual forays to keep the revs up, the temperature in all of the cabins rose rapidly. In the engine compartment itself it was as high as 50°C. The cabin became oppressively hot and we lay drenched in sweat, hot and smelly, trying to sleep, but without any success.

I awoke just before dawn with the certain feeling of dread that something was wrong. Battling with my befuddled senses, it was a second or so until I realised that the engine had stopped. It was the heavenly silence which had awoken me. Beside me, Iain came instantly awake also for the same reason.

'What is it?'

'We're stopped. The engines have stopped.' Then the children sat up. Now all awake, we lay and discussed the possibilities. Iain went up to enquire what was happening and returned with the news that no-one really knew much more than what was quite apparent—trouble with the engine. Half an hour later the engine half-heartedly restarted and we all went up on deck for the cooler air. After a while, I ventured down to the galley where I found the engineer taking a spell from muttering abuse at the ship's working parts.

'Feeling better?' he asked.

I must have been. I'd managed to shower in the enclosed foul-smelling lavatory-shower cubicle in which the toilet bowl had been half choked. I'd changed into a fresh tee-shirt and shorts and, most wondrous of all, I'd cleaned my teeth. And while not exactly bright-eyed and bushy-tailed, I could nibble on a piece of dry cabin bread and sip at a mug of tea which Arch, the cook had given me. I felt almost OK, just so long as I didn't look at the two eggs and large hunks of bacon swilling about in a layer of grease and tomato sauce which had just been served to the engineer for breakfast. I nodded.

'You'd feel better still if you ate something,' he said, demolishing the quite awful looking meal with gusto. 'Settles your stomach and at least you have something to throw up if you need to.'

Lance Simiona was a 23-year-old, large, muscular and endearingly foul-mouthed Cook Islander. His language has to be expurgated for print.

'Rolls like an old cow, doesn't she?' He sopped up the remains of his breakfast with large hunks of bread, thickly smeared with butter and jam. I agreed heartily. 'Should have been on board during Hurricane Charlie, shouldn't she mate?!'

Ian Nesbitt, the New Zealand electrician, joined us at the small table bringing with him a replica of Lance's greasy breakfast. Ian, who was in his late 20s, was employed by the Cook Islands government on a three-year contract. He'd made several trips to the islands in the southern group which are accessible by plane and this was only his second visit north. The first time was apparently the occasion when they were hit by Hurricane Charlie. They regaled me with horror stories like men recounting tales of war.

'It came up too quick for us to have a chance to run anywhere,' Lance revelled in the memory. 'We just had to sit it out. Eight and a half days we were in it...just going wherever it took us. Damned dangerous in these parts with so many reefs.'

'Bloody seas were so mountainous,' Ian helped him along, 'that she'd climb to the crest of a wave,' he demonstrated graphically with his hands, 'and then couldn't make it, so she'd slip back down. Thud!'

Lance slurped his tea.

'The passengers lost all their luggage,' Ian continued. 'Washed overboard. Everybody, deck and cabin passengers, all crowded into the cabins. Should have smelt it. Christ! All that puke and sweat. Never known what they meant by the smell of fear till then. Christ!' He finished off his food.

'Remember that trip, Arch?' Ian called to the cook, who came to stand in the doorway between the galley and the dining area. He stood there sucking his teeth.

'Don't remember a bloody thing mate. Wiped myself out. Only thing to do. Don't fancy drowning sober.' He scratched his back, inflamed with prickly heat, on the door jamb.

'I don't know how you could bring yourself to make a second trip,' I said to Ian.

'It's a job, isn't it. They say go, and I have to go. Anyhow, the doc says that the most important thing to do is to keep up your fluid intake. I damn near snuffed it last time. In those eight days I lost 2½ stone [16 kilos]. Had to be hospitalised when we reached Raro. I was so dehydrated, I was fed with drips and all that stuff.'

Lance laughed derisively at this display of 'weakness' and I reflected on how different men are from women.

'What's so important that they need to send an electrician up here anyway?' I asked.

'They just had the PM through here. He flew to Apia and came back down through the northern group by boat. Only way to get to them. First time *ever* that these people have had a visit from their own prime minister. He promised them all sorts of stuff in the way PMs do and one thing was to wire up Rakahanga. While they stop off to load copra I have to wire seven houses, the church and the wharf!'

'But how long will that take?' I could see this trip stretching on for weeks.

'Dunno. But I'll tell you something. . .and that is, that you'll all just have to wait till it's done. Cos this old tub's not leaving without me. I'm not getting stuck up in these parts for three months or more until just maybe another boat comes through.'

'She's no bloody tub, mate,' Lance interjected. It seemed that it was permissible for him to bad-mouth the *Mataora,* but not anyone else. 'A tub would never have seen that hurricane through.' He turned to me. 'He thinks he's been in rough weather with her. But by Christ he should have been on board when we brought her out from Europe.'

'Were you on that voyage with Don Silk?' I asked.

'Yep. Just the two of us. And rough?!' He snorted. 'That North Sea is something else. Apart from the snow and ice on the decks. Christ!'

'How much time do you spend at sea?'

Lance gave me a curious look. '*All* the time.'

'But aren't you entitled to so many days at home after doing so many days at sea?'

Again the curious look. 'This is my home. When we get into Raro I might sleep at Mum's place a couple of nights. But that's enough. Gives me the fidgets. Quite often I don't bother to go ashore while we're in harbour. She's not a bad old bitch really.' He slapped the table with the same proprietorial affection some men display toward women.

As if irked by this lack of respect, the *Mataora*'s engines coughed and spluttered and threatened to stall again. Lance swore vociferously and got to his feet. With greasy rags spilling from the pockets of his greasy shorts, he clattered down the companionway into the noisy bowels of his true love.

Ian went to his cabin to fiddle with his large radio. I had the feeling that, despite his carefully-manicured, blasé manner, he was attempting to pick up radio stations in

Western Samoa which might have more accurate and longer-term weather predictions!

'Not going to eat any breakfast then?' Arch asked, still scratching in the doorway.

'Perhaps just a piece of toast if I may,' taking up his offer more from politeness— after all, I was a deck passenger and not entitled to his breakfast—than from any desire to eat.

'They're right you know,' he said. 'You'd feel better with something in your stomach. Food, or if you're like me, grog.' It was a defiant and yet pitiful statement.

'How long have you been on the *Mataora?*' I asked.

'A year or so. Never cooked a meal in my life before that. I was in the New Zealand Army for 20 years. Signed on as a lad. Came up to Raro last year on an aid project with the army. Building bridges and upgrading the roads. Met this local girl and fell in love.' He scratched harder. 'Left the service to stay on with her. And then she upped and died on me. Been on a bender ever since.'

Lance eventually got the engine working again but it was clearly not going to last very long before another breakdown occurred. For most of the day we sat up on deck reading, sleeping and keeping our ears attuned to the slightest change in the throb of the engine. On several occasions it would slow right down, cough and splutter a bit, then pick up its rhythm again and continue, but for how long nobody knew.

The captain, 'Bo' Berg, a slightly-built, sandy-haired Swede of about 40 years, seemed unconcerned by the whole procedure. We observed him consulting Lance a few times and at one stage he lifted his eyebrows and shrugged his shoulders as if to say, 'Ah well, if that's the way it's got to be. . .'

Bo was what I suppose you'd call a 'free-lance' skipper. He'd apparently worked previously for several years with Silk and Boyd but had left them to sail around the Pacific in his own boat, a large, home-built cruising catamaran which, we learnt later, was moored in the yacht harbour at Tongatapu in the Tonga group.

Silk and Boyd had cabled him in Tonga and asked him to come back for a while to work on the *Mataora*. He'd done so and, after only a short while, had had an accident and slipped a disc, which forced him to spend several weeks in hospital. This was his first trip since then and it was obvious from the way he moved about the bridge and the upper deck that he felt very cautious about his back.

During the afternoon the engine began to slow and cough more frequently until the vessel was only travelling at about one-quarter speed. The problem, according to Lance, who surfaced from time to time from the furnace-like engine room, for a breath of fresh air, was being caused by water in the fuel.

'It's the centrifugal separator,' he said on one occasion, as if we should know what that was. 'It's clogged up. . .not working. Means the fuel is full of shit.'

At about four in the afternoon the engine slowed even more ominously. . . chugged along very slowly for about half a minute, then finally stopped. Lance made three attempts to restart it. Nothing. His language, which could be heard on the top deck, smoking up through the funnel-shaft, was X-rated and grew more and more purple as he worked away on the recalcitrant engine.

There was nothing anyone could do to help him. We could only sit around and appreciate the comparative silence as we drifted in a relatively calm sea. I decided to try to fashion a scoop for the porthole of the cabin we'd been sleeping in. If we could get a bit more air coming into the room during the night maybe we'd be a little more comfortable. By cutting up a stiff cardboard box and shaping it to the porthole, so that about 30 or 40 centimetres protruded beyond the side of the ship, we might have an effective air-conditioner. But there was no way of telling if it would work, not until we got underway again. Wallowing listlessly as we were, there was not enough breeze to try it out.

It was quite a strange feeling really, drifting on an open ocean...nothing but dark blue sea for 360 degrees around the horizon, and the knowledge that the water beneath us was tremendously deep, over five thousand metres to the bottom!

As dusk came on and the sun set, there was still no indication when we might be on our way again. The skipper came out onto the outer bridge with his sextant to 'shoot' various stars and later we heard him on the radio in the chart-room talking, first to Rarotonga, then to Manihiki.

'We're 75 miles [120 kilometres] to the south of you,' he said. 'We have a little engine trouble, but we should be off the entrance by about seven or eight in the morning.'

Trish and I were standing outside the bridge with a few of the other passengers and crew who were listening to the conversation. I turned to Trish, doing a little mental arithmetic. 'I think we do about 10 knots when we're going properly...that means he doesn't really expect us to get underway again until about midnight. We might as well sleep on deck again.'

After fixing ourselves a meal of cabin bread, tinned meat and cheese, we spread the big, rolled tarpaulin out again and stretched our sleeping bags out on it. Because of the lack of motion and wind, we slept reasonably well, until around 1.30 a.m. when the engines suddenly throbbed to life. She had a couple of false starts and then the ship began to gather way. There were a few desultory cheers heard from various parts of the vessel and after a while we slowly drifted back into a less easy sleep. It was comforting to know that the engine was running again, but even my untrained ear could tell that it was not running on all six cylinders.

At about 3.30 in the morning we suddenly hit a heavy rain storm. We tried, as before, to weather it out up on deck but it became too much for us and again we had to seek refuge below. This time, however, we went straight to the cabin we'd been using previously. The first thing we noticed was that it was considerably cooler than it had ever been before. I wanted to feel that it was as a result of my scoop but it was almost certainly only because the engine had been stopped for so long. This was born out when, within a few hours, the temperature in the cabin had risen to almost boiling.

At 6.00 in the morning, in the pre-dawn dark, I gave up and left the cabin to stagger back up onto the poop deck where I slung a hammock and tried to grab a few more moments sleep. At least it was cool there and the rain had long since stopped.

Seven or eight o'clock, our projected arrival times in Manihiki, came and went without any sign of the atoll. We were making only about half speed. The engine was still sick.

We showered and ate some breakfast, keeping our fingers crossed that she would keep chugging along. Eventually, not long after nine, we sighted Manihiki, a low string of green islets stretching across the horizon. The day was beautiful: no clouds and a flat-calm sea. Gradually we drew closer. But then, when we were still about 10 or 12 kilometres away, the engine suddenly slowed again. Everybody looked up and listened expectantly...waiting. The engine chugged slowly to a halt...and that was that.

Down in the engine room Lance began to let loose with his string of curses. He tried to start it up again, but nothing happened. He emerged for a conference with the captain out on deck then returned to his furnace-hot engine room, while the skipper went to the bridge to call Manihiki on the radio, telling them in effect, 'We'll see you when we see you.'

We all settled down to wait again.

There was a strong current which was pushing us on an angled course towards the atoll, so that as the morning wore on, the small, uninhabited, palm-covered islets that formed the southern rim of Manihiki's lagoon grew steadily nearer and larger, but there was no sign of anybody on them. We had thought there might be some copra workers who would see us drifting but no. Perhaps we would just drift on...into the central Pacific.

The day became hotter and hotter. We were only 10 degrees below the equator now and, with no breeze and the sun reflecting off the mirror-like sea, the heat was beginning to get to us. A few of the crew were sitting around on the poop deck playing guitar and singing Polynesian songs. One of them, we discovered later, was not a crew member, but a government doctor who was travelling to Rakahanga (the next island), to see a dangerously ill patient there.

Suddenly George, the steward, appeared in his bathing costume and without a moment's hesitation, clambered up onto the deck rail and hurled himself out into space. He gave an ear-splitting yell as he executed a rather fancy-looking dive and plunged into the water about seven or eight metres below.

From the moment we'd first met George he'd struck us as a 'mover'. He was only about 23 or 24 years old, but he was always full of beans and enthusiastic about almost everything, particularly about the prospect of returning to Manihiki, his home island, after several years in New Zealand. It was quite probable, we thought, when we saw him going over the side, that he intended to *swim* to Manihiki, but he was just cooling off.

Within seconds the other members of the crew had followed him, with whoops and shouts of laughter, into the water, one of them fully-clothed in his greasy overalls. A big rope was thrown overboard for the swimmers to grab hold of and climb back on board.

'Are you going in, Dad?' Sean asked.

'Sure,' I said, although I had some doubts. The water, even though we were so close to the island, was apparently over 3000 metres deep! Not that the depth really matters...it's what's in it that counts. Anyway, Sean and Zara and I all joined in. Herman also. It was terrific. Leaping off a ship in the open ocean is quite a sensation. The water was crystal clear and we could see the underside of the *Mataora* as though it were floating in air. But below it, the water went through varying shades of blue, down into what we knew were tremendous depths.

Both Zara and Sean leapt off the side time after time, until finally everyone tired of the fun and we clambered back on board wonderfully cooled and refreshed, just in time to see two or three power boats on the horizon heading out from Manihiki towards us.

# 12  MANIHIKI
A quarter of a million dollars in black pearls

When he took off his large floppy straw hat, the young man, whom we had watched career out from shore to the *Mataora* in a small outboard-powered aluminium dinghy, flicked back a shock of blond hair, which came as a surprise and contrast with what we'd become used to in the islands.

He shook hands with us. 'I'm Max Cumming,' he said with the self-consciousness of youth, multiplied by the embarrassment of meeting total strangers who were nonetheless from his world. He accepted the boxes of fruit from Peter and Mum and shot back to shore, weaving his expert way among the other slower dinghies. Several of these were overburdened with people from the island who couldn't wait until the long anticipated relatives or friends, passengers on the boat, came ashore. Instead they all came out to greet everybody on the *Mataora*. There were shouted, happy reunions, much hugging and laughing and casual throwing into the dinghies of personal possessions. We watched with amusement as one young woman was greeted and then motored back to shore amid half a dozen friends, while she clung for dear life to a full-sized oven she had brought back with her. At about this time Lance managed to revive the ailing engine. It turned over sluggishly just long enough for us to limp the remaining couple of kilometres to an anchorage off the break in the reef where we began to unload cargo and passengers with a will.

Herman was going on to Rakahanga where his wife had relatives who were expecting him. We decided that we'd go ashore on Manihiki and hopefully see Rakahanga later.

What a sorry quartet we looked as we stumbled out of the dinghy after a rolling, 300-metre ride in through the pass in the reef, then up the small quay, our legs buckling under the mixture of the unaccustomed weight of our packs and the unnerving steadiness of dry land. I could fully understand why survivors of shipwrecks, or even European sailors coming ashore on 'new lands', after long voyages, staggered ashore to fall down and kiss Mother Earth!

The little crowd of onlookers lounging at the end of the wharf, enjoying the spectacle of the unloading of the boat pointed us in the direction of the Cumming home, a short distance away through the small settlement of Tauhunu. They took it for granted that, as we were obviously foreigners, we had come to visit the Cummings who were the only Europeans on the island.

Back in Raro, Peter Cusack had told us a little about the Cumming family. Five years ago they had sold up everything in New Zealand to start an amazingly ambitious scheme: the only cultured pearl farm in the South Pacific not run by Japanese. Only remarkable people manage to live in such an isolated situation and when we walked the 200 metres from the wharf to their largish, tin-roofed, weatherboard home, we were greeted like long lost friends. Even though they were not expecting us and knew nothing at all about us, they took us at face value, which is saying a great deal for their generous spirits, considering how our faces, and the rest of our bodies, must have looked!

'You'll stay with us,' Peter helped me off with my pack. 'In our Kikau "Motel".' Kikau, he told us, is the local word for palm thatch. He led us around the side of their house to a wonderful little residence with a thatched roof and walls, where they put up their friends on rare visits. It was built on stilts and equipped with a fantastically comfortable double bed.

'The children can sleep next door on mats,' he said, 'and here's the bathroom.'

It had a wondrously clean cement floor with soap and toothbrushes, deodorant and shaving gear neatly laid out along shelves attached to the tin walls. In the corner, a 44-gallon drum of cool, clean, fresh rain water.

'No worries about water, we have plenty. And the lavatory is over there under the coconut palms.' (I soon discovered it to be a sweet-smelling non-moving, properly functioning facility!) 'Have a clean up while we read our mail and we'll start dinner going. How about barbequed fish?' Fantastic.

Half an hour later, clean-skinned, glossy-haired and freshly clothed, though still somewhat shaky on the pins, we made our reappearance, to the sounds of Elgar. Peter was organising the barbeque in the yard beside the house.

'New tape. Came up on the boat.' Peter put the tape recorder behind a small hibiscus bush. It was for all the world as if there was an orchestra playing just for us in the exclusive dining room of a five star hotel! 'Alwyn will be out in a minute, she's still reading mail from home. It's a great day when the mail arrives.' He stoked the glowing embers of a small fire and put the fresh fish on the grill. 'You watch those, son,' he said to Sean and turned to Iain. 'Now what will you have to drink? Will you join me in a beer? It will be quite a celebration for me. Been off the drink for a year. Had a bad attack of hepatitis.' He snapped open a can of Leopard. 'We had a team of doctors through here making reports on health care in the northern islands and one of them gave me a grand dose of hepatitis. How's that for a bad joke. Course, he didn't know he was infectious at the time and he was very apologetic afterwards. But I had to go down to hospital in New Zealand and leave Alwyn on her own here with the two boys to cope for three months. They managed magnificently.'

On cue, Alwyn appeared. 'I'm sorry to have been so long,' she smiled. 'It was rude of me, but I wanted to read the news from my mother and the rest of my family. Our older boy, Andrew...he's at uni. in Townsville now, doing marine biology. We miss him terribly.'

We quickly assured her that we understood completely about how important mail is when you're isolated, because we had felt the same while we were travelling.

Max arrived with more boxes from the *Mataora* helped by another young bloke, slightly older, whom he introduced as Steve Craig from Russell in New Zealand. 'Steve has been living and working with us for a year,' Peter explained, 'ever since Andrew went down to study.'

With the orchestra playing familiarly patriotic music in the background and the fish sizzling away, we settled down to get to know our hosts and new friends. Peter, who was Australian, told us that he had spent 20 years in the Australian Navy. (So that was how come the whole shabang looked so shipshape and Bristol fashion.) He had met Alwyn, a New Zealander, who had sung for two and a half years with the Australian National Opera in 1957 when she was singing in André's, a Sydney night-club.

'He was so handsome in his uniform,' Alwyn smiled at the memory as she told us.

From the way they talked, it was obvious that this love at first sight had blossomed into a lifelong friendship. I feel heartened when I meet the rare couple who have made it like this. Both of them had lived full lives before meeting each other and have gone on doing so ever since, both professionally and personally. They are proud of each other's achievements.

'Alwyn was the first woman to appear on television in Australia!' Peter said.

'That was in 1956. I was on the Johnny O'Keefe show which was broadcast from a church hall in Surry Hills, Sydney, for Channel 9.'

Alwyn's maiden name was Lechie, which immediately gave her a common interest with Iain Murray MacKenzie Finlay. They were obviously both late of Scotland—about four generations late! At the time of her marriage to Peter she was performing in the Olympic Follies in Melbourne. Iain swopped tales of those days with them both because it was at the 1956 Olympic Games that he first began to work as a journalist.

'My last play was *Move over Mrs Markham,*' Alwyn said. 'I toured with Honor Blackman in New Zealand and Moira Lister in Australia. After that, Peter and the boys and I moved to Malaysia.'

Malaysia is one of our most favourite countries and we found we had quite a number of friends in common. Peter and Alwyn were there during the dodgey early days of independence. Derek, now Professor Llewellyn-Jones of *Everywoman* fame and his actress wife, Liz Kirby, were there also and naturally, Liz and Alwyn, being in the same business, became good friends. Finding more and more friends in common, we laughed over how small the world is.

'So how come you ended up here?' I asked.

'Not *ended* up, please!' Alwyn came back quickly.

'It's the sort of scheme which has always appealed to me,' Peter put in. 'And in the sort of place which has also always appealed. When the opportunity to buy into it came up, we talked it over, did some sums and here we are. It's been slower to get started than we thought it would be, but it's been a great experience and an adventure and we're still sure it's a goer. Tomorrow the boys can take you out and show you the farm and the lagoon. And you kids,' he turned to Zara and Sean, who were beginning to drop in their tracks, 'can go out in the outrigger or on the windsurfer if you like. I suppose we should let you go to bed. You look just about all done in.'

'It was quite a trip,' Iain said, 'and we haven't had much real rest.'

'How well I know,' Alwyn smiled. 'To start with, Peter came up here on his own to see whether or not it would be feasible for the boys and me to live here. We didn't hear and didn't hear...for ages. Communications are pretty difficult. So in the end, I decided to come on up anyway. I got onto that boat with the two boys, they were 13 and 15 then, and all our luggage. No cabin. We just wedged ourselves under the tarpaulin, determined to sit it out. Oh boy, was it rough. It's always rough, I've learnt that much. I dread each trip down and we only go once a year at the very most. It was just before Christmas and I planned to be up here *by* Christmas, but of course that wasn't how it worked out. On Christmas Day she was moored off Aitutaki and the whole crew was too plastered to move. I had brought along a small canned chicken and also some canned vegetables and a canned Christmas pudding. So while all the crew were carrying on, the boys and I had a little party of our own up on deck. They didn't invite us in for a drink or anything. And it was so rough! She was wallowing about and shipping water. I was desperately trying not to let the boys see how frightened I was. The cook became so drunk, he was useless and then, and only then, they sent up a message saying that if I agreed to cook for the rest of the voyage, they would make cabin space for us. If it hadn't been for the boys, I would have told them to go and jump. But for their sake, I took the job on and we finally made it here on New Year's Eve. What a celebration we had. Didn't we Peter!'

'Determined lady!' He glowed with admiration.

Despite feeling physically tired, we found the conversation so stimulating that we sat outside under the stars talking until almost eleven, before going to our beds in the 'kikau motel'. Zara and Sean had long since disappeared to collapse on the attap mats laid on the floor of the little hut where we were quartered. We had the double bed—incredible luxury after the type of beds we'd been trying to sleep on over the past four or five days. The moment our heads hit the pillow, we were asleep.

We were awoken just before dawn by the sound of someone, or some*thing*, walking and rustling around on the crushed coral path just next to our hut. I couldn't make out what was causing the noise and, as it had woken me completely, I slid out of bed and stepped to the open doorway. A very large pig was rooting around amongst the shrubbery in the garden. I leaped out, picked up a stone and hurled it at the animal, chasing it out of the garden. I recalled that Peter had mentioned that he was constantly chasing the schoolmaster's pigs off his property and he had made a powerful sling-shot just for this purpose.

I went back to bed for a while and lay there watching the dawn gradually lighten the interior of the hut. The air was beautifully cool and fresh, although it had been warm enough to sleep without any covers.

Later, we showered in the tin shed bathroom by throwing buckets of fresh rainwater over ourselves...wonderful. The Cummings had constructed two huge cement water tanks in the yard and they held an enormous amount of water. They aimed at being as nearly self-sufficient as possible...and not only with water.

'Take a look at these fluorescent lights,' Peter had said to me on one occasion during the previous evening. 'They are running on solar power.' He pointed to a 12-volt battery on the floor which was connected to the lights. 'The telegraph office here has a solar-powered fuel-cell operation which converts sunlight directly to electricity. When they've got all their own batteries charged up, they usually let me charge a couple also.'

Living in such an isolated situation requires tremendous forward planning and also a considerable outlay on supplies. Peter and Alwyn took us on a guided tour of their house which was crammed with food and other stores that could not be bought on the island. All of their dried food was stored in tins, or five-gallon plastic containers, in quantities at least 15 to 20 times larger than the average household would keep in its cupboards. With just three or four ships a year calling at the island, it was the only thing to do. We began to see some of the difficulties inherent in living in such a remote place.

'Take the fridge, for example,' Peter said. 'There's no general electricity supply here. Okay, so there's refrigerators that run on kerosene, but not big ones...only those little ones for caravans and the like. They just don't make big ones any more. This one must be almost 20 years old. It's good, but it uses four gallons [18 litres] of kerosene a week. At $2 a gallon, that's $8 a week—over $400 a year just to *run* the thing! You've really got to be careful with everything. We never throw anything away—not even cardboard boxes. When the time comes to pack up everything and leave, we'll need them. There's nothing available on the island. The same with the garbage. We keep all our vegetable and humus-making scraps for the garden and we plant all the seeds from our fruit. Already we have more paw-paws growing here than anyone else on Manihiki.'

After breakfast at a table in their backyard, Peter showed us their workshop, virtually all of one side of the house had been allocated for it. 'We have to do all our own repairs on everything,' he explained. 'There's no-one else here who's going to do it for us. That means we have to carry spares for just about everything.' He pointed to four outboard motors sitting on a rack. 'I'm sure you know how easy it is for these things to pack up. We're always losing props on the coral heads. We have to be able to do complete repairs and overhauls, or else we'd be out of business.'

We'd talked about Peter's and Alwyn's 'business' the previous evening and, naturally, we'd been fascinated by their story—after all, it has all the ingredients of most people's South Sea island fantasies: a tropical paradise, independence, escape from the rat-race, pollution etc., yet still includes the chance of making a lot of money. So far we hadn't seen any of the results of their venture into pearl farming, but now Peter led us out into the yard again where we'd observed piles of wooden fruit boxes stacked under sheets of corrugated iron.

'We make our money from three sources really,' Peter said as we walked towards the boxes. 'There's the shell itself...for mother of pearl...' He slipped a clam shell from one of the boxes as he spoke. It was about 12 or 13 centimetres across and glistened like silver. 'These are the black-lipped shells we have here. They are very much sought after. You see the way the outer rim is black, but it gives rainbow colours as it changes to the silver of the centre.' He pushed the shell back into its box through the open side. 'But there's not a great deal of money in this form for us unless we sell them like this...' He pulled another shell from a different box. It was the same as the previous one, but there was a huge half-pearl, perhaps two centimetres across, sitting near the edge. 'These are what we call "blister pearls",' he said. 'When you cut it out of the shell, it is only half a pearl, so you can't use it on a string. It's used in brooches, earrings, rings. . . that sort of thing.'

'How much do you get for these?' I asked.

'Well, the price is depressed at the moment. The Japanese are trying to squeeze us. They are the main buyers, you see. They should be paying us at least $20 each, but it's down to $10.'

I gazed at the rows of boxes.

'There's more than 18 000 there,' Peter said, anticipating my next question.

'$180 000.' I whistled softly.

'Which should be $360 000,' he added.

'And the third way you sell them,' Trish asked, 'is presumably the whole pearl?'

'Right. But that's the tricky one. It's a very different and more difficult job to grow a whole pearl than these blisters, much more difficult. But of course, with a far greater return. I've got this year's harvest ready to go down to New Zealand in a couple of months. Like to have a look?'

Peter disappeared into the house and rummaged around in a chest, emerging a few minutes later with a couple of large coffee jars filled with pearls. . . white, rainbow and black. Alwyn brought out a velvet-lined tray in which to spread the pearls as Peter took them from their bottles. There were at least 2000 beautiful pearls there. We looked on in amazement and wonder as they glistened and shone in the bright sunlight. I took several photographs.

'They're nice aren't they,' Peter said matter-of-factly, as he picked up an almost perfectly round black one. 'This is a 13-millimetre black. . . worth thousands of dollars on its own. The others are individually worth many hundreds each. . several of them over a thousand, but when you sell them in large quantities like this, you've got to sell the good with the bad and take a bulk price. . . probably around $100 each.'

'So that's another $200 000,' I said.

'Yes, but once again, the Japs are squeezing us. They're only offering $30 at the moment. I'm thinking of by-passing them and going to Europe to sell direct. You see up till now all the pearls that go on the market in Europe have come through Japan. . . they've had the market sewn up. We'd be cutting out the middleman if we sold direct.'

Peter waved his hand in a gesture of frustration. 'We just can't afford to accept their prices. This place has been tremendously expensive to set up— at least a quarter of a million has gone into it—you'll see how the whole thing works this morning, when Max takes you out in the boat. It also takes a lot of money to run. So if we took what they're offering, we'd go broke.'

'But surely that's not likely,' I said, 'when you've got all these pearls and the shells to sell? You've proved that it's a viable proposition.'

'Well, yes, that's true. We've had a few setbacks along the way, that have affected our pearls, but usually we've discovered what's happening and rectified it quickly. We've also brought a good deal of prosperity to the island—up to $40 000 a year in income for the islanders working for us; $40 000 total, that is, far more than copra has ever brought in for Manihiki. In addition we give the Island Council three or four times the amount of money they get from their own government in Rarotonga, so the people of Manihiki are very happy with the setup. All we've got to do is get around this Japanese stranglehold.'

About an hour later we learnt a little more of how the Japanese have kept control of the cultured pearl industry when Max took us in one of the open, outboard-powered launches to the 'pearl factory' on one of the other little motus across the lagoon. The island was several kilometres from the main village and the Cumming's home. This was where they had located their pearl 'workshop'. It consisted of a group of low, open-sided sheds with thatched roofs which were clustered along the shoreline in front of a grove of coconut palms. After pulling in to a small wharf, we walked up to one of the sheds where Max introduced us to four islanders who were sitting cross-legged on the floor in a circle. They were chipping and cleaning large piles of the blister pearl shells. We chatted with them for a while and then left to explore the rest of the 'factory'.

'How much are they paid?' I asked Max.

'$40 a week', he replied. 'With three weeks paid holiday a year. This makes them by far the best-paid workers on the island . . . even civil servants in the government in Rarotonga only get $20 a week.'

We moved to another shed where several tables were lined up in a row. On each was a stainless-steel device which was bolted to the tabletop. They were small, but very strong clamps. These were the devices by which both the blister pearls and the round pearls were first implanted in the living oysters.

As Max and his friend Steve demonstrated, we could clearly see that the process of starting the blister, or half-pearl, was vastly more simple than that of making a whole pearl. With the half pearl, clams are taken from the water, where they hang in plastic cages, placed in the special stainless-steel brace and forced open about a couple of centimetres. Then a small half-sphere of either soapstone or epoxy resin is slipped in with a pair of tweezers, the flesh of the animal is lifted up and, with a special fast-acting glue (which costs $20 for a tiny bottle), the foreign implant is stuck down to the inner surface of the shell. The clam is then returned to the water and, within about eight or nine months it completely covers the foreign object with a thick layer of mother of pearl.

'The process for the round pearl is something completely different', Max explained. 'The Japanese have kept the technique to themselves ever since Mikimoto started the cultured pearl industry there ages ago.'

The conversation was interrupted briefly while Max took some ointment and sticking plaster from a medicine cabinet in the shelter to put on his foot. He'd cut it on the coral several days earlier and it had become somewhat inflamed and swollen. He finished the task and returned to where we were examining the steel clamp.

'If the Japanese have kept the technique for round pearls a secret,' Trish asked him, 'how did you make the ones we saw this morning?'

Max laughed. 'We don't do the implants for those. We've got to get Japanese technicians to do it for us.'

'Here? On Manihiki?' I said in surprise.

'That's right. Each season we bring two Japanese experts here for about six months and they do nothing but operate on oysters every day. They make a clear $10 000 each, then take off back to Japan.'

'But', I said, 'surely you can do it yourself? Is it really that difficult?'

'Well, they've kept the finer points of the technique a close secret and they generally make a practice of not telling anyone the real tricks of the trade, but from watching them work this season and from conversations I had with them while they were here, I think I've got it taped. I've implanted about 200, but it'll take about two years before we know if I've succeeded. The round pearls take that long.'

'Why is it so different?'

'Basically because it's a much more delicate operation. It's microsurgery really. You have to insert a tiny piece of implanted tissue, it's a nucleus of Mississippi River pearl shell, right into the byssus muscle of the oyster, or into its gonads. You've got to do it just right, or the oyster will die. Either that or the pearl won't form properly around the tiny irritant.' He turned to head back to the small wharf where the boat was moored. 'Come and see the rest of the "farm", where the pearls grow.'

'There are several locations,' Steve explained, 'in different parts of the lagoon. We're always experimenting to find the best water, where the currents and nutrients are best. Also to find the best depth.'

The first 'garden' was not far from the 'factory', only a hundred metres or so from the shore. A row of yellow floats, which were anchored to the floor of the lagoon, stretched off in parallel lines for several hundred metres. Slung beneath the floats in nylon mesh bags, only 20 or 30 centimetres under the surface of the water, were hundreds of large oyster shells. They apparently don't try to attach themselves to anything as they would in their natural state but hang free in their nylon bags, just allowing the nutrient-laden water to pass through them.

The next 'garden' was more remote, out in the deeper water near the centre of the lagoon. After a brief run in the motor boat, we manoeuvred around for a few minutes while Steve and Max lined up a couple of landmarks on the surrounding rim of the lagoon.

'This is our deeper, experimental station,' Max said. 'All of the nets and shells are suspended at a depth of about 13 metres.'

'Are they on the bottom?' I asked, as there were no buoys or floats visible on the surface.

'No. We've got floats anchored to the bottom, which is about 20 metres deep here, but the floats stay under the water and keep the nets at the correct depth. You'll see in a minute.'

We put on our masks and flippers and slipped over the side of the boat into the clear water to watch as Max dived easily down to the nets on a lungful of air. There was no way we could do it. We just hovered close to the surface, breathing through our snorkels, watching as he checked the line of nets, surfaced and dived again, repeating the process until he had completely checked the whole line. This, Steve told us while Max was busy, was a necessary job that had to be done regularly to see that none of the nets had been torn of broken and that the oysters still appeared healthy.

From there, we cut back across the lagoon to the main village and the Cummings' house where Peter was talking to a dark, muscular villager. He introduced us.

'This is Ionue,' Peter said. 'He is my chief employee on the island.'

Ionue smiled broadly and extended his hand. It was hard and calloused and he had a grip of iron. He was, I would say, about 45 or 50 years old, but incredibly fit. There appeared to be not an ounce of fat on his body which rippled with muscles. He was, we learnt later from Peter, one of the greatest underwater divers in the South Pacific. We were to hear more of Ionue's diving achievements later, but at the time of our first meeting, it was suggested that he join us and the Cummings for the evening meal. He accepted readily, but immediately offered to go to his fish traps and collect some fish to cook.

Ionue asked me to come with him in his outboard-powered boat to the traps which he had constructed out of coral in a shallow part of the lagoon a couple of kilometres north of the village. It was nearly dusk as we approached the extensive network of tidal pools he had made by piling up long, low walls of broken coral in the water. The idea was that the fish would be led into successively smaller pools from which they could eventually find no escape.

'Sometimes we have two or three hundred fish here,' Ionue said, as we waded from the boat through the shallows. 'Sometimes we feed the whole village from this pool . . . but this time . . . huh!' He turned up his nose. 'Almost nothing.'

Almost nothing to him would have been a superb catch to anyone else. There were probably 15 fish ranging from 15 centimetres to half a metre long, as well as a one-metre-long shark! Ionue watched the shark and then, waiting for an opportunity as it swum past, grabbed it by the tail and with one quick heave, slung it out of the pool into the shallows. Within five more minutes he had deftly netted half a dozen fish and, after tossing them into the boat, we were on our way back again with our dinner for that night.

'Shall we bow our heads in prayer.' I gave Sean a firm nudge and made eye signals. Caught off-guard, none of us knew that among his other qualifications, Ionue was also the Catholic pastor for the island. We quickly laid down our knives and forks and bowed our heads while Ionue gave a simple prayer of thanks for the delicious meal we were about to consume.

For the rest of the evening he kept us entranced with stories of island life and his diving experiences. Peter would feed him lines like, 'Tell them about how you left them gaping in Tahiti, Ionue.'

Ionue would smile modestly. 'That was when I represented the Cook Islands in the South Pacific Games. We have only a small population so that the spear-fishing team consisted of just one person, me.' He looked at Peter.

'And Ionue caught more fish in one hour than the Tahitian team of three caught in five hours!'

'And he had a bout of 'flu at the time too,' Max added.

Ionue regularly dived to 36 metres on only a lungful of air and could stay down for an incredible four and a half minutes. 'I've timed him,' Steve told us in admiration. He has also taught Max all he knows about diving.

'I'd never done any diving before I came here,' Max said. 'But Ionue is a master. Underwater, he is much more than just another fish, because after all, he also has the intelligence and other abilities of man. I remember one time I was down with him and he was aiming at a fish, when a small shark swam up beside him. Without taking his other hand off the trigger, he caught hold of the shark by the tail and pulled it sharply out of the way. Then he fired and caught two fish on the one shot.'

'Aren't you afraid of sharks?' Zara asked, impressed. Ionue explained what we had heard before, from Nanua on Rangiroa and other islanders; that it is possible to sense if a shark is feeling frisky or vicious.

'But I have been afraid.'

'When?' Sean demanded.

'See these fingers.' Ionue held up the first two fingers of his right hand. They were thinner than the others, badly scarred and rather crooked.

'That happened when I was a child. Younger than you. I was fishing with my father on the reef and when we had enough and were just about to go home, I walked out a little way into the water, about up to my waist, to cool off and I saw a slight movement in a rock pool. I thought it was a fish and I reached down to try to catch it and my hand was grabbed by a moray eel.'

'Oh!' Zara shuddered.

'What did you do?' Sean was open-mouthed.

'I yelled out to my father, but he had already walked on along the beach and even if he heard me, I expect he thought I was fooling about, not wanting to come home. So he kept on walking. The eel backed into his hole and held so tight, that I was forced to bend over. The tide was coming in fast. When I looked under the water at him I could see he was a real monster...must have been three or four feet long [over a metre] at least. He just held tight and, if I had stayed still, the tide would have come in and drowned me. I was already having trouble getting my head above the water to take deep breaths of air. So I summoned up all my strength and tore my fingers out of its mouth.'

We all flinched.

'...as hard as possible. The flesh was stripped away...down to the bone...but at least I got away.'

As he talked we realised that it must have been Ionue about whom George, the steward on board the *Mataora*, was talking when he had told us several stories.

'Oh yes, I taught George to dive,' Ionue said when we asked him. 'And many other young boys too. But they all leave. Down to Raro, or New Zealand.' He looked sad. 'I don't blame them for wanting the bright lights and the girls.' He smiled at Steve, who shifted uncomfortably.

Obviously Steve had told Ionue what he had also confided in me, while we were out on the lagoon. That although he was fascinated by the work and loved the simple lifestyle, he thought that at the end of the year, having spent 12 months on the island, he would probably head home.

'I miss the social life,' he told us, referring in a delicate way to there being no girls. There were girls of course—a few even of the right age and inclination among the population of 350 Manihikians. But it would be very much frowned upon by the islanders if Steve or Max became involved with any one of them without there being a serious long-term intent. So much for the myth about the lax morality in the South

Pacific! Alwyn had already told me that shorts were not really acceptable on women and bikinis were a definite no-no.

'What about bringing a girlfriend up from New Zealand?' I had asked Steve.

He shrugged. 'I don't know any girl who would want to spend a whole year in such an isolated place. Do you? In abstract the idea appeals. But to actually do it. That's another thing.'

Lying in bed that night, my mind racing with stories of sharks and eels, pearls and holding your breath for four and a half minutes (you try it!), I mulled over Steve's words and thought them a fairly depressing comment on the female of the human species.

'Look what I've found.' Zara slowly opened her carefully clenched fist the following morning to reveal a large black pearl.

'Where did you find it?'

'In the chicken yard,' she said proudly. 'I was cleaning up. Can I keep it?'

'I think you'd better show it to Peter.'

'It must have been thrown out accidentally,' Peter said, eyeing the pearl. 'It's worth about $500.'

Alwyn looked slightly guilty. 'The boys and I go through all of the flesh of the oysters not once, but twice. Still we must have missed this one. A chicken probably ate it and it's been right through and out the other end.'

Zara looked more carefully at the beautiful black stone and wrinkled her nose.

'I tell you what,' Peter said. 'I'll swop it for three little white ones.'

'Four,' Zara smiled winningly. 'Then I can stick one each on a pipi shell [a small white oyster shell] for the Robb girls for Christmas presents and keep one for myself.' The bargain was struck and Zara spent the rest of the morning happily cleaning up the small shells on the Cummings' grinding wheel and sticking her little white pearls in the middle of the shells to make presents for some of her close friends in Australia.

Iain was busy making a metal porthole scoop from an empty cabin bread tin to replace the cardboard one we had on board the *Mataora*. It had made quite a difference to the temperature in the cabin, but, in the rain, it had become rather limp and tired. Sean was off fishing from the outrigger and I was still trying to catch up on my notes which, not surprisingly, had fallen behind on the voyage up. Max was supposed to be studying for a maths exam he was taking that night but his infected foot had ballooned frighteningly to an ugly size and was giving him so much discomfort that he had been given antibiotic injections by the island nurse, the only medical officer on Manihiki. He was resting on his bed listening to a tape from his brother which had come with the latest mail.

'Max is crying,' Sean reported when he returned from hauling the canoe up out of the lagoon. 'He misses his brother.'

In a while I went over to see how Max was feeling and hopefully to cheer him up a bit. 'How's the foot?'

'Okay', he said stoically.

We both looked at the offending appendage as if it was a recalcitrant *enfant terrible* with a mind of its own. 'I guess you get pretty lonely sometimes and miss other young people,' I said.

He shrugged his shoulders. 'I don't have time to think about it often. Though I do miss Andrew and I'm looking forward to joining him at uni. But...' he added quickly, in case I thought he was being disloyal, 'I don't regret having grown up here.'

We talked for a while about the advantages and otherwise of living on Manihiki. No peer group pressure, but no social life. A simpler life, but one with a smaller number of choices.

Approaching, as the Finshep family was, the teenage years of confrontation and growing independence, I wondered whether spending these years, which are invariably anxious ones of trial for both parents and children, in a place where there were fewer causes of dissension between grower-up and grown-up would be a loss or a gain— whether to become a mature adult *requires* a period of trauma.

I came to a conclusion—it does not!

Iain, who was now busy with Zara in the kitchen, he making his speciality, pizza, and she making hers, a cake, came by to say that he and Peter were off to the CAO (Chief Administrative Office) to buy some beer and whisky before it closed.

'We may be too late already,' Peter said. 'The *Mataora* is back from Rakahanga and when the boat's in, the CAO locks up the grog supply so the crew don't get drunk and the work gets done.'

It was locked up and the CAO was down at the quay. But Peter explained to his wife how we were 'important visitors' from distant lands and how it would be inhospitable not to allow us to buy some booze! The persuasive way he talked made us sound as though we couldn't last without! Having broken the rules by unlocking the place, she threw caution to the winds and took us on a tour, first the liquor bond and then the court house, an adjoining single room which managed to exude an air of justice not only being done but being seen to be done. The bench, the judge's chair, the dock and, on the walls, unsmiling down, faded photographs of ex-New Zealand governor-generals and their good ladies in dated formal fashions; elbow-length gloves (the ladies) and plumed hats (the fellows). Beside them was a picture of Queen Mary, the present Queen of England's granny; Edward the Eighth when he was, according to rumour, the gallant and charming Prince of Wales; and Queen E. herself, looking 30 years younger than now. Odd to see them looking down on a place they have never clapped their eyes on and more than likely have probably never heard of.

Iain's pizza was a great success, and Zara's cake too. I remember those few evenings on Manihiki with a special affection. They had an aura. A soft air, and a welcome cool after the day's blistering heat.

Max went off to sit in solitary confinement, locked into the spooky court room by the CAO's wife to write his maths exam which had come up on the *Mataora* and had to leave with us the following day. The boys' entire high school education had been achieved in this manner, with Alwyn keeping them to a regular schedule of study. When Max returned at 11 p.m., his foot still very swollen and painful, he told us how in the middle of the time allotted for the exam, an inebriated islander had come hammering on the door demanding to be let in. There can't be many students who sit their exams under such off-beat circumstances.

In the morning while I was packing up our gear so as to be ready to leave at a moment's notice when we got word that the *Mataora* was loaded, Iain called out to me from the main house and I went over to find him and Peter and Alwyn busy exchanging gifts. We always travel with a few opals to give as thankyous and, having done so, Peter proceeded to load us with beautiful half shells of black-lipped oyster. 'They make very good dishes for seafood entrees', Alwyn recommended. She was right, but at that moment entrée dishes seemed rather remote for us!

No sooner had we stashed these in our bulging packs, along with our freshly-washed clothing, than Ionue arrived with more gifts of oyster shell and there was more swopping and thankyous.

When word came that the *Mataora* was ready, Peter insisted on loading our packs into the wheel barrow, perhaps he thought we still looked a little weak-kneed, for the short walk to the wharf. We said our goodbyes and thankyous to Alwyn and Max and Steve. Hospitality seems to be infectious in the South Pacific, rubbing off on even new residents. The Cummings had certainly been so kind to us, that we shall always remember them with affection and their 'kikau motel' with pleasure. All we can hope is that they visit us so that we can return their generosity.

As Ionue guided us out to the *Mataora* in his small boat, Peter stood on the wharf, came to attention and gave a smart naval salute.

# 13  RAKAHANGA
## Paradise exacts its price

In the Pacific you soon get used to the fact that nothing happens immediately. When we clambered back on board the *Mataora,* we sat wallowing beneath the afternoon sun about 100 metres from the edge of the fringing reef for a further three hours before we took off in the direction of Rakahanga, some 40 kilometres (about three hours run for the *Mataora*) to the north.

In earlier days there used to be considerable traffic between the two islands, with inhabitants sailing back and forth to visit relatives or to trade, but the practice has been banned as, on a number of occasions, boatloads of islanders have been swept away and lost at sea. There is a particularly strong westerly current passing between Manihiki and Rakahanga, a steady three or four knots, and if an outboard motor breaks down during a crossing, a small boat and its passengers can be carried relentlessly away from the two islands and very quickly lost from sight.

In 1965 a group of Manihikians set off in a small launch for Rakahanga and met with just such an accident. The story of their struggle for survival during 65 days at sea in their open boat as it was swept almost 3500 kilometres across the western Pacific to Erromanga Island in the New Hebrides, is one of the most remarkable survival epics in the annals of the sea. A book, *The Man who Refused to Die,* tells of the extraordinary courage of Techu Makimare, the hero of the voyage who continually urged his companions to hang on to life—not to give up hope.

As it happened, Techu's nephew, a man called Tutai, was a member of the crew of the *Mataora.*

Night had fallen by the time we were half-way to Rakahanga. The sea was flat-calm with practically no swell and the equatorial stars shone down from a completely cloudless sky. We sat on the upper deck in the cooling breeze just soaking up the atmosphere. Through the rear window of the wheel-house we watched as Zara questioned the skipper, Bo, about the charts. A message crackled through on the ship's radio. It was the CAO from Rakahanga enquiring about the *Mataora's* expected arrival time. Bo answered and from the conversation it was clear that there was some conflict between him and the CAO. He told the man that we would be arriving off Rakahanga during the night and would be ready to start loading copra at first light but that he wanted to leave the island before noon. The CAO informed him that that would be impossible. There were 38 tonnes of copra on the island that were to be loaded onto the ship and rather than load half of it for shipment back to Rarotonga, he would let the whole lot stay until the next ship came by in three months time.

'Thirty-eight tonnes?' Bo said into the radio microphone. 'On Manihiki they had 104 tonnes and they loaded in eight hours. You should be able to do 38 tonnes in three or four hours.'

A pause at the other end and then, 'Impossible,' the Rakahanga CAO said sharply.

'Well, take it or leave it,' Bo said. 'We'll be ready for you at first light.'

They both signed off and the skipper stepped out onto the outer bridge deck where we'd been standing. 'They're a lazy lot here at Rakahanga. Well. . . not really lazy I suppose. It's just that the CAO owns all the boats and he pays the men so little that they don't want to work. On Manihiki they're all private boat owners contracting to do the loading and offloading so they work hard, competing to get more loads for themselves—just different systems, that's all.' He smiled. 'There's a moral there somewhere.'

This running backwards and forwards between the two islands was apparently an unusual procedure for the *Mataora.* On most trips she, or the other Silk and Boyd ship, the *Manuvai,* would just stop off once, unload, load and be gone. But on this trip the whole thing was complicated by the fact that Ian Nesbitt, the electrician had had to be dropped off first at Rakahanga, so that he could do his wiring job and then be picked up later. Also, the doctor had to be dropped off as soon as possible on Rakahanga and then picked up at the last moment with his desperately ill patient. In addition, there was still more cargo to be picked up from Manihiki, from the smaller settlement of Tukai on one of the other motus on the rim of the atoll. Evidently we had to return to Manihiki once more. On discovering this, we thought that perhaps we should have stayed there and waited, but then we would have missed out on Rakahanga. It was a crazy setup and we could see that Bo was irritated by the fact that he had to shuttle back and forth like a ferry. That the *Mataora* had to struggle along on its still sick engine didn't help matters.

Trish and the children went to bed while I stayed up on deck for a while talking to Bo and drinking a few cans of cold New Zealand beer which he produced. He had bought about half a dozen cans of beer each for the whole crew as a thankyou for the way they had worked over the past few days. There was a kind of magic about the night. The moon had come up on our starboard and the sea was glistening silver. Bo talked about his own boat, the big catamaran he had left moored in Tonga.

'Will you go back to it eventually?' I asked.

'Certainly. I intend to continue my voyage before long.' He had spent more than half his lifetime in the Pacific and although he spoke perfect English, there was still the strong lilt of a Scandinavian accent in it. 'There is too much to see and do,' he said with an easy laugh. 'I couldn't stay on the same run forever.'

'But your boat...is it all right? I mean, is it safe...just left moored in Tonga?'

'Oh, yes, there is a Scotsman living on the boat next to it. He is keeping an eye on it for me. When you get to Tonga, you can stay on it if you wish.'

I thanked him and said that we weren't sure when we would be in Tonga, or whether or not we could take up his offer. But, in any case, we'd check on the boat for him to see if it was still all right.

At about 9.30 p.m. we came up to Rakahanga. On the glistening, silver sea, it was just a long, dark strip, lying flat on the horizon—no lights to be seen anywhere. The captain ordered the engines stopped, but instead of dropping anchor, he let the vessel drift. With the steady westerly current carrying us away from the island, there was no chance of us drifing onto Rakahanga's reef and there was no other island or atoll for hundreds of kilometres in the direction we were drifting. By about four in the morning we were some 20 kilometres to the west of Rakahanga, drifting silently on the low swell. The engines were started up and we motored back towards the island in time to be back off the entrance through the reef by first light, as Bo had promised the CAO.

There were no boats in sight, nor any of the islanders. We saw Bo on the bridge and he smiled and made a gesture with his hands, turning both palms up, as if to say, 'See, I told you so.'

Finally, after almost an hour, a few people arrived at the little concrete jetty and a couple of boats came out with some bags of copra. Having got our swimming gear together, we jumped into one of them to go into shore for a while to look around the island.

Our Austrian friend, Herman, had been here on Rakahanga for three days, having decided to stay here, with his wife's relatives who lived on the island. As there was only one village of about 300 people, we felt sure that we'd be able to find Herman without too much trouble.

Stepping ashore onto the concrete pier, we began to walk slowly towards the village which was about three or four hundred metres back from the seashore, along the edge of the lagoon. At only eight in the morning the day was already very hot and we kept to the shade of the tall coconut trees along the small road, as we walked.

It was Zara who spotted Herman walking along a path near the lagoon. He saw us at the same time and turned quickly across to us. 'I want you to come with me,' he said after we'd exchanged greetings. 'I want you to meet my friends.'

He took us along the path beside the lagoon, further away from the village centre to a small complex of huts and houses built of wood. On the steps of one of them, an open-sided, thatched-roof structure, a group of people sat singing softly to the tune of a guitar. They stopped as we approached and one of them, an attractive woman in her early 50s wearing a large hat stood up with a smile to say hello.

'This is Turi,' Herman said, 'Turi Bishop. She has returned to Rakahanga for the first time in 32 years.'

'Thirty-two years!' I echoed. 'Where have you been for all that time? In Rarotonga?'

'No,' she laughed. 'In New Zealand.' Immediately she spoke, you could hear her strong New Zealand accent. 'I married an English engineer...he comes from Bath. He is retiring soon and we are thinking of coming back here to live.'

'So you'll be going back to New Zealand again first?' I asked.

'Oh, yes...I must. I am coming on the *Mataora* with you.' She turned to introduce us to the others, first, the couple sitting on the steps beside her. 'This is my cousin, Mahia Tupou,' Turi said, 'and another relative, Mary Amarama.' We shook hands. The man, Mahia, was about 50. He was bare-chested and brown, with a number of tattoos on his arms—obviously very fit. Like Ionue on Manihiki. 'He is a fisherman,' Turi told us.

Mary was about the same age as Mahia, but she showed it more than he. She had a not-unattractive face, but when she smiled or sang, she revealed a practically toothless mouth.

Off to one side another woman sat weaving a rito hat from thinly-sliced coconut leaves. 'My sister, Patesepa Poroto,' Turi said with a wave of her arm. We examined one of the hats she had already made and remembered Papa Raui's comments on Mitiaro about the rito hats of Rakahanga. The fibres Turi's sister was deftly weaving were incredibly fine. Young coconut leaves are cut into thin slivers, then soaked and bleached until they are soft and pliable. We could see from the amount of work that she was putting in and from the end product how the Rakahanga hats have earnt the reputation of being the finest in the Pacific. Turi tapped my arm.

'And finally,' she said, 'my daughter, Elizabeth, who came with me from New Zealand.'

Elizabeth stood, small and demure, to one side. She was 18 and beautiful. She also smiled and said hello to us and then sat down quietly at one end of the group. We discovered later that she wasn't exactly in her mother's good books as the first thing she'd done on their arrival in the Cook Islands was to fall pregnant to a young civil servant in Rarotonga. So while Turi was travelling on with us on the *Mataora,* Elizabeth would stay on the island to have the baby.

Turi picked up the guitar. 'Sit down,' she commanded everyone and then launched straight into a Polynesian tune. Mary and Mahia, who were sitting beside us, began singing—harmonising wonderfully, not unlike the church singers in the two services we'd attended on Mitiaro and Aitutaki. We sat on the little open verandah of the house for half an hour, listening, entranced as they all played and sang.

After the first couple of songs, Turi had handed the guitar to Mahia and, while he played, she stood in front of us all and danced, swaying and moving in typical Polynesian fashion, her arms undulating gracefully in front of her and to the side.

'Oh, I wish sometimes that I could be two people,' she said, still dancing. 'I am so happy to be here on my home island. One half of me wants to stay and the other half wants to go back to my home and my family in New Zealand.'

I looked at Mahia and Mary. Mahia just raised his eyebrows for a moment, but they both kept on singing.

If it takes extraordinary people with vision and a sense of adventure to put themselves outside of a comfortable society and go set up a pearl farm on an out-of-the-way island like Manihiki where they will be the only Europeans, think how even more courageous is the person who goes it alone, with no backup, no support system other than her own resources. Such a person is Glennis Hill.

She didn't *look* out of the ordinary as she came along the blinding-white coral path to the house where Turi and her friends were playing, singing and dancing. But she did sound very different from the girl next door and probably very different from how she sounded when she first went to Rakahanga, a whole, long year before.

She was introduced as an Australian and at first I thought perhaps she was a migrant who had learnt to speak English as an adult. But then I realised that it was a pidgin-accented English she was speaking and when she told us that we were the first English-speakers she had talked with in the year she had been on the island I understood why her speech was so unusual. Glennis was simply speaking English the way northern Cook Islanders do. Most of them invariably speak their own Maori language between themselves, unlike those in the southern group where there has been considerably more contact with foreigners.

'You are more than likely the first tourists to ever visit Rakahanga,' Glennis told us.' 'Government employees and people from international aid agencies and so on have called here, though not in the last year, but never people who are just visiting for pleasure. What made you want to come here?!'

'I could well ask you the same question!' I laughed. I already knew from the Cummings, who had met Glennis when she came through on the boat to take up her post, that she was in her early 30s and an 'AVA'—an Australian Volunteer Abroad— working as a teacher.

'If I had known what I was letting myself in for, I might well not have come!' Glennis laughed. 'And if there had been flights out of here, I might very well have *left* long before now.' She grimaced. 'I probably don't really mean that to sound as strong as it does, but it's a relief to say it. I haven't been able to say it since I arrived. There's been no-one to whom I could say it. It's a bit like discussing the value of aid programmes, the pros and cons— disrupting the culture perhaps, but on the other hand, widening horizons. I get tired of the endless talk about these issues when I am with other aid people, but when I am *not* with them, I get sick of not being able to discuss them! Stupid.' She chastised herself.

There was a general move in the direction of the wharf. We had all heard so many horror stories of passengers being stranded on islands and having to wait for weeks, months even, for the next boat to come by, that we were very anxious to keep an eye on how the copra loading was progressing. As we walked, Glennis talked.

'Tell me if I am boring you,' she asked with disarming frankness, 'it's just that it's so pleasant to have someone from outside to talk to.'

'You make it sound like a prison.'

'It has some aspects. But no. I don't mean to. Perhaps seeing you and your family like this has reminded me so sharply that there is another world out there. It's possible to live here and forget that. Most of the time I am perfectly happy to be here. I am very glad I came. It's just that occasionally I get lonely. Not that I'm ever alone. . . just lonely. No-one to bat ideas around with. Always having to set an example and be on display.'

At the wharf, it was obvious that loading was going to take some time longer. A large percentage of the population of 350 were there. Those who were not helping to unload cartons and drums of cargo, or to load the bags of copra, were enjoying the diversion of the boat's rare visit by giving advice to the workers. Others swam in the water around the wharf, dodging the small boats as they ferried the copra out and the cargo in.

The men and boys swam in their shorts, the women and girls in their modest dresses, which, when wet, clung to their bodies most immodestly. Elizabeth, Turi's daughter, went in her jeans and tee-shirt. Zara and I peeled off our clothes to reveal our bikinis, much to the surprise and interest of the others. 'I used to wear bathers,' Glennis said, floating around, her dress ballooning out in the water, 'but it's easier to go with the local custom.'

After a while, the loading still continuing, we strolled back along the rocky foreshore to her house. 'It's not much, but it's mine, as they say.' The small wooden one-room house was like a student's room at college. Posters and photographs, books and momentos. A bed and a small cooktop completed the facilities.

'Where do you. . .?'

'Over there.' She pointed to a small enclosure with no roof, but walled to neck-height. 'It's toilet and shower combined. The shower is just a scoop over effort. When I first came here, I lived with a family for a few months. I was supposed to stay on with them, but I knew I'd go crazy if I didn't have a space to call my own. It was embarrassing, because naturally the family thought they had done something wrong, and no matter how hard I tried to explain, they didn't understand. A woman, living on her own. . .it just isn't done.'

'People *do* go crazy. . .' I suggested. We had heard about an AVA teacher who had to quit Manihiki after a year because he just couldn't take the isolation any longer and, according to local gossip (which abounds on all the islands we visited in the South Pacific), he began to show signs of instability.

'Yes. I know what you mean,' Glennis was not one to gossip, 'though I didn't see him before he left. People might say nasty things about him, but I'd like to see how they would cope with it!'

'Why did *you* choose such a remote place?'

'I'd taught as an AVA before, in the New Hebrides, down on one of the southern islands there. I loved it and I thought, if I go to the Cooks, I'll do the same thing. Not stay on Raro, where there's little to be learnt professionally or personally. I thought I'd be more useful out here.'

'And are you?'

She was silent for a moment and then, 'The terrible thing. The worst thing,' she paused again, 'is that I don't think I'm much use, even here. The simple truth is that I can't teach them about what they need to know—how to improve their diet, how to cook and sew and run a home efficiently. How to care for children. Family relations. Adjusting to a changing society. The things I *can* teach them, like straight education, are of no value to them.' She looked at me as if wanting me to contradict her, to at least say something, even if it were to agree.

'It must be of value to some of them,' I said and told her about Temu Okatai, the Tourist Authority fellow in Raro. Rakahanga was his home island and he was receptive enough to the education he received on it to want to go on down to Raro, to finish high school and then on to take his degree in New Zealand.

'Trouble is, I wonder if even that is a real success story,' Glennis said, 'or if we shouldn't be educating them to see the values in their own society instead of making them feel they have to leave it to take further schooling.' She sounded a bit like Dawson Murray, the Aitutaki headmaster whom we'd met. 'But for my own personal sanity, I have to agree with you. That I should be opening their eyes to that world. It's the only way I can keep going here.'

Before taking up as an AVA, Glennis had travelled widely in Europe, India and Asia. When this particular job came up she arrived in Raro only to be told that single women were disqualified from taking solitary posts on isolated islands.

'The intimation was that, whereas a man might be able to stand the strain, a woman wouldn't. In the light of what happened on Manihiki, that's rather ironic. Anyway, when they said that, it persuaded me more than anything else to insist on coming here—I wasn't going to be discriminated against! Now I am paying the price for my determination to prove myself as good as any fellow. And for the same reason, I couldn't possibly pack it in. Serves me right!'

After soaping up and swilling off in her open air 'bathroom', we sat for a while outside her house. The world and his brother came by and stopped off for a chat and to look over the newcomers. I could see what Glennis meant about never being alone. After half an hour we walked back to the wharf where the loading was almost over and Glennis introduced us to Temu Okatai's sister and her husband, the local cop.

Turi was supervising the loading of her vast piles of luggage. Bo came ashore for a last check to see that all the cargo had been taken aboard and then it was time to leave. We said goodbye to Glennis and wished her luck and the stamina to see out her last year on Rakahanga. Then we all crammed into a dinghy, with the last bits and pieces, to be motored back through the pass in the lagoon to our floating home.

At the ship's side we had to wait while other people and goods were loaded and I almost fell into the water laughing at the message on one of the crewmen's tee-shirts. It read: BOGNOR REGIS. . . THE LAST RESORT. You have to be English and to have spent a summer holiday in Bognor to fully appreciate that!

As the *Mataora* weighed anchor and the crowd on the shore waved, poor Turi burst into tears. It was all too much for her. Leaving behind the other half of her persona, along with her pregnant daughter, not knowing when she would see either again. A South Pacific paradise exacts its price.

We finally sailed from Rakahanga at 6.30 p.m., far later than the skipper's noon deadline. He had bowed to the inevitable and kept the *Mataora* positioned off the island until all 38 tonnes of copra had been loaded. It took 12 hours instead of his estimate of three or four. The Rakahangans *were* slower than the Manihikians, but, to be fair, it should be said that they had to negotiate a much narrower and more dangerous channel through the reef than their neighbouring islanders.

However, we were still not yet finished with either Manihiki or Rakahanga. We returned to Manihiki, first to the main village of Tauhunu at about 9.30 p.m. for more passengers and mail. Peter Cumming came on board with two more letters for us to post in Apia when we got there. We talked for 15 or 20 minutes before saying goodbye again, as the ship was making ready to move up the coast a way to the only other village on Manihiki, a much smaller settlement called Tukai which was near to the fish traps that Ionue had taken me to after our first meeting.

At Tukai we picked up some more passengers, including an amazing *rei-rei,* as they call them in the Cook Islands—a homosexual man who was also a transvestite. As he was dressed in women's clothes and it was dark, it wasn't until the following day that we realised that the woman we'd seen coming aboard the night before was in fact a man. His-her name was Suwarrow (which is also the name of one of the Cook Islands' more remote, uninhabited atolls) and despite his sometimes rather bizarre appearance, we found, over the next few days that he had a most engaging personality; he seemed always to be happy and was popular with everybody on board.

By about 11 p.m. that evening, after picking up the extra passengers from Manihiki, we were ready to return to Rakahanga again for the last time. On this occasion it would only be for a brief stop to pick up the sick patient we'd been hearing about—a man called Humurua Mehau who was evidently close to death from starvation. The doctor, Auemetua Taurari, who had gone ashore on Rakahanga four days previously, did not want him on board the vessel until the very last minute. The plan was to take him on the boat to Apia in Western Samoa, then fly him down to hospital in Rarotonga.

At 2 a.m., after waiting offshore at Rakahanga in the darkness for some time, we saw a light on the wharf which meant that the patient had been brought there and was about to be ferried out to the *Mataora* in a small boat. Trish and the children were below, asleep, but I had stayed up, talking to Bo. We stood there watching from the bridge as the little vessel chugged out from Rakahanga's darkened shore. Pulling alongside, the crew and several of the sick man's relatives struggled to lift a large mattress on which the man was lying aboard the *Mataora.*

I helped them as they manoeuvred it up the narrow steps to the poop deck at the rear, laying it down on the deck where the man's wife stretched herself out beside him. She was a big, fat, jovial woman who must have weighed at least 100 kilos. He, by contrast, looked shocking, like an inmate from Belsen. It was a warm night, even at this time, and there were no bed clothes over the man. He seemed like a skeleton. He could have weighed no more than 40 kilos. We'd been told that he was only 35 years old but he could have been 135.

I remember thinking to myself, poor bugger, he hasn't got a chance. Apparently his son had died about six months previously and he had become very morose and upset over the boy's death and for some time had refused to eat. Then, so the story goes, he had contracted some illness—an infection of the larynx or the tonsils, which then *prevented* him from eating anything, even if he'd wanted to, and he began to rapidly waste away, with no improvement in his illness. There was no doctor on Rakahanga, but evidently some paramedical official had begun giving him tablets which were only intended for patients with heart disease, a course of treatment which only aggravated the poor man's condition. When the doctor arrived on the *Mataora,* he immediately put the man on a 'drip' to feed him intravenously and began dosing him with antibiotics. The doctor seemed to think there was a chance that the man might pull through. But it would be touch and go.

At 2.45 a.m. the little launch pulled away from our side and the *Mataora's* engines began to throb rhythmically to life as we gathered way and put the island to our stern. In the wheel-house the skipper scribbled in chalk on a small blackboard near the helmsman—240°—our course for the next three days; over 1000 kilometres of ocean to Apia. After a while up on deck in the breeze, I went below and immediately noticed the coolness of the cabin. The air was coming in through the porthole much more effectively than before. My tin scoop was working like a charm.

The following day was a lazy and comfortable one. It was extremely hot as the sea was calm with very little wind. We slung the hammocks up on deck and alternately read and slept there. The sick patient, Humurua, lay quietly on his mattress nearby, while his wife ministered to him. Not that there was much to be done, except constantly fan him. Most of the time he neither moved nor spoke. And yet he *had* shown signs of improvement. On two occasions he made feeble attempts to eat a little fruit and succeeded. His wife also fed him some spoonfuls of meaty broth which Arch, the cook, had sent up from the galley. Hopeful signs.

The Manihiki/Rakahanga to Samoa sector of the trip was technically an 'international' journey, whereas the previous part from Rarotonga was considered 'domestic'. On this section we were now officially cabin passengers and entitled to eat ship's food instead of our own provisions. We began to take advantage of the various tea and coffee breaks which were held in the small dining saloon, and of course, the main meals. The first lunch after leaving Rakahanga was steak and onions. It was a very nice meal, except that, in the tremendous heat of the day, it tended to sit a little heavily in our stomachs and we all became so drowsy that we had to go to sleep again in the cabin.

Later in the afternoon we sat around in the saloon with Turi Bishop, Ian Nesbitt, the electrician, Herman, the German, and Suwarrow, the transvestite. Suwarrow wore a low-cut singlet (which tended to advertise the fact that he had a chest that was decidedly more feminine than masculine) and a piece of material wrapped around his waist which looked more like a short skirt than a sarong. His legs were hairless, but although his face was closely shaven, he could not hide the line of his beard.

I can't remember what we talked about, there in the saloon, but I know we all laughed a lot and later, when we went up on deck to watch a brilliant sunset, Zara said, with a very adult look about her, 'Boy, I'm going to have a lot to write in my diary after this trip!'

In the early afternoon of the second day out from Rakahanga we went up to the aft deck. It was like a scene from a war movie. 'Dead' bodies littered inelegantly on mats on the deck and in hammocks, immobilised by the immense heat.

The sick man's wife had fallen asleep, fan still in hand. Zara, lying on her back, mouth open, was stretched along the table. Sean and Iain were sunk motionless in hammocks. All around us the ocean was empty. Oily-calm. Reflecting the overhead burning sun. I perched on the rail and stared out. I'd read that the Pacific Ocean covers a third of the globe's surface. That's how it looked.

May Grimsdale, a young New Zealand Maori woman who had come aboard at Manihiki and who was travelling with her two-year-old daughter, Rewa, got up from her mat and came over to the rail to talk. I felt great sympathy for May, though I would never have let her know, because I quickly realised that she would have dismissed such a feeling as paternalistic and racist, whereas actually it was based on an affectionate understanding of other women. May, an attractive woman of 23, was suffering that loss of identity which the majority of mothers with young children go through. Always mother, wife, housekeeper—never able to be just yourself. It was tougher for May than for most, because she was most definitely her own worst enemy.

In the four months she had been on Manihiki she had rubbed everyone up the wrong way. 'They're a lot of narrow-minded fools,' she dismissed them angrily. She seemed to have a great deal of pent-up anger. 'They didn't like me being friendly with the young men. They're so small-minded and petty. I came up here to be with my own people and to learn the language. I've been so destroyed by "papalangi" [the New Zealand Maori word for whites] like you that I don't speak any Maori at all.' She paused. 'God! How awful! I'm not saying they're as lousy as whites, but they come damn near.'

I said nothing. It was too hot and the blue Pacific too beautiful to defend the indefensible.

'I'm not sorry I came,' May went on, 'even though I am being thrown out and the government won't renew my visa. How's that! One of their own people. They prefer to let people like *you* in.'

May's husband, who, I discovered later, was a 'papalangi' (what guilt was he paying for?) and their other small child, were in New Zealand. 'I told him, "I need to go away for a while. To be with my own people." What a laugh! I can't wait to get out now.'

'Did you learn any Maori?' I asked, hoping that something positive had come out of her visit.

She shook her head. 'No. They would only talk to me in English. They saw me as a New Zealander. How's that?!'

Distressing. That's how. I had African friends in London who had experienced the same rejection when they'd made a long anticipated return 'home'. We'd met American blacks in East Africa who had suffered the same rejection. The lesson, of course, is that there's no going back. What's done is done. The past is gone. And that your colour and the shape of your eyes, or the texture of your hair does not determine your present, only your past.

We were thankfully distracted from our conversation by the first mate who had climbed to the top of the mast and was scanning the horizon for the island of Puka Puka. We weren't calling in there, we just needed to avoid it. A problem, because it is so small and so flat and there are dangerous reefs in the vicinity. In fact Puka Puka is also known as Danger Island.

The crew came out to line the rail and keep an eye out. The captain stood anxiously by the wheel-house. All the activity and the air of tension wakened the rest from their deadened state. Shortly we sighted the island, adjusted our course slightly and, after a while, any potential danger cleared. The temperature also dropped.

Because of the calm I was able to eat a reasonable amount of Arch's evening meal. (Boat trips like this are a great way to lose weight.) After the meal, Iain and the kids and I sat out on deck and watched the sun set in pink perfection. At that particular moment, I even entertained thoughts of being able to sail the oceans in our own vessel. It would have to be well organised, half the problem with the *Mataora* was that there was nowhere we could sit without getting greasy. After a couple of days, Sean looked like an engine-room hand. But there was no way I could nag him. We all felt dirty, and though the lavatories in the shower cubicles were no longer choked, the cramped compartments were hardly conducive to frequent bathing—too claustrophobic.

In the middle of the night a storm blew up and I was extremely glad that I hadn't been foolish enough to confide in Iain my tentative dreams of cruising the world, because he has been trying to persuade me for the last 15 years that it's the only way to go and that it would be great fun etc. I would have been accused by him of being a fair-weather-sailor, which is what I am.

Rain, heavy rain, bucketed down. The sick patient was carried, on his mattress, first down to a cabin, where he damn near suffocated in the heat from the engine, not to mention the abominable noise. . . then up again and into the wheel-house, where the captain had to step gingerly around him. The sea got up and several times Iain's metal scoop collected a load of water which swooshed right into the cabin. Eventually he took it off.

None of us talked to the others as the *Mataora* rolled and pitched and tossed its way across the huge ocean. But I am sure that we all had the same thought: What happens if the engine packs in now? It sounded as though it was only firing on half its cylinders and every now and again it would almost not turn over, stutter, pause, and, with only great labouring, manage to summon up enough power to get going again.

All the next day the seas kept up. Fortunately, so did the hesitant engine. I lay on my bunk reading Paul Scott in spells and taking anti-seasick tablets periodically. A request was sent down from May for some tablets. Lance could be heard cursing the engine. Iain and the kids came back and forth to the cabin sporadically.

'How much longer?' I asked Iain on one of his visits to check my state.

'Tomorrow. We'll be there tomorrow.'

I thought of my Latin mistress.

Morning came. At last. And once we were in the lee of Upolu, the main island of Western Samoa, now clearly visible and much larger than I had imagined, the swells lessened and I managed to crawl up, blinking like a mole after the winter hibernation.

'Don't walk in there,' Arch, stone-cold sober, ordered. I'd never seen the floor mopped before. Outside, the companionways were awash with sudsy water. Even the greasy deck was being given the once-over. Captain Bo had on a clean shirt and shorts. An air of respectability was abroad.

'A couple of hours and we'll be in Apia,' the captain told us. 'The health people will be coming out to give us clearance.' Ah, so that's why the spring clean.

We also cleaned up as best we could. Immigration officials in every country are hopelessly prejudiced against people who don't smell of aftershave and deodorant. Then we stowed our gear in our packs and went up to the bow to have our first glimpse of Apia and, after a month in the Cook Islands, a new country. It was difficult to believe. The trip seemed to have gone on for so long.

Suddenly, as we stood at the very tip of the bow, the sea around erupted with gleaming, smooth, grey backs. Porpoises! Easy to believe that they had come out to welcome us. They frollicked effortlessly around the metal hull, and surfed on the bow wave. Smiling as they leaped and dove. Congratulating us on having made it.

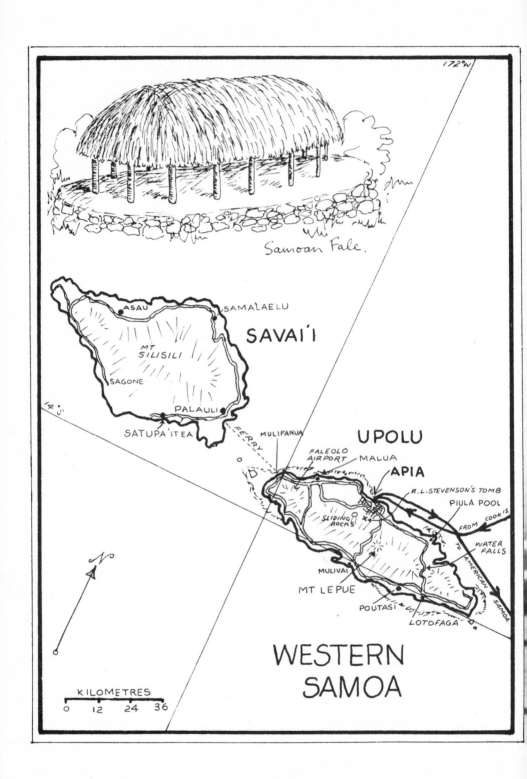

Samoan Fale.

SAVAI'I

ASAU · SAMALAELU

MT SILISILI

SAGONE

PALAULI ·

SATUPA'ITEA

FERRY

MULIFANUA

UPOLU

FALEOLO AIRPORT · MALUA

APIA

R.L.STEVENSON'S TOMB

PIULA POOL

SLIDING ROCKS

FROM COOK IS.

WATER FALLS

MULIVAI

MT LE PUE

POUTASI

LOTOFAGA

TO AMERICAN SAMOA

172°W

14°S

N

WESTERN SAMOA

KILOMETRES

0   12   24   36

## 14  UPOLU
'And the hunter home from the hill'

In no island or island grouping of the South Pacific are the history and traditions of pre-European Polynesia more entrenched and preserved than in Western Samoa. Of course, the Western world has made a tremendous impact. First the missionaries and blackbirders, then the traders and colonisers and now, as with the rest of the world, the all-pervasive materialist-consumer-pop-oriented society of the late twentieth century is reaching into the remotest corners of the once innocent Pacific.

But Western Samoa somehow seems to have been able to retain much of the old traditional lifestyle of the early Polynesians and, for many, this is something to be guarded jealously.

Little is known of Samoa's pre-European history but it is believed to have been the area in which Polynesian culture originated around 3000 years ago, after previous migrations from Melanesia. Samoa is also considered to be the starting point for the great eastward spread of Polynesia through the Cook Islands, the Society Islands, the Tuamotus, the Gambiers, the Australs and Marquesas, right across to Easter Island.

The first European navigator to visit Samoa was, as it happens, the same man who 'discovered' Easter Island—the Dutch admiral, Jacob Roggeveen. He passed through the Samoan group in 1722. During the next 100 years only two or three other Europeans called. These included the French sailors Bougainville (1768) and La Perouse (1787) but they did little more than land to replenish their supplies of fresh water and fruit.

In 1820 the ubiquitous Reverend John Williams of the London Missionary Society landed on Savai'i, the biggest island in the Samoan group, where he once more set himself to the task of Christianising the inhabitants. Between 1840 and 1880 there were many Europeans who came to settle in the Samoan islands and a three-way struggle for control of the group developed between Germany, Britain and the United States. The time was one in which almost any nation could claim sovereignty simply by raising a flag. It unfortunately coincided with a period in Samoa when there was continual rivalry and squabbling between the five great Samoan chiefly families.

In the early 1870s an extraordinary character, Colonel A.B. Steinberger, came to Samoa as an agent of the US Government to help arrange a formal peace between the warring tribal factions. But in 1875 he suddenly severed all his connections with the United States, drafted a declaration of rights and a new constitution for Samoa under which he became the premier and virtual dictator of the islands.

Acting together, Britain and the United States arranged for Steinberger to be arrested by Captain Stevens, the commander of the British warship, HMS *Barracouta.* Steinberger was deported to Fiji where he proceeded to sue the British government for damages.

For the next quarter of a century Britain, America and Germany continued to vie for dominance in the area until, in 1899, a number of treaties were drawn up between in the three powers. Under these, Germany was permitted to annex Western Samoa, that is, the two big islands of Savai'i and Upolu and the half a dozen or so adjacent smaller islands. America would take the island of Tutuila and a few smaller ones nearby, while Britain agreed to withdraw completely from Samoa on condition that Germany surrendered, in favour of Britain, all her rights and claims in the islands of Tonga, Nuie and the Solomon Group.

Incredible, when you think of it—the way the major powers just go around carving up the world to suit their own interests.

Germany held control of Western Samoa for only 15 years, because shortly after the outbreak of the First World War a New Zealand task force occupied the islands. But in those 15 years Germany had made a very big impact. The legacy of her rule is still there. At the time of their takeover of Western Samoa in 1899, the Germans were already well established commercially in the islands. They immediately set about organising the agricultural economy of Samoa with typical Teutonic thoroughness and efficiency. They built roads, bridges, water supply and sanitation facilities. They organised large cattle ranches and laid out, in long serried rows, the largest planned coconut plantations in the world. However, in doing so, they used more than just gentle persuasion on the paramount chiefs in order to muster their workforce and they ruthlessly suppressed any political opponents or agitators. Their approach to discipline was totally foreign to the Polynesian way of life and the German administration was far from popular at the time of its collapse and surrender to the New Zealand expeditionary force.

The New Zealanders, however, proved even less popular. There was endless political trouble. The Samoans were unhappy with the methods of the New Zealand military officers who led the administration. The impression given was that these officers had no understanding of the Samoans' national feelings. To them, Samoans were little more than ignorant savages and so the record of New Zealand's administration of the territory prior to World War II is not a happy one.

After the war, though, things seemed to change and the New Zealand parliament began to prepare the way for self-government in Samoa. On January 1st, 1962, Western Samoa gained its independence. It was an event of immense importance for all of the island people throughout the Pacific, for this was the first island nation to become fully independent.

Upon our arrival in Apia harbour on board the *Mataora* we shouldered our packs and wobbled down the gangway onto the pier. Herman joined us, carrying a dufflebag, as we walked away from the *Mataora* towards the town. He was leaving the ship here also and, after a few days, would take a plane back to Rarotonga to meet up with his wife and daughter again. He was, however, also travelling on a budget and looking for some reasonably cheap accommodation, so we decided to do our looking together. There were no big 'goodbyes' to all our companions on the *Mataora* as we'd arranged to meet them later in the day at Aggie Grey's Hotel for a drink. The ship was expected to stay at least a day in Apia.

We found a large tree on the waterfront road, outside of the port area and, as the day was hot and the tree was shady, we decided to leave our gear there. Trish and the kids would stay and look after it while Herman and I walked into town to try to find a place for us to stay. Half-way around the broad, sweeping curve of the Apia foreshore we came to Aggie Grey's, one of the most famous 'watering holes' of the South Pacific. We went in just to check the prices. It would have been great to stay there because there were so many stories and so much local history attached to the place, but it had been re-developed over recent years into a fairly jazzy tourist hotel and the room rates ($66 for the four of us) were just too expensive.

Herman and I continued on into the centre of town. It had a nice feel to it. Despite the oppressive heat, the Main Beach Road along the waterfront was relatively busy—by island standards, although by Western yardsticks it would probably be described as casual, relaxed. . . even lazy. The road was lined with large shady trees and many people sat in the cool of the shade just watching the passing parade. They all smiled and said a friendly 'hello' as we walked by. Even the policemen, who were dressed in an extraordinary uniform consisting of a powder-blue, short-sleeved bush-jacket tunic with a matching skirt (*lava-lava*) and a white London-bobby-style helmet, greeted us with a smile.

We noticed immediately that there seemed to be a much greater attachment to traditional Polynesian costume amongst the average people in the street than we'd seen elsewhere. Many men and boys wore *lava-lavas* instead of long pants or shorts and a good percentage of schoolboys we saw were wearing *lava-lavas* as part of their school uniform.

Ninety per cent of the population of 160 000 are full Samoans, which means that the two islands of Savai'i and Upolu contain the largest concentration of full-blooded Polynesians in the world today. More than 70 per cent of them live in and around the capital, Apia, which is really the only town of any size on the two islands.

Herman and I eventually located the Government Tourist Office which gave us a list of more reasonably-priced places to stay in Apia. The best of these seemed to be Betty Moore's Guest House, which, according to the map, was back in the direction we'd just come. It was off the main street and that was the reason we'd missed it. It was a large, old house that had been converted to take guests at $5 each a night, children half-price. It was next door to another large house which had just been taken over by the People's Republic of China to use as an embassy, their first in the South Pacific. It was also just around the corner from Aggie Grey's, close to the waterfront and the centre of town. It seemed ideal for us...unfortunately it was full. However, Betty Moore herself, a small, jovial woman in her 60s, was very apologetic. She spoke almost as if she was under an *obligation* to accommodate us.

'Never mind,' she said, 'I will find you somewhere to stay. I will ring my cousin.' She disappeared inside to use the phone and then returned a few minutes later. 'Yes,' she said, 'my cousin Francis will take you. She has a nice house...a little farther out.'

With that, she ushered Herman and me into her little Suzuki van and, after picking up Trish, Zara and Sean and our packs from beneath the big trees on the waterfront, drove us a couple of kilometres to her cousin's house, where we were given three bedrooms—two for us and one for Herman—for the same price we would have paid at the guest house.

After settling in, washing up and changing our clothes, we all took a bus back into town to have a good look over the place. We posted Peter Cumming's mail, had a hamburger, then walked down to Aggie Grey's to soak up a couple of drinks as well as the atmosphere.

Aggie Grey is a fairly remarkable woman who, at the time of this writing, is well into her 80s. No-one, of course, can live forever, but when Aggie dies, there'll be little for her to regret. She's already crammed several lifetimes into one and become an institution in Samoa and something of a legend throughout the South Pacific.

Her father, William John Swan, a chemist from Yorkshire, came to Samoa in the 1890s and met up with a beautiful local girl called 'Pele' who was to be Aggie's mother. 'She couldn't speak English,' Aggie says, 'and he couldn't speak Samoan. But that was no problem. They didn't need words...they spoke the language of love.'

It was World War II that made Aggie's name a byword in the Pacific. She was running a small bar called the 'Cosmopolitan' on the waterfront. In 1937, when she was in her late 30s, already twice widowed and with six children, she had fought and won a long battle with the New Zealand colonial authorities for a permit to operate this licensed club which eventually won international fame not as the 'Cosmopolitan', but simply as 'Aggie's'.

Aggie played hostess to thousands of American servicemen, either based in Samoa or on their way either to or from the Pacific battle zones. To them, the beer and the dark-eyed Samoan girls in Aggie's were a welcome respite from the harsher realities of army life and the war.

Aggie still talks of the wild parties with American officers and the young marines seeking companionship—when the bar rocked with the sound of music and the laughter of the servicemen and the local girls. The bar's reputation in those days was hardly 'lily-white', but it was apparently a lot of fun. One of the officers Aggie remembers from the time was a young Naval lieutenant called James Michener and it's been suggested by some that he based the character 'Bloody Mary' in his book, *Tales from the South Pacific,* on Aggie Grey. But the Bloody Mary of the book is mean, uncouth and foul-mouthed—the antithesis of Aggie. Michener himself says Bloody Mary is a composite figure, several characters rolled into one.

But Aggie's not really worried. The connection, whether true or not, brought a lot of publicity to her place and, in the years since World War II, it's grown into a very successful hotel; over 100 modern rooms in beautiful grounds, a swimming pool, the lot. The centrepiece of the complex is a huge traditional open-sided Samoan *fale* or meeting hall which is constructed of magnificently-carved and patterned timber. The big logs are bound together completely by twine, without any modern nails or screws, so that the inner ceiling forms an intricate and beautiful pattern of interwoven battens.

The hotel and grounds would, of course, be unrecognisable now to the original habitués of Aggie's old Cosmopolitan Club. They would almost certainly bemoan the loss of character that all the mod cons have brought, but for a grand old dame like Aggie, who has heads of state and prime ministers turn up to her birthday parties, and who's lived it all anyway, the past is the past and now is now.

Ian Nesbitt, the electrician from the *Mataora*, came into the bar and joined us. Shortly afterwards, Bo, the skipper, walked in, accompanied by Don Silk, the ship's owner, who'd flown in from Rarotonga because of the engine breakdowns we'd had. He'd airfreighted a couple of large parts up to Pago Pago and they would be fitted there when the ship went to American Samoa. We sat and talked for a while about the ship and the voyage.

'What happened to the sick man?' I asked.

Bo answered, 'He's in hospital here now and he'll fly down to Raro in the morning.'

Other people from the *Mataora*, both passengers and crew, were due to arrive at Aggie's shortly, but we left at about 6 p.m. to return to the house where we were staying. The ship would now be in port for a couple of days and we knew we'd see them all again before they left. But for the moment we all felt like having an early night—in a decent bed. Having come ashore and begun to relax a bit, the cumulative effects of a couple of weeks on the *Mataora* were beginning to catch up with us.

The next day the four of us, plus Herman, squeezed into a hired two-stroke Suzuki jeep, which cost $20 a day with unlimited mileage, and took off to explore Upolu.

Going clockwise around the island, the first thing that struck us was the uniquely unusual style of the oval-shaped houses or *fales* (pronounced fahlays), as they are called in Samoa. Nothing more than a thatched roof, or in too many cases a tin roof, supported on bare poles, and open to the floor. Between the poles were hung plaited blinds, rolled right up to the roof in fine weather and let down to keep out the rain. It was really hardly any different from living in the open. Because there were no walls there were no shelves, so all possessions were stacked on the floor, along with bedding, which was just a mat and a cover. In these one-room houses whole families lived. Not much room for privacy—or hang-ups. Most Pacific islanders would never have heard of Freud. He's a product of colder climes.

The other striking feature of the villages we passed through was the churches. Painted white, often with elaborate wooden fret-work picked out in pink or blue, these almost cathedral-sized structures dominated the scene.

Home and church. Family and god. That says most of what Samoan life is about.

Samoan culture is strong because family life is strong: strong to a point which many Westerners would find intolerable. To an outsider it may seem as though there is not much room for individualism. The society is based on the chiefly or *matai* system. Each *matai,* whose position is invariably hereditary, is the head of an extended family, an *agia* (pronounced eye-ing-a). There are about 10 000 *matais* and they choose among themselves only the 45 *matais* who will go forward to represent the people in the central parliament. The people have an opportunity to vote directly for only two members.

The system can hardly be called democratic—more a form of paternalism—but it seems to be acceptable to Samoans because there's no groundswell of opposition. Mostly perhaps because the system ensures that no-one goes hungry or neglected, for that would bring disgrace on the *agia*. It also means that if you don't want to push yourself, you don't need to because your support system will carry you. It's an ideal which many people in Western societies find very attractive, but it is one that has its price...the subjugation of individual achievement. To make it work, Western Samoan society is rigidly structured. Each person knows his or her position within it and shows great respect to elders and betters. Rules of etiquette demand that one does not speak while standing in a *fale!* You must sit down and either cross or cover your legs, as it is considered rude to point your feet at anyone. Nor should one eat while walking in a village or standing in a *fale*. It's considered impolite to drive or ride past an open *fale*. One should walk and, if you're carrying an umbrella, lower it as a sign of respect for the *matai*. Tipping, as everywhere else in the South Pacific, is taken as an insult and, above all, one should remember that Sunday is the Lord's Day and that it is not for nothing that the Samoans are known as the 'Irishmen of the Pacific'.

Samoans of every class go to church on Sundays; the men wear their best *lava-lavas* and brilliant white shirts, the women, their best dresses and hats. They take their religion (49 per cent Protestant, 45 per cent Catholic, a few SDAs and a few Mormons) very seriously. For instance the women do not wear flowers on their hats. But this is not to say that Western Samoans lack the traditional Polynesian warmth and exuberance. Whenever we stopped to look at a particularly impressive church, we were immediately surrounded by dozens of laughing and chattering young children.

As we drove through the villages which cling to the rim of the island, leaving the interior very much underpopulated, we began to pass clusters of women waiting on the roadside with large baskets overflowing with mangos. They were obviously waiting for an expected truck to pick the fruit up for sale at the central market. There was such an abundance of the fruit, which happens to be my favourite, that the road was littered with ones which had escaped and no-one bothered to pick them up. My frugal spirit was sorely tempted, but as they cost only 20c for six, I restrained myself. It would have appeared too mean for words! Instead we bought dozens of them, eating four, five and six each until we were in danger of overdosing. The worry is that with such heady-tasting fruit, it's possible to make yourself sick and then be unable to ever touch or smell, let alone eat another mango again and that would be a tragedy. They were also gorgeously sticky and stained our faces and hands so yellow that we shortly stopped off for a swim...under a church.

The church of the Methodist College of Piula is built on a cliff over the outlet of a small, underground stream of crystal-clear, fresh water. Where the water runs into the lagoon a small rock wall has been built to dam the flow and you can swim, on the one side, in fresh river water and then, merely by slipping over the edge, in salt water. The river has worn out a cavern so that the adventure is to swim into this cave, dive down a couple of metres to where there is a small hole just large enough to admit an adult body and squeeze through this into the next cave along, which also goes out to the sea. Oh dear! It helps if you yell. It relieves the fear. . . and frightens away the nasties in the dark water. Hopefully!

Refreshed (well, at least revitalised from all that extra adrenalin) we drove on around the coast to a village where the road peters out and where we watched as 60 or so schoolchildren, most of them barefoot, and ranging in age from 5 to 15, did marching drill under the scrutiny of a man in a semi-military uniform.

When we left we began to climb up over the mountainous eastern end of the island. Conditions in the back of our jeep were pretty uncomfortable and noisy, so we stopped every half an hour or so to change over and to take turns in the back. One of these stops was to watch the traditional Samoan travesty of a game of cricket. No bails, stumps (or rather three rough sticks) a metre tall, bowling end alternating with each ball, a soft ball, no overs, and a batting style to make a former serious cricketer like me wince. But fun. The pitch was just the open grass between huts with a strip in the middle worn down by constant running. The ball, whacked with an oversized, roughly-hewn bat, sailed over the huts and in among the coconut palms almost every time.

Once they had us as open-mouthed spectators, there was plenty of good-natured chaffing. I guess the game is a leftover from when the Brits were pushing their weight around in the area, but it surely has developed a style all of its own and, as the MCC were so upset by Kerry Packer, they would most definitely choke with indignation over cricket Samoan style!

Our next stop was made to admire two of the largest banyan trees I've ever seen and the next was at a small roadside shop to buy some soft drinks. Although it was overcast, the day was very hot and Zara and I, at least, were still recovering from the boat trip. We felt rather drained and disembodied. Zara felt the worst because she also had a sore throat and when I looked inside her mouth I could see that it was infected. 'I'll give you something when we get back home,' I reassured her and she didn't complain again, though it must have been painful. Both children have learnt from their travelling to stoically sit out situations like these.

We clustered around the top step which ran along the front of the shop and talked to the girl who worked there. Along with other goodies, the shop sold Mr Snickers, Babe Ruth, Hershey bars and additional American confectionary. We asked her if there was much demand for American products.

'Oh yes,' she nodded. 'After all, many Samoans work over in American Samoa—the wages are much higher. They develop a taste for things American. Also of course we see advertisements on the TV, which we pick up from Pago, so it's not really surprising.'

That evening, having started Zara on a course of antibiotics, we left her and Sean at home and went out to meet up again with the *Mataora*'s passengers and crew in the main bar at Aggie's. They were full of the news that Arch the cook had become so plastered in the bar during the afternoon that he had literally had to be carried back to the boat, and that Turi had cooked the evening meal for them all. Poor lovesick Arch.

After a while we decided that we'd go and check out the Tusitali Hotel. Herman and Turi came also. The rest were too firmly entrenched to move. The Tusitali, at the other end of the waterfront, is the only other hotel of international standing in Apia. It is modern and attractive and its patrons are conspicuously different from those at Aggie's. The Tusitali gets the younger, Samoan set. There was quite a crowd standing around the main dining area which had been cleared of tables and chairs for the evening's show. It was a magnificent *fale,* with handhewn posts and cross beams wrapped with sennit cord in elaborate patterns, but Turi was very dismissive of the girls.

'They call that dancing!' She wrinkled her pretty little nose. 'I could do better than that.'

I'm sure she could have. It was far slower and lacked the vitality and aggression of Cook Island dancing and music. The one good part was a display of fire dancing by a man who was heavily tatooed from his waist to his knees in traditional Samoan style. We were told that during the colonial period this art form very nearly died out, as indeed it has done in New Zealand, but that with the coming of independence in Samoa, it once more became acceptable.

When it was over, leaving him with at least one painful singe on his thigh and me with the worry that if this happened frequently enough, he might burn off his patterns, the four of us went out onto the patio around the swimming pool where we talked for some long time. Turi, still aching for Rakahanga and for the half of herself she'd left behind there...Herman, still unsure whether it would be possible for him to make a life in the islands for himself and his family.

'I love it here,' he said, 'but I'm not sure I could make a permanent home here. My wife wants to, of course. It's her home. But I would miss Europe and the snow. I love to cross-country ski and I have a good life there. There's my job...it's not that bad...and my friends.'

'If you think of it that way,' Iain said, 'it's too difficult a step to take. Better not to think of it as a final step...cutting yourself off forever, that sort of thing. After all you can always go back. Europe won't disappear.'

'My job would if I gave it up.'

'But you could always find another. Doing something...anything. That's the great thing about being fortunate enough to have been born when and where you were. You own your own home. You're not going to starve are you.'

'No.' He was a little hesitant. 'But...well...it's a big step.'

'Into the grave is a bigger one.'


Although I wasn't expecting it to be, the following morning proved one of the most aesthetically satisfying of my life. I know Trish feels the same way... and Herman too. Zara and Sean probably don't, although it will, I hope, stick in their memories...something to think about later.

A few kilometres from the centre of Apia, along one of the roads leading across the island, is a beautiful old nineteenth-century mansion called Vailima which has been preserved and well cared for over the years and is now the official residence of the president of Samoa.

Early in the morning, after we'd had breakfast, we drove out to the house and along a tree-lined road beside it called 'The Road of Loving Hearts'. At the end of the road, which is less than a kilometre long, is a small, but beautiful botanical garden. It sits at the foot of Mt Vaea, a steep, jungle-clad mountain. We parked the car under a tree.

The morning was cloudless and already very warm as we began to follow a narrow path that wound its way into the dense rainforest and up a long valley. We knew we were in for a fairly long walk...about half an hour or so, we thought, but within a very short time, as we were cut off from any cooling breezes, and the damp jungle gave off more and more of its moisture, we began to sweat profusely.

'How far have we got to go?' the kids were asking.

'Until we get to the top,' we kept telling them. 'It can't be far.'

But the track just kept winding and zig-zagging upwards...seemingly endlessly. The humidity was oppressive but the surroundings were wonderful. The foliage was green and dank, but it was also large and luxurious. It had a primaeval, prehistoric quality. There were huge ferns and tangled vines, spectacular sprays of tree orchids and shiny leaves on enormous trees. Occasionally, as the path climbed across the steep face of a hillside, there would be a clear break in the foliage through which we could glimpse other parts of the rugged hills and valleys, without seeing any signs of habitation. Apart from the occasional sound of a 'whip' bird and the whistling of other birds, there was a wonderful silence.

Finally, after almost an hour, we came out on to a big spur near the top of the mountain, from where we looked out over a magnificent panorama... Apia harbour below us in the distance and the sea, sweeping off to a far, blue horizon. To our right and hundreds of metres below us, was Vailima, the presidential mansion we'd passed earlier. It sat, small and white, in the centre of spacious lawns. To our left, beside us in the middle of the spur on which we were standing, was the tomb of the man who once owned the grand house below—a tomb which bears one of the most famous epitaphs in the world and which was the reason for our long trek up the mountain.

It reads:

Under the wide and starry sky,
Dig my grave and let me lie.
Glad did I live and gladly die
And I laid me down with a will
this be the verse you grave for me
here he lies where he longed to be
home is the sailor home from the sea
and the hunter home from the hill.
*Robert Louis Stevenson 1850-1894*

Stevenson, the masterful author of *Treasure Island, Kidnapped, Dr Jekyll and Mr Hyde, The Master of Ballantrae* and many others, came to live in Samoa in 1890. He was dying of T.B. and he knew he had only a few years to live. But by the time of his death he had endeared himself so much to Samoans that they enshrined him as one of their own heroes. 'Tusitale' they used to call him...'the teller of tales'. He was so widely loved in Samoa that when he died there was universal grief throughout the country. Great crowds of weeping mourners carried his body up the hillside to its present burial site. Eventually his American wife, Fanny Van der Grift Osborne, was also buried beside him with an epitaph that Stevenson had written before his own death:

Teacher, tender comrade, wife,
A fellow-farer true through life
Heart-whole and soul-free,
The august father gave to me.

*1914*

And there they lie together, in what must be one of the most beautiful settings for a grave in the world.

*Kidnapped* had been one of the books we had read with Zara and Sean during our stay in the little cottage in Somerset over the previous 12 months, so when the children put two and two together, they were impressed.

The idea that the man who had written about a desperate chase and murderous happenings in the Scottish Highlands could have been living here on this remote tropical island was quite something. They copied the inscriptions down to be transferred later into their project books.

At the bottom of the hill, after a much easier walk down, we swam in the clear, cool fresh waters of a mountain pool before taking off on a drive deeper into the mountains to a spectacular gorge in which a tumbling river had cut a series of beautiful pools and waterfalls. The water from each pool poured over a succession of sloping rockfaces down which you could slide...if you were game enough. The place is called, appropriately enough, 'Sliding Rocks', and is a favourite picnic and play area for locals on the weekends. When we arrived, however, it was deserted. We had asked directions from a Samoan woman at the top of the valley and then clambered down a steep narrow path through dense jungle towards the sound of falling water.

It was an idyllic spot with three different 'slides' of varying steepness. Zara and Sean were first to go, with screams of delight, followed by demands that we try the slides also. Soon both Trish and I and Herman had all slid down the various falls and the valley was echoing with our shouts and laughter.

After a while we paused for a lunch of mangos and bananas we'd bought at the market earlier in the morning. Then, after another half an hour or so of swimming and sliding, we left the place for another drive, this time heading towards the western end of Upolu Island.

The road, lined with simple Samoan houses, the open-sided *fales*, was absolutely beautiful; lush, tropical vegetation all the way, with scores of brilliant flame trees in blossom. You'd wonder why anyone would ever want to leave...and yet they do...in droves.

Although Western Samoa is the most populous Polynesian nation in the world, there are large numbers who have left their native islands to live in other lands—some 70 000 altogether. Of these, 17 000 are in Hawaii, 20 000 in the United States (mainly California), 20 000 in New Zealand and the remainder in Australia and other Pacific islands.

At the western tip of Upolu, which we reached before long (the whole island is only 80 kilometres from end to end), we could see in the distance the huge, ragged bulk of the big island Savai'i. Its irregular skyline loomed in the midday haze across the 20-kilometre-wide strait which separates it from Upolu. Savai'i, although it is 50 per cent larger than Upolu, has only about one-third of the population. It is a rugged and, as yet, little-developed island with mountains reaching almost 2000 metres in height . . . several of them are active volcanoes.

At Mulifanua, as we rounded Upolu's western tip, we began to skirt the vast coconut plantations operated there by the Western Samoa Trust Estates Corporation (WSTEC). This is one of the largest plantations in the world—certainly the largest in the South Pacific. It was laid out—tens of thousands of trees—in perfectly straight lines by the Germans during their years in power in Samoa prior to the First World War. It has apparently been remarkably successful and productive, which is just as well, because Samoa's economy has been heavily dependent on its exports of copra, as well as cocoa and bananas, *too* dependent perhaps. Fluctuating prices on the world market have sharply cut returns to Samoa over the past few years and forced them to look to new industries. Timber and cattle farming apparently hold considerable promise as it has only recently been discovered that conditions for raising beef cattle in Samoa are amongst the best in the world and the industry is growing rapidly.

On our way back to town we came upon a second freshwater spring, similar to the one in which we'd swum at Piula, near the Methodist College. Here, on the opposite side of the island, the large pool of wonderfully clear water also ran from under the rocks into the sea, but in this location a dozen or so people . . . men and women . . . were using it for their daily ablutions and also to wash their clothes. One of the men, like the Samoans of old and the man we'd seen at the Tusitale Hotel, was tattooed all over his body, from neck to knees.

That evening we said goodbye to the *Mataora* which was almost ready to sail for Pago Pago. We went on board and chatted for a while with Arch the cook and Lance and Bo . . . as well as Turi Bishop and Suwarrow. I experienced a sharp pang of regret. I felt . . . and Trish said later that she did too . . . that a little piece of my life was slipping away.

About every couple of months or so I am compelled, by being physically unable to do otherwise, to spend a day in bed. Ideally with a bunch of grapes and the *Women's Weekly,* back issues only, nothing as demanding as a recent copy. The following day was just such an occasion. No good fighting it. I knew from the moment I awoke. All the symptoms. I hate my body for not living up to my demands, but I might as well give in. I'm more trouble than I'm worth if I try to stay upright.

We were awoken at 5 a.m. by desperate knockings from Herman. The taxi which was supposed to have picked him up at 4.30 to take him in to Aggie's, there to connect with the airport bus, had not arrived. Would Iain please drive him in? I slid back into unconsciousness.

During the rest of the morning I was aware of Iain coming and going; parcelling up stuff to send ahead to Australia, research material, books, black-lipped oyster shells, etc.

It was oppressively hot, as if building up to a storm and, believe it or not, I *was* able to retreat to three-year-old issues of the *Women's Weekly*; yes, they even reach the islands of the Pacific. In my debilitated condition, the people in the photographs, the articles, the advertisements, all looked comfortingly familiar.

In the early afternoon Francis asked if we would like to move across to the rather more private cottage at the far end of the large garden. Perhaps she thought that if I was going to fade away, it would impinge less on the family if I did it there! The people who had been staying in the cottage had moved out, leaving only one young New Zealand doctor. Iain packed up and carried our gear across and I moved from bed to bed like some poor version of the wilting Lady of the Camellias.

Iain had checked on transport to American Samoa. The boat, a ferry, would leave the following evening, for an overnight journey to Pago Pago at a cost of $7.00. 'Or would you prefer to fly?' he asked. That took 15 minutes and cost $30.

'You decide,' I said pathetically and retreated to a short story, secure and happy in the foreknowledge that, as ever, good would triumph over bad. It did and I slept some more and awoke feeling considerably better.

Iain had cooked a meal and, as the doctor, Peter Coleman, had returned, we ate together and then sat talking for a while before he went back to the hospital.

Later that night the temperature suddenly dropped and the storm broke. Violent and tropical-heavy.

It seems to me that during this narrative we've mentioned 'heavy downpours' on more than one occasion. . . tropical rainstorms in which the heavens have opened and water has bucketed down with a vengeance. It becomes a little difficult, when you experience these things, to believe that they can become any heavier and that you can find new superlatives to describe them. Sean's comment is perhaps as good as any. He said, 'This is something else.' My notes for that Saturday night and the following day read: 'Incredible rain. . . the heaviest we have ever seen. Fantastic!'

'Is it like this at the beginning of every rainy season, do you think?' I asked Peter Coleman, who had just come from the hospital.

'Well, I don't really know, but I think this is a bit unusual. They say there's a tropical cyclone coming.'

'Oh great,' I muttered. 'Great. Just when we're going to take a boat for Pago. Do they say where it is? Has it been on the radio?'

'Somewhere to the northwest and coming this way, but I don't know if they've made any predictions about when, or if it will actually come over Upolu or Apia.'

'Well, at least we'll be heading east. . . away from it,' Trish put in. 'I hope the ship can travel fast enough.'

'It's only about eight or nine hours to Pago. . . so you should be well in front of it.'

After finishing our meal of chicken and vegetables and cleaning up in the little flat, we said goodbye to Peter and then sloshed across the lawn to pay Mrs Moore and to ask her to call a taxi to take us to the wharf where we were to board the big inter-island ferry, the *Queen Salemasina*.

It was dark and still teeming with rain as we struggled out of the cab to carry our packs onto the vessel through the frontloading vehicular access ramp, only to find we had to stand and wait in a long queue...(fortunately just out of the rain)...to pass through immigration departure proceedings. At the head of the queue there was an empty desk...no immigration officer in sight.

Things got a little fraught amongst the hundred or so people standing in line. A few scuffles broke out between those who'd been waiting in one position for some time and others who tried to jump their places. Several policemen arrived to quieten things down and bring some order to the situation, which was beginning to have overtones of Gilbert and Sullivan. The immigration official eventually arrived and, after a further 20 minutes we were finally 'processed' and allowed to climb to the upper deck...an enclosed area filled with rows of moulded plastic chairs and tables.

It was clear, even before we moved from our moorings, that neither the tables nor the chairs were going to be used for the purpose they were originally intended. Everybody simply lay down on the floor, wherever there was room. We wondered if perhaps they knew something we didn't. In any event, realising that there was obviously not going to be any entertainment, refreshments or any other diversion for the duration of the voyage, we too staked out our claims on some floor space, underneath one of the tables. Sean chose a section of the luggage rack.

Just before we sailed, the intercom came to life and a scratchy record was played. It was sung in Samoan but it was quite recognisable as a hymn. Perhaps it was just because it was Sunday, but then again—maybe it was intended as a prayer for those in peril on the sea. The whole thing was acquiring an atmosphere which was not really conducive to our peace of mind.

Soon the *Queen Salemasina* slipped her moorings and we headed slowly through the darkness out of Apia harbour towards the open sea. Within minutes we knew why everyone had gone to ground...there was a big sea running. It was not so much a storm, just a huge swell, which tossed us around like a rowing boat. We all dosed ourselves with Drammamine anti-seasick tablets and settled down to try to sleep through it all.

It was extremely difficult, as we were rolled and thrown all over the place. Several people were sick, but fortunately we weren't among them... probably because of the pills. We even managed to get some sleep on the hard deck floor before we eventually came into the lee of the island of Tutuila. We followed the coastline, about a kilometre offshore for about an hour until, around 6 a.m., we eventually turned into the magnificent harbour of Pago Pago.

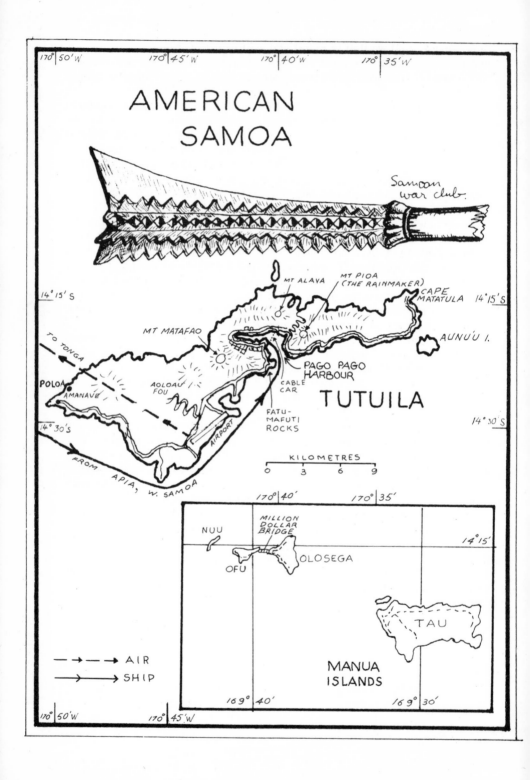

# AMERICAN SAMOA

Samoan war club.

MT ALAVA
MT PIOA (THE RAINMAKER)
CAPE MATATULA

14° 15' S                                           14° 15' S

MT MATAFAO

AUNU'U I.

TO TONGA

PAGO PAGO HARBOUR

POLOA

AMANAVE

AOLOAU FOU

CABLE CAR

TUTUILA

FATU-MAFUTI ROCKS

14° 30' S                                           14° 30' S

AIRPORT

FROM APIA, W. SAMOA

KILOMETRES
0    3    6    9

170° 40'                 170° 35'

NUU

MILLION DOLLAR BRIDGE

14° 15'

OFU

OLOSEGA

TAU

AIR
SHIP

MANUA ISLANDS

169° 40'                          169° 30'

170° 50' W            170° 45' W

## 15 TUTUILA
### 'A battle for survival'

'This is the Power of the Pacific...Radio WVUV, saying hi there to all you sleepy heads.' I flicked the switch cutting the hard-sell announcer off in his prime.

'Aw gee Mom,' Sean mimicked. He was energetically engrossed in the invariable inspection tour which he and his dad instantly make of any new hotel room; opening drawers and wardrobes (after all some careless guest might have left a bar of gold or at least an old magazine), turning on taps, light and power switches, swishing back curtains and exclaiming over the view, trying out the beds and the easy chairs, plugging in the electric kettle, looking to see if there were any 'free' drinks in the fridge and of course simultaneously turning on radio and television and flicking through the channels.

'No.' Sean's hand had reached out again for the switch and I fixed him with my special look. It was all too much for me so early in the morning and so suddenly in a new and very different country.

'You should see the pool!' Zara yelled from the balcony.

'Pool!' Sean exclaimed and they were gone, leaving me to collect my thoughts and adjust to the idea of having a room in the Rainmaker Hotel overlooking Pago Pago harbour which vies very closely with Moorea's Cook's Bay for the title of the most beautiful harbour in the South Pacific.

So, how come we were staying in such a swish place? Well...when the *Queen Salemasina* docked, it was only 6 a.m. and even after the immigration officials had inspected every stamp in our passports (the more you've travelled the more suspicious they are) and made Iain unpack his painstakingly done-up parcel which he had been unable to post in Apia because the post office had been closed, it was *still* only 6.30 a.m. The rain was bucketing down, we were pretty strung out from the crossing and we were hungry. When we asked where we could get some breakfast, everyone shook their heads and said nothing opened until at least 7.30 a.m.

'The Rainmaker might have something open,' one of the seamen said.

'Let's lash out and have a slap-up breakfast there,' I suggested. Iain and the kids looked so woebegone, I thought it would give us all a lift. We sloshed our way for about a kilometre along the small main street, which I found pleasingly low-key and most unlike what I had geared myself up to expect...a milder version of Waikiki. The hotel was also a happy surprise. It's the best, in fact it's the only real hotel in town as the other places there are more like guest houses.

From the menu in the snack bar downstairs, we chose flapjacks and honey. Well, why not. When in Rome and all that. But first up, bacon and eggs and to follow, those strange, completely tasteless pieces of aerated stuff which resemble the material from which egg cartons are made and which Americans call bread.

Back up in the lobby of the hotel we were asking if we could stow our packs while we looked around town for some place to stay when a huge man, and I mean huge, like nearly two metres and built like the proverbial brickhouse, came out from an office behind the reception desk and introduced himself as Tony Brown, the hotel's manager. He wanted to know where we were from and all the rest. We asked Tony about himself too. 'I'm from here originally,' he said, 'but I went to school Stateside for a while and then I joined the police force in Hawaii.'

I made some comment about him being the right build for the job; I was getting a crick in my neck just looking up at him! He smiled. 'Yeh. But size ain't everything. One day I got shot up...'

'How?' Sean wasn't going to let a remark like that slip by...and listened open-mouthed to Tony's recounting of the bank hold-up in which he played heroes and was shot for his trouble.

'Then my Mom, she says to me, "Tony, it's time you quit and got yourself a proper job." So I did.' (Difficult to imagine a man that size paying such attention to his 'Mom!') 'I went back to college and trained in hotel management. Worked around the place, then came back home here and opened up a nightclub of my own. Last year I was asked to take over The Rainmaker and so here I am. Where you folks staying?'

We explained that we were travelling for several months and that, although his hotel looked just great, we would have to look for someplace more moderately priced. 'You're going to stay here...for free,' Tony insisted. 'After the travelling all of you have done, it will be my pleasure.'

So that's how come we got to stay in The Rainmaker in Pago Pago (please pronounce Pango Pango). It's called falling on your feet.

It seemed as though it might rain forever so the only thing to do was to ignore it, which is what the kids had done as they lapped up and down the hotel pool. Tony pointed us in the right direction for the almost adjacent tourist office and when we arrived there, having run from sheltered spot to sheltered spot, we found that he had phoned ahead and we were therefore greeted by Chief Makaa Nui like honoured guests and offered a sightseeing trip in their office car later in the day.

When I say chief I should explain that Makaa Nui is not a talking chief. The social system of both the Samoas is so complex that even the Poms could learn a thing or two from it! So that, while being a chief carries a fair amount of clout, it's not so august a position as being a talking chief. We tried over and over again, by asking many people, to understand how the scale worked, whether one slid or was pushed up or down, whether one was to the manor born, so to speak, or could have greatness thrust upon one. But being English and unable to explain my own country's class system to an outsider, I should have known better than to try to come to grips with the Samoans'. It was good enough that Makaa Nui was as helpful and friendly as Tony Brown.

In downtown Pago Pago post office—the full American deal complete with mail clerks in uniforms—we queued among the Christmas decorations to finally post ahead to ourselves our big parcel. Christmas decorations? The first we had seen. So incongruous in that tropical place were the snow scenes of Santa Claus and sleighs drawn by reindeer.

We took a bus, a smaller version of Tahiti's 'le truck'—glassless windows and blaring music—to the far side of the harbour, past the scores of white-uniformed workers coming off shift from the fish-canning factory which is the next largest employer after the government.

Nearly half the labour force, about three and a half thousand people, work for the government. The canneries employ around one and a half thousand. The minimum wage is between $1.25 and $2 an hour. All of this is unique in the South Pacific; large-scale government and private employment and minimum wages. But then, American Samoa is unique. Its nationals are also nationals of a country 10 000 kilometres away. It is an unincorporated territory of the USA administered by the US Department of the Interior. The flood of money from the mainland is almost embarrassing. There are, in fact, not enough goods and services on which to spend it all. A combination of national fashionable guilt over 'owning' a Pacific island, so unfashionable in the latter half of the twentieth century, and a desire not to be stuck with a charge of exploitation, has driven the Americans to deluge the Samoans with such lavish care and hard cash that, in the course of only a generation or two, the people have almost totally deserted their own way of life. American Samoans no longer produce copra. But then why the hell should they when it's such back-breaking work for so little reward.

We ate lunch in a Chinese café surrounded by other gringos. . .average working Americans, nothing glamorous. We could have been taking a lunch break in downtown Dallas.

The rain, which hadn't stopped but which had eased up slightly, burst forth with renewed vigour as we took the bus back, so that by the time we reached the centre of town, which is strung out around the bay, we had to jump from the vehicle across the spreading pools of water which were quickly covering the road. From the comparative protection of the post office porch, where we sheltered, we were to witness a half-hour spectacular as Pago was hit by the edge of the tropical storm which Peter Coleman had warned us about in Apia. Thank heavens we weren't still at sea.

High winds buffeted the palm trees lining the road, shredding their long fronds. Traffic came to a standstill and people, their light clothing drenched and clinging to them, ran for shelter. The road became a river, glistening in the moody grey light. Lightning flashed, thunder rumbled. And we were made uncomfortably aware of how puny people and all their quite pathetically paltry concrete achievements are. Not to be too poetic about it all. . .it was as if a giant stalked, whistling down the main street, by his sheer size disturbing the air. And all of us little ant-sized people moved tremulously out of his way. Just as suddenly as he had come, he went, the air rushing in behind to fill the vacuum created by his passing, and everyone came off the walls, laughing a little nervously, to resume again their self-important lives.

'This is the village where five people were killed in an avalanche a month ago.' Moana stopped the car under a large flamboyant tree. She had driven us during the afternoon from the Tourist Office, where she worked, along the road which, as ever in the South Pacific, clung to the coastal rim, to the western end of Tutuila.

American Samoa's total land area is only 200 sq. kilometres, compared to Western Samoa's almost 300 sq. kilometres. Tutuila, the main island of American Samoa, is really on the top of several ancient volcanoes. It has a land area of only 134 sq. kilometres with its highest peak, Mt Matafao, rising to just over 700 metres above Pago Pago harbour.

One effect of Tutuila's steep terrain is that there is very little flat cultivable land. Another is that heavy rain inevitably washes large quantities of soil down the mountainsides. Surprising, really, that this tragedy which Moana told us about was the first time in many years that people had been buried alive in a mudslide.

'Look.' Moana pointed and we saw where the thick, red volcanic soil had torn a path through the heady green of the jungle. It lay like a tear running down the face of the mountainside. 'The dead people were all of one family,' she said. 'The earth slid right through their house, which used to be there.' She indicated a scattering of timber frames 100 metres away. 'It happened in the middle of the night, they were buried as they slept.'

Moana had lived 'Stateside' as they say. . . as also had almost every other American Samoan to whom we talked. 'I went to college for four years in L.A. I loved it. But this is better. For a start, it's home and, apart from that we have the benefits of being American added to the joy of being a Pacific islander. What more could anyone want?'

When we ran out of road (the rest of the northern coast is served only by boat), we turned around and started back and Moana showed us around her home village of Amanave. As in all the other villages we had seen, there were no traditional *fales:* just regular rectangular wood or fibro places with tin roofs. They had a suburban look about them, as though misplaced from the outskirts of a large American city. No family graves in the front garden. No taro patch out back and only small, forlorn-looking, neglected coconut plantations.

By the time we got back to Moana's office in time for her to knock off at 5 p.m. (9 to 5 in the South Pacific?!) the rain looked as though it might be going to give it a rest for a while, so we walked back to town.

Actually what most visitors call Pago is really a combination of two small towns: Pago Pago and Fagotoga (pronounced Fangotonga), plus the even smaller settlements of Utulei, Anua and Lepua. Twenty thousand of the territory's total population of just over 27 000 live in this small area which is spread around Pago Pago harbour and nestles under the looming sides of the Rainmaker Mountain, the 563-metre high Mt Pioa.

I first heard of the Rainmaker years ago when I read Somerset Maugham's novel about Sadie Thompson, a lady of repute. I then had no idea where Pago Pago was, but it sure sounded exotic and now that I had eventually got there, of course we had to go see the actual Sadie Thompson's boarding house in which Maugham set his scene. An unimposing, flat-faced, boxlike weatherboard structure with the words 'Max Haleck's Godown No.1' painted along its decidedly unexotic exterior. A supermarket warehouse. Sadie has turned up her toes and the waterfront has been cleaned up, and that's progress, or something.

Samoans are beginning to realise that all this is happening so fast that unless they capture its passing, it will be gone and forgotten. In order to prevent this, there is, on the waterfront, the Jean Hayden Museum, named after the wife of an ex-governor. The odd thing about this museum is that, unlike most museums, a visit there is like stepping forward not back in time. Forward because this is what will eventually happen in the rest of the Pacific, inevitably. Sealed in glass display cases are examples of arts and crafts which are lost to American Samoans and yet are still a part of every-day life in most other islands of the Pacific. I wondered what the one-armed pastor on Rangiroa would have made of the explanation of copra production and what Ionue on Manihiki would have thought about their information on fishing and diving techniques in the Pacific. Very soon, in Tonga, we would see whole villages involved in producing tapa cloth. In the Pago Pago museum it was treated with the reverence reserved for an ancient art form.

In the middle of the warm night, sleeping with the balcony windows wide open onto Pago's harbour, I was woken by a foul smell. It took me a while to realise that it was the stench of fish coming from the cannery.

In the morning the rain had abated somewhat but the sky was still overcast and there were heavy showers every now and then. Nevertheless the temperature was warm and although when we went out and walked into town we wore our rain jackets we soon found it was too hot to keep them on.

After another American breakfast of flapjacks and maple syrup at a small café in the town, we went again to the tourist office to meet up with one of the other officials, Misi Tialavea, who had volunteered to take us on a drive around the rest of the island in the office's pick-up truck.

We drove off to the west again... covering some of the road we'd been over on the previous afternoon with Moana. But Misi, a large man who was in his mid-40s, wanted to take us this time to a small town in the mountains at the centre of the island. As we drove along the coast road, before heading inland, we passed two dramatically beautiful islets of grey volcanic rock that were standing clear of the water probably 20 metres tall—like thumbs sticking out of the lagoon. They were only 40 or 50 metres away from the shoreline and the road. Their sheer sides were covered, from about four or five metres above the water to the top with lush vegetation and both had a fringe of coconut palms at the top.

'Those are the "flower-pot" rocks,' Misi told us as we drove by. 'They have a very interesting legend attached to them. Do you know of it?'

We shook our heads.

'The story is that, many years ago in the olden times of Samoa a couple came from the western islands here to Tutuila by canoe. The man was very old but the woman was young and beautiful. As they approached the shore, the old man, exhausted by the ordeal of the voyage, began to die. The young woman stepped out of the canoe into the shallows, and attempted to bring it in to land. But the local villagers, who had gathered on the shore, began throwing rocks at the couple and eventually stoned her to death. The canoe was tipped over and the old man fell into the water where he also died. The two bodies... so the story goes... turned instantly to stone, becoming the two islands we see now... two pillars of stone as a constant and shameful reminder to the villagers of this awful murder.

'Both the rocks and the village... here it is now...' Misi pointed as we drove, to a small, tidy collection of bungalows on either side of the road, '...are to this day called "Fatumafuti" which in our language means man (fatu) and woman (mafuti).'

We drove on for a while in silence and it occurred to me that many of the old Polynesian legends I had heard or read about revolved around either thwarted love or tragedy...most of them seemed to contain at least some element of great sadness.

In ancient times of course, American Samoa was not a separate entity from the rest of the islands that make up the independent nation of Western Samoa. But in the centuries preceding European arrival Tutuila was apparently a subordinate island to Upolu in Western Samoa and was used as a place of banishment for troublesome chiefs. Perhaps one such incident formed the basis of the Fatumafuti legend.

The whole island grouping of Western and American Samoa is believed to have been settled at least 2500 years ago. Although no significant archaeological research or exploration has been carried out in American Samoa, Lapita pottery found in Western Samoa has been dated as far back as 800 BC.

We drove on under a lowering sky heading for Apaloau Fou, the highest village on the island, where we would have had, Misi assured us, had there been ideal conditions, a superb panoramic view of the western end of the island and the sea beyond. As it was, the sky opened and the rain poured down in torrents. Zara and Sean who had been sitting in the back, crowded into the cabin of the truck to sit on our knees, while Misi turned the vehicle around and drove back towards town.

As we drove, he told us one or two more of the old myths and legends associated with the island's past and we felt again the strength of the bonds that unite the Polynesian people across the Pacific. Whether they be technically American citizens, French, New Zealand, Chilean or whatever, they are first Polynesians. One feels, at times like this, that the overlay of European society imposed during the past few centuries is really quite superficial...and that it has hardly touched the inner core of the Polynesians.

The first European in the area was, once again, the Dutch admiral who discovered Easter Island and Western Samoa, Jacob Roggeveen. He turned up at Tutuila in 1722, at the same time that he 'discovered' the other islands in the Samoan group. The history of American Samoa from that time onwards is basically the same as Western Samoa's (see pp. 137-8), until the partitioning of the island group by the big powers, Britain, Germany and the United States in 1899. At that point, when the US took over Tutuila and six other small islands, including the Manua group, some 100 kilometres to the east, it had no real machinery to run a colony, so President McKinley declared the islands to be the responsibility of the US Navy.

In many ways Tutuila was a great prize for America. The deep-water harbour at Pago Pago is unquestionably one of the finest in the Pacific, if not *the* finest, and in the late nineteenth century American shipping interests foresaw its increasing use in the proposed trans-Pacific shipping services. For the US Navy it would prove important as a coaling station for their warships. But with the advent of oil and major shifts in strategic and trading patterns, Pago Pago never achieved the prominence expected of it at the turn of the century.

Although the island had been ceded to the United States by the Samoan chiefs, the US government did not accept it as a territory, but as a protectorate, which remained under Naval administration, with the commander of the Tutuila Naval Station, as it was called, designated as governor.

During World War II a huge influx of American marines suddenly changed the quiet Naval station into a strategically important training and staging area in the war against Japan. Although the US had technically run the place for 40 years, the lives of the Samoan people had remained basically quiet and undisturbed. But, with the presence of such a large force of American military personnel, their way of life could hardly continue uninterrupted. For the first time Samoans got a real taste of 'the American way'. Certainly there were modern roads, airstrips, docks and modern medical facilities built, but there was also beer, chewing gum, swing music, plenty of money and scores of other aspects of Western culture which tended to disorient, if not immediately fragment, Samoan society.

But then, in 1945, the marines left almost as suddenly as they had arrived and Samoa returned to the quiet, peaceful place it had been before the War, leaving large numbers of local people a little distracted, somewhat disaffected and in general, wondering what had struck them.

In 1951, President Truman declared that the US Navy should hand over administration of the islands to the Department of the Interior and that American Samoa, now an 'incorporated territory' of the US, be run by a civilian governor. However, despite the switch-over, there were few real changes in the way the place was administered. Certainly, from the people's viewpoint, there was practically no difference and, over the next 10 years there was a period of relative quiet and practically no development.

In 1961, however, the scene changed almost overnight. The then recently-inaugurated President John Kennedy sent out a new governor, H. Rex Lee, to Samoa with specific instructions to 'get the place moving!' Lee arrived in Pago Pago and launched into what he described as a 'complete rehabilitation programme to correct the lagging economic and social development' in the territory. With special funds allocated by congress, American Samoa was forthwith plunged headlong, once more, into the twentieth century. During the six years of Governor Lee's administration the islands were put through a massive and dynamic modernisation programme which brought new harbour facilities, new roads, a new hospital, widespread electrification and sewerage schemes, good schools, a jet airport, a luxury hotel (The Rainmaker) at Pago Pago, a thriving fish-canning industry and television broadcasts for schools.

But all these new developments also had some bad side effects. Older Samoans saw the imminent breakdown of their old social systems. As one Samoan leader said of the steam-rolling Americanisation of Samoa, 'We are engaged in a battle for the survival of ourselves as a people, for the things that are dear to us and for the way of life that has sustained us since the beginning of our history.'

Looking at the place now, almost 20 years after Governor Lee's crash programme, one feels very mixed emotions about American Samoa. It *is* very Americanised, and without doubt one of the most affluent islands in the Pacific, with more facilities, comforts, mod cons etc. than almost any other island grouping. But in moving towards this seemingly enviable position, the people of American Samoa have had to accept such large doses of paternalism from 'Uncle Sam', that, as Trish has already pointed out, there are now virtually no indigenous industries on the islands at all. Almost everybody works for the government or for the two giant US-owned fish-canning factories, Van Kamp and Starkist.

There are some quite amazing examples of unnecessary and probably counter-productive American largesse. As soon as anyone reaches the age of 50, for instance, they become eligible for a good 'old-age' pension and substantial weekly food handouts of chicken, tinned meat and fish. Residents of the territory's Manua group of islands, to the east, who attain the age of 50, also become automatically entitled to free airfares to and from the main island of Tutuila whenever they want to fly—as often as they like! In the same islands, the US government has built a $1 million bridge linking two small islands which have a combined population of only a few hundred. Only six or seven cars a day are expected to use the bridge.

Then there is the crazy situation of Samoan supermarkets being filled with cans of tuna that have been caught in local waters, canned in Pago Pago, shipped to the US mainland and then back again by the big American supermarket chains. Even sadder, though, is the fact that it was not Samoans who caught the fish in their own waters. They have no local fishing industry. The two big canning factories are supplied by Japanese, Taiwanese or Korean fleets of fishing boats.

Despite all of this, however, American Samoa has, for the visitor, an extremely pleasant aura about it. Samoan culture is still alive and, although it may not be quite 'well', Samoans are nevertheless still very proud of their heritage and traditions and, in the face of a deluge of American culture, seem to be moving towards a reasonable blending of the two lifestyles.

At present, surprisingly, the territory does enjoy a considerable degree of independence. The legislature of American Samoa consists of 18 senators elected by the county councils and 21 members of a house of representatives, also elected locally. They introduce, debate and pass legislation affecting the whole territory as well as expenditures for the annual budget, which is around US$42 million a year, (a staggering figure for only 30 000 people). Until 1967, almost all bills were suggested and sponsored by the executive branch...that is, the governor.

Now the governor, who is also an elected Samoan, only signs the bills into law. At the time of our visit to American Samoa the governor was a popular figure...Peter Coleman (coincidentally the same name as our doctor friend in Western Samoa), the first elected Samoan to fill the post of governor. He *had* served as governor previously (from 1965 to 1971), but for that period he had been directly appointed by the US Government.

'This is a new road to the other side of the island,' Misi said, as we continued around the island. He turned off the coast road and began climbing a steep, well-surfaced road that ascended a saddle between Mt Alava and Mt Pioa (the Rainmaker). We had returned from the western half of the island, passed through the town, circled right around Pago Pago Harbour and we were now making for the eastern tip of Tutuila island.

'I haven't been up here myself,' Misi told us as we came to the end of the tarred surface and began sliding on a muddy, unfinished road. 'We may not be able to go all the way now. But when it is eventually finished, it will be the first good road linking the southern side of the island to the north.' He handed us a map. 'As you can see, the existing roads all run along the southern shore. There is nothing on the northern side.'

We slithered to a halt. 'We can put some stones in the back to give us weight,' Misi said and we all began collecting large rocks from the roadside. I didn't think it would make much difference, but the additional weight over the truck's rear wheels gave them a better purchase on the slippery road and we managed to climb the rest of the way to where it levelled off at the middle of the saddle.

We stopped there, in misty and overcast conditions, to gaze out over a great sweep of jungled mountains running down to a virtually empty coastline on the northern side of the island.

One often tends to think of the Pacific as having been completely populated and thoroughly explored, yet often during this journey we came upon relatively large areas that were still untouched and unaffected by civilisation...wilderness regions of considerable beauty.

The road running down the far side of the saddle had not been sufficiently graded for us to negotiate it without a four-wheel-drive vehicle, so we backtracked and continued our drive around the sea-level coastal road to the eastern end of Tutuila, passing all the while through a succession of small villages consisting of western-style bungalows. Again we noticed that there were practically none of the open-sided *fales* that were so much a part of the Western Samoan village scene.

'That is my house,' Misi said, pointing to a small, but comfortable-looking, low bungalow opposite a magnificent beach and coral lagoon. Anywhere else, it would have been a million-dollar site. Here, it was just par for the course. Everybody in American Samoa has a great view...from wherever they live.

The only sour note to our drive was the large quantity of litter and garbage we saw in several places along the way: beer and soft-drink cans, food tins, wrappers and cartons. The problems of a Western, consumer-oriented, pre-packaged society, in a paradise like this, seemed totally out of context.

Later that evening we had hamburgers, done with real American flourish, in the café of The Rainmaker Hotel, then relaxed in the cane chairs of the Sadie Thompson bar while Zara and Sean sat glued to the colour TV set in the lounge watching some numbing American soap opera.

The next day we walked up Solo Hill, behind Government House, to the station of the cable car which swings its way out across Pago harbour and up to the top of Mt Alava where there is a giant TV-transmitting aerial. For a while there in the early 70s,

American Samoa had a large-scale programme of television education (Governor Lee's crash programme!). The kids were used as guinea pigs in this new method of teaching, but because of the compact environment and the relatively small number of pupils, it was fairly easy to gauge the results and, after only a few years, it was clear that they were so poor, especially when compared with the expense, that the idea was dropped and schools reverted to the good, old-fashioned teacher/pupil style. A lesson.

The cable car swung out. Way below us, a British container vessel was unloading in port. The actual bird's-eye view. The cable ran ahead for almost two kilometres; one of the longest unsupported cable spans in the world. It looked like a long way down to the water. Plenty of room, you'd think, to fly a plane underneath...if you were crazy enough to want to pull a stunt like that. Well, a few months after our visit to Pago Pago, on Flag Day, a national holiday, that's exactly what some fellow did. An American service pilot, with a crew of seven on board his Lockheed Orion, part of the Stateside contingent for the celebrations, flew under the cable, as he had boasted the night before in the Sadie Thompson bar, that he planned to do. He miscalculated, the tail plane hit the cable, and, out of control, the plane plummetted to the ground, demolishing the entire right wing of The Rainmaker Hotel, all 76 rooms (one of which we had stayed in). Fortunately most people were attending the national day celebrations in the stadium. But one Japanese visitor, standing, minding his own business in the foyer of the hotel, was killed: as were, of course, all the crew members and the gung-ho pilot. No doubt it will come out that he was a Vietnam veteran who found non-combat life pretty tame.

Looking back, I'm rather glad that this event, if it had to happen at all, occurred after and not before our visit, because I would have been even more nervous in that little swinging car than I was pretending not to be. The view from that height was superb and made possible a full appreciation of the dramatic beauty of Pago Pago Bay. The deep blue water, curving back so far into the body of the island that it almost cut it in two, was absolutely spectacular. It also happens to provide just the sort of port in a storm for which all sailors must yearn.

Half-way across, and climbing, we passed over a fleet of moored fishing boats waiting their turn for service or overhaul in the Pago shipyards which are regarded as the best in this part of the South Pacific. Still climbing, we then could see below the two large fish-canning factories, fairly humming with activity and, even at this height, their smell reached us. Then it was into the cloud which hung over Mt Alava.

At that height, just under 500 metres, it was considerably colder and, when we stepped off into the mist, we could quite easily have been on a Scottish moor (on a good day in spring). Skirting the transmitter station, we walked to a look-out point from which, through a break in the cloud, we could see parts of the island rearing up out of the glistening sea below us on the northern shore stretching off into the distance. It was very obvious how empty it was. Surprising how little impact 30 000 people can make, and it's consoling how quickly you can reach areas where they've made no mark at all.

On the way back it was even more discomforting for nervous-of-heights-ninnies like me, because it's a downhill run and impossible not to worry about the efficiency of the braking system. The little cab was crammed with workers from the TV relay station, and only a quarter of the way down, there was a loud shout and the cab jolted to a halt, swinging rather wildly in the air some 300 metres above the water. Oh, dear.

The men kept laughing, even when the car started to climb back up to the top of the mountain again.

'What's the matter?' Sean asked.

As he always teases me about any momentary qualms I may display, I remained outwardly calm and said, 'Nothing much. I expect they just have to fix something.'

'Suppose we'll have to sleep on the mountain,' Zara said matter of factly. 'And I haven't brought my toothbrush.'

Covering nerves with a display of excessive casualness is just one of Zara's little masterpieces.

The car swung into its dock, banging against the metal step, the door was flung open and in jumped another young man, laughing and flushed. The rest all laughed even harder and joshed him in Samoan. . . I guess about the fact that he is always late and that one day they won't come back for him.

Our next planned stopping place after American Samoa were the islands of Tonga. But we particularly wanted to try to enter the group through the 'back door'. . . via its northern islands Vava'u and Ha'apai which were far closer to the Samoan islands than to the main Tongan island of Tongatapu and, so we'd been told, far more beautiful. However, after a couple of abortive 4 a.m. trips to the airport attempting to get standby seats on the little Britten Norman Islander aircraft that flew there, we gave up and decided to fly directly to Tongatapu. It seemed that there were just too many people already booked and wanting to get to these northern islands of the Tonga group and, with Christmas approaching, it was obvious that the situation could hardly improve.

We had checked on what boats were travelling in that direction. There was no regular shipping line, although small ships and fishing craft occasionally carried passengers to the islands. We learnt that we had just missed a boat that had left Pago only a few days before our arrival. Now, with no shipping heading that way within the next week, and with flights fully booked, we had to start thinking of by-passing Vava'u and Ha'apai and going direct to the main Tongan island of Tongatapu and the capital, Nuku'alofa. Hopefully, we could back-track from there to Vava'u and Ha'apai. . .but it would be a 1400-kilometre trip instead of only 800 the more direct way.

Strange how the knowledge that you can't get out of a place, or that it might become difficult for you to leave, tends to make you hasten your arrangements and to leave probably a good deal earlier than you might have under more controlled conditions. This was certainly the case with us in American Samoa. We were now determined to take the next flight to Tongatapu. It would mean flying back through Apia in Western Samoa, but on this main route, operated by Polynesian Airlines, the planes were bigger; De Haviland prop-jet aircraft with around 40 seats which meant that the bookings were not quite so heavy.

We were able to make a booking for ourselves on a flight that evening to Apia and, once it had been arranged, we could relax for the remainder of the day. The weather stayed clear. It was warm and sunny and the sky was a brilliant blue. The harbour, with its dramatic, green mountains rising on all sides, looked particularly beautiful. It was almost as if the place was saying, 'see what you're going to miss', now that we had decided to leave.

We lay for an hour or so on the small harbour beach near the hotel and swam in the clear water. Then, leaving the children swimming, Trish and I walked into town and strolled through some of the little back streets that climb the hillside on the edge of the central area. When we returned, Zara and Sean were full of excitement.

'There's a man here who looks like Ryan O'Neal,' Zara said.

'Maybe it *is* him', Trish said. 'Where did you see him?'

'By the pool. It isn't the real one though, he just looks very like him. And he's Irish. . . I heard him speak. He has a very nice voice. . . and he looks very nice.'

'They're having an Island Night tonight,' Sean put in, 'with dancing and fire-eating and everything. You should see the way they've decorated the whole place. . . around the pool.'

'Do we have to leave tonight?' Zara asked quietly. 'Can't we stay longer?'

'Well. . . we've already got the tickets.' I was a little surprised at their reaction. Obviously there had been other places where we'd all felt like staying a while longer, but this seemed a little different. It was the first time they'd put it quite so definitely. I wondered if we might be pushing the pace along too quickly. . . and if our being constantly on the move was getting to them. Or was it Ryan O'Neal?

'Couldn't we leave on another day? We like it here,' Zara pleaded '. . . and it's going to be fun tonight.'

'Zara,' I began, 'look, my love. . . you know what we've been through during the past couple of days, trying to get to Vava'u and Ha'apai. Now we've got tickets to go to Nuku'alofa and. . . .' I looked at Trish, who gave me one of those looks which says. . . don't be so heavy. . . then turned back to Zara who was clearly close to tears. I hesitated, not knowing what to say. It was a situation that hadn't really presented itself in any way before. Most of the time we just charged on and Zara and Sean happily (or *seemingly* happily) fitted in with *our* overall schedule. Of course, on our previous journeys with them through Africa and South America, they'd both been younger and it was more understandable that they should just fit in with our plans completely. Now, with Zara just turned 13 and Sean almost 12, their independent feelings were being felt more often, but this was the first time they had said that they did not want to move on and that it had become (at least in Zara's case) an emotional issue.

But, there was really no way we were going to change our plans. We. . . that is, Trish and I. . . had taken the bit between our teeth again and we were already looking forward to Tonga. Nevertheless, Zara's feelings were hurt. . . and she was not about to be mollified easily.

In the evening, when we prepared to leave for the airport, she was quiet. . . not sulky. . . just subdued. The situation wasn't helped by the fact that the preparations for the Island Night festivities on the patio around the hotel pool were very attractive and the light over the harbour as dusk approached was almost unbelievably beautiful. The sky turned from a deep blue to a wonderful purple colour. The air was still and warm and all the

Hawaian oil lamps were burning in readiness for the big barbeque and dancing. The whole area was garlanded with flowers and the scent of frangipani and tiare tahiti was heavy on the air. It seemed crazy to have to leave a setting of such beauty.

In the taxi, which took us to the airport, we were all quiet—Zara in particular. I turned from the front seat and saw that, once again, she was almost weeping. I said something like, 'Oh Zara, my love, you mustn't be upset. There're lots of other nice places we'll be going to on the way from here...' But I saw, as I was speaking, that I was only making it worse. There was another piercing look from Trish which said...don't say any more. Just let it be. It was one of those moments where one feels totally inadequate in coping with another person's emotions...and just one small confirmation of the fact that Zara was no longer a child.

A little over an hour and a half later...after a delay in the flight...we were in the air and on our way.

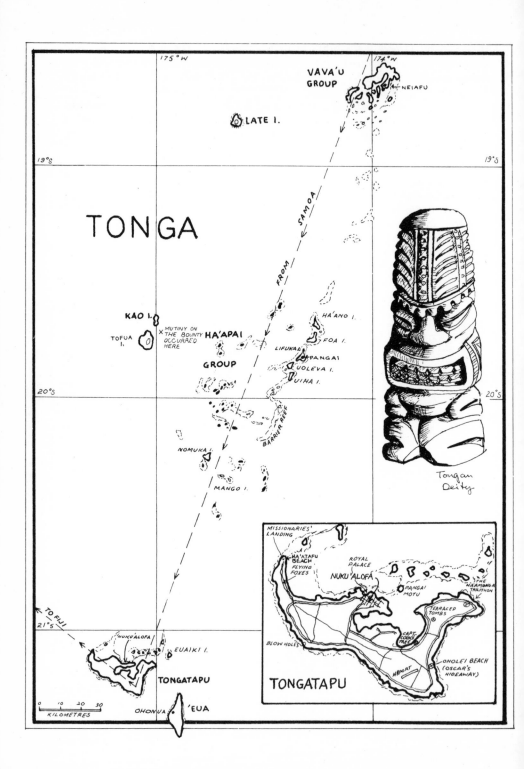

TONGA

175°W
174°W
19°S
19°S

VAVA'U
GROUP
NEIAFU

LATE I.

FROM SAMOA

KAO I.
MUTINY ON
THE BOUNTY
OCCURRED
HERE
TOFUA I.
HA'APAI
GROUP
HA'ANO I.
FOA I.
LIFUKA I.
PANGAI
UOLEVA I.
UIHA I.

20°S
20°S

BARRIER REEF

NOMUKA I.

MANGO I.

Tongan
Deity

TO FIJI
21°S
NUKU'ALOFA
EUAIKI I.
TONGATAPU
OHONUA
'EUA

0  10  20  30
KILOMETRES

MISSIONARIES'
LANDING
HA'ATAFU
BEACH
FLYING
FOXES
ROYAL
PALACE
NUKU'ALOFA
PANGAI
MOTU
THE
HA'AMONGA
TRILITHON
TERRACED
TOMBS
CAPT.
COOK'S
TREE
BLOW HOLES
AIRPORT
OHOLEI BEACH
(OSCAR'S
HIDEAWAY)

TONGATAPU

# 16 TONGATAPU
## To church with the king

After just an overnight stay in Apia, we were on our way again the next day to Tongatapu.

It was rather a strange experience though, to take off on a flight in the middle of a Friday afternoon and land, two and a half hours later, to find that it was early Saturday evening. Crossing the International Dateline like that, from east to west, leaves you feeling that somehow you've been cheated—a whole day gone out of your life—just like that!

'Dad,' Sean said not long after the flight began, 'if you could make a trip over the dateline from west to east every day, then you would *gain* a day, every day...and you could live twice as long.'

It seemed an interesting possibility.

During the flight down to Tongatapu, we passed over the islands we'd been trying to get to—the Vava'u and Ha'apai groups. We gazed enviously out of the windows of the aircraft, down at the magnificent pattern of colours made by the sprinkling of scores of coral and volcanic islands. There are two separate collections of over 70 islands in these northern Tongan groups, only a few of which are inhabited. (Of the total of 169 islands that make up the whole Tonga group, only 36 have people living on them permanently.) As we were passing the Ha'apai group we saw through the window, far off to the right, on the horizon, two volcanic islands which, almost two centuries ago, formed the backdrop for history's most famous mutiny...the mutiny on the *Bounty*.

The *Bounty* had arrived in the Tongan group from Tahiti, carrying a cargo of breadfruit. The ship's commander, Lieutenant William Bligh, was 'relieved' of his command by the mate, Fletcher Christian and the mutinous crew. Bligh and 18 other men were cast adrift in a 23-foot (7-metre) long-boat, while Christian and the rest of the crew sailed off in the *Bounty*. The castaways were given 19 gallons (85 litres) of water and 150 pounds (68 kilos) of bread. They tried to land on Tofua for provisions of fresh fruit but were driven off by hostile natives who killed one of the crew, John Norton, the quartermaster.

He was clubbed to death. Bligh then set off in the tiny boat to make for Timor, some 3000 kilometres away! It was the only other landfall he knew of and thought he might be able to reach with the prevailing easterly winds.

He made it in 48 days.

The hostess on the plane brought around sandwiches and coffee for the passengers. It was the standard airline fare. . . pre-packaged, no different from what you might get on any other airline in the world. But then the steward came by behind her to follow up with boiled taro and plates of tinned corned beef! It was as if the locals, the Samoans and Tongans, would not be able to get by without their daily dose of these staples. Not exactly exciting stuff, but at least it was different and you could see from the faces of the Tongans and Samoans, as they took it from the offered tray, that they appreciated the gesture.

Travelling on the plane with us to Tongatapu were the two American boys we'd met weeks earlier on Moorea, Bob Rhodos and Tom Kunz. Both Zara and Sean had been delighted in Apia, when we returned to the airport there after our overnight stay, to find Tom and Bob waiting to catch the same plane to Tonga. We hoped that perhaps this would make Zara feel a little better at having left Pago Pago. . . and it did.

We exchanged news and stories and learnt that they had stayed for a couple of weeks in French Polynesia and then flown to American Samoa. After a short stay there they had moved on to Western Samoa where they had been for about three weeks. . . spending most of the time in small villages on the big island of Savai'i.

It was after 4 p.m. by the time we landed at Fua'amotu airport on Tongatapu Island. Bob and Tom had told us that they'd heard on the 'student grapevine' that Leo's Guest House was a good place to stay in the Tongan capital. . . cheap too. So, when we saw Leo's bus at the airport, offering free transportation to anyone who was staying at the Guest House, we took it. After a 40-minute drive over unmade roads we pulled up at Leo's place, a simple, white weatherboard house on the waterfront, only to discover that there was no room for us there.

'You could try Herman's place.' A large, brown woman who stood at the doorway of the house, pointed along the waterfront. 'It's called "Fasi moafi",' she said, 'and it's only a few hundred yards along.'

We shouldered our packs and walked along the road, past the island's main hotel, the International Dateline, to another small wooden house that had been converted into a guest house. Here we met Herman. . . another Herman. . . a very different one from our companion on the *Mataora* and in Western Samoa. This Herman was a slim, greying German of about 50. He had a grey beard which was neatly trimmed, Abraham-Lincoln-style, without a moustache, around his jaw.

There were only two rooms available, so Bob and Tom took one of them and we the other. The place was old-fashioned, but at least it was clean and, for only $10 a night for the four of us, we could hardly complain. We had some doubts about Herman, who seemed unusually abrasive, particularly towards Tom and Bob, once he realised that they were Americans, but we put it down to the fact that he hadn't slept well the night before, or perhaps his lunch had disagreed with him. Anyway we didn't stay around long enough, at that particular time, to find out. We went out to take a walk around the town and to buy some groceries before the market and the shops closed down. Herman had shown us a rather dilapidated old kitchen at the back of the house in which we could cook up breakfast and whatever meals we liked.

The town of Nuku'alofa is quite small, about 40 000 people, and it's not particularly attractive. Its streets are very dusty and we noticed immediately that the people were considerably poorer than their neighbours in Samoa or the Cook Islands. We had been told previously that the other islands in the group, Ha'apai and Vava'u, were far more attractive and that as little time as possible should be spent in Tongatapu. Nevertheless, apart from what I've just said about the town, our initial impressions were very favourable. Admittedly, the island is not dramatically beautiful physically—like Samoa or French Polynesia—but we found that in Nuku'alofa we immediately felt at ease. The people in the streets were friendly. . .they smiled and said hello. And, in the market where we bought two huge papayas for 20 cents each, a large bunch of bananas for 20 cents and a kilo of tomatoes for 20 cents, we were made to feel welcome. That sort of situation tends to affect your view of a place, so, right from the beginning, we knew that we were going to like Tonga.

On Sunday in Tonga you go to church. Partly because everyone else goes and if you didn't, you'd feel so conspicuous in the empty streets. Church is the only place open and there's nothing else to do, but also it's an event, an occasion, and an opportunity to see the king.

We'd made breakfast in the simple kitchen at the back of the house under Herman's watchful eye and acerbic tongue. I was determined not to let his manner upset me, but tried instead to tell myself that beneath his decidedly abrasive exterior beat a soft heart of gold! Difficult when he yelled at me for using the 'wrong' frypan!

Tom and Bob, who were not prepared to make these allowances for Herman, kept up a stream of sarcastic muttered guttural remarks to each other and to Zara and Sean which had them in barely suppressed fits of giggles. But when Herman asked if they were intending to go to church with the king, they stopped in their tracks and, over their faces came that sort of suffused golden glow with which almost every American I've ever met becomes transfixed when the words king or queen are mentioned. For all their egalitarian and democratic ideals, they seem irresistibly drawn towards the idea of royalty and noble families.

I doubt if this actually crossed Bob and Tom's minds when Herman mentioned the king, probably just that it would be 'neat', and something to write home about. Zara and Sean, I think, anticipated diamond-studded crowns and trailing regal robes because, having insisted that they put on their least travel-wearied clothes and scrub and brush themselves into something approaching respectful tidiness, when the king entered the church to stand in the pew opposite us across the nave, they turned to me in amazement, with 'That's the *king?*' written all over their faces.

His Majesty, King Taufa'ahau Tupou IV, exudes kingship in a way few others in that dwindling band of royalty around the world manage, except when tarted up in all their regal clobber. But here he was in a simple, white, high-collared, tieless shirt, *lava-*

*lava* and sunglasses (which he kept on throughout the service), a veritable embodiment of regal power. This aura is no doubt helped along by his bulk, which is so stupendous (he admits to 175 kilos), that when he travels abroad, forward arrangements include efforts to ensure that there are cars, chairs and beds large enough and sturdy enough to contain him!

When he sat, everyone sat and even though the rest of us alternately stood, sat and occasionally knelt throughout the service, King Tupou never moved again except once, when he stood to read the lesson. An aide brought in a portable electric fan and adjusted it so that it played directly onto him... and no-one else. Beside him, Queen Halaevalu Mata'aho kept cool by waving her own plaited straw fan.

Centenary Church, big though it is, isn't really a church at all, because the majority of Tongans are Wesleyans and therefore go to chapel. My Gran and Gramps were chapel and my Dad too, till he left home, though he could never shake off chapel mores and their attendant attitudes of guilt. So I felt quite at home in the deliberately spartan (thou shalt make no graven image), but still attractive surroundings and gave loud voice, much to my children's embarrassment, to the familiar hymns. I sang John Wesley's words in English, while the rest of the congregation sang in Tongan.

Another translation to Tongan values was the manner in which the congregation was rigorously segregated; men to one side of the aisle, women to the other, with children under 16 sitting on the floor in front. Many of the men wore spotless white shirts and plain ties under dark suits, shiny with a lifetime of being 'saved for best'. The rest wore shirt and tie and knee-length *tupenu* or *lava-lavas*. The women's *tupenu* were ankle length. (Modesty is the password in Tonga, where it is illegal for any man over the age of 16 to appear in public without a shirt on.) Both men's and women's *tupenu* were overlaid with finely-woven, coconut-fibre decorative mats which are worn as a traditional sign of respect on many occasions.

Between the sexes was a brass band in a British marine-like uniform and a choir in madonna-blue gowns. They played and sang beautifully under the guidance of their conductor who stood on a chair in front of them. Their rendition of the Hallelujah Chorus, sung of course in Tongan, would take a lot to better.

As in French Polynesia and the Cook Islands, the minister welcomed his foreign guests in English and apologised that the sermon, which naturally would be in Tongan, would be difficult for them to follow. (I wondered, in how many English or Australian churches, would the obvious foreigners be welcomed in their mother tongue.) The resounding oratory dramatically delivered in deep, resonant Tongan and taking 40 minutes, contained references to Australia, Britain, New Zealand, America and Iran. We were kept fully alert trying to guess what it was all about.

Opposite us, the king, bulking majestic, sat immobile: all emotion masked by his sunglasses.

'Is he asleep?' Sean asked.

It was more difficult to see that, than to appreciate that something had happened which made it necessary for the king's minister of religion to make explanations from the pulpit. A blatant tie-up between church and state. It was like stepping back 800 years to the era of Thomas à Becket and Henry II! Mind you, it's only when you move away from your own society and view other cultures as an outsider, that aspects of your own come into focus. So it wasn't until I lived away from England, that I could see the still uncomfortably close ties between the British monarchy, parliament and judiciary. Another reason to travel.

The last hymn was, of course, 'Rock of Ages' and no sooner had it ended, than the king was on his feet (so he hadn't been sleeping at all!) and with an unexpected display of nimble-footedness, was off through his private side entrance. Though we followed with the rest of the congregation moments later, he was already pulling away in his big black Mercedes 600 by the time we were out.

Back at Herman's we were surprised to hear that there was an excursion which we could join to one of the small islands, a few kilometres offshore from Nuku'alofa.

'But I thought nothing like this was allowed on Sundays,' Iain asked. 'No taxis, no buses, nothing.'

'Ah,' Herman said with a look of world-weary wisdom, 'but this island you will be visiting belongs to the king.'

The seven-metre boat we went out on was owned by Earl Emberson, a blond Tongan of regular good looks and unusual parentage. 'My mother was half-Tongan, half-English and my father half-Danish and half-Polynesian mixture,' he explained. 'I was born in Tonga and keep Tongan citizenship,' (and evidently an 'in' with the king I thought).

Earl charged $3.50 each for the boat trip out and an additional $4.50 for a very good barbeque lunch. We opted for just the boat trip. He had already delivered two boat loads to the island, so obviously it wasn't a bad little business. He also hired out bikes for a dollar a day from his waterfront home a couple of doors up from Herman's.

Pangai Motu is a small flat island with superb white sand beaches facing onto the capital and a mangrove swamp on the far side. The afternoon passed too quickly. It wasn't often enough on this journey that we actually just lay about on a beach and we waited till almost all the other people had gone, many of them in their own little boats, and Earl was doing his last run back, before we too left.

We were sitting up on the deck, to more fully enjoy the flush of sunset, when a young fellow, with noticeably blues eyes behind his spectacles, and a large, full, D.H. Lawrence-style beard, asked Iain, with a trace of a German accent, if he would take a photograph of him with his own camera, so that he would have a picture to send back to his Mutter und Vater.

'Sit up close to Trish,' Iain suggested, 'and you can tell them she's your girlfriend. That'll give them something to worry about.'

'Thanks!' I said.

The photo taken, the young man introduced himself and brought out a visiting card which was printed: 'Hans Jorg Hämmerling. Student, Globetrotter, Lebenskunstler.' And his address in Germany. He was pleased, I think, that I had some comprehension of what the word lebenskunstler meant. Lover of life. Free spirit. That sort of thing. Only it sounds better in German.

During the following morning, we tried to see if we could get a flight to Vava'u or Ha'apai, from this direction but there were long queues of people waiting at the town office of the airline so we gave up and took off to explore the town and the shops more fully. On Saturday when we arrived it had been late in the day before we'd gone to the market and then on Sunday, everything had been closed. That Monday morning, even by about 9.30, the day was hot and humid. There were clouds in the sky, but no rain. The wet season had not yet reached Tonga. We seemed to be a few days ahead of it...or just catching the beginning of it, all the way across the Pacific. The streets were still dusty and dry despite the heavy air, but they were full of people bustling back and forth—many of the women carried large, black umbrellas to protect themselves from the sun.

Although Tonga is considerably less affluent than some of the other South Pacific island groupings, no-one is so poor as to be without proper food or shelter. In the Western sense there appears to be substantial unemployment in Tonga, in that only about a third of the workforce of about 50 000 are in income-producing jobs. But statistics here can be misleading, because the balance are not unemployed or 'on the dole', but involved in subsistence agriculture. Under the Polynesian system of community property, there are always jobs to do and no-one lacks the essentials of food, housing, adequate clothing, medical attention and education (which is free and compulsory to the age of 14). However, since there is traditionally no pay for this kind of communal work which is undertaken for neighbours, friends or relatives, many young Tongans have been tending to drift away from the old way of life to seek paid employment. But there are few jobs available.

Tonga's economy is not a strong one: it is basically an agricultural country, with copra and bananas as its main crops. There is no significant manufacturing industry to provide extra jobs. The government civil service is the largest employer, with the commercial shops and business in Nuku'alofa absorbing the rest. There are not enough jobs around though to prevent many young people from migrating to New Zealand or to neighbouring American Samoa, or Hawaii, in search of better opportunities.

It's often difficult when you see a system that has worked well for centuries having to face the difficulties of coping with and adapting to the twentieth century. In the face of the onslaught of Western culture, should it cling to the old ways and reject the modern intrusions into its lifestyle...or leap headlong into the ways of the West, accepting the drawbacks as well as the benefits?

Tonga, more than most of its island neighbours, has tended to, if not reject, then accept more slowly, the Western way, even though this has meant it lagging behind (in the Western sense) as far as development is concerned. The main reason is undoubtedly its rigidly stratified social system...a system which has been compared to that which existed in Europe during the feudal and medieval ages. King Tupou himself has compared it to nineteenth-century Prussia.

This ancient Polynesian hierarchy of king, paramount chief, high chiefs, chiefs, paramount orators (or talking chiefs), high orators, orators etc. is a direct equivalent of the European system of earls, dukes, barons, counts and knights. It is a pyramid system of social rank that was in operation throughout all of Polynesia at the time of the first arrival of Europeans in the Pacific. Despite the Westernisation of the region, its influence has remained intact almost everywhere; except perhaps Hawaii, where the very large influx of Asians and Europeans has diluted the Polynesian tradition. Even in Tahiti, where the French have pushed hard for complete adoption of the European way, the chiefs are still the dominant force.

Tonga, though, remains the stronghold of the tradition—understandably so, as it was the cradle of the social rank system which spread from Tonga throughout the rest of Polynesia.

King Taufa'ahau Tupou IV is the absolute ruler, at the top of the pyramid. Beneath him are two broad layers—the nobility and the commoners. Within these layers there is further stratification. In the nobility layer, for instance, there are nobles who hold large estates and privileged positions while on the next rung down are chiefs who have no hereditary estates or rights to representation in parliament, but nevertheless hold important positions in social life. The commoners' layer, which includes the bulk of the population, contains (in descending order): men of wealth, church leaders, the educated elite, heads of government departments, heads of institutions, and, at the lowest level, villagers and citizens.

One would think that the villager would have a fairly rough time, but under the system there are some quite extraordinary rights enjoyed by the ordinary citizen... well, at least *male* citizens. For example: every male Tongan, when he turns 16 becomes entitled to a 'bush allotment' of about three hectares of land, as well as a town block measuring about 40 metres by 40 metres. He pays the equivalent of round $4 a year for the allotment and no rent at all for the town site. By law every landowner is required to plant 200 coconut trees within 12 months of acquiring the land and is obliged to keep it free of weeds.

In addition, because Tongans practise the Polynesian philosophy of community property, personal wealth matters much less to the ordinary citizen than to most Westerners. In theory a villager owns everything in the village, but he also owns nothing, because whatever he owns belongs to everyone else as well. He can take or be given any amount of food and clothing for his personal needs, as well as obtain free labour to build his house, but all of these things he must also be prepared to *give* in return within his clan or to visitors.

This free giving and taking system was a source of amazement to the first European arrivals and has always been in sharp conflict with Western legal attitudes towards property. Sad really, because the Polynesian way clearly represents a less selfish and more humane approach than the one on which much of the rest of the world has operated for thousands of years.

At a small café in town, while having a sandwich and a cup of coffee, we met Hans Hämmerling again.

'Are you doing anything this afternoon?' he asked. 'There is a graduation ceremony at the college where I teach. The king will be presenting the prizes... and there's a big Tongan feast afterwards.'

'But surely that's only for invited guests?'

'Oh no, it's for everyone. It's provided by the families of all the students... and there's no real way of knowing who's invited and who isn't. Anyway, *I'm* inviting you.'

As we left, we called in briefly to the Tonga Visitors' Bureau, which was right next door to Herman's guest house. We wanted to collect some of the various brochures and other information published by the office about the island and, while there, we met the Bureau's director, Russell Marriott. Russell was a tall, quiet man with grey hair... in his 50s I imagined. He was an Australian who had spent many years working for the Australian Government Information Service in the United States. He took on the directorship of the Tonga Visitors' Bureau in the late 70s.

He was most helpful to us with advice and information about things to do and see in Tonga and offered to provide us with some transportation around the island on the following day. We spent about half an hour with him before heading off to the graduation ceremony.

The Atenesi College is a private secondary school which takes students up to Australian or New Zealand university entrance level. The ceremony was already underway on a small patch of lawn in front of the main building and a temporary stage had been set up for the king and assembled guests. A policeman stopped us about 200 metres from the proceedings and, after leaving our cab, we walked the remaining distance between some small cottages and coconut trees to the edge of the grass where we sat and watched the ceremony which included a number of traditional Tongan rituals demonstrating obeisance to the king. King Tupou, still sheltering behind his dark sunglasses, sat giant-like in centre stage, flanked on his right by his son, Crown Prince Tupou To'a and on his left by Mounga Loa, the president of the Tongan Wesleyan Church (the man who had delivered the Sunday sermon at the church), and a red-bearded European, the New Zealand principal of the college. Once again an electric fan also sat on a chair nearby, directing its breeze onto the king.

From where we were we could see our friend Hans dressed in what must have been his best Sunday suit, sitting amongst some other teachers in the front row facing onto the lawn. He nodded and raised his hand, indicating that he had seen us. We had missed some of the show: on our arrival, a group of tribal leaders were seated cross-legged on the grass in front of the king, chanting in Tongan and clapping their hands. Then a huge roasted pig, garlanded with flowers and banana leaves, was carried in and placed in front of the king, accompanied by more chanting and singing. Then, after what seemed like a sort of dedication, the pig was carried off, to await the later feasting, and the graduation-ceremony-proper began.

The students, in scarlet satin robes and mortar boards were called, one by one to receive their diplomas from the king. The head student gave a speech, which was followed by one from the king, praising those who were graduating and exhorting others to further study and greater academic achievement. The king himself is a former student of Newington College in Sydney and an honours graduate in jurisprudence at the University of Sydney and Oxford.

Almost immediately after the speech ended, a Tongan girl, dressed in a patterned *tupenu* danced into the centre of the enclosure to the accompaniment of a rhythmic drumbeat. Her chest, back and arms were covered in coconut oil and they glistened as she moved, slowly undulating her hips in a dance that appeared to be vaguely Hawaian, but also very Asian, in the way she moved her hands. . . not unlike a Thai dancer.

Then, in a local custom we saw only in Tonga and Western Samoa, members of the audience began walking out into the arena and, as the girl continued her performance, seemingly oblivious of what the others were doing, they started slapping banknotes onto her oily skin, leaving them sticking there as they returned to their seats.

Next, after the dance had finished and she had picked up all of the notes that had fallen to the ground, the mothers and relatives of all the graduating students came in from the sides bearing huge bolts of intricately-patterned *tapa* cloth. . . some of them 20 to 25 metres in length and up to 5 or 6 metres wide. These were made from beaten bark by the people from the students' home villages and are traditionally given to the king on occasions such as this. The king apparently receives so many huge pieces of *tapa* that it is an accepted practice for him to pass them on—to give them away again, usually to visiting dignitaries, or important foreign guests, as a gift from the people of Tonga. What you do with a piece of *tapa* 6 metres wide, by 20 metres long, if you're given one, I don't really know.

Anyway, we all sat entranced at the proceedings, not really knowing what to expect next. We could hardly have been prepared for what did come: after an overture by the Tongan Police Band we were treated to an abbreviated performance by students of the college of Gilbert and Sullivans' 'Trial by Jury'. . . in Tongan! Dressed in incredible costumes, with fuzzy afro haircuts powdered white, and heavily-made up, they sat in the centre of the lawn in front of the king and sang the whole story through. . . to the delight and much laughter of the audience.

The king left shortly afterwards in a khaki-painted Unimog of the Tongan Defence Force. . . a sturdy-looking vehicle, in keeping with the monarch's immense proportions. He was followed, in descending order by the various official guests, the last being the diminutive figure of the Taiwanese ambassador.

Then came the food. Hans came over to greet us and to lead us around the back of the college building to a gargantuan feast which had been spread out on long tables outside the building. We had never seen anything like it before. Apparently Tongan feasts are famous for their variety of food and enormous size. This one certainly lived up to the reputation.

On every table there were several *polas*—long trays made of plaited coconut fronds on which were laid out crackling brown suckling pigs, chickens, roast beef, lamb, pork, huge whole fishes which were either barbequed or grilled, trays and trays of lobsters, crayfish, beautiful crabs, prawns, abalone and octopus. In addition there was an immense variety of vegetables; kumera, taro, and avocado as well as piles of tropical fruit: mangos, papaya, passionfruit, bananas and pineapples.

We were stunned by the array, but not for long. It was quite clear that the hundreds of guests did not intend leaving it there as a visual display. They were hopping into it with a will and, although there was no chance that we might miss out on something to eat, we quickly joined in, trying to sample a bit of everything. . . an impossible task, but a pleasant one to attempt.

There was impromptu singing and dancing all around and, though we were really outsiders, everyone was friendly towards us and we enjoyed ourselves immensely. After about three-quarters of an hour, when everybody had at least eaten *one* good meal, we said goodbye to Hans and left. Many of the students' families were preparing to leave anyway. They were packing up what remained of their food, making ready to repair to their separate villages where they would continue the feasting into the night. Although a veritable army of people had been fed, there was still sufficient food left to go on for several days.

# 17   TONGATAPU
## Oscar's hideaway

'...*the friendly behaver [sic] of the Natives who seemed to (vie) with each other in doing what they thought would give us pleasure...*' as Captain James Cook wrote at the time, caused him to designate Tonga as 'The Friendly Isles' a name they have kept ever since his first visit in 1773. The irony being that these 'friendly natives' were in fact plotting to kill him!

'This is the place where Captain Cook landed.' Ver Fonua pulled the van over to the edge of the unsurfaced road and the four of us piled out to follow him. We read the inscription on the metal plaque attached to a piece of wood which, so they claim, comes from the tree under which Cook rested when he came ashore.

There is no break in the reef at the spot so it must have been a trifle hairy landing. Exciting to imagine him, the great Yorkshire navigator, exactly half-way around the world, being rowed in to step ashore in those buckle shoes and white hose, cut-away jacket and sausage-curl white wig. Disregarding the imperial politics of the men in Whitehall and the crown, under whose name he sailed at that moment in time...clambering up the beach into the unknown. You must admire the courage of the man and be envious that you weren't there too.

'He went to a lot of places didn't he,' commented Sean.

Ver, a man in his mid-20s, worked for the Tonga Visitors' Bureau and had been asked by Russell Marriott to show us around the island. We had called into Russell's office again early that morning and while Ver organised his day so that he could spend it with us, we had talked some more with Russell who told us a little more about his work for the Australian government in various parts of the world.

'I'd got as far as I was going to go with them,' he said, 'and I decided the time had come to make a break. So here I am. I have far more responsibility than I'd ever have had if I'd have stayed on waiting till retiring time and for my superannuation. This is wide open. Carte blanche. Very exciting. I have the personal backing of the king who wants to encourage tourism as a source of much needed revenue. Though of course he...and the rest of us, know that the process has to be carefully monitored, because the Tongan way of life must be preserved and this is a very fragile thing. There is no immediate danger of our being swamped with more people than we can handle, because we're not on any of the major airline routes. So there's no package tours. No Club Mediterranée. No cheap rates. Though of course, you must have noticed how everything is so inexpensive here anyway. We are working on long-range plans and our comparative isolation may, in the end, be our greatest draw card. We may very well eventually be the only place left in the world where you really *can* get away from it all.'

Following the coast eastwards for a couple of kilometres, we came to Mu'a, the former capital, and to the terraced tombs of Langi, the burial place of an ancient dynasty of kings, the Tui Tonga, dating back to 950AD.

The Tui Tonga was of divine origin, the son of the sun god, Tangaloa (remember our fully-equipped Tangaroa in the Cook Islands?) The right to rule was passed down through 500 years of Tui Tonga until, at the height of the dynasty's power in the thirteenth century its domain included part of the Lau group (now in Fiji), Rotuma, Futuna, 'Urea, Tokelau, Samoa and Niue. But there was the inevitable internecine strife—wars and murders—so that by the time Europeans arrived on the scene (Schouten and Le Maire in 1616, Abel Tasman in 1643 and others like Wallis and Cook in the 1700s), the system was so weakened, it was ripe for outside gods. The Tongans took to the Wesleyan branch of Christianity (propogated by the seemingly omnipresent LMS), like ducks to water, when it was first introduced in 1822.

Even so it was none of these outsiders, but rather a remarkable Tongan, who managed the mammoth job of hauling the islands into the nineteenth century where, by the present king's own admission, it has happily stayed put: that man was King George Tupou I, a descendent of the royal lines. He became ruler of his native Ha' apai in 1820, of Vava'u in 1833 and of Tongatapu in 1845. Tupou I, the great grandfather of the present king, was two metres tall and, after converting to Christianity, he took the name George in honour of King George III of England. His wife was christened Salote, the Tongan version of Charlotte, after mad George's wife, the English queen.

From the Langi it was only a matter of another few kilometres to the Stonehenge of the South Seas; the 700-year-old large coral limestone archway called the Ha'amonga trilithon. The two pillars, with a mortised crosspiece, were built, so the story goes, by King Tu'itatui as a monument for his two sons whom he feared would quarrel after his death. The uprights represent the sons, the crosspiece the yoke of brotherly love. It's a pleasant enough story, with a certain appeal to any parent with siblings who squabble! But the present king had an idea that there was more to it. He had seen Stonehenge, on England's Salisbury Plain, and had read about Egypt's Abu Simbel and knew that both of them were used as forms of calendars. Perhaps ancient Polynesians used the Ha'amonga in the same manner. He had the arch cleared of vines and found a small bowl-shaped depression on the top, with a groove pointing toward the east. A path of vegetation was cleared in line with the groove and on June 21st, 1967, the year of his coronation, King Tupou went out to wait for the sunrise. The sun came up out of the sea at the end of the tunnel of greenery.

Beyond the trilithon the surrounding dense foliage had been cleared so that when we looked through the arch we had the impression of looking along a telescope pointed to the horizon.

We recalled the 'hitching post of the sun' in the Inca temple in the high fastness of Machu Picchu which was used in the same way. And when you stop to think about it, for people living centuries ago, the fear that the days would go on growing shorter and that eventually the sun would slip from its hitching post and never return, must have been very real. Even as I write this piece, in my ancient marrow I am aware that tomorrow is the shortest day of the year in this hemisphere and I know that I shall be glad when it has past and we roll on to lengthening days. Perhaps some of that primitive fear never leaves us. Singing down through the generations, the basic instincts are stamped into our very being.

Zara and Sean were impressed with the trilithon because, having seen Stonehenge, Abu Simbel and Machu Picchu, they probably feel the vibrations of mankind's basic desire to comprehend the ineffable.

The unmade roads made conversation pretty limited; they would also jolt the poor van into a shuddering early retirement, but we managed to talk a little to Ver as we drove on through the very simple, small settlements. He told us that he had only just begun working for the Tourist Authority and that he liked it very much. Just as well, because Russell Marriott told us later that we would be embarrassed if we knew how little he earnt.

'What's all that banging?' Zara called from the back seat. For a moment I had fears for the van's tappets.

'*Tapa,*' Ver said, matter of factly, as if it was an everyday occurrence, which no doubt it almost was for him.

'Oh let's stop and go back,' Zara cried, but by then we were through the tiny village.

'There will be plenty more,' Ver assured her, and he was right. In nearly every one of the string of hamlets along the road, we could hear the rhythmic tonk-a-tonk-a-tonk of the iron-wood mallets bashing the bark from the paper mulberry trees.

In one village we stopped and, by following the sound, came to a small hut where a woman and her daughter were sitting cross-legged on the ground in front of a medium-sized tree trunk across which they had laid the bark and were busy pounding away.

Ver spoke to them in Tongan. Many more people seemed to be less than comfortable with the English language on Tonga than in the other island groups we'd visited, but as always, a great deal can be communicated without actual words. The woman's husband, who came across to see who the visitors were, showed us with great agility, how to strip the bark from the mulberry sapling, holding one end of it between his toes. He then removed the hard outer coating and passed his wife the white inner layer which she put in a large wooden bowl full of water.

'The saplings have been cut and left to soak for a few days,' Ver explained, 'and now the lining itself will be left overnight for a further soaking.'

The woman made the beating, which naturally spreads the 5-6 cms-wide bark strip out to perhaps 18 to 20 cms, look very easy. Smiling, she offered me the hammer.

'She wants you to try,' Ver smiled too.

As I quickly discovered, along with Iain and the children, who followed my pathetic attempt, it's not easy. I guess there's a knack to it which comes with practice. But apart from anything else, the noise and the monotony would drive me crazy.

Once stretched to its final capacity, the bark strips are glued together with highly sticky manioc root juice to form pieces almost a metre wide and as long as the occasion demands. We asked the woman who she was making the *tapa* for. Through Ver, she answered, 'For the visit of the cruise ship.'

A few villages farther along, on our way across the island heading for the west coast, we stopped again and Ver led the way to a small community hall where all the women of the village were involved in the communal work of decorating a long piece of *tapa*. The material had been stretched over a curved-topped low table which ran the entire length of the hall, which was perhaps five or six metres long and whose surface was covered with various raised designs made by laboriously stitching hibiscus bark and coconut fibre to a pandanus leaf base. The women, 10 to a side, again cross-legged on the floor, rubbed the *tapa* with pandanus fruit brushes dipped in dye. The stain coloured the raised designs. We asked Ver what dyes the women used to produce the traditional brown patterns outlined in black.

He spoke to the women and after much smiling and gesturing, translated back to us, 'The black comes from boiling rusty iron nails in a bark dye. The brown is ground ochre.'

In Tonga, more than in any of the other Pacific islands which we visited, *tapa* is still very much a living part of the culture. Tongans make it for themselves, to give away as a sign of respect—as we had seen at the graduation ceremony—and to sell to visitors on cruise ships. Watching these women making *tapa,* it was obvious to us that it was far more than just the end product that was important. The social get-together, the women talking and joking as they decorated the cloth, was the equivalent, in our society, I suppose, of ladies' tennis mornings, or Tupperware parties!

Farther on again we made another stop where we saw many metres of finished *tapa* laid out to finally dry in the sun. We asked around to find out who owned these long strips and tracked down a smiling friendly woman called Meliame 'Otufanga who was delighted when we asked if she would sell us some. For the embarrassingly low price of $5, twice as embarrassing because we had seen what time and patience was required for its making, we bought a piece 6 metres long and promised to send Mrs 'Otufanga a photograph of how we used it as a sort of decorative frame right round the top of our bedroom walls in our own house.

Next it was the blowholes at Houma, where the constant pounding of the Pacific surf has worn holes in the coral limestone reef and spouts up with terrific force through these openings like geysers, and then Ver took us to Kolovai. There he showed us the hundreds of flying foxes—a euphemism for bats—which make their homes in a grove of casuarina trees. Difficult to feel warmth towards bats, I always find. Still I guess they, too, have their place in the overall system and these bats were one up on most others, seeing as how they belonged to the king and on Tonga are considered sacred. Sacred or not, they smelt something terrific and they were not above fouling the road, or anything, or anybody foolish enough to stand beneath them, as they hung upside down and chattered madly in a most unregal manner. In fact their only royal aspect was their size: some of them had wing spans of a metre!

On the very tip of the western arm of Tongatapu there is a neat plot of land surrounding a plaque commemorating the landing there of the first Christian missionaries to Tonga. Religion being a geographical accident (if you had been born in India you'd more than likely be a Hindu, in Iran a Moslem, in Ireland a Catholic), one can't help feeling something approaching awe for the drive these men and women displayed in their determination to break geographical boundaries and, at great personal risk, offer up their own particular brand of religion.

As I've said before, Tongans embraced the Wesleyan faith with great ardour. My Gran, in whose house on Sundays I was allowed to do nothing more active than read the Scriptures or embroider religious mottoes, would definitely have approved of the fact that, despite pressures from other countries and the airline industry, no flights are allowed to take off or land in Tonga on the Lord's Day. This is no small matter when considering a visit to Tonga and it's made more confusing by the loss or gain of a day, depending on where you're coming from. Best, I think, to play safe and stick to a Wednesday. The other wickedly delicious aside to this authoritarian religious fervor is that the Seventh Day Adventists, less numerous here than in other Pacific nations, who normally celebrate their sabbath on a Saturday, in Tonga must do so on Sundays!

Back in Nuku'alofa, which I don't think I've mentioned before as meaning, 'The Abode of Love', we paid our respects to the king's palace. It's right on the waterfront, on the edge of the town; a white painted, wooden fantasy of cupolas and gingerbread, straight out of a fairytale. What is most remarkable about it is that alongside is a chapel, the king's private place of worship; equally ornate and only marginally smaller than the palace itself. On the lawn beside the entrance, 22 men in brilliant whites played cricket.

We dropped Ver off at his office, as he had surely done more than his bit for the day. It was already approaching 5 p.m.; we walked a couple of blocks back to the enclosed royal cemetery where the most recent kings and queens of Tonga, most notably Queen Salote, lie at rest.

As a child I remember her big, happy face, smiling through London's grey drizzle when, despite the weather, she drove in an open carriage, en route to Queen Elizabeth II's coronation in Westminster Abbey. With her magnificent 2-metre bulk, sunny disposition and, by comparison, bright clothes, she brought a welcome burst of Pacific sunshine and made the rest of them look very drab and overdressed. The mass of the British G.P. loved her almost as much as their own queen and were greatly saddened when she died in 1965 after ruling her islands for 47 years.

Cows quietly ate the verdant grass around the base of the tombs and then stared at us, vacant-faced, as they chewed the cud.

'Why are cows allowed in to eat the grass round the royal tombs?' Zara asked Herman when we returned later to Fasimoafi. Her expression was one of disapproval.

'Because,' Herman gave a thin smile, 'they are the king's cows.'

The next morning we spent a quiet few hours sitting in the sun in the back yard reading and then watching other people fishing with lines from the sea wall across the road from the guest house. Then, in the early afternoon, Russell Marriott appeared.

'I'm going to take you to see a rather unique place, and to meet a friend of mine,' he said. 'He's called Oscar. And the place is known as "Oscar's Hideaway".'

'Oscar's Hideaway?' Sean was immediately interested. 'What is it?'

'Well, I'll let you see it first. You'll need to bring some money. It's not exactly cheap...$8 each, and half for children...but, I can assure you it's well worth every penny. It doesn't really start until sunset, but if we leave now, you can meet Oscar and his family and you'll have time to swim and sunbake on the beach...Oholei Beach is one of the loveliest on the island. It's completely deserted.'

We left shortly afterwards in Russell's car for the half-hour drive to the southeastern coast of Tongatapu where, after leaving the main road, which was itself unsurfaced, we followed an even narrower and dustier road through thick tropical bush to a small grove of coconut trees on low cliffs, about 100 metres from the shore.

On the way, Russell had told us something of Oscar and his 'Hideaway'. Oscar Kami had for many years been the head footman and then personal valet to Queen Salote of Tonga. Having left the queen's service in the 60s, he and his family now ran a weekly traditional Tongan feast and dance night in an amazing network of caves which fronted onto Oholei Beach.

'It's better to come early like this,' Russell said, 'so you can see the place in the daylight. It's really quite spectacular.'

As we left Russell's car, which he had parked in a small clearing, we saw a group of people unloading supplies from a Kombi van nearby. It was Oscar and his family. Russell introduced us. Oscar had a round, smiling face. He was dark-skinned, of medium height and, like most middle-aged Tongans, portly. . . if not exactly fat. He welcomed us to his place and, after a brief chat, suggested we go down to the beach to swim and snorkel on the reef for a while. 'I'll see you later,' he assured us.

Russell led us down a winding, narrow path which was almost completely covered by high, tropical undergrowth of vines and bushes. It was dark and had an eerie feel about it, even in the daytime. The path wound quickly down the black volcanic cliffs to the sand at beach level, where we found ourselves in an extraordinary honeycomb of open-fronted caves overhung by high coconut trees and other types which grew more densely in weird and grotesque shapes. The whole area was in shade and the air was quite cool, despite the heat of the afternoon. There were pathways in the hard sand marked out with thick poles. Some rough wooden structures, including long tables and benches, were spread through the trees and Hawaian oil lamps on sticks were dotted everywhere. Through the trees, we could see the brilliant whiteness of the beach and a glimmering turquoise lagoon.

'I'm going to leave you here,' Russell said. 'It doesn't start until after the sun goes down, so you've got some time to yourselves, before other people start arriving.'

We said to Russell that he should stay, but he said that he had other things to do and that we'd enjoy it anyway, so we said goodbye and as he made his way up the path again, we headed for the beach. Zara and Sean went exploring the caves and the foreshore, while Trish and I went for a short walk along the beach and a swim in the lagoon. We swam out through shallow water to the fringing reef where a series of blowholes were sending fine jets of spray high into the air. From where we sat on the jagged coral outcrops, looking back to shore, we could see that the beach was totally deserted and the whole stretch of coastline, for as far as we could see, had no sign of habitation. It really had the feel of a tropical paradise.

At sunset we made our way back to the area where Oscar's feast was to take place. Zara had already made friends with Oscar's daughters and had been helping them prepare some of the food dishes, but, at the time of our return everything had been thrown into a state of temporary confusion by Sean. One of Oscar's sons, a boy called Pakofe, was kneeling on the ground giving medical treatment to Sean, who's foot was covered with blood. He had apparently leapt from a high rock onto the sand and taken a large slice out of his big toe on a sharp piece of coral. Despite the copious amounts of blood, Sean seemed to be taking it all in his stride. Two of Oscar's daughters stood by watching as Pakofe busily made use of a brand new medical kit. 'I bought it only this morning,' Pakofe grinned.

Sean's toe was successfully bound up just as the first of the other guests began arriving. A mini-busload of people from the International Dateline Hotel, another from Leo's guest house and some more in cars from a couple of other small guest houses. Not many people. . .about 40, I suppose, although we'd been told that Oscar had catered for up to 300 people on occasions when cruise ships called at Tonga.

A group of Tongan musicians strumming on guitars and beating wooden drums began to play from a small platform built into a tree above the tables and benches. The Hawaian lamps were all burning, the drinks were being passed around and the feast was about to start. Two big suckling pigs had been turning over slowly on a spit over an open fire. The 'umu', or underground oven, in which other food and meats had been cooking away all day, was being opened up...the sand shovelled away, then a canvas covering removed, then the palm leaves, then the food, sitting on more palm leaves on the hot rocks underneath.

Oscar's daughters, sons, nieces, nephews, cousins etc. then set to work to serve it all. It was really fantastic...in fact my mouth waters just writing about it. Roast pig, chickens, lamb, octopus, hot clams, crabs, wonderful salads, taro, yams...as much and more than we could eat. And with it all, an ebullient Oscar hovering everywhere, supervising, laughing, telling stories...singing with the band, sitting talking with his guests and generally making everyone feel relaxed and welcome.

Oscar had been doing the rounds, talking to his guests as they tucked in to the huge feast. With a big smile on his face, he stopped at our rough-hewn, wooden table and sat down to talk. After a few minutes of compliments to him over the food, I asked him about the period he had spent working for the queen of Tonga.

'Well,' he laughed, 'I first came to Tonga when I was only eleven years old.' He shook his head. 'I could never have believed then that all this would happen to me. I came with my parents from Vava'u, about 200 miles [320 kilometres] away in a fourteen foot [4½ metre] boat. It took us two weeks to get here. Then I started work as a galley-boy and deck-hand on English and Dutch ships and then I eventually landed a job here in Tongatapu as a page-boy in the royal household.'

'And you stayed in that job for how long?'

'Oh for many years...many years. I became the queen's favourite...her head footman and valet. I was personal valet to Queen Elizabeth of England when she and the Duke of Edinburgh stayed here,' Oscar said proudly.

He picked up a piece of octopus from one of the dishes made from split banana tree-trunks and slipped it into his mouth. 'But as I grew older, I longed for my home island of Vava'u. I wanted to be independent. I told Her Majesty that I must leave her service.'

'Did she try to stop you?' Trish asked.

'Oh yes...for a while. But she saw that I really wanted to go. She tried to persuade me to at least stay here on this island, Tongatapu. She offered me any piece of land I wanted on the island...eight acres [3 hectares] anywhere I wished. I didn't have to make up my mind immediately, she said. Any time I was ready.

'When I left the royal household, I went to Sydney to learn all about hotel catering. I trained at the Carlton-Rex hotel there and then came back here to be catering manager at the Dateline Hotel. But all the while I had in mind doing something like this...to be independent. I had mentioned this offer of land, that the queen had made to me, to a friend in Sydney...an Australian ...and he came to Tongatapu to help me decide where to choose my land.

He went all over the island, from end to end and advised me to ask for this piece here at Oholei.

'The Minister for Lands, Prince Tuipelehake, the present king's brother, who is now the prime minister of Tonga, was amazed when I pointed it out on the map. "But there's nothing there," he said. "No roads, no facilities, no villages, no arable land. . .just cliffs and the beach. We can find you something much better than that." But I insisted. It was the scenic beauty that I wanted. Then, when I told people what I planned to do with it, everybody laughed. It would take too much money they said. But I went to American Samoa, where the money is much better, and I worked at The Rainmaker Hotel there. . .running all their bars and restaurants. . .for over a year, saving all my money. Then I came back here, hired a bulldozer and pushed a road through to my land. That was back in '69. Still they laughed at me. During '70, '71 and '72 my whole family worked with me to make the place right. It was slow, but in '73 we started to make a little business and from then on we have only gone forward. Now it is one of the most successful tourist attractions in Tonga.'

Success seems to run in Oscar's family: of his five sons, one is studying science at the Australian National University Canberra, the second is manager of a Chinese restaurant in Nuku'alofa, another is a senior air traffic officer with Air Pacific Airlines, the fourth is the chef at the Dateline Hotel, while the youngest son and Oscar's three daughters all work in the hotel industry as well as being dancers in the traditional group which performs regularly at his own functions at Oholei Beach and at others in the island's hotels.

At the end of the feast it was time to see the dancers to their performance, so Oscar led everyone along a torch-lit path into a huge cave. The band of drummers climbed up onto a rocky outcrop behind us where they could only just be seen in the flickering light of the oil lamps. The dance routines, in a variety of Tongan and Polynesian costumes, were dramatic and exciting, but the pièce de résistance was the finale. . .a fire-dancer who put on a show of spectacular contortions and acrobatics with blazing torches which brought gasps from the crowd amongst whom we were sitting on the rocky floor of the cave.

All the way across the Pacific, from the very beginning of our journey, we had seen dancing of one kind or another, basically Polynesian hula-style dancing, with local variations in style and pace. I found it interesting that we never really had to make any great effort to see these dances. . .they are just so much a part of Polynesian life, so common in the everyday existence of the people, that literally everyone dances. . .from fat, old men on Aitutaki, to 80-year-old Aggie Grey in Samoa. The dance is integral. Without it, Polynesia just wouldn't be the same. It's a nice feeling to have it happening all around you. Even if you can't do it yourself, without disclocating something, it's great to watch.

We left Oscar's Hideaway at about 11.00 p.m., feeling full of good food, drink and entertainment. In the mini-bus on the way back to town, one of Oscar's daughters led the whole group of people in the bus in a sing-song, so that by the time we were dropped off at Herman's guest house, Fasimoafi, we were all feeling decidedly positive about life in general. A few more Oscar Kamis around the place would make a big difference to the world, we decided.

'Ere... where d'ya reckon I'd find a chiropodist? Me bloomin' feet is killin' me.' The man with the strong Cockney accent, the painfully sunburnt nose and the British-length shorts, grimaced as he alternated his balance to stick out first one and then the other offending extremity for our inspection. 'Ooooh,' he wailed.

We had been walking along the main street, the following morning, when this man, who was in his middle-60s and quite obviously a visitor to Tonga, suddenly accosted us and, without any preamble, had launched into a tirade against his feet.

Having not a clue as to the whereabouts of a chiropodist on Tongatapu, but keeping to ourselves the strong suspicion that there wasn't one, we suggested to the fellow that he hobble on around to ask Russell Marriott, who seemed to have a good idea about most things on the island.

The man thanked us for the suggestion and began moving slowly off, muttering about how he thought he'd better start heading back home. 'Oim missin' me goat,' he added. 'I 'ave one wots 'ouse-trained. I takes 'im fer walks an' all an' I worry 'e'll fret 'i'self away wiv me gawn. Nice place though this Tonga, ain't it?'

Conversations for the rest of the morning, which we spent searching for gifts for friends, were a decided anti-climax after that.

Laden with pieces of *tapa,* wooden masks and statues, woven baskets and shell earrings, we staggered back to Herman's and Iain began to display his impressive skill as a parcel-maker-upper and wrapper. My role in these operations is to keep the cardboard boxes, brown paper, string and sticky tape rolling in. Perhaps if my maths mistress had told me that I should persevere with the struggle, as a comprehension of basic maths helps with spatial recognition, which in turn would one day enable me to pack up awkward shaped artefacts in Tonga, I would have seen the point. But then again maybe I wouldn't.

After wrestling the end products along to the post office, we visited the philatelic bureau and invested in some rectangular coins and some banana-shaped stamps. On the way back home, we picked up our airline tickets for the following morning's flight to Nadi (pronounced 'Nandi') and finally repacked our packs.

Russell had told us that there was a Japanese film crew in town and, wanting to know more about why make a Japanese film in Tonga, we had called by at the Dateline where the crew were based and arranged to meet the director, Takashi Nomura, that evening for drinks.

'I'm sorry that my English is not so good,' Takashi Nomura said, dismissing a skill with a second language which very few native English speakers ever bother to develop. We apologised for *our* total lack of Japanese.

'This is my translator, Mishi.' Takashi introduced the young woman who sat beside him, wearing zappy casual gear and looking a million dollars. Mishi spoke softly with a noticeably American accent. 'I went to college in Maryland for three years,' she explained.

Takashi in his kimono (not a bad sort himself) nursed his beer as he told us about the film he was directing. 'To put the story very basically, it's about a Japanese boy and his father who are visiting Tonga and go out fishing with a Tongan boy and his father. The Tongan man is washed overboard and the Japanese man does not rescue him. The story revolves around the Japanese boy's attempts to reconcile his natural love for his father with his contempt for him over what he sees as a despicable act of cowardice. That's it, very simply.'

'Very Japanese,' I suggested.

'Yes,' Takashi smiled. 'Very Japanese. Always inspecting our hearts. Great emphasis on a man being a man.'

'Why Tonga?' Iain asked.

'Why not? It is so beautiful. It's also cheap and we have no problems with unions. And, best of all, Tongans are naturally gifted actors because they are an unsophisticated people with none of the guile and artifice which comes with being, what should I call it, more complex. More aware.'

We asked if there had been any problems.

Takashi shook his head. 'Nothing by comparison with how it would have been if we had been shooting this film at home.'

'The language?'

'Well, at first it was a little difficult because the Tongan version of English is so different from the Japanese version of English! But we improvised a lot. No, it's been a good shoot. Most of the crew of 60 have gone now. We have all but finished. Just a few things to tidy up. To be frank, the only reason why I shall be glad to leave is because I am sick of taro and yams and taro and yams and taro and yams. The food is too basic for my tastes!' He laughed. 'But otherwise I shall be sorry to go. The lifestyle is so simple and gentle. It is how we are supposed to live.'

This was the first film Takashi Nomura had made outside of Japan, though he had made many at home. 'This one is already sold in Japan and in the United States,' he said, 'and I hope to branch out now and do more filming away from Japan.'

We asked if the young boy in the movie had school lessons while he was on location.

'Oh yes. He has a fulltime tutor travelling with him. It is very expensive, to bring so many people and so much equipment down here, but I think it will pay its way.'

We were joined by three other Japanese members of the crew who all appeared to be incredibly fit. They needed to be, as they were the divers and underwater photographers.

'We built a complete boat for *$10,000* and then sank it!' they boasted. 'It's down there off Panga Motu, if you want to look at it.'

One of the divers spoke in Japanese and they all laughed. We looked enquiringly at Takashi who smiled.

'He was just saying, as long as you don't dive down to it on Sunday. It is a joke only. Because you see he was arrested.'

'Arrested!?'

'Yes.' Everyone smiled and laughed. 'There was a group of us and we were all arrested. Because we were filming on a Sunday! We had been warned not to, so we took a picnic to make it seem like an innocent outing and there we were filming away like crazy when. . . bang, out of nowhere, came the police and 20 or so of us were put in jail. Didn't Russell tell you?'

We shook our heads.

'He was with us. He was arrested too. I think it was only because of him and his influence where it matters, that they kept us only for just a few hours and let us off with a warning not to do it again. Can you imagine this happening anywhere else in the world? Never on Sundays.' Everyone laughed.

Back at the guest house, Herman brought out his guest book, which he had decided Iain should have the honour of drawing in. 'But don't you touch the first two pages,' he ordered. 'Those are left empty in order that one day His Majesty and the nobles may sign there.'

We looked through at some of the contributions made by other guests. A few of them were far from complimentary. Obviously these people had suffered under Herman's acid tongue. But he didn't seem to mind. 'You write what you like,' he said to Iain, 'and please do not lean back on the chair like that.'

I bridled, but Iain's nicer nature prevailed and he sat down to draw a large Fasimoafi guest house, towering above a diminutive Dateline, to which we all added our thankyous and goodbyes.

## 18  VITI LEVU
'Good evening, sir. What have you in that bottle?'

I suppose there've been times when the reader of these pages has felt a degree of envy; the idea of a voyage through the South Pacific...blue lagoons, waving palms and white sands...is for many an often-dreamed-of, once-in-a-lifetime odyssey. For most it is a dream that is never achieved. But I would just like anyone who does feel small twinges of envy to know that, from at least one point of view, it's not all beer and skittles. There is sometimes a considerable cost, not only in money, but in terms of the worry associated with money.

Not that Trish and I are overly security-conscious anyway, but one does have to make a living and, shortly after our arrival in Fiji, we received some disquieting news in this respect. Fiji was one of the places in the Pacific we had decided to make a mail pick-up point. As we knew we would be moving around a great deal in the Cook Islands, Samoa and Tonga, we arranged for all our mail after Tahiti to be sent to the American Express office in Suva. So, as soon as we arrived at Nausori airport, we took the bus into town, left our packs at the airline office and walked along Victoria Parade to collect our mail.

A nasty shock in a letter from our bank. The overdraft had gone way beyond the agreed limits and the manager informed us apologetically that he had no option but to refuse payment on any future cheques...including the mortgage payments on our house. Great!

What to do? We flicked through our travellers cheques. Not that we didn't know exactly how much we had left anyway...it was just a nervous reaction. We had enough to complete our journey as planned to Australia if we were careful. But then, there'd be nothing at all for when we arrived, we'd be deeply in debt and there'd be no money coming in—at least not for some time.

While Zara and Sean prowled around the duty-free shops lining the road, we sat in a park and talked...gloomily. Should we cut short the trip, head for Sydney and try to get jobs as soon as possible? Or continue on for another

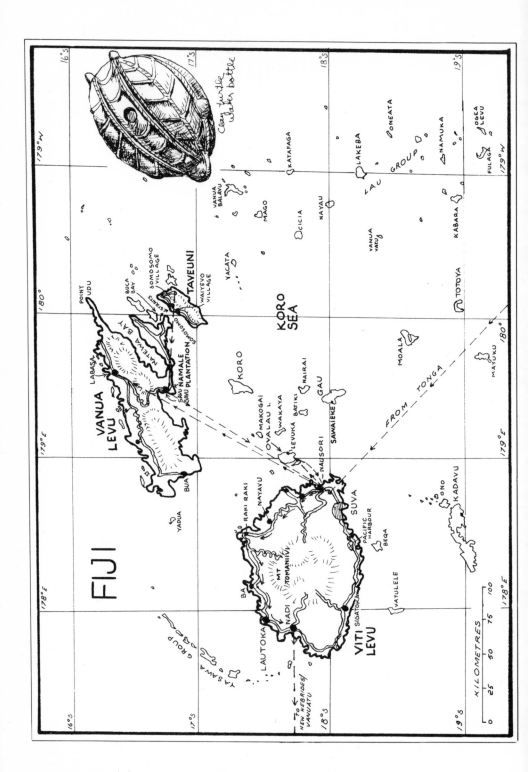

Clay turtle water bottle

FIJI

VANUA LEVU

TAVEUNI

KORO SEA

VITI LEVU

LAU GROUP

KILOMETRES
0  25  50  75  100

three weeks or a month to visit Fiji, the New Hebrides and New Caledonia, and then arrive in Australia broke and behind the eightball?

I was overcome with feelings that we were crazy to be spending our money like this—completely irresponsible. But in the end, we were both agreed. There was no real choice. We had to continue. Nevertheless, the whole situation had taken a turn we didn't like at all. It left us with an underlying feeling of concern, which, for a while, took the edge off our enjoyment of Fiji. Fortunately, the human mind being what it is, our worries eventually began to drift into the background and surfaced only occasionally. If we'd been getting a letter like that every day from the bank, I'm sure we couldn't have lasted.

The point of all this chat about money is that while some readers might have felt those slight twinges of envy I mentioned, for what seems an exciting and interesting lifestyle, the majority would not be prepared to toss in their security and let things go to the point where those final letters start coming from the bank manager. And yet, it seems, that unless one has vast amounts of money, that is what is sometimes necessary.

Despite this rather gloomy first hour or so in Suva, we still experienced, on a different level, a degree of excitement and interest at having arrived in Fiji. The contrast with the other islands through which we'd been travelling couldn't have been more striking. The whole place was considerably more modern, buildings of 8 and 10 storeys and more and the streets were busy with people and cars bustling back and forth. A very polyglot society, all sorts of faces, plenty of Europeans, Chinese and Polynesian islanders, but of course, the most prominent were the darker-skinned Melanesians—the indigenous people of Fiji—big people with round, generally happy faces and big, smiling mouths. . . and the Indians. Right across the Pacific we had seen hardly any Indian people. Now, we saw them everywhere.

Another thing about Suva that made us feel we were moving back into a more twentieth-century, Westernised society was the strike. All of the city's banks were on strike for higher pay. None of them were open and there were people walking back and forth in the streets carrying placards. Just like home!

We booked into The Town House, a hotel close to the centre of town. At about $25 a night, it was out of our normal bracket, but comfortable and handy and, after all our bad news, we thought, to hell with it, perhaps a comfortable hotel would boost our morale a little.

There was another welcome boost to come; a little later in the afternoon at the Fiji Visitors' Bureau we met Malukai Gucake, the director and his executive manager, Isimeli Bainimara. The Bureau office is in a beautiful old building right in the centre of the city. To the credit of the city council, the old colonial-style structure has been preserved and renovated, while high, modern office blocks have risen all around it. The Bureau itself was in a mild state of chaos when we arrived due to the fact that they were in the midst of their high tourist season and Christmas was fast approaching. But both Malukai and Isimele were extremely friendly and helpful to us. Malukai, a short, chubby, brown-skinned man with a moustache and ever-ready smile, was apologetic that we should see Fiji in such a crowded condition.

'So many tourists,' he said. 'It would probably be better if you had come in the off season.'

We explained that we'd been to Fiji before and seen some of the regular tourist destinations, but on this occasion we wanted to seek his advice about out-of-the-way places—islands not frequented by hordes of tourists—and if you look at the map of Fiji, that's not a very difficult request. Of the 320 islands in the group, less than a dozen are visited by significant numbers of tourists and only one, the main island of Viti Levu, contains the major tourist resorts and attractions.

'We thought we'd like to go to Vanua Levu and Taveuni,' I said.

Isimele's eyes lit up. 'Ah,' he said with a wide grin, 'Vanua Levu is Malukai's home island and Taveuni is mine. If you go to Taveuni, you must visit my family. They will show you the real Fiji. They live in Somosomo, a small village there.'

Malukai was also pleased that we should want to go to these two islands instead of the regular resorts. I think it was almost a pleasant change for them to sit down and discuss the things to do and see on their home islands, which by comparison to some of the other 'glamour' spots in the Fiji group, are all but ignored by visitors.

Fijians are intensely proud of their heritage and, although they are amongst the more economically advanced Pacific nations and they experienced just on a hundred years of British colonial administration, their ancient traditions are still strong.

Prior to the first European arrival, the islands of Fiji had been inhabited for some 3000 years. The Dutch nagivator, Abel Janzoon Tasman, was the first Westerner to sail through the islands in 1643, when he reported trouble in negotiating his vessel, the *Heemskerck* through the dangerous reefs in the northeastern part of the group. But it was more than 130 years before another European, Captain Cook, came anywhere near Fiji. He reported sighting the small island of Vatoa in the southeastern corner of the Fijis in 1774, but didn't land. Another 15 years passed before the main islands were sighted and that was when William Bligh and some of his crew were making their celebrated voyage in the open long-boat from Tonga to Timor, following the mutiny on the *Bounty*. A Fijian war canoe chased them. Bligh came back three years later, in 1792, on HMS *Providence* and made a more thorough investigation of the group.

From then on European visits became more frequent. With the discovery of sandalwood in the Fiji group, traders began operating in the area in the early years of the nineteenth century and then the official exploring expeditions of several nations completed the discovery and charting of the group. These were from Russia, under Thadeus Von Bellinghausen; from France under Dumont d'Urville; from Britain, which sent the survey ship HMS *Victor*, and from the United States which organised an exploring expedition led by Commodore Charles Wilkes.

Then, of course, the missionaries arrived on the scene, but, because of a basic disinterest, if not open hostility on the part of the Fijians, they did not make much ground in their first years in the Fijis. The situation in the group was complicated, as it seemed to have been in many of the other island groupings in the Pacific at the time, (or perhaps it had always been that way) by constant tribal bickering and fighting. In Fiji there seemed to be almost continual tribal warfare.

In the mid-nineteenth century, Cakobau, a Fijian chief of the island of Bau, had considerable success in extending his influence to the islands of Viti Levu, Lomaiviti, Taveuni and Lau and foreigners were beginning to address him as Tui Viti (king of Fiji). His fortunes waxed and waned and his power and prestige were constantly under threat from other tribal leaders. Seeking for a way to solve his problems in one fell swooop (he was also heavily in debt to various American residents of the islands) he offered Queen Victoria the opportunity of Britain taking over Fiji by deed of cession. That was in 1858.

Through years of indecision and an endless succession of 'possibles', 'maybes' and 'perhapses', Britain finally agreed that Fiji should be ceded to the crown in 1874, almost 20 years after Cakobau had first made his offer. And then it was really only because Britain had no choice. Large numbers of British settlers had swarmed to Fiji during the intervening years, anticipating eventual British sovereignty over the islands, and they were exerting considerable pressure on Britain to move. Then, during the American Civil War, when cotton supplies to England and Europe from the American south had dried up, Fiji suddenly became an important source of raw cotton, and consequently more valuable to Britain. In addition, the practice of 'blackbirding'—that is the virtual kidnapping of Fijian natives to work as indentured labourers on plantations in Fiji and other islands and also in northern Australia—was causing increasing concern and arousing international criticism. This, combined with the other factors, prompted Britain to finally act on the offer of cession.

Without any doubt, the most significant impact of Britain's century-long colonial rule was the controversial and contentious decision of the first British governor, Sir Arthur Gordon, to bring Indians to Fiji to work as labourers. With the end of the American Civil War and the revival of the cotton trade from the American south, Fiji's fortunes in this area had declined, but the settlers had shifted their crops to sugar. Governor Gordon, however, was against the idea of Fijians working for Europeans in their own country, and authorised the importation of labourers from India under a five-year indenture system. At the end of five years, the Indians would be free to return to their homes *at their own expense,* but, if they chose to remain for a second five-year term, the Fiji government would pay their return passages. Alternatively, at the end of 10 years, they could opt to stay in Fiji if they wanted to.

The first load of 500 Indians arrived in Fiji on May 14th, 1879 and from then on there were about 2000 immigrants each year, until 1916, a total of more than 70 000. They had a difficult time, and worked under deplorable conditions. Yet many Indians still felt that their situation was far better in Fiji than it would have been had they returned to India. So they stayed on after their 10-year indenture period to become independent farmers on land leased from the Fijians...and, of course, traders. In this century, the Indian population has grown far more rapidly than that of any other ethnic grouping in Fiji, so that now, indigenous Fijians of Melanesian extraction are actually outnumbered by Indians in the ratio of roughly 300 000 to 260 000. The remaining 40 000 that make a total population of about 600 000, are Europeans, other islanders, Chinese and people of mixed race.

Fiji gained its independence from Britain in 1970. Ratu Sir Kamisese Mara who had been chief minister under the internal self-governing situation that preceded independence became the first prime minister. The first British governor-general, Sir Robert Foster, was succeeded in 1973 by a Fijian governor-general, Ratu Sir George Cakobau, the great grandson of the King Cakobau who had signed the deed of cession of Fiji to Britain.

After collecting as much information as possible from Malukai and Isimele at the Visitors' Bureau, we thanked them both and then went out to try to arrange a few things for Christmas. If we went to Vanua Levu and Taveuni, we would be spending Christmas and New Year on one or other of the islands. It would be the first time for many years that we would not be with either friends or parents for Christmas and at least we had to get *some* presents for Zara and Sean. Both of them had been talking about getting a portable radio-cassette player when they got back home, so Trish and I decided that, although it was more than we could afford considering the precarious condition of our finances at the time, that it would be a radio-cassette player each for them—but nothing else.

A bit of a bare Christmas. We were finding it very hard to get the right feeling. We had been on the move for so long, and the South Pacific isn't very Christmassy anyway; it was difficult to believe that it was really going to overtake us. Nevertheless, Trish and I went out on our own, while Zara and Sean wandered around Suva, looking the place over. Of course there are hundreds of photographic and electronic shops in Suva, all selling 'duty-free' stuff, so we had no difficulty in finding places that sold what we were looking for, only difficulty in finding the right price. They all varied so greatly and it was necessary to bargain, but eventually we found the right type at an acceptable price and bought two of them. We weakened a little and also bought them a pocket calculator and a music tape each. Then we returned to the hotel with them all heavily wrapped, but quite clearly to the eagle eyes of Zara and Sean, presents of some sort. They were, however, forbidden to touch them until the right time—several days away.

If, like me, you are a public market freak then in Suva a visit to the large market at the other end of town from the big shops, but still within easy walking distance, is a must. Crammed with stalls selling fresh fruit and vegetables and fish in a staggering variety it fairly hums with life. The Fijians stick to selling the basic staples such as yams and bananas while the Indians go for the less prosaic peppers and chilis. Also, at many of their smaller stalls outside the main open-sided building, they sell paper twists overflowing with peanuts fried in curry powder and an array of very sweet, small cakes and biscuits, variously spiced and made of coconut and honey.

I should warn you now that I'm fairly wrapped in Fiji. As Iain has said, we've visited a couple of times before and each time I like it more. It has for me what I like to find in people, an exciting mix of intellectual and physical stimulation.

We bought too much, unable to resist the temptation of all that delicious fresh food, but we were unable to find any soy sauce for sale. A couple of people suggested that we try the Chinese café over the road where the daughter of the owner very kindly dispensed some from the kitchen's large container into an empty soft drink bottle, and then wouldn't take any payment for it. With armfuls of goodies, Iain carefully carrying the unstoppered bottle half filled with soy sauce, we started heading home and were so engrossed in talking about what we had seen that day that we didn't notice two policemen, one Fijian, one Indian, large and slight like Mutt and Jeff, until they barred our way along the footpath.

'Good evening sir,' the Indian said in Peter Sellers accent and with English bobby politeness, 'what is it that you have in that bottle?'

Startled, Iain smiled and told him, 'Soy sauce.'

'Yes sir,' the officer said in tones of disbelief. 'Well, would you please to be so kind as to not drink in the street. It is not the custom in Fiji.'

'It is to put on our food, not to drink. Here have a smell. It's soy sauce.' Iain proferred the bottle, but the Indian gave that little sideways nod of the head which is such a universal gesture among Indians that when you visit India you find yourself doing it, and over his face came a weary expression which said, 'I've heard it all before.'

'Yes sir,' he reiterated politely. At this point his big Fijian colleague stepped forward and would have taken up Iain's offer of a sniff if the Indian hadn't turned to give him a warning look—'don't encourage them...' and he stopped midway.

'Really,' Iain persisted, 'it's just soy sauce.'

'Just so long as you do not drink in the street, sir. Good evening.' And he walked on, followed, somewhat reluctantly I thought, by his offsider.

It was difficult not to laugh, but we daren't because, apart from appearing rude, it would have confirmed his opinion that we were rolling along the main street knocking back neat rum or some homemade concoction. No doubt visitors behaving in just that manner are not beyond his experience!

We woke next morning to the sound of church bells. Opposite us, the Catholic cathedral had opened its doors and the early morning congregation streamed in, all wearing their Sunday-best. Indians, Europeans, Fijians, of all ages. We lay and listened to the carols. 'Oh Come All Ye Faithful', 'Oh Little Town of Bethlehem.' I could feel the Christmas blues beginning to descend and so forced myself to get up and make breakfast.

At 10.30 a.m. they all came out again, the priest on the top step shaking hands and smiling; the outgoing congregation greeting the incoming one. There was more bell-pealing and another carol service. It's mind over matter, I told myself as the terrible pangs of homesickness raged.

We cleaned up and repacked our packs. Iain and I carried the tape recorders in their obvious wrappings, still being eyed hopefully by the children who knew better than to ask about them. We were the only people on the bus on the way to the airport, which was driven by an Indian man in his late 40s. We sat up front, and, after exchanging a few pleasantries he launched into a vitriolic attack on his employers, a private bus operation. 'I started work at five this morning and I will not finish until after ten tonight.' Remembering the union demonstration we had seen in Suva, Iain said, 'But you'll get overtime for that won't you?'

The man shook his head vehemently. 'No overtime. They don't pay overtime. Just a flat daily rate. Start when they want you and finish when the last plane comes in. Sometimes that's not till midnight.'

I said, 'But surely your union...'

The driver cut me short with a grunt of disgust. 'I am not with any union. This company will not employ union members. The only union drivers are those who drive the government buses.'

'Why don't you get a job with them?'

'I have tried. Believe me. But they want younger men. All that is left for me is to work for private companies who will employ older men, but only if they do not belong to the union. So...' He took his anger and frustration out on the driver of a small car who had got in his way. Horn blasting, he cut in on the poor bloke who, as we re-passed him, looked as terrified as I'm sure I do when several tonnes of metal moving at 80 kmh comes within a centimetre of my offside!

'Who owns the company?' Iain asked.

The Indian spat out a very Indian name.

'Oh. I see,' Iain said.

'Yes,' the Indian replied, pulling up abruptly outside the terminal. 'No Fijian would run a company in that manner. They're not sharp enough businessmen.'

The plane was delayed. (So what's new.) I had Paul Scott; Iain had the latest edition of *Time,* which, after a preliminary flip through I had decided not to read, but rather to cling to my illusion of a sane and pleasant world until the last possible moment! Zara and Sean went off to case the terminal shops and returned with the news that there was the most gorgeous-looking Indian girl all dressed up in red and gold and that the man with her had 'masses of gold coins around his neck.'

Sean was impressed. 'Come and look,' they begged, 'and tell me how much you think the gold is worth,' Sean added.

The newly-married couple (for that was patently obvious what they were) sat conspicuously at the far end of the waiting room, looking remarkably out of place in that spartan building. She was indeed gorgeous looking in her red and gold: the soft silk of her scarlet sari shot through with gold thread. A red dot on her forehead and so much gold jewellery, I couldn't help wondering if she would topple over when she tried to stand up. He, by contrast was soberly dressed in a brand, spanking new, smart grey business suit, white business shirt and formal tie. All of which made the necklace of glittering gold sovereigns hung around his neck appear even more startling.

'He has no socks on,' Zara, a stickler for detail, commented, with a touch of disapproval. The brand new shiny, shiny, black laceup shoes did indeed have the laces removed and were worn on bare feet.

'That's so he can slip them on and off easily to be barefoot for the temple and for private houses too,' I explained to her. But I could see she still awarded him a demerit.

'Isn't she beautiful,' they both exclaimed and I smiled at the couple, hoping they wouldn't take our obvious interest as rudeness. All our conversations had been conducted *soto voce,* while pretending not to look!

Our flight was called and imagine the children's delight when the couple boarded the same plane and sat behind us and beside Zara and Sean who couldn't keep their eyes off them. The plane was a very snazzy Bandurante: a Brazilian plane which carries 18 passengers and is shaped like I feel planes should be shaped; long and thin and streamlined. Elegant, with seats of real leather.

We rose, circled and, turning northeast, were immediately over the sea which was silver in the late afternoon sun. Islands everywhere. Beautiful! We had settled back to enjoy the flight when we heard the young bridegroom ask Zara what her name was and the pause of delight before she told him. They began to talk, both Zara and Sean asking questions only children can ask and not be thought rude!

He explained that they had been married near his home on Viti Levu that morning and that now they were going to her home on Vanua Levu for a repeat performance.

'Can I feel those gold coins?' Sean asked.

The young man good-naturedly leant across and said, 'Those were given to me by friends and family. You see my wife,' he said the word softly, 'has the same.'

'Oooh,' both the children exclaimed in delight over the bride's necklace of coins of equal size and number which lay half-concealed in the splendour of her sari.

'How much are they worth?' It was Sean again, at which point we thought it politic to intervene. We turned around, introduced ourselves and congratulated them.

'I am Chandrika Prasad,' the young man shook hands. 'And this is my wife.' The handle was stressed now.

The beautiful young woman smiled and opened her bright, black, kohl-smeared eyes just a little wider. We answered his questions about our journey and then asked about them.

'I am a civil servant,' Chandrika said with pride. 'I am in the quarantine department where I am a vet. My wife' (there it was again) 'she is a teacher of English.'

He was so friendly, so pleasant, that I plucked up the courage to ask what I had been longing to know. I tried to put it in a tactfully roundabout way. 'Many Indian marriages are still arranged aren't they? Is it still that way in Fiji?'

Quick as a flash, he picked up my impertinent meaning. 'Quite often.' His grin broadened and his face...I can only describe it this way...sprang alive with happiness. 'But ours is a *love* marriage.'

At Labasa's tiny airstrip a busload of relatives and friends waited their arrival and we waved them off to their new life. Happiness is as infectious as sorrow and we all felt we too had been given a present just by meeting them.

# 19 **VANUA LEVU**
## A Christmas landmark

Labasa (pronounced Lambasa), came as something of a surprise to us. The bus dropped us off outside the Hotel Takia which is on the main street and we clambered out to stand on the sidewalk where we were almost swept away by the press of people, all of them Indian. That's not true. Not quite. Perhaps one in 20 was Fijian. But the overwhelming impression was of an Indian population. It was like being suddenly transplanted from a Pacific island to the Indian subcontinent.

We checked in, left our bags and were out again as quickly as possible, anxious to enjoy the atmosphere. Fortunately, all four of us thrive in this sort of place. It was 7 p.m. and the shops were still open and crowded with opulently-fleshed women in swishing saris, smelling of heady perfume. There were children everywhere, their bright eyes kohl-rimmed, either being carried or running in and out of a forest of legs.

We went from shop to shop, exclaiming over the quite monumentally horrendous, but therefore very enticing goods! Indian gods, made out of plastic, their flesh a revolting pink, the paint of their brightly-coloured clothes gawdy with splashes of glitter. Replete with painted toenails and caste masks. Very tempting! Glass bangles, oily perfumes, lengths of sari material. Tee-shirts with fluorescent messages, plastic sandals and everywhere shopkeepers pressing us to buy. I wanted to hug them all, so over-excited do I become in such a place!

Exhausted, we found a small café crowded with fairly inebriated gentlemen where we ate curry and rice with our hands, washing them first in the sink in the corner. For less than a dollar each we ate fit to bust and then strolled home through the still-crowded streets, resisting Sean's pleas to go to one of the half dozen cinemas. All of them were showing those quite marvellously melodramatic Indian dramas, the ones in which good always triumphs over evil, though not without a great deal of heart-rending tragedy along the way, and in which the lovers' lips never quite manage to meet!

Christmas Eve! Yet none of us felt in the least like Christmas. Zara and Sean did perhaps, a little more than Trish and I, but it was clear that they too felt the same disorientation in time and space that we did.

The streets of Labasa were hot and dusty, even at 8 the next morning, as we walked along to another small café a short distance from the hotel. Some of the Indian stores had a sprinkling of tinsel and Christmassy slogans amongst the wares displayed in their windows, but they were rather desultory and could hardly have inspired a festive spirit in anyone. Still, at least we couldn't complain about the prices in Labasa: a breakfast of fresh orange juice, boiled eggs, bread rolls, jam and coffee for four people came to a total of $1.93!

Back at the hotel we met Paul Jaduram, the manager and part owner. He was small and slightly built, in his mid-30s and very friendly. He had been born in Labasa, where his parents, like many other Indians, were traders. But Paul had also spent some time working in England. His family had bought a cinema and Paul was sent to London to work in cinemas there so as to get to know the business. While he was there he met and married an English girl, Stella, who had come back to Fiji with Paul and they now had a couple of young children. We didn't meet Stella immediately, but Paul said he hoped we could meet her the following day in Savu Savu. We had told him we were going to take the 80-kilometre bus ride to Savu Savu which is on the opposite side of the island, later in the day.

'We will be there too,' he said. 'My wife and I. We are going across with a bunch of the people who are doing the new construction work on the sugar refinery here. We'll see you there. Are you having Christmas dinner at the hotel?'

'Er...ah, well yes, I suppose we are,' I said. Not having even thought about it. 'That would be nice...sure.'

'You can sit at our table...I'll organise it. I'm sure you'll really like it. They put on a big spread and all sorts of people come to it. Locals as well as visitors...from different parts of the island. It's better than anything in Labasa.'

'Great,' I said, feeling my spirits slightly lifted. At least one part of Christmas was organised.

Labasa and Savu Savu, on opposite sides of Vanua Levu island, had only recently been linked by road. It was a fairly rough, unsurfaced road across the rugged central spine of the island which took about two hours to traverse. We knew it would not be the most comfortable ride in the world, but nevertheless we were quite looking forward to the trip when we made our way, shortly after noon, down to Labasa's central market where we would catch the bus. The market was terrific: a great mass of people swarming amidst a fabulous assortment of fresh fruit and vegetables, meat and fish and all manner of clothes, shoes, luggage, toys, cooking utensils and Indian oddments, glittering bangles and sari material.

We bought a more-than-ample supply of fresh fruit to take with us on the journey and, when our battered old bus pulled into the market, we piled our packs into a couple of open compartments in the side of the vehicle, only to have them quickly covered with huge clumps of taro plants belonging to villagers who had come into town to do their marketing and extra shopping for Christmas.

The bus was fully air-conditioned: it just had no windows! or rather, no glass in them, which was just as well, I suppose, because the day had become scorchingly hot.

The road across the island was dusty and bumpy but, as we'd been told by Paul Jaduram, the scenery, as we climbed into the mountains, was spectacular. Vanua Levu is the second largest island in the Fiji group, being about 180 kilometres long, with the only significant population concentrations being in Labasa (20 000) and Savu Savu (around 5000). The rest of the people live in small villages and towns dotted around the rim of the island. The centre is very sparsely populated, being mostly tropical rain forest, very beautiful though, particularly in the mountains, where the long white plumes of several waterfalls can be seen plunging into virtually in-accessible valleys.

We stopped by a small waterfall on the mountain road about half-way across the island for the passengers to drink and freshen themselves with water to gain some relief from the powerful heat of the day, before continuing on to Savu Savu.

The road approaches Savu Savu around the rim of a wide bay, fringed in parts with mangrove swamps. The green mountains in the background give the place a setting of considerable beauty. It is only a tiny town, a few shops, a wharf and a cargo shed sprinkled along the waterfront, which faces onto a two or three-hundred-metre wide channel separating the mainland from a small island which is covered with thick vegetation. The first thing that met our view, resting on the sands of the island, was the rotting hulk of an old sailing vessel, a three-masted brigantine that had been wrecked on the beach. It looked like a scene from a Joseph Conrad novel.

The hotel, which we reached after a short, steep climb from the waterfront road, was only one-quarter full, despite the fact that it was the only hotel in town and this was supposed to be the high season for tourism in Fiji.

We all had a brief siesta before going back into town to look it over. Zara and Sean went prowling through a small supermarket while Trish and I walked to the far end of the settlement where we found an old white-painted wooden church.

'I wonder if they'll have carols tonight?' Trish said, almost to herself. 'Christmas isn't Christmas without carols.'

'I don't like your chances,' I said, trying not to sound too discouraging. She was feeling the lack of any Christmas spirit more than any of us. The previous Christmas we had spent in the west of England, in Somerset, where Trish had grown up. In the little stone cottage where we'd been staying we'd had the full treatment for that Christmas—a big tree, lights, snow all around, turkey, Christmas pudding, Christmas cake (all our own work) and lots of friends to visit us. This was quite a contrast.

On the way back into the town, having discovered from the man across the road that there would be no carols, we found a little Indian curry restaurant where the four of us ate well for $3.

Later, we went downstairs into the small bar of the hotel where Trish and I had a drink while Sean and Zara played billiards on a miniature table in the hotel's recreation room. A very large Fijian man in white pants and a white, short-sleeved, open-necked shirt came across the room towards us. He was with a dark attractive woman, also in white.

'Excuse me,' he said, 'are you Mr Finlay?'

'Yes,' I replied, standing up. I had not really expected him to talk to us.

'My name is Peter May. I am the manager of the hotel.' He turned to introduce his wife, whose name was Betty and I introduced Trish.

'Mr Bainimara of the Fiji Visitors' Bureau cabled me to say that you would be coming here. Are you staying for our Christmas dinner tomorrow night?'

'Yes we are,' I told him. 'We're looking forward to it. Please. . . sit down.' I motioned to the lounge chairs beside us.

They both sat down and Peter began to tell us a little about Savu Savu and how they came to be here. He had been a rugby player and then worked for several years with Qantas Airlines before returning to Vanua Levu, his home island. When he first arrived, he'd taken on the job of managing Savu Savu's public bar, a pretty rough joint we'd seen earlier at the bottom of the hill near the waterfront. I'm sure he would have had no trouble keeping everyone there in line. He wouldn't be the sort of person you'd pick a fight with. . . unless you were crazy. He was over two metres tall and built like a tank. When the hotel had been built, he was asked to take over as manager.

As the hotel was owned by an Australian group, we talked for a while about foreign investment in Fiji and then about land ownership.

'There is only a very small percentage of Fiji's land. . . less than 10 per cent, that is freehold land, land that can be owned by foreigners,' he explained. 'The rest is owned by us Fijians.'

He said it in a noticeably proprietorial manner and I knew that by 'us Fijians' he meant Melanesian Fijians, not Indian Fijians, or Fiji Indians, as they are called. They cannot own land and the law goes to some lengths to prevent them from doing so.

'It is all we have left,' Peter said, voicing a sentiment shared by tens of thousands of indigenous Fijians. His comment brought into focus the sharp divisions that exist in Fijian society. Native Fijians not only feel they are being threatened by the sheer number of Indians, but, through their natural aptitude for trade and small businesses, the Indians now virtually dominate Fiji's second-level commercial world. The top level, that is, the major businesses, lies firmly in the hands of Australians, British and New Zealand companies and, of course, the ubiquitous multinationals.

The native Fijians' lack of interest in the commercial world has led, over the years, to their being forced to one side, to become, in effect, strangers in their own house. Their only strength has lain in politics and the land. Because of the ancient chiefly system and the constitutional arrangements in force when Fiji gained independence from Britain in 1970, the indigenous Fijians have been able to hold on to considerable political power and they have taken steps to ensure that they are not further swamped by the Indian population. In doing so, however, they have met with criticism for what are undeniably undemocratic processes. Land ownership is an example: it is all but impossible for a Fiji-born Indian, even one who is a second or third generation Fijian, to have perpetual title to any piece of land. He can buy into the 150 000 hectares of existing freehold land, which continully changes hands anyway (even non-Fijians, Europeans, living out of the country, can buy into this limited supply of land), but the vast bulk of the islands' 18 272 square kilometres of land remains firmly in the hands of the native Fijians.

'Another thing that has made it difficult for us,' Peter said, 'is the gradual breakdown of our culture.'

'But that's not the Indians, is it,' I said. 'That's us. . . Europeans. . . Western civilisation. . . the twentieth century.'

'Right. We all want the things that Western society has, but we forget that there is a lot we have to give up for it all. . . the collapse of the village system for instance. Before, we had no problems with law and order. The chiefly system was respected and people knew what was right and what was wrong. Nobody would step out of line for fear of being ostracised by their friends or neighbours. But then, the chiefly system was replaced. . . at least as far as the law was concerned. Policemen in uniform were sent to live in the villages and towns, to take over the role of guardians of the peace. . . but no-one really respected them in the same way they did the village elders and this led to disorder. Then, when people saw that authority had shifted permanently from the chiefs and elders, there was a loss of respect for them too, which only aggravated the breakdown of the system. Then, when drinking regulations were lifted, there was a great deal of drunkenness. It is a big problem.'

For some time the sound of a rock band had been coming through to the bar from another part of the hotel.

'Where is the music coming from?' I asked.

Peter's wife smiled. 'It's from a disco. We have a small, open dance floor outside in the garden. Normally, we have a dance here on Saturday nights, but this is a special one for Christmas Eve.'

'Shall we go out to see it?' Peter said and we left the bar to walk out of the hotel towards the music.

Twenty or 30 couples were already dancing on the floor and there were 60 or 70 other people who sat drinking and talking at tables which were spread around the floor.

We also saw, as we arrived, Zara and Sean leaning over a low, thatched wall watching the band play. They waved to us as we took a table on one side of the floor near the entrance.

The dance was in a *bure,* a large, open-sided hut with a high, thatched roof in traditional Fijian design. There were several people we had seen earlier, who were presumably guests of the hotel, but the majority of the dancers and others sitting at the tables seemed to be locals . . . mainly Fijians, including a few Indians.

We danced a few dances and sat talking with Peter and Betty and, before we knew it, it was midnight and the band was playing 'Save the last dance for me'. Then, from the shadows on the lawn, a number of people . . . local Fijians . . . emerged in a group, stood facing the *bure* and suddenly burst into song: '*Hark the herald angels sing, Glory to the new born King . . .* '

'Carols!' Trish exclaimed in delight. 'We're going to have them after all.'

Looking around us, we saw people smiling and talking animatedly amongst themselves. They seemed as surprised as we were.

Did you know this was happening?' I asked Peter.

He laughed and shook his head. 'No. They're from a local Presbyterian church, I think. I had no idea.'

The group, about 20 men and women, sang well . . . 'Good King Wenceslas', 'Silent Night', 'O Come All Ye Faithful' . . . all the old traditionals which we recognised, even though they were all sung in Fijian.

Then suddenly, almost as abruptly as they had appeared, they stopped, bowed to their audience, said 'Merry Christmas', and began to disperse and walk off.

'What a shame the children weren't here to see it,' Trish said, as we walked back to our room. They had long since gone off to bed and, when we came into the room, they were there, sound asleep.

A funny sort of Christmas for them, I thought, as we switched out the light.

'Happy Christmas, Dad! Happy Christmas Mum!' For the first time in their lives the children had waited until we were awake on Christmas morning before greeting us. 'Come and look at the rainbow,' Zara implored, 'it's beautiful.'

'It is,' Sean confirmed. 'Come and see.'

We stumbled out of bed, still only half awake, and onto the small balcony from which we had a view across the water to the wreck, the small island and beyond. And there, arched over the horizon, was the most gloriously perfect rainbow, each colour bright and distinct, and inside it another paler one. Even for a non-religious person it seemed to hold a special promise to it that Christmas morning.

We stood for a couple of minutes drinking in the view and coming awake and then, as we turned to go back into the room, 'Happy Christmas', they both chorused again and for the first time we saw, in the corner of the balcony, an amputated branch done up as a miniature Christmas tree, decorated and hung with cards, with parcels around the bottom.

'Do you like it?' Sean asked eagerly.

'It's wonderful,' I said, feeling the tears start in my eyes as I grabbed his hand and then Zara's as she stood proudly beside their surprise.

'It's the top of a branch from a tree in the garden and these,' Zara touched the tinsel and glass balls, 'are from the big tree in the lobby.'

'We just *borrowed* them,' Sean added hastily.

Right then I wouldn't have cared if they had robbed a bank to get them, it was such a fantastic gesture of the real spirit of Christmas. I felt I had been offhand and niggly with them all over the past few days, indulging myself in feeling blue and low, homesick and deep-down lonely because this was the first Christmas since my Dad had died. But they had loved me enough not to mind—to go ahead and plan such a beautiful surprise for Iain and me.

'This is for you.' Sean gave me a card showing a woodcut print of a Fijian woman weaving a basket. Inside he had written, 'Happy Christmas Mum. I love you. I promise you won't ever again have to shout at me to take a shower and wash my hair! Sean.'

'And this is for you.' Zara gave a card to Iain showing a woodcut print of a Fijian dancer. Inside it said. 'Happy Christmas Dad. Thankyou for Africa. Thankyou for South America. Thankyou for the Pacific. And here's to the next one! All my love Zara Saskia Fionnleagh!'

I was still teary-eyed over these when Sean thrust a parcel into Iain's hands. He unwrapped a tee-shirt with 'Bula Fiji' and a stencil print of a Fijian policeman on the back. Next came a necklace of sea-urchin spines for me. And then Iain was given some aftershave. 'Read what it says on the label,' Sean ordered.

'Now every man can have Sex Appeal,' Iain intoned. 'Well, I'd better slosh it on,' and we all laughed.

'And here's yours, Mum.'

'Ginseng, Fragrance of Youth,' I read from the blurb accompanying the spray bottle. More laughter. 'We should go well together,' I said.

We gave them their tape recorder-radios and they feigned surprise. Then their calculators and taped music, so that we were immediately blasted out with 'Don't Walk, Boogie On.' Zara's tape recorder didn't work correctly and Iain accidentally wiped a small blank spot on her music tape while trying to fix it. Neither incident upset her; she took it all in a very mature manner. Nevertheless we assured her we would see about changing the machine when we got back to Suva.

It was as though we had turned a corner and they had changed from being children into being young adults. Sure, we've had plenty of to-ing and fro-ing between the two conditions since then but that Christmas will ever remain a landmark for me.

A short while later, when they had gone off for a swim and we were back in bed wishing each other a Happy Christmas, I remarked that it was a turning point, that from now on nothing would be the same. 'Here they are decorating the tree and waking us up. Pretty soon the roles will be completely reversed and they'll be making allowances for and looking after Mum and Dad. It's strange, isn't it, how quickly it happens, without us hardly noticing?'

'What I think,' Iain said, in that affectionate but decisive manner which means he thinks I am being too introspective, 'is that it all seems like a change for the better and that, instead of worrying away at it like a dog with a bone, we should go down and have a Christmas drink in the bar!' Which is what we did.

The bar was filled with a gregarious crowd whose only common denominator was the sugar mill in Labasa. All the men were employed by Reddy Fletcher, a New Zealand construction company, who had won a recent government tender to enlarge and modernise the refinery. The women and children were camp-followers...sort of twentieth-century equivalents of the women who followed the Crusaders. Forward into an economic, rather than a religious battle. They were an interesting self-sustaining group which could have been picked up holus-bolus and put down anywhere in the world, while still remaining the same tightly-knit community; there to get on with the job, finish and move on to the next one.

They covered all fields of the operation, from brickies (brick-laying for a kiln, which has to withstand immense temperatures, is rather different from putting up a patio wall), to engineers and trouble-shooters. They were a very international team—a Dutchman married to an Indonesian-Chinese, a New Zealander to a Samoan, a Brit. to a New Zealander, a couple of Australians. What they had in common was that they all found life in their home countries pretty tame and restricting. They enjoyed the uncertainty and the lack of the claustrophobic heavy hand of government and unions. They were cowboys. The only difference was that in Westerns, the cowboys don't have kids. This crowd had dozens between them.

In the convivial, festive season atmosphere we were soon absorbed into the group and we asked them why they had come over from Labasa to spend Christmas in Savu Savu.

'A lot of us are keen divers,' George Muir, the project manager told us, 'and we've been told that the area around here has some superb spots to dive. Tomorrow we're going over on the wreck and then around to Namale. Those who don't dive just come along for the ride. There's not exactly heaps to do in Labasa.'

We told him about our journey and he invited us back to Labasa to look around the refinery. 'It's pretty impressive,' he smiled.

'Where else do Reddy Fletcher have projects underway?' Iain asked.

'Indonesia, Iran, Borneo. We're flat to the boards with work. We have to get this job done by the middle of next year because there are other projects coming up. We'll go back to New Zealand from here and wait to see where we are sent.'

'I guess you earn pretty good money on these jobs?'

'Not as much as if I stayed home and worked. But I like working for them. There's no mucking about. No bullshit. They give you your head and you get on with the job. All the places I've been with them, the feeling among the fellows has always been high. They all work like stink. Long hours. No overtime. They take pride in getting the job in on time and under cost. There's none of that back home. No pride in workmanship. All they talk about is working less hours and getting more money and what they can make on the side. The result is that the country isn't only standing still, it's going backwards. Everybody wants something for nothing. I don't want my kids to grow up with that as their model. All my mates back home think I take these jobs for the soft life. I say, "listen mate, if I wanted the soft life I'd be staying here, for as long as it can last, going mad with boredom." '

The conversation widened to include several of the men and women and they all basically agreed with what George Muir had said.

'How do Fijians feel about outsiders coming in to do the job?' I asked.

'Every man-jack of us has had to apply for a work permit,' George explained. 'Even though it was the Fijian government which awarded Reddy Fletcher the contract, we had to satisfy them that we could not find a Fijian to do each of the jobs we are doing. And then we were only given work permits for six months, which will only be renewed if we can prove we are still indispensable. There's no coming the heavy white man act here. And fair enough.'

Gradually people drifted off to settle their kids down for afternoon naps and to take a siesta themselves in preparation for the evening's dinner and party. We followed suit but not for long, because the afternoon's rain came. The wet season was just about to happen in Fiji and Iain and the kids insisted that the place to enjoy it best was in the pool. They were right. There's little to beat floating on your back, while large, fat globules of water pound onto your body, burst and are instantly replaced. The noise of the torrential downpour striking the water in the pool all but drowned out our shrieks of laughter.

Zara swam over to me, her long blonde hair plastered to her body, and ordered, 'Dive down and lie on the bottom face up so you can see the rain coming down.' I did so and was rewarded with a remarkable sight as the heavy pieces of water struck the surface and shot through it like bullets for some millimetres before being amalgamated into the main watery mass.

That evening we had Christmas dinner with the Reddy Fletcher crowd in the hotel dining room. It wasn't the best, but the company made up for it and it couldn't have been too bad because Sean managed two meals. He ate with the smaller children and then, an hour later, with the adults!

There were crackers with mottoes, plastic jewellery and tissue paper hats. The wine flowed, along with the jokes and the reminiscences. A band started up and there was sporadic dancing. Zara and Sean went off to bed, having done one of those things I admire most about them—made the most of the day—which, after all, was not every child's idea of Christmas.

Early on in the festivities we met Paul Jaduram again and he introduced us to his wife Stella. We had not seen them earlier when we'd been down in the bar because they had arrived late in the afternoon. I was immediately attracted to Stella, who was about my own age and who I was delighted to find had a very strong north London accent.

'Tottenham,' she answered my query. 'Actually I was born in Wales but I grew up in London. I've been here for almost 10 years now but I still can't get rid of the accent.' She gave a broad smile. 'I'm sorry I missed you when you were in Labasa. Paul told me he'd spoken to you and I've been looking forward to meeting you because we don't have many outside people visit. Most of our business is government people over from Suva. After all, you couldn't really call Labasa a tourist resort could you? Paul is building a new hotel though...on one of the islands offshore, which we hope will encourage more tourists to come. Are you coming back to Labasa, because I'm sure Paul would like to show you around?'

I told her that we hoped we could and then asked how she and Paul had met.

Even her laugh had a London accent! 'Paul was over home on a course in cinema management. I think he told you that the family own a couple of cinemas here and, at that stage, he was going into that side of the business. I was working in an office in Tottenham, earning peanuts as a little typist, and my girlfriend and I wanted to go on holiday in Europe, but we couldn't afford to unless we took a second job at night. So we did. As usherettes in this cinema where Paul was learning the business.

'I could tell straight away that he fancied me, but he didn't do anything about it for weeks and weeks and then, one evening after we'd finished, and me and my girlfriend were waiting at the bus stop, he pulled up in his car, said he was going our way and could he give us a lift home? It wasn't until months after that I found out he wasn't going that way at all! He dropped my girlfriend off first, and then took me home and asked me for a date,' another infectious laugh, 'and that was that! And here I am in Fiji! Who'd have believed it? Our Stella from Tottenham, winding up in Labasa! Most people back home think it's a lot of savages speaking mumbo jumbo and eating each other out here.

'Two years Paul and I courted, before we got married. And even then Paul's family would only let him marry me if I agreed to come and live in Fiji. Fair enough I suppose. But it meant leaving my Mum. My sister lives in Australia. I've visited her lots of times and I'd love to live there permanently, but Paul's life is here and we have the two kiddies now. Still, I do feel bad about Mum, poor old dear, she's on her own now. Dad died of cancer earlier this year. It was a horrible death. My sister and I have asked Mum to join one or other of us, or to divide her time between the two of us, but she says she's lived all her life in London and she might as well die there.'

We talked on, Stella and I, refugees that we were, about the pleasures and pains of being separated from home and family. It helped a great deal.

In the morning, we were up early and, after finishing off what fresh fruit we had left—a couple of delicious mangos and papayas—we hitched a lift with a couple of the Reddy Fletcher people around to Namale plantation, a small place with limited guest facilities, which was on the coast road several kilometres around in the same direction that the others would be travelling.

Malukai Gucake of the Fiji Visitors' Bureau had told us about the place, which we discovered to be in a spectacularly beautiful setting on a small cliff promontory, only 10 or 12 metres above white sandy beaches and a stunning lagoon enclosed by a fringing reef. A number of small guest *bures* were spread through the grounds around a central dining and recreational area in a building that was originally a private plantation home. The gardens were a profusion of tropical vegetation and huge banyan trees.

The place was run by Robin and Lynette Mercer, both born in Fiji of New Zealand descent. They owned a small coconut plantation farther along the road but some years previously an American had bought the headland where the guest house now stood and asked the Mercers if they would manage it for him. They agreed, and it has been a singular success, with most of the visitors to it coming under special booking arrangements from Europe, the United States and Australia. Once again, it was well beyond our budget, but having heard so much about it, we thought we could at least spend a couple of days there.

We had been told that the reef just offshore was particularly beautiful. The lagoon, which stretches out from the shore 100 metres or so to the reef, is only a metre or so deep, but once you reach the reef, there is a sheer underwater cliff plunging some 20 metres to a sandy bottom and then, a little farther out, it dives sharply down into the ocean, an abyss over 1000 metres deep!

On the afternoon of our arrival, after meeting the Mercers and settling in, we contented ourselves with the lagoon which was itself extremely beautiful, being filled with multi-coloured coral formations and fish of every description. We snorkelled and then lay on the beach, writing letters while Zara and Sean swam and explored further along the shore. Later in the afternoon we returned to our rooms to wash and change. Our *bure* was in a marvellous setting...almost like a tree-house. It was sandwiched in between two banyan trees and, while it could be entered at ground level on one side, on the other, which was reached by walking through the bedroom and out onto a wooden deck, you found yourself seemingly suspended ten metres high in the air. The whole structure was built out into the trees over a cliff, below which there were more gardens and hibiscus trees. The *bure* was decorated in very rustic South Pacific style; bamboo, pandanus leaves, thatched roof, straw matting on the floor. But it had two comfortable bedrooms on either side of a central bathroom with modern facilities. The bedspreads and curtains were of bright, floral design and the place felt very light and airy. We could easily have settled in for several weeks.

Over dinner, a buffet curry surrounded by an incredible variety of fruits and spices, we met some of the other guests; a German family who were living in Sydney on assignment for Unilever and a retired British professor who had been dean of the Department of Oceanography at the University of British Columbia in Vancouver. For the past 15 years, he told us, he and his wife had come out annually to the South Pacific to go skin diving in various remote places. 'This is one of the best', he assured us.

The next day, after a delicious breakfast, Robin introduced us to Levaki, his young Fijian assistant, who had offered to guide us to a nearby waterfall. 'Bring your swimming things', he suggested.

We set out along the road, accompanied by the German couple, Hans and Ruth Kosch and their two sons, Stefan and Cristian, who had decided to join us and, after a kilometre or so, we cut up through the side of the plantation, across rough country and into the thick jungle. Despite the upward climb and the day's heat, we were not uncomfortably hot because the heavy canopy of jungle greenery gave plenty of shade. The sun penetrated only in fine shafts, smooth and strong enough for a fairy to slide down.

Along the way, Levaki, who was barefoot and wearing only shorts despite the stony track and the groping undergrowth, pointed out various trees and bushes, giving their proper and colloquial names and explaining some of the uses to which they were put either as medicines, foodstuffs or building materials. Thick liana vines, of Jack and the Beanstalk capacity, hung down, seemingly suspended from the sky, for we couldn't see their starting point. Naturally everyone had to have a swing from at least one.

When we reached the waterfall and the deep pool into which it plunged we all wanted to stop and swim but Levaki made us continue on, up to the very top from where we were rewarded with a splendid view of one jungled crest after another, stretching off into the distance. Then it was a matter of a mad scramble down to see who would be the first to plunge into the pool. Actually I didn't exactly try to be in the lead, as the pool was dark and I thought it wiser to leave it to someone else to find out how deep it was and what it might contain! 'I can't even reach the bottom', Iain surfaced, 'and the sides are just stony, no weed.' Reassured, I took the plunge.

For a quarter of an hour we frolicked like wood nymphs under Levaki's eye, as he sat on a big boulder at one side. Suddenly he sprang to his feet and executed a perfect, high, arching dive right into the middle of the pool. He stayed down breathtakingly long and, just as we began to feel slightly anxious, he surfaced and we clapped. Obviously he had been waiting until our first pleasure with the cool water was sated and he could then rely on us being an attentive audience.

'Look how the water sits in his hair like raindrops,' Zara said, when Levaki surfaced. He shook his head and the water spun off in a shower of sunlit droplets. 'It's so thick it can't get through. Oh, I'd love to have hair like that.' Zara sighed.

Levaki performed a few more daring acts, a routine I imagine that he went through whenever he brought visitors to his pool. We all joined in with our own pale imitations and I thought how basically simple people are; what amount of pure pleasure they derive from natural acts, such as this fooling around in a jungle pool.

In the afternoon, following another superb meal, Robin took us all to visit his plantation. It was very much a working plantation; apart from supplying all the food for his family and their guests, it also produced enough excess copra and vegetables, fruit, eggs, chicken and even rice, to send to market.

One of my dreams is that if I were excessively wealthy, I would fly my friends from all around the world and have them all together in one spot for an open-ended holiday. Namale would be a perfect spot to stage such a pleasure. Actually you wouldn't even need to be madly rich and, as it can only accommodate a little more than 20 people, the whole thing is not entirely beyond imagination. Of course it would be even more easy to organise if they paid their own way. Lynette says this happens fairly often. But a booking would have to be made some considerable time in advance because they are fully booked more or less continually. It is without doubt one of the most beautiful places I have seen anywhere and there's plenty to do for those for whom lying around in the sun isn't enough.

The final *frisson* of perfection for me was the reef. It had taken me a long time, too long, to work up my confidence. I should, at that point, have turned around and gone back to all the places in which I hadn't been relaxed enough, or brave enough to fully enjoy. But at least there was the reef off Namale and me in a conquering mood! What I especially liked about it was that the water was shallow enough, even at high tide, to walk only knee-deep across 100 metres or so to the edge of the reef and from there it was relatively simple, if you carefully gauged the incoming surge of the water, to leap off and enter that other world.

Oh, it was wonderful. Wonderful. The face of the reef fell away steeply, and all down it there was a magic array of coral and, darting in and out amongst it, an exciting profusion of multi-coloured, multi-sized fish. And from the reef face out, the sandy bottom drifted away to slowly increasing depths, with huge coral trees sprouting from it and great boulders of beautiful brain coral spread about on it like giant marbles.

I don't wish boastfully to give the false impression that I was without fear in this watery underworld. Far from it. It was more that I was so enthralled with what was going on down there that, for slices of time, I could forget my fear. Every 15 minutes or so I would suddenly remember where I was and then I'd have to get out, trying not to tear pieces out of my body on the treacherous reef wall as I did so; difficult, when lumbered with over-sized rubber feet. Then I'd stand for a while watching Iain's snorkel, hearing his muffled cries of delight and seeing him jack-knife down into the water for a closer look at whatever new treat he had discovered. Then I couldn't bear it a minute longer and I'd jump back in, paddling like crazy to reach him in the touching faith that he would be able to protect me from horrors of the deep!

In this manner we spent an idyllic morning, the highlight being the sighting of a turtle. Until that moment I'd been under the mistaken impression that they were ungainly, lumbering creatures. But, by golly, in the water they are like a winged Adonis. No way could we keep up with him, or was it a her?

It was a wrench to leave Namale, but if we went on paying those prices for food, even though it was of gourmet quality, we'd be penniless in a matter of days. The prices were only what you would pay in a medium-priced restaurant in Australia, but that in itself put them outside of our travelling budget. Putting it high on the 'next-time-round' list, we said goodbye to the Mercers and hitched a lift back into Savu Savu.

Scruffy little Savu Savu looked pretty good because it was real. Even though I had enjoyed Namale so much, it was a place apart and basically I enjoy being a part *of,* not apart *from.*

It seemed a little strange to be going back across the island to Labasa, but we did want to see the sugar mill and, fortunately, the weather was considerably cooler than it had been on the day we had crossed the island from Labasa to Savu Savu, so the trip passed quickly.

At the Hotel Takia we looked up Paul and Stella Jaduram again and Paul immediately offered to take us to the mill which was about six or seven kilometres out of town.

On the way to the sugar mill, Paul stopped the car at a small Hindu temple by the roadside.

'This is the Temple of the Snake,' he said. 'A very sacred place for Indians here.'

It was a small unimpressive building of cement which looked more like a little suburban house than a temple. It had been painted in rather garish colours. At the doorway we slipped our shoes off and left them outside while we stepped into the one main room of the building. It was almost filled, from floor to ceiling, with a huge, natural rock. In fact the whole structure had been erected over and around the rock, which quite clearly resembled a giant cobra with its head upright and its hood spread wide.

'The story is that the stone is growing,' Paul said quietly. 'People come from all over Fiji—and even from India, to see it. They believe that it can perform all manner of miracles, from curing sickness, to bringing rain for their crops. It is famous throughout Fiji as a rain god and it's also supposed to bring babies to sterile couples!'

We circled around the great figure for a few minutes, watching several sari-clad Indian women placing incense sticks in sand containers and pressing their palms together in silent supplication to the Snake God.

'My grandmother used to bring me here,' Paul whispered. 'She told me all the stories about it . . . because she believed it . . . every bit of it. She was very traditional in her ways. She came to Fiji when she was only eleven.'

We had moved around the stone and back out onto the small verandah where we began to put our shoes back on. 'Did all of her family come at the same time?' I asked.

'Oh, no. None of them came. She was pinched from her village in India...kidnapped.'

'But why?' Trish said, amazed. 'Surely not to work here.'

'No, of course not. As a bride.'

'A bride! At eleven!?'

'Yes. There were so many men who were coming here as labourers that there was a flourishing black market in illicit child brides.'

'But couldn't her family do anything?'

'They never knew what happened to her. She never saw them, or heard of them again.'

'But, how terrible. What happened to her? Obviously things turned out reasonably in the end, because you're here...and...well, as you said, she used to bring you to the temple and so on. Did she stay married to the same man?'

'Yes. And eventually, after his period of indenture was over, they grew to be very rich and influential. It is a real success story.'

Obviously there is much more to a story like that, but there's no doubt that the original Jadurams on Vanua Levu made the best of a bad job, because the name Jaduram is all over the town of Labasa. There are streets named after various members of the family, Jaduram office buildings, cinemas, and also creches, which the old lady, Paul's grandmother founded and ran for Indian women in poorer situations than she. She was quite obviously a remarkable woman, and it was equally obvious that Paul thought so too and, for all his Western ways, gave the strong impression that he shared his grandmother's beliefs in the power of the Snake God.

When we reached the sugar refinery Paul left us in the hands of one of the plant foremen, Babu Ram, who was to take us on a brief tour around the mill. I had only once previously visited a sugar refinery, about 25 years ago, up in the North Queensland cane country near Cairns, and I remember it as an extraordinary experience, like entering a maelstrom of noise, activity and motion.

The main crushing plant assaults your senses. The sound is incredible; a cacophony of machinery grinding, steam jetting and pistons pumping. You can hardly hear yourself think. Then there's the thick smell of raw sugar, mixed with industrial odours of oil and chemicals—all of which combines with the sight of enormous pieces of machinery, gigantic metal fly-wheels, five metres or so in diameter, spinning at tremendous speeds, huge crushing wheels tearing and shredding tonnes of sugar cane to tiny bits, movement everywhere you turn, in a mist of shrieking steam. It is like walking straight into what you might imagine the Krupp steel works to have been in about 1850.

Not that a new mill would be greatly different. I think even the most modern mills still have to have these great pieces of machinery pounding, whirling and grinding away. It was just that the whole thing set us aback slightly. Zara and Sean stood open-mouthed for a few moments after we entered the main crushing hall, as if to say, what on earth is all this about?

Surely you don't need all this stuff just to make sugar? I couldn't help feeling that myself.

But then, as we were led through the other parts of the mill to see the various refining processes, where the brown, watery juice is channelled away into huge vats, boiled down and refined, filtered and processed, by-products like molasses extracted and brown sugar spun out of its liquid suspension in high-speed centrifugal drums, we began to understand the complexity of what seems to be a very simple product, a product we lift so casually from the supermarket shelves and dump into the trolley.

A very pleasant and friendly Indian man, Gaya Prasad, who was an industrial chemist employed by the mill, took us through the chemical section, explaining the processes step by step, as well as something of the story of sugar in Fiji. Sugar has long been, and still is, Fiji's most important agricultural export, bringing in around $70 million a year in foreign earnings. It is also the product which, more than any other, has shaped the pattern of Fiji's social development in the twentieth century. As we've already pointed out, it was sugar that brought Indians, by the tens of thousands, to Fiji as indentured labourers.

From the time the first refinery was built in 1882 by the Colonial Sugar Refineries Company (CSR) at Nausori near Suva, the industry in Fiji was dominated by this Australian organisation. It very quickly expanded colonial Fiji's sugar production, built three more refineries, including the one at Labasa, and established huge estates to grow the cane.

The CSR company remained in control of Fiji's sugar industry until 1973 when the Fiji government took it over by purchasing the company's mills and freehold land for about $14 million. From then on, the industry has been run by the Fiji Sugar Corporation, a public company which is run on commercial lines, but whose shares (all but 2.2%) are owned by the government. Despite some decline in production and sales during the 70s, the industry is expanding considerably at the moment with the modernisation of several mills, including the one at Labasa, and the opening up of large tracts of virgin crown land on the island of Vanua Levu for sugar planting.

Rick Farmer, one of the people from the Reddy Fletcher company whom we had met in Savu Savu, showed us over the new steam generator they were building. It was a multi-million-dollar facility that stood almost 10 storeys high next to the crushing plant.

Sugar processing needs great amounts of water and steam and the old mill, built in the nineteenth century, was in need of a more up-to-date steam generator. Then, after clambering through the maze of pipes and scaffolding for 20 minutes or so, trying to absorb some of the details of how the whole thing worked, we had a steam-generated cup of tea in Rick's site office before he gave us a lift back into the town, from where we caught a bus back across the island to Savu Savu.

At 5534 sq. kilometres, Vanua Levu is just over half the size of Viti Levu but it is still a very big island. It took us all the next morning to travel in a beaten-up bus along the road, which clings, as is usual in most Pacific Islands, to the coast, from Savu Savu to Buca Bay at the far northeastern tip of the island. The journey cost $1 for adults, 50¢

for the children. Cheap, yes, but very hard on the posterior.

It was a Sunday again and the bus kept stopping to pick up and put down people, almost all Fijians, in their best clothes and carrying large black umbrellas to ward off not the rain but the strong sun. Little girls came out of jungle settlements, immaculate in pink or white stiffly-starched party dresses, blinding white ankle socks and shiny patent leather shoes. They were accompanied by their Mums in equally spanking, neat attire and their Dads, wearing suit jackets and collars and ties over below-knee-length skirts and good sturdy sandals.

There was no more of a settlement at Buca Bay than anywhere else along the road we had come; just a couple of flimsy houses. But at Buca Bay there was, in addition, a small wharf to which everyone who was left on the bus (about 10 or so) made a beeline, so we followed suit.

An Indian man in his 30s wearing shorts and a tee-shirt poled his way towards us in a tiny dinghy. Moored behind him, about 30 metres offshore was a single cabin boat of perhaps six metres with an outboard engine and an obviously handmade wooden canopy over the open rear deck. There was already such a crowd of people on the deck that we wondered where all our fellow bus passengers would fit. The Indian, who made himself known as the ferry operator, began to cram people into his dinghy and pole back out to the moored boat. Three trips like that he did. And each time the dinghy came perilously close to capsizing. The water wasn't deep, so there was no danger of drowning, but I knew from Iain's anxious look that he was thinking not about our safety, but about his 50 rolls of film!

Having reached the ferry without a dunking, we peered into the cabin and were met by 25 or 30 pairs of doleful eyes staring up out of the gloom. There must have been 20 or so people in there even before he'd started loading the bus passengers in. The rest of them sat up on the deck. Iain manhandled our four packs into a corner of the cabin, apologising as he squeezed his way around and over people and their bundles. I couldn't help noticing that he made sure his own pack was the most easily accessible and checked that the zipper on the bottom large pocket where he stored his exposed and unexposed film was free to be opened quickly.

Then it was up with the anchor and a tugging on the rope to start the reluctant engine.

I had an idea that the voyage to Taveuni would take a half or at the most, three-quarters of an hour. It took *two!* And it was not in the least pleasant. We very quickly left the lee of Vanua Levu and were immediately hit by strong swells and buffetted by wind. As each big swell approached I braced myself in an attempt to ride it like a bucking bronco. The cabin was soon awash at ankle depth. One of the young men was detailed to pump the bilges like blazes, but the best he could manage was to maintain the watery status quo.

The sky was leaden, the wind kept up. Land seemed too far off and I was too busy concentrating on not being thrown overboard and encouraging the children to do the same, to have any time to be seasick. At last, at long last, we came into the lee of Taveuni and the pounding, thumping, rising and falling stopped. Just like a switch had been thrown. We all looked at each other in relieved disbelief and at the skipper who shrugged his shoulders and gave an apologetic smile.

Another half hour and we were sliding up the smooth beach of Waiyevo, stumbling out into the water to haul our packs up onto dry land and thanking, yes, *thanking,* the skipper.

# 20 TAVEUNI
## 'At the stroke of twelve all hell broke loose'

Waiyevo has one hotel which is the only place to provide accommodation of any sort at all on the entire island of Taveuni. There are not even any guest houses. It's the Travelodge or nothing and never did a Travelodge look so good, though I bet we didn't look so good to the staff of the Travelodge!

We checked into our rooms, had hot showers and unpacked our gear, which miraculously, because we had such good packs, was hardly damp at all. The children discovered the pool, which was right on the edge of the small beach running down from the hotel, a two-storey building which was spread along the shoreline. The view was terrific out over the Taveuni channel which we had just crossed and which looked deceptively somnolent.

At about 4 p.m. the phone in the room rang. It was something of a shock as it had been a very long time indeed since we had had a phone call. Iain spoke to a voice which introduced itself as belonging to Isimele Bainimara's brother, Robert. Isimele had told us to look up his relatives on Taveuni, but we had hardly expected him to phone ahead and ask them to show us around which is what Robert offered to do.

Robert, large and talkative, arrived in a car driven by a smaller, far quieter man, whom Robert introduced as Enasa, also Isimele's brother.

We took off southwards, once again along the only road, which again clung to the coast. Taveuni is known as the Garden Island of Fiji because the volcanic land is so fertile that almost any tropical produce will grow there.

Enasa drove a short distance outside Waiyevo, which consists of the hotel, a separate public bar (which, as in Savu Savu, is also owned by the hotel) and a small Burns Philp store. Don't blink or you'll miss it all. We pulled off the road at a point where we could see a signpost which had two arms. The arm pointing to the east was marked 'Yesterday', the arm pointing to the west was marked 'Today'. Written beneath was a notice which read, 'This is the only motor road in the Southern Hemisphere crossing the 180th meridian, where each day begins!' Of course we had to take photographs and I reminded Zara and Sean of our visit earlier that year to Greenwich Observatory on the Thames and explained that this place was exactly half-way around the world from that spot. It think I was more impressed than they were because it seemed like we had covered an awful lot of territory for there still to be as much again left to complete the circle. Lord knows how much of all my geography lessons they take in, but I can be very boring about insisting on telling them!

A little farther on there was a large seminary setup on the hillside, overseen by an enormous cross.

'That place,' Robert told us, 'the land and everything, belongs to the Catholic church.'

It's very unusual in Fiji for anyone to own land other than Fijians, except in a very few small areas of existing freehold parcels, but this land was given to the church by a grateful chief who received a blessing and a cross to carry into a fight from a priest before doing battle against invaders from Tonga. He won and killed all the enemy and, in gratitude, he gave the land to the church to keep forever.

Suddenly the unsurfaced road became smooth with tarmac. 'This is Soqulu plantation,' Robert announced in explanation. 'Here, foreigners can come and buy land, freehold, and build a home for themselves. I will show you some.'

Enasa guided the car up a winding, beautifully surfaced, kerbed and guttered road, past dozens of partially cleared building sites. The magnificent large trees had been left on site and, as we went higher, the view out over the ocean to distant Vanua Levu became more and more spectacular. Occasionally we passed a house. Splendid in its isolation.

'That belongs to an Australian,' Robert said, as if this would give it special significance for us. 'A Mr Arnott. I think he makes biscuits.' (Well, not Mr Arnott, himself, I thought, enjoying the image of the man up to his armpits in dough (pun) and working night and day to churn out millions of 'Arnott's Better Biscuits'.) 'And that one too,' Robert continued. 'It is an Australian's home. He is a doctor. A ladies' doctor.' (I bettcha.)

The road wound on and round and up and then we began the descent, all the time with Robert extolling the virtues of the place and how little was left for sale and how prices were going up and so it was a good investment. More like a real estate agent, he sounded, than a Pacific Islander.

'And what do the locals think of all this,' I managed to squeeze the question in.

'Oh, they are happy,' Robert assured me. 'It brings a lot of money to the island,' and then he added, unaware of the implications, 'and they all stay here, they do not come to the rest of the island.'

In other words, it's all right with the islanders if rich, retired, gentlefolk wish to buy up a lump of land and build an opulent, out-of-character house high on a hill at one end of their island. Just as long as they don't come clattering down into their villages. Fair enough. It's the equivalent of take the money and run. But for me Soqulu is a no-no. It's beautiful, sure. There's fishing; Robert showed us the small wharf where a large, powerful boat rode at anchor. The owner, he assured us, can get from Suva harbour to Taveuni in 40 minutes! Then there's the reef, snorkelling, swimming, a club house (Robert showed us this too) with a pool and tennis courts and a golf course, all of it open and ready for action. But who would you get to meet? Who would you interact with? Other people just like yourself. Rich and retired. (Not us!) It's one of those up-market retirement villages and they give me the creeps. No snotty-nosed kids (those who visit their grandparents in the holidays will never have snotty noses), no bored teenagers (they'll all be in the process of being groomed to become captains of industry). No brawling wives and husbands (more the well-honed stilletto thrust). No life, be out of it. No, thanks.

Just before the tarmac turned back again to dusty gravel we spotted the most amazing Hollywood-style home down off the road on a little wooded peninsula which jutted out into the sea.

'Stop,' Sean shouted. Enasa reversed for us to have a better view.

'Who lives there?' Zara breathed.

'That used to belong to the original developer, a man named MacIntyre,' Robert told her. 'But when he sold the land to another real estate company, they insisted that he sold them the house too, so now it belongs to them and no one lives there. It has sunken baths and a swimming pool and private tennis courts and huge rooms looking right out on the ocean.'

The children stared. 'I'm going to have a place like that,' Sean sounded dreamy.

'Oh yes,' his prosaic sister snapped, 'and a white Rolls Royce!'

As he dropped us back at the hotel, Robert invited us to visit a waterfall with him in the morning and to spend the following evening, New Year's Eve, with him and

Enasa and his family in their village of Somosomo. We accepted with delight. 'First there is a church service,' Robert said, 'and then at midnight the children and the adults, everyone, goes mad. You will see.'

Robert and Enasa arrived at 9.45 a.m., about three-quarters of an hour later than they said they would be. Car trouble. Nothing serious... points and plugs, according to Robert who, from the beginning, had taken over the role of talker, leaving the driving to Enasa. The car was a white Toyota, about five or six years old and in pretty good condition, considering the state of the roads on Taveuni.

'It is our brother's car,' Robert informed us. 'We look after it very well.'

'Your brother? You mean Isimele...in Suva?'

'No, no. Another brother...Epele. He is in the Fijian Army...a lieutenant.' There was a note of pride in his voice. We nodded approvingly.

'How long has he been in the Army?' Trish asked.

'In the Fijian Army, only three years,' Robert replied, 'but before that, he was 17 years in the British Army. I will show you some photographs later. He was in Hong Kong and Singapore...then Cyprus and in Dorset, in the U.K.'

'And now?' I asked. 'Where is he now...in Suva?'

'Oh no. He is in Lebanon.'

'Lebanon?'

'Yes, with the United Nations peace-keeping force. Fiji has a contingent there, you know.'

'Of course,' I said, although I had forgotten. One tends to associate the Swedes and the Canadians with U.N. Peace-keeping forces and forget that many of the smaller nations have contributed to these often dangerous and nearly always thankless tasks. Fijians, we discovered, are very aware of their own Army's participation in Lebanon where they are trying to bring order out of a chaotic nightmare. Several young men have been killed by senseless sniper fire in Beirut while on patrol and their deaths have resulted in unprecedented displays of public grief and mourning throughout Fiji.

'It is a dangerous place to be...Lebanon,' Robert said seriously. 'We wish Epele was back here. We are building a house for him. You will see it today.'

'Is the family building it for him?' I asked, thinking that it might have been the classic example of traditional family unity in the islands...everyone working for everyone else. But it was apparently Epele himself who had initiated the construction and was paying for it.

'Epele has always saved his Army wages well,' Robert explained. 'He bought this car and a taxi licence for us to use it for hire. We can make a living from it and also put aside some money for Epele. That and his wages go to build his new house in the village.'

We were driving north on the coastal road, the only road on the island, which is roughly rectangular...about 40 kilometres long, by about 10 or 11 kilometres wide. The road actually runs along only one side of the island, the western side, as the east is totally undeveloped and uninhabited with nothing but jungled cliffs plunging down to the sea.

'This is Somosomo, our village,' Robert said, as we rounded a bend in the road and, after crossing a bridge over a fast-moving stream, began passing through a small village of simple brick and timber houses...mostly of conventional Western design, but with one or two buildings sporting the more traditional thatched roof.

'You would like some tea,' Robert said. It was more of a statement than a question, and Enasa had already turned off the road anyway, to drive down a narrow track towards the seashore and a group of three or four small houses.

'This is where we live,' Robert waved his hand. 'And that is Epele's new house.' He pointed to an unfinished house of concrete blocks and shiny tin roof, which nestled tightly between two other buildings. From one of them, a large, round woman with a smiling face emerged.

'And this is my sister, Maria Bainimara...Enasa's wife.'

Ah. Things became a little clearer. Enasa, Epele and Isimele were brothers. Robert was a brother-in-law.

Enasa smiled and ushered us into his home, but still said nothing. It wasn't as if Robert tried to dominate the conversation, it was simply that Enasa's English wasn't as fluent as Robert's. He understood everything, but preferred to leave the talking to his brother-in-law.

Somosomo is the home village of the deputy prime minister, Ratu Sir Penaia Ganilau, Robert told us as we sat down in the small, but comfortable lounge room of the house. Maria bustled back and forth, brewing up the tea and putting out a plate of cakes and biscuits.

'He is here now, to spend the New Year with his relatives and friends. It is very important, here in Fiji for all politicians and chiefs to spend this New Year period with their people.'

After we had finished our tea we were shown through Epele's unfinished house, and then continued on our way, towards the northern end of the island.

'Where that road finishes, there is a beautiful waterfall,' Robert said. We rounded the northern tip of the island and, for a short while, the dusty road ran inland, about a kilometre from the coastline. We could still see the sea, however, over rolling hills that were being used as pasture land and coconut plantations.

'These are nearly all expatriate plantations,' Robert said as we drove. He gave no hint as to whether he approved or disapproved. 'Australians mostly...one American, a military man, Colonel Cobb, and of course the big companies; Burns Philp and Morris Hedstrom.'

'The Australians,' I asked, 'have they come here recently?'

'Oh no, they have been here for many years...and their families before them. The Hennings family are Australian. They have hundreds of acres of copra plantation here. They've been on Taveuni for almost a hundred years. Then there's the Tartes and the Douglases...also Australians.'

A hundred years, I thought. They're hardly still Australian, but it was interesting that Robert and presumably the other locals *thought* of them as Australians. I wondered how the people in question thought of themselves.

We began to pass through some more thickly jungled country where lush, tropical bush was growing close to the edge of the road again. Rounding a bend, we saw a group of men walking along the road ahead of us in single file. The leader, a big Fijian man dressed in a white safari suit was carrying a high-powered rifle slung under his right arm. As we passed, Enasa gave a wave, which was returned by the man with the rifle.

'That is the deputy prime minister, Ratu Sir Penaia Ganilau,' Robert said. 'He is going to kill one of his cattle for a feast. It is for his village. Every year he does this.' We turned to look at the little group through the rear window, just in time to see the man in white point into the scrub to the right of the road and head off into it.

The waterfall, when we reached it, was particularly beautiful. It was about a kilometre's walk from where we left the car near the tiny village of Bouma. We followed a narrow jungle path which led eventually to the head of a small valley where we were presented with the sight of a thin stream of white water plummetting over a 25-or 30-metre-high cliff into a large, deep pool of clear, fresh water. Within moments we had slipped into our swimming costumes and joined three or four young village children who were already swimming in the pool. Robert came too, although Enasa sat rather demurely on a large rock by the side, just watching. We swam out toward the centre of the pool where the waterfall was pounding down with such force that it was almost impossible to reach because of the flow of water pushing us back. By swimming underwater however, we could come up directly beneath the falling torrent. It was not something we could take for more than a few seconds though, as the water pounded down so fiercely on our heads and shoulders that it was quite painful. And we couldn't avoid the fear that perhaps a small rock or river stone might also come flowing over the top with all that water.

The pool was incredibly clear and, with a snorkelling mask which Sean had brought, we could easily see the whole of the bottom of the pool which sloped up from a depth of about 10 or 12 metres. We heard a shout from Robert and looked up to see that he had climbed over the rocks to a ledge in the cliff-face, about six or seven metres up, behind the waterfall. With another shout and a wave, he leapt out and into the deep water. Sean and Zara were already heading for the rocks to climb up also. I followed and, shortly we were all leaping off the ledge into the water.

We spent a pleasant three-quarters of an hour horsing around like this, before resting on the rocks and eating some fruit we'd brought with us. Shortly afterwards, we dressed and reluctantly made our way back along the track to where we had left the car. It was such an idyllic spot, we felt we could have built a little shack there and stayed for years.

A short distance along the road we came upon a man carrying a huge, bloody section of a slaughtered beast on his shoulders. 'My God,' I gasped at the rather bizarre first sight of it. There was blood everywhere, running down over the man's back as he jogged along the road with his gory load. A little farther on there were two more men with equally bloody sections to carry.

'The deputy PM got his cow,' Robert smiled. 'A good feast tonight.'

A few kilometres farther on we passed by some of the big, company-owned coconut plantations that Robert had mentioned earlier. It was the same road we had travelled along in the morning, but Robert had not pointed them out to us on the way through. This time he gestured towards a row of green-painted corrugated iron huts, nestling in amongst the coconut palms.

'Those are the "coolie lines",' he said.

'Coolie lines?' Trish asked. 'What do you mean.'

'They are the barrack rooms for the plantation labourers. In the old days when the Indians were brought out to work the plantations, the Europeans used to call them "coolies" and these are the "coolie lines".'

'But surely these aren't the same...they don't still...I mean, surely things have improved since then?'

'There's not much difference,' Robert said. 'Oh, the pay is better than it was in those days, although it's still very low...even by Fijian standards. And, of course, now they can leave whenever they want to. But they are still very bad conditions and we feel that the big companies and the other white plantation owners hold back Fijians by keeping the pay-scales down.'

There's not a great deal you can say or do at times like that...except perhaps sink a little lower in your seat.

That evening, when Robert and Enasa picked us up at 7.30 and brought us back to their village, a group of their neighbours were sitting around on the grass nearby, drinking some kava and talking. We were taken over and introduced to them and then invited to squat cross-legged on the grass to join them for a drink of kava.

The cup, a half-coconut shell, was passed to me first. It was half full of the muddy, brown liquid. I've had kava or yagona (pronounced yangona), as they call it in Fiji, on a couple of previous occasions so it was no surprise to me...but I can't say it is something that I'd walk more than a hundred metres for. There's not much taste to it...just a funny, tingling feeling on your tongue as you swallow it, and after a while, your mouth tends to feel a little numb. It's not alcoholic and they say that it's not hallucinogenic, but I do think it tends to be habit forming. In any event, it is extremely important to Fijians as a traditional drink and is used ritually in a great many official functions and other ceremonial occasions, as well as being drunk socially by the bulk of the population.

On this occasion however, we didn't stay long enough for our mouths to become numb, but left after a quarter of an hour to join Maria in brother Epele's new house for a real Fijian dinner. We sat around on the matting floor while Maria produced a great array of chicken, prawns, mutton, taro, casava and salads of lettuce, cucumber and tomato and also the leaves of the big swamp taro plant, which are delicious when boiled up in coconut milk. We talked easily and casually with various visitors coming and going throughout the dinner to say hello or chat for a while. Then, at 10 p.m. they said it was time to leave for the New Year's Eve service, which was to be held in a makeshift church in the school hall across the road. The main village church had been so shaken about in a recent earthquake, that giant cracks had appeared in the wall and parts of it had crumbled away.

We were the only non-locals at the service and the congregation was rather amazed to see us walk in and take our seats. A buzz of conversation rippled through the small crowd and several of them smiled and called hello to us. The service was long (two hours) and for us, rather boring—only because, naturally enough, it was all in Fijian. After a while, Zara and Sean began to get a bit fidgety and when two or three of the other Fijian children were allowed to go out of the hall, we let them slip out too...with instructions to return by 11.30 p.m. A number of the other children who remained in the hall began to drop off to sleep where they sat as several speakers took it in turn to drone on in rather soporific tones. Their speeches were interspersed with conventional Western hymns—sung in Fijian, of course, as well as several carols. Things weren't made any better by the fact that the hall began to get very hot and stuffy.

Then, just before midnight, the service was rapidly wound up and, at the stroke of 12, all hell broke loose outside in the village. A pattern of wild drumbeats erupted from several directions. We all went outside to listen. Then cars began arriving down the main road with their horns blowing, either continuously or intermittently. Children were tearing through the crowds laughing and yelling. And then came the water. They were hurling buckets of water over everybody they could get close to.

'This is a tradition in Taveuni,' Maria explained to us, while dodging a stream of water. 'They do it every New Year's Eve.'

As a result of some nifty footwork, we managed to make it to Enasa and Maria's house with only a few splashes, much laughter, and some loud, good-natured joshing from the village kids.

We sat around and sipped some more kava, but by 1.30 a.m., Zara and Sean were fading fast, not to mention Trish and I, so we headed back to the hotel, where we came upon a few bedraggled and sopping wet revellers who still remained from the party there. They had either jumped, or been pushed into the pool at midnight and were sitting around keeping the bar open. They waved to us to join them, but we were too far gone ourselves, so we declined and made our way back to our rooms, collapsing into bed where we hoped to get at least some sleep before facing the first day of the New Year.

The next day the hotel looked very much like the morning after the night before. And the staff looked like it too. It had obviously been some party. They didn't exactly hold their aching heads in their hands as they sluiced down the patio area around the pool, nor did they groan and wince as they bent down to gather up the litter scattered about the garden. But they looked as though they wanted to and they had the slow deliberate movements of people for whom just working their muscles was a great effort.

The guests didn't look any happier with themselves either. A couple of the men managed to open the doors onto their patios and spread their pool-drenched clothes out to dry. The others kept their doors shut, curtains drawn and air-conditioners humming until very late in the morning.

We unfortunately had a plane to catch so it was time to pack up yet again.

On our way to the airport we stopped off at Enasa's home in Somosomo to say goodbye and thankyou once more to Maria. She was ready for us, with armfuls of beautiful frangipani flower leis, which she must have made fresh that morning. The effort involved in making them after such a late night made then an even more special gift. That's another thing one learns from real travel...that people who have the least, give the most; of their time, of their emotions and even of their worldly goods. It's a terrible truth that the more people have the more they want, the more they are frightened of losing it and the less they are willing to share.

At the airport we learnt that a cyclone was forecast and was heading our way. The plane was late...in fact there was some doubt that it would come at all. But it did, looking like an improbable metal bird, as it dropped into Taveuni's small grass strip which is spread out across the side of a steep hill.

For the trip back to Suva I sat up front and had a really fabulous view of the variegated ocean. We picked up passengers from Savu Savu, which meant that we came in low over 'my reef' at Namale and I would have boasted to the pilot about my snorkelling exploits but he was wearing his headset and couldn't hear me. All the way back to Suva we flew really low, perhaps because of weather, and it was the most glorious trip. The best in the whole Pacific journey. Perhaps it was just that my vibrations were more than usually in sync with what was going on around me, but I clearly recall the blues of the ocean and the sky and the white puffs of cloud and the green islands fringed with white surf foaming on reefs. Sitting up there with an unobstructed view was the next best thing to flying the plane myself. And learning to fly moved up the list of future projects. When people intimate that they are bored, I wonder how this can possibly be, when there are so many things to see and do and learn about. There's no way that one lifetime could possibly be enough.

## 21  OVALAU
### 'A slow and dignified slide into obscurity and decay'

Levuka, I think, is a little like some beautiful women you read about...a dancer or singer perhaps, whose attractions have faded with time and whose admirers and lovers have deserted her. She is a little sad and neglected maybe, but still retains an air of dignity, old-style charm and inner beauty.

Levuka, on the island of Ovalau, was the old capital of Fiji. It was the main trading centre of the islands until the capital was moved to Suva in 1882. From that moment on, Levuka went into a gradual decline until it became what it is now—basically just a sleepy little village. Apart from the Japanese fish-canning factory on the edge of town there is practically no activity in Levuka. In touristic terms, no-one goes there...a great pity, because it is truly a charming and beautiful place. We decided on Levuka as our next stop after Taveuni for that reason...that nobody goes there, and also because of the fact that it had been the old capital. It was a little bit of history, preserved, we were told, almost unchanged since the early part of this century.

After overnighting in Suva at the Outrigger Motel, we spent the morning picking up more mail, exchanging Zara's defective radio and then packaging it and Sean's up to send off to Sydney by sea-mail, so that we wouldn't have to carry them around with us. We also checked into the Fiji Visitors' Bureau to see Malukai Gucake and Isimele Bainimara again. We thanked Isimele for the hospitality his relatives had shown us on Taveuni and passed on the message to him that *he* must also visit them soon. It had been two years, they said, since he had been back to his home village.

By lunchtime, it was raining heavily. Clearly a result of the cyclone system. We were going to *fly* to Ovalau island because we had missed the morning ferry. It was only a very cheap, 10-minute flight over about 20 kilometres of water but we were worried that the weather might force the flight to be cancelled. The rain had come down in absolute torrents during the bus ride out to Nausori airport and when the scheduled time came for the plane to leave, we were still standing inside the small terminal building gazing out at a grey mass of rain tumbling from dark and heavy clouds. The plane, a Britten Norman Islander, hadn't even arrived and no-one seemed to know when it would.

Our plane did eventually arrive about an hour later and, although we had been impatiently cursing its lateness, when the pilot turned it straight around on the tarmac and we were told to board...still in the pouring rain...we didn't feel too happy about going. We started having second thoughts. 'How the hell can he fly through this?' I said to Trish. 'It's like pea soup.'

Trish said nothing. We paused a moment or two, then shrugged and all together dashed out to the aircraft carrying big umbrellas, which an employee folded up and returned to the terminal when we were inside the aircraft. Within minutes the pilot had the plane moving and we were tearing down the runway which was half awash with water. We lifted off and then flew the whole way to Ovalau at a height of about 200 metres, over shallow reefs and small islands, which we perceived vaguely through the rain and mist and cloud, eventually coming in to land on a tiny airstrip which, like the one on Taveuni, had been cut out of the jungle on one side of Ovalau.

The rain didn't let up. We got our packs unloaded and under cover and then waited for half an hour or more for a mini-bus to arrive. There was some suggestion that the 20-kilometre road between the airport and the town of Levuka had been cut by flood waters, as it apparently often is, but the bus turned up after a while and by 7.15 p.m., more than four hours after we'd left Suva for the airport, we arrived in Levuka.

As the bus trundled into town we could see immediately, even though it was dark and rainy, that we would like the place. It was small...really only one main street along the waterfront...and its buildings and shop-fronts...old wooden structures with verandahed walkways, looked like something from a turn-of-the century movie set.

There was only one hotel in town, the Royal...the last survivor of a veritable horde of hotels that once served a busy and thriving port city. Now, at the height of the tourist season in Fiji, it was all but empty. Of its two dozen rooms, only four were occupied—two of them by us. The hotel was built in 1883 and, architecturally, has nothing to recommend it. It is a rambling, two-storey wooden structure that has been added to and changed over the years. But we found it scrupulously clean, eminently comfortable, dry, in the midst of all these torrents of rain and, best of all, exceedingly cheap...$10 for the four of us.

Our rooms on the upper floor had open verandahs around them and, for a while, we just sat there in the dim light, listening to the rain pounding on the roof and watching it pour off the overhang in sheets. We could quite easily have gone straight to bed there and then, but, plucking up our courage, donning our rain jackets and taking off our shoes, we ventured out, running from one shop shelter to another to find a place to eat. Nothing was open. The restaurant we'd been told about by the hotel proprietor was closed, but, fortunately, in a back street, on our way back to the hotel, we found a small Chinese café that was open. We had a hearty meal of chow mein and curry. Curry?? Well, the Chinese are nothing if not pragmatic and, with so many Indians in Fiji. . . what could be more natural than Peking Duck Vindaloo?

The public rooms in the Royal Hotel are crammed with memorabilia: photographs of Australian and New Zealand rugby teams which visited Fiji in the 60s line the walls and on every conceivable perching place there are knick-knacks and souvenirs. They have nothing in common, other than being personal memories from which, with a little imagination, one could piece together a composite picture of someone's lifetime habits, interests and friendships. They had a masculine feel to them and I was sure they had been collected by Mr Ashley, who, we had been told by Isimele, owned the Royal Hotel and knew a large number of fascinating stories and historical lore about his home island. But when we enquired after Mr Ashley from the young woman who appeared to be in charge of the kitchen, she replied, 'Dad's not here. It's just Mum and me.' And the way she said it, flatly, with no emotion, indicated that he was not expected back. I couldn't quite gauge, though, whether he had just gone walkabout, or taken a more permanent step into the future.

Whichever it was, the partially-crippled woman cleaned the concrete  proof that he had at one time existed, with an energy, driven I thought, more by a desire to prove to herself that she could still control a diminishing number of her muscles rather than an affection for the articles themselves. For the finishing touch she filled the numerous vases of random taste with flowers which she created by alternately threading a hibiscus bloom, then frangipani flower onto stalks of split bamboo. The determination with which she performed this meticulous feat seemed like a challenge to the infinite ingenuity of the Almighty; an expression of dissatisfaction that he hadn't come up with such a flower design himself!

To walk off the large breakfast of fruit, fried eggs, toast and coffee (which for the four of us had cost just $4.50!) we went along to the far end of the township of Levuka, a distance of not more than a kilometre. On one edge of the poorly maintained road was the sea and on the other side a row of single-storey buildings. A couple of these wooden places were totally deserted and in a state of near collapse. It's always sad to see abandoned dwellings and Levuka has more than its fair share. It is teetering on the edge of becoming a ghost town.

The sea was grey and sullen, the air fresh, as it is only after heavy rain, but it was fattening up with the heavy individual perfumes drawn from the still dripping vegetation by the already increasing heat of the day. In the small graveyard, behind a startlingly incongruous English-looking little stone church, were headstones with barely decipherable inscriptions. They bore the names of men, soldiers, civilians and missionaries who had come to the riotous greenery of this Pacific island from a grey little island on the other side of the world to serve their own particular vision. There were the graves of women who had accompanied them, in their own line of duty, and even of the small children of these unions.

Most had, according to their markers, died of 'the fever'. I guess the isolation would have claimed a few too. One of them had been born in a Somerset village near my own birthplace and his granite gravestone carved 100 years ago by a company of stonemasons whom I knew still to be in business. Even in death these people still had the self-importance to have a tombstone sent all that way from 'home'.

Down on the waterfront we climbed up a little promontory to read the names listed down the sides of a stone memorial to men from Ovalau who had died in battle during World War I. All the names were European. Later in the afternoon we would see another such marker at the other end of town, only this time all the names were Fijian. Who believes that death is the great equaliser?

In the mounting morning heat we wandered slowly back to the hotel. There's nothing 'to do' or 'to see' in Levuka. You make your own entertainment. In the lounge we talked for a while to an elderly American woman from Juno, Alaska, who was travelling alone and who was the only other guest in the hotel, and to three members of the American Peace Corps who were working on the island and had dropped in to have a drink. The hotel was very much the town's social centre.

For a couple of hours, while the children went off to search for a gift for an expected baby of a friend in England (and returned with a tee-shirt suitable for a two year old), Iain and I sat out on the verandah adjacent to our bedroom and wrote notes and letters to our friends and our bank manager.

The rain started again, heavy and tropical. Our windows had no glass, just heavy wooden shutters which we propped open with pieces of wood. The rain drummed hard on the shutters and we could see it doing the same on the sea. The wind got up, bringing a welcome coolness, shredding the palm leaves and whipping up small waves. We sat in our ricketty planters' chairs, which would have done justice to Somerset Maugham. The creaking floorboards sloped towards the walls.

'This is perfection,' Iain sighed, and I knew what he meant. The slight acid smell of mould and tropical decay. Death in life. Life in death. Very comforting.

Feeling that to do our duty by Ovalau we must explore the other end of the township of Levuka we ventured out again when the rain eased.

Along past the few Indian, or Chinese-owned, sparsely-stocked shops and the memorial to Fijian soldiers, we came to the most significant site on the island, if not in all of the Fijian islands. A neatly-mowed grassy patch, enclosed within an iron railing, and in the centre, a flagstaff flanked by three bronze plaques. Plaque One read, 'The instrument ceding to Queen Victoria, her heirs and successors, the possession of and full sovereignty and dominion over the Fijian islands and inhabitants thereof, was signed here on 10th October, 1874.'

Plaque Number Two read, 'To commemorate the visit to Levuka of His Royal Highness the Prince of Wales on the occasion of Fiji's independence, 12th October, 1970.'

At that time I remember there was a great deal of loose talk about unavoidable racial strife; blood in the streets and general mayhem. It didn't happen. Fiji's transition from colony back again to fully-fledged independent nationhood is a tremendous success story. It has developed into a self-confident, adult nation, looking forward, with energy and enthusiasm and back, with pride. This is shown by Plaque Number Three, 'This stone was unveiled by His Royal Highness the Prince of Wales on the 9th of October, 1974 to commemorate the 100th anniversary of the signing of the deed of cession on the 10th of October 1874.'

At six in the morning, the rain, which had been bucketing down all night, was still heavy and the girl in the hotel warned us that there might be no flight out because the expected cyclone—Cyclone Peni—was now approaching Viti Levu.

We picked up a copy of the *Fiji Times,* which, incidentally, carries the slogan, 'The first newspaper published in the world today'. (Suva is just west of the international dateline, where the new day begins.) The banner headline read: *Cyclone Peni on way.* It went on: *The Nadi weather office reported that last night the cyclone was between 500 and 560 kms northwest of Labasa and warned that it was on track for areas in the north and east of Fiji with winds increasing to storm force 55 to 60 knots.*

We asked the clerk who ran the one-person operation Air Fiji office (in a shop shared with a general merchant) what he thought of our chances of getting a flight out. He was very pessimistic. Nevertheless, after 10 minutes or so, when two other passengers arrived, he led us out to the airline's little mini-bus and we all set off for the airfield.

As we sloshed along the road, the scene was eminently dismal. The sea and sky became one indistinguishable mass of heavy, soggy grey and several times there were sections of the road that were so flooded by swollen streams which had burst their banks that our driver slowed the vehicle almost to a standstill to inch his way carefully through the water at well over axle-level. We passed some small settlements where people stood around disconsolately with the flood waters lapping at their knees outside their already inundated homes. I couldn't help feeling that we might be in for a longer wait at the airport than we'd expected. If the plane didn't come and the rain kept up like this, it was quite possible that we wouldn't even be able to make the return trip to Levuka, let alone fly out. We'd be marooned at the airport.

The prospect didn't really worry us. We found that we really liked the island and the township of Levuka. Compared to some of the glossy, expensive resorts in other parts of Fiji, the old capital was streets ahead in atmosphere and beauty.

When we discussed it, it was difficult to decide what we would do to the town and the island if we had a magic wand. It was that same old dilemma of progress versus way of life. You know, the place has loads of 'potential'... that is; history, character, atmosphere, friendly people, and physical beauty. Under the right direction it could be made one of the prime tourist spots of Fiji. But then, maybe it's better left to just continue its slow and dignified slide into obscurity and decay.

Reaching the airport we were told that there was no radio contact with Suva because of the storm. It would just be a matter of wait and see...wait and see if the plane arrived that is. We sat down in the small airport shelter. The wind and rain continued unabated and, sitting gloomily under shelter, looking out at the strip, we began to hope now that the plane wouldn't come. I didn't really fancy the prospect of flying off into that solid bank of ominous grey which blotted out everything. It was worse even than the day we had arrived.

But of course, the plane did come. Typical. When you want them to be on time, planes never are. When you wish they wouldn't arrive, they do. As we ran from the little airport hut out to the plane, we could only pray that it had sufficient working instruments to see us through. The fact that it leaked, with the rain dripping through onto the seats, didn't do much to bolster our confidence.

The pilot was a Brit. It probably sounds a trifle prejudiced, but it made us feel a little safer. Certainly Trish relaxed marginally. Even so, she asked whether it wouldn't be advisable to sit the storm out, here on Ovalau. The pilot smiled, 'Don't worry. We'll fly low and stay under the worst of it. But this will definitely be the last flight of the day.'

As things turned out, the flight wasn't too bad. . . all things being relative. We did stay low. . . around 100-150 metres above the lagoons and coral reefs which now, without the sunshine reflecting and refracting in their waters, looked grey and gloomy. The surface of the water was whipped by the wind, which also tossed the plane around uncomfortably on a couple of occasions. . . particularly on the landing approach to Suva's Nausori Airport.

As the little craft taxied to a standstill on the airport's rain-slicked tarmac, the pilot removed his headset and leant back in his seat. I realised, as he let his hands drop from the controls and relaxed, how intensely he had been concentrating during that short, but not really pleasant flight.

'Well,' he said laconically, 'that was some trip!'

To add to all the rain and the uncertainty, I was, conveniently as usual, suffering from menstrual cramps like you wouldn't believe and had a strong desire to pull a blanket over my head. Instead, we scrambled on a bus going to the township of Nausori where we waited for an hour, sheltering as much as possible in the doorway of an Indian general merchant shop. It was here, next to the marketplace that we were hoping to catch another bus that would take us some 300 kilometres to Nadi at a point almost exactly opposite our present position, on the western side of the island.

Easily disoriented idiots like me are very appreciative of Viti Levu's road system, because it is impossible to become lost. The Queens Road runs from Suva clockwise around the south of the island to Nadi. That's the one most visitors travel and that way lie the major tourist resorts and hotels. The Kings Road runs from Suva anti-clockwise around the northern shore of the island to Nadi. It's unsealed, and there are no great tourist spots. That was the way we were going. It was expected to be an eight-hour trip.

The bus, open-sided, but with roll-down side tarpaulins, was crowded with people and baggage. Again and again, when we travel, we bless our backpacks. Imagine getting onto a bus like that with a hard-edged, angular, regular suitcase. Very out of place and awkward to handle. Packs can be squished, squeezed and shoved into crannies and nooks, sat on, leant against and generally abused and still not show signs of permanent distress.

At 10 a.m. the bus pulled out of Nausori and the rain, which had eased for a while, started up again with renewed vengeance. Down came the side tarpaulins and with them a dank and musty smell. The inside of the bus darkened, as in a cinema before a film showing and in the gloom, the motion of the bus was accentuated to a nauseating degree.

I tried to doze and actually did manage to slip into a state of semi-consciousness from which I was aroused by the pulling up of the blinds and the bright sunlight streaming in. It was like waking to another world. Gone were the omnipresent palms and tropical luxuriant green, replaced by flat open country; the beef and dairy cattle country round Nayavu. The houses were neater and, rather than the scrappy settlements we had seen elsewhere, they were grouped together almost like English villages, with walled gardens.

At Rakiraki, where the road turns west, the bus stopped and we all piled off to buy nibblies from a wide choice of Indian restaurants. Big, doughy rolls filled with hot, spicy, who-knows-what which tasted delicious, especially when followed by fresh fruit and soft drinks. I was starting to get an old familiar craving, which grows and grows when we travel, for a large glass of fresh cold milk. Funny that, because once at home, I don't actually drink so much milk, but then when we're on the road, I also dream of biting into a large juicy, tender steak... and I'm not so much of a meat-eater either. I think it must be that, as we eat more or less anything, anytime, and anywhere, when we travel, I begin to yearn for simple, good, nourishing food.

It was immediately apparent, looking up and down the main street of Rakiraki, that the storekeepers were all, almost without exception, Indian. In the small farming communities we had come through the people were almost all Fijian.

Iain has already pointed out this gradual takeover of Fiji's second-level commercial world by the Indians, but the situation seemed to be more sharply defined in this part of Fiji than some of the others we'd seen. It was almost as if there had been a demarcation line drawn.

The Fijians point to the fact that the Indians run the businesses as an example of what would happen if they were allowed to buy land. The Indians, they warn, would take over the land in the same way, and native Fijians would be ousted. Race relations are not helped by the fact that a Fijian child can fail his or her school leaving certificate three times and still be given another chance at it, whereas the first time Indian students fail, they are out on their ear. Also, Melanesian Fijians hold *Fijian* identification papers while Indian Fijians hold papers which say they are Fiji *Indians*.

While visiting the country, even though often asked, we didn't volunteer any opinions on this very divisive subject. After all, we were guests. But from all we saw and heard, I think I would have to agree with the decision that Fiji Indians should not be allowed to buy land. Yes, I know it is discriminatory and morally wrong. If only life were more simple. But there are no easy answers, only easy questions with complex, sometimes unpalatable solutions. It is difficult not to agree with the Fijians when they worry that the naturally more aggressive nature of the Indians would make it virtually certain that, once allowed to buy land, they would very quickly become the major property holders, with the Melanesian Fijian population reduced to being second-class citizens in their own country. (Indians point out that this is precisely what *they*, the Indians, already are, legally.) What one fears is dispossession, which is what has happened to Australia's aboriginals, which would hardly be acceptable, especially when the world has had the historical advantage of that experience.

Back on the bus and off again with the intermittent heavy rain squalls necessitating frequent raising and lowering of the blinds. The topography of Viti Levu is dramatically influential on the climate of the island. The prevailing currents and wind patterns mean that rain-bearing clouds bump into the mountains of the volcanic heartland, unload their contents and then breeze on along. The result is that the

10 390 sq. kilometre island is divided, climatically, in two. The eastern half gets deluged, while the western half is positively dry.

We had crossed the invisible dividing line and, even though still suffering from the after effects of Cyclone Peni, the change was quite startling. It was the first temperate region vegetation we had seen for months.

The next sizeable town, Ba, is rather more Chinese than Indian. Same busy effect, but different smells. The Chinese are later-comers than the Indians, but have shown the same industrious qualities which make them good citizens anywhere. They are decidedly less interested in politics than are the Indians and not at all anxious about racially discriminatory laws, just as long as business is good. Considering their proportionately tiny number of around 5000, they've made quite a visible impact on Fiji.

By the time we reached Lautoka, the sugar capital of Fiji, I was only holding on by my fingernails, which are insubstantial at the best of times. The last half hour run into Nadi passed in a darkening blur, as the dusk came down like a curtain. After covering that distance, through bad weather and over lousy roads, we still came into Nadi on time at 6.30 p.m. Sometimes I am most appreciative of punctuality.

At the Gateway Motel I had a long, hot shower and fell into bed, past caring about food or wanting to talk to anyone. As I drifted off, I heard Sean, who had returned from a preliminary exploration of the hotel, badgering Iain to have a game of pool with him. Makes me laugh when people ask, 'how do the *children* cope with travelling!'

When we eventually arose the next morning at a leisurely pace and at the unaccustomed hour of 8 a.m., we were well refreshed by a good night's sleep and also pleased to see that the sky was clear and blue once more. Cyclone Peni had apparently dissipated itself on the eastern side of Viti Levu and some of the islands in the Koro Sea. There had been considerable property damage, according to the news, but fortunately no loss of life.

After breakfast, we took a bus into the township of Nadi to do some shopping.

I looked around and eventually found a super digital watch, a sports version for my older boy Guy, who lives in Sydney and was about to turn twenty-two. But that's all we bought...the rest was just window shopping.

During the afternoon we sat around the hotel's small pool, reading, swimming and generally relaxing. There were definitely plenty of other things to see and do in the Nadi/Lautoka area, but we just felt that we'd been on the run for quite a while and wanted a static day.

That evening, after a light dinner of a piece of pineapple and a couple of sandwiches, and after Zara and Sean had gone to bed, Trish and I went to settle the hotel bill and then went upstairs to the bar for a drink. The shuttered windows of the bar and lounge area were pushed wide open and the warm, humid night air flowed around us. There were only three or four other people in the lounge. The lights were low and it was very quiet. Although we had been in many more beautiful places on our way across the Pacific, I remember feeling that night a sense of appreciation of the tropics...a relaxing sensation (it wasn't the booze, I hasten to point out, as I only had one beer)...a sense of comfort, of belonging...an almost womblike, enveloping warmth. A feeling of wanting to stay in the South Pacific and not go back.

We were moving on the next day to the New Hebrides (or Vanuatu as it is now). Only two more stages and then . . . and then Reality with a capital R. It was hard to believe it was coming to an end. We wanted it to go on forever.

# VANUATU (NEW HEBRIDES)

## 22 EFATE
### 'We are moving shortly'

'If you get sick, you have a choice; for good nursing, you go to the British Hospital, for good food, you go to the French Hospital.'

We laughed at Michael Pusinelli's joke. But he didn't. For him it wasn't a joke... just another aspect of life in Vanuatu (New Hebrides)—a chain of beautiful islands with a tragic history, a complex present and an uncertain future.

At the time of our arrival, the islands were still technically the New Hebrides, but elections had been held, the local Vanua'aku party had won and the place was just sitting out the last few months before final independence from France and Britain, who had jointly ruled the territory since 1906 under a unique political system called a 'condominium'. All of the fuss and farce of the rebellion led by Jimmy Stevens on the island of Espiritu Santo, which hit the headlines around the world, was still in the future.

From conversations we had with various people while we were in the capital, Port Vila, however, it wasn't too difficult to see that there was trouble brewing...that underneath what seemed to be a quiet and sleepy exterior, there were many issues and grievances bubbling away that would eventually surface as major problems for the new nation of Vanuatu, as it was eventually to be called.

Vanuatu is one of the bigger island groups in the South Pacific, being spread over some 725 kilometres of ocean and totalling almost 15 000 square kilometres in land area. Port Vila, as the capital, is naturally the largest town and it was here, on the island of Efate, that we landed to spend what turned out to be too few days. The New Hebrides deserved more than we could give it. We really wanted to spend much longer, but our money supply was now getting very low and the really sensible thing, I suppose, would have been to have flown straight to Sydney from Fiji. But we were determined to eke it out for long enough to spend a week or so more on the road and, in any case, it would be madness to overfly the New Hebrides when it was so close to independence. There was also the fact that Michael and Marie Pusinelli were expecting us. So we reasoned away our nerves, shouldering the future aside until tomorrow, when it would no doubt, as it had always done before, take care of itself.

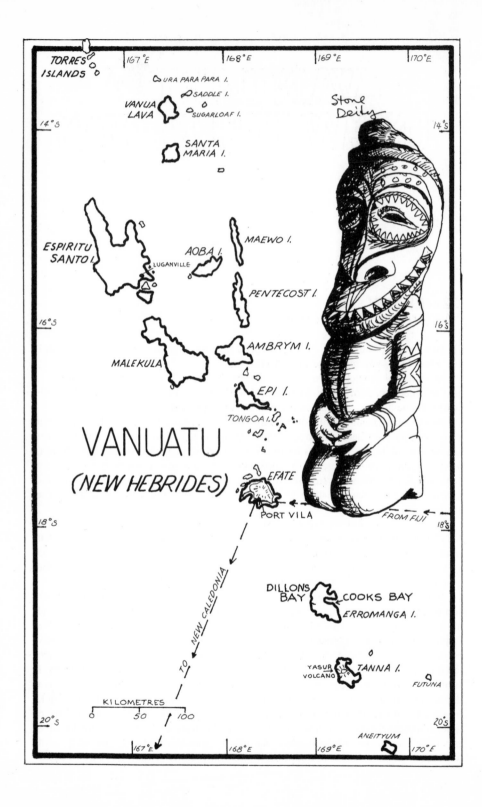

TORRES
ISLANDS

167°E     168°E     169°E     170°E

URA PARA PARA I.

SADDLE I.

VANUA
LAVA

SUGARLOAF I.

14°S                                                                    14°S

SANTA
MARIA I.

Stone
Deity

MAEWO I.

ESPIRITU
SANTO I.

AOBA I.

LUGANVILLE

PENTECOST I.

16°S                                                                    16°S

MALEKULA

AMBRYM I.

EPI I.

TONGOA I.

VANUATU

(NEW HEBRIDES)

EFATE

PORT VILA                              FROM FIJI

18°S                                                                    18°S

TO  NEW CALEDONIA

DILLONS
BAY        COOKS BAY

ERROMANGA I.

YASUR     TANNA I.
VOLCANO

FUTUNA

KILOMETRES

0        50        100

20°S                                                                    20°S

167°E                168°E     169°E     170°E

ANEITYUM

The Pusinellis were friends of Tom and Jenny Moxon, the Australian couple we had met months previously on Easter Island. Tom had cabled us in Fiji from his home in Brisbane to tell us that the Pusinellis were expecting us to look them up when we got there. It always helps a little when you know you're not going to be a total stranger in a new country, not that we'd experienced it very often in any of our previous travels, but we were, nevertheless, quite looking forward to meeting Michael and Marie Pusinelli.

When they weren't at Port Vila's little airport to meet us, as arranged, we took the bus into town and checked ourselves into the cheapest guest house we could find. It was called simply 'The Guest House' and was the private home of Ron and Kate Graham, an Australian couple who had lived in the New Hebrides for some years and who were in the process of extending the house in order to accommodate more guests. The half dozen or so other people staying with them were mainly young students and other single travellers—Australians, Americans and New Zealanders, in their early 20s, who were out enjoying the Pacific and doing it on the cheap.

Kate showed us the bathroom and communal kitchen and apologised for the piles of planks and bricks which were stacked on one side of our large, door-less bedroom. At 900 Francs (about $15) for the four of us, we could hardly complain. We assured her that the piles of building materials didn't worry us in the least.

'It's just like home,' Zara commented.

We asked directions to the Pusinelli's house and set off walking. Although it was only a little after nine in the morning, the heat and humidity were very high and what was intended as an easy stroll became something of a long haul. It was all up-hill and wasn't helped by the fact that our directions weren't very concise. When we turned off the main road to follow a smaller one up an even steeper hill, we were confronted by a fork in the road which we hadn't been told about. One led around a big spur of the hill overlooking Port Vila bay, the other, a dirt road, climbed towards the peak of a hill. The air was very still. There was the buzzing of flies and insects and an occasional bird call, but apart from that, everything was silent. No traffic and no people in sight, although there were a few houses set off the road on either side.

The directions we'd received from Kate Graham did say that the Pusinellis' house was 'very high up', so we decided to take the left-hand fork of the road, the unmade one leading to the top. As we walked, the view became steadily more spectacular. We could see the whole of Port Vila stretching out along the edge of the bay, which is a very attractive harbour. At the top we approached a small, unprepossessing house sitting in a fairly dry bush garden, the vegetation being very similar to the Australian bush, not the lush tropical greenery of Fiji. There was no sign of movement, nor any sound. We began to feel embarrassed about calling on complete strangers at this time on a Sunday morning. Perhaps they were at church—or maybe they were still in bed after a late night out. How could we know?

There was no answer to our knock on the door, so we walked around to the front...or perhaps it was the back of the house...anyway, it was the one with the view facing out over the bay. There was a broad, open patio space where a slim, attractive woman in a bikini was swinging in one of those suspended couches reading a book, while a young, blond child of perhaps 18 months scrambled around amidst a pile of toys beneath her.

'Excuse me,' we called to her. 'We're looking for Michael Pusinelli. Is this the right place?'

She gave a slight start, got down from the swinging chair and came towards us with a smile. 'Yes, it is,' she said. 'But I'm afraid Michael isn't here. He's gone to the airport to meet a family who are arriving on this morning's plane from Fiji.' She paused, looking at us, then at Zara and Sean. There was a flash of revelation. 'You wouldn't be that family, would you?' She smiled even more broadly.

'I'm Marie,' she said and invited us through the child-gate onto the patio where she sat us down and then bustled around for a few mintues preparing some iced coffee for us and lemonade for the children, before sitting down herself again to talk and laugh over the fact that Michael had missed us and was probably scouring the town to find us.

When he eventually arrived, after almost an hour, we learnt that that was exactly what he'd been doing. He looked surprisingly calm after what had been a fairly exasperating start to the day. When he couldn't find us at the airport, he had checked with the immigration officer and found our cards on which we had given the name of the best hotel in town as the place where we would be staying. We'd seen the name on one of the brochures on the plane, but there was no way we would be staying there. I mean, we could hardly put down on the form, 'We'll be looking around for the cheapest place possible.' That sort of official question always begs you to stretch the truth. Anyway, when Michael checked the hotel, of course we weren't there, nor were we in any of the other three or four decent hotels in town. So he'd eventually given up the search and come home.

'Where *are* you staying, then?' he asked.

When we told him, they both expressed surprise...if not quite shock.

'But good heavens...why did you pick that place,' Michael said.

'Simple,' Iain laughed. 'Because it's cheap. It's also perfectly all right. It's reasonably clean and comfortable...and that's all we need.'

'Well, you'd better stay and have lunch with us,' Marie said in a tone of commiseration, as if, because we were staying at the Guest House, we couldn't afford to eat!

It was a delicious, English-style Sunday lunch. Roast beef and veg., but with roast taro in place of potatoes. Michael obviously had absolutely no intention of 'going troppo'...an attitude which I think not altogether without merit. While we ate, he told us how it was that he had come to the New Hebrides.

'I was working with Barclays Bank in England and they offered me the opportunity of coming out here to open their office in Port Vila. I stayed with them for eight years.'

While he talked, I worked out that, as he was not yet 30 (the Moxons had told us this) he must have been only in his very early 20s when he was given the manager's position, which meant that he must have been a fairly highly-regarded young man in the banking world.

He was strikingly handsome, with a well-tended beard, and he looked as Italian as his name suggested. In fact, he told us that he did have Italian forebears, but was now, and his family had apparently been for generations...British to the bootstraps.

Marie, who, we understood, was in her mid-20s, also had an interesting and mixed family background. She grew up in Fiji where she attended a Catholic girls' school.

'It was while I was with Barclays,' Michael was saying, 'that the New Hebrides became a tax haven...mostly for Australians.' He laughed. 'I remember one day a man came in carrying a grip and wearing a haversack. He put them down on the floor and began producing money. We finally counted up a half a million dollars in used Australian banknotes.'

'Wow!' Sean was goggle-eyed.

'We accepted it of course. It was a legal deposit. But it posed us some difficulties. It all had to be sent back to Australia, because officially we can only have a total of two million Australian dollars in circulation here at any one time, so it would have been dangerous for us to release another half million, just like that. We made him wait until we cleared it all back to Australia before we started paying him interest. It took about three months, but I guess the wait was worth it for him. He seemed quite happy about it.'

The intricacies of the whole arrangement were a bit beyond me, but just the idea of this fellow walking into the bank with half a million dollars...cash...was mind-boggling enough. We longed to know his name, but of course, Michael was not able to tell us.

When he left Barclays, Michael took up a job with Trammel Crow, a large American company which is heavily involved in hotels and real estate in the Pacific, and was still the local manager for the organisation at the time of our visit. When we asked, he was not quite sure what changes independence might bring to the New Hebrides but said that he and Marie were just going to sit it out to see, as he put it, 'which way the wind blows.'

Such waiting requires a certain phlegmatic spirit, I feel, not to mention considerable nerve and patience.

'The little troubles we've had,' he said as we quickly finished our ice-cream dessert before it melted in the heat, 'are blown up out of all proportion by the press. Particularly the Australian press. They turn stink-bombs into grenades and sticks into rifles. We listen to Radio Australia and when they report what's happening here it's like listening to them talk about some place we don't know.'

It's not difficult to understand people wanting to stay on. The islands are very beautiful and Port Vila itself, although relatively small and unsophisticated, has great charm. There have, of course, been crazy conflicts and anomalies caused by the joint rule of Britain and France. But the influence of the two cultures has also had its benefits—from the British side a legacy of respect for the rule of law and a well-ordered and relatively uncorrupt civil service. From the French a slightly more cosmopolitan approach to life and a more civilised attitude towards such things as public eating and drinking, liquor laws and so on.

The French wine we had drunk at lunch with the Pusinellis had been a delightful claret, but by 2 in the afternoon, when we left them, both the wine and the intense heat and humidity of the day were beginning to have their effect...on *me* anyway. We walked back down the hill to the Guest House and all had a long afternoon siesta.

In the cooler air of the early evening we took a local bus for the two-kilometre ride into the township of Port Vila to look the place over. All of the major shops and offices are spread along the main waterfront road, Rue Higginson, which fronts onto Vila Harbour, a fine and picturesque sheltered bay. There are two large islands in the harbour, Fila and Iriki. Iriki, at the time of our visit, was the site of the residence of the British commissioner. The French commissioner's office was on the mainland.

The two governments, which were constantly competing with each other, spent a considerable amount of money on public works and building along Rue Higginson in beautification programmes for the waterfront. When we walked through the town that Sunday evening, it could hardly have been more beautiful. Across the harbour, the sun was setting behind the island of Fila. A couple of cruising yachts lay moored close to the shore. There were a few people about, mainly visitors or locals who were just enjoying, as we were, a quiet evening stroll. At one corner of a large, open area which fronted onto the sea wall, a group of gospellers began singing hymns in pidgin English to a sort of rock-rhythm and the accompaniment of guitars. We joined some of the other people to watch and listen for a while.

There was a small Chinese general store not far from where we were staying so, the next morning, we were able to buy some provisions and cook up a hearty breakfast in the Guest House's communal kitchen whose walls were adorned with small notices which had been left by previous guests recommending various cheap places of accommodation right across the Pacific. We wished we'd seen it before we started *our* trip.

We went in to the town again to make contact with a couple of people whose names we'd been given in London before we left for the South Pacific. They were two people who, in a way, crystallised the picture for us of the complex changes the New Hebrides was undergoing as gestation progressed towards the birth of the new nation of Vanuatu. One of them was Chris Turner, a man who had spent almost 25 years in the British colonial service and was, at the time we met him, chief secretary in the Ministry of Finance of the condominium government.

The other was Calcott Matas Kelekele, a representative of the new guard—a young, but influential member of the Vanua'aku Pati, the party which was already the government-elect of the islands and would take power as soon as the day of independence arrived and the ceremonies were all over, in a few months time.

Unfortunately, we were unable to see either of them that morning, but were told, when we called their separate offices, that Chris Turner would be available later in the afternoon and that we could meet Calcott Matas on the following day.

We decided to fill in the time until we could see Chris Turner by taking a bus for a short distance out of town to Erakor Bay for a swim at a beach there. It was pleasant enough; the sun was warm and the water refreshing but it was rather crowded with both locals and tourists and we felt that perhaps we should have gone farther around the island.

Chris Turner turned out to be one of those now anachronistic figures who, although they were quite common in many parts of the world right up till the '50s and early 60s, are a dying breed...the career British colonial civil servant. He had spent 13 years in Tanganyika (Tanzania) then the past 10 years in the New Hebrides.

'I like to keep as far as possible from London,' he smiled. 'In fact, sometimes I even wonder if they know I exist out here.'

We were sitting in his small office in the condominium administration building on Rue Higginson and it was clear that he had got rid of what paperwork he'd had to do for the day, which was now over for him, apart from this chat with us. He was tall and slim...in his mid-40s, I guess, although he looked younger. He was dressed in tropical white shorts, a white, open-necked, short-sleeved shirt, long white socks and, leaning back in his chair, he seemed relaxed, despite the evident frustrations of working for the condominium.

'This is the world's most ridiculous form of government,' he said. 'It's neither one thing nor the other. It's extremely difficult to get anything done here in the normal colonial way, because we've really had *three* governments.'

'Three?' I said. 'You mean French, British...and the new provisional government?'

'Oh no,' he laughed. 'That's made it four. But at least it won't be like this for much longer. With independence, it'll be only one. No...you see, for all the years that I've been here, there've been three administrations...the British, the French and the *joint* government. The British and French have each operated completely separate, and therefore duplicate police forces, health facilities, and education services...to name just a few. But then there have been the joint services where we both co-operate. We join forces in such areas as road building and maintenance, port operations and all of the various forms of transport and communications.'

'One would think,' Trish commented, 'that having the choice between French and British education systems would be a good thing...the competition would keep people on their toes...'

'Yes, you'd think so, but it's been farcical most of the time. I mean having two policemen, a French one and a British one, on point duty directing traffic is a bit ludicrous, don't you think? And yet that has happened here. It became a willy-nilly competitive situation in which Britain, unfortunately, couldn't keep up. You see Britain has *never* spent money on its colonies, but here it has been shamed into doing things and spending money that would never have been done, or spent if France hadn't been pouring it in.' He leant forward across his desk as if offering a confidence. 'Look, since 1970, France has spent more on education here than Britain has in the entire time we've been here. France has spent huge amounts of money on new schools, new teachers, free food, showers in the schools, free boarding schools...it's incredible.'

'Winning hearts and minds,' I said.

'Yes, but it applies also right through the government. The total budget for these islands is about $50 million a year. Of that, about $15 million comes from local revenue, France puts in $25 million, while Britain puts in less than ten! The British tend to treat everyone in the colonies as if they're in some great game park: "Splendid-chaps-out-there; don't-interfere-with-them... just-let-them-get-on-with-it" sort of approach. The French, on the other hand, are quite lavish with their money. Their civil service is very well looked after.'

'You sound a little bitter about it?' I noted.

'No, not bitter,' he smiled. 'I enjoy it here. I have a good life. But, if you're a district agent on Santo, for instance, and you see your French equivalent, often doing only half the amount of work you're doing, but getting *six* times the salary, you can't help feeling just a little put out. Anyway, it's all academic now...there'll just be one government and one civil service.'

'What about all the French and British administrators...people like yourself...will they stay on? Will you stay on?'

'Well, I'm hoping to. I'm hoping for some sort of job in the new government...perhaps in the finance ministry again. I think the new government will need some of the expertise that's been developed here over the past few years.'

'You mean in the tax haven business?'

He paused. 'Finance centre has a better ring to it, I think,...but...yes. The new government will probably offer taxation concessions to Australians and other businessmen who bring money here, but it's got problems also. There was a danger at one time of the Mafia moving in...casinos, all that sort of thing. And the land situation almost got out of hand.'

'How?'

'Well, for a while, foreign land developers...speculators really, began to move in and buy up land. One in particular, an American—Eugene Peacock— bought huge tracts of land...thousands of hectares, from locals at ridiculously low prices, then subdivided them and began offering them for sale in Hawaii and the United States on the 'never-never' plan. But the condominium stopped it all. They could see that he would have created a series of Hawaiian-type towns, full of Europeans, or Americans, where the locals, the indigenous New Hebrideans would have been just the domestic servants...the gardeners, cooks and so on...and then, naturally, as the differences in lifestyle became more apparent, it would also breed thieves and petty criminals.'

'But how could people...foreigners...just come in and buy land like that? In most of the Pacific islands we've seen....Fiji in particular, the locals have a very tight grip on virtually all the land.'

He leant back in his chair again, putting his hands behind his head. 'It's been different here. Foreigners have been allowed to buy land from local owners and then, after waiting for two years, apply to have freehold title approved for it. But that's all changing. In fact the Vanua'aka party, the new government elect, promised in their election platform that they would resume a lot of foreign-owned land.'

'That'd be a bit of a shock for overseas investors, wouldn't it?'

'Right. But that's what's likely to happen...and I suppose we'll just have to wait and see how everybody reacts.'

These conflicts between the Europeans and the *indigènes,* and also, as it happens, between the locals themselves, in the islands are probably more deep-seated than they would seem in Port Vila, the relatively cosmopolitan and Westernised capital. On the island of Espiritu Santo (or Santo as it is called more commonly), the secessionist movement led by Jimmy Tupou Patuntun Stevens...the self-styled chief president Moses, was more than just a joke. The world was to discover this, only weeks before the New Hebrides independence, when he launched his revolution and declared Santo's secession from the rest of the islands in the group.

On several of the other islands also the inhabitants are not particularly friendly to strangers...particularly Europeans and, in some areas, they are surprisingly primitive. For instance, there are the islanders on Pentacost, north of Efate, who are world-renowned for their daring 'land diving'. In a real dice with death, the men tie one end of long bush vines to their ankles, the other to the top of a 25-metre-high timber tower, then hurl themselves from the tower to plunge, head-downwards towards the earth. Hopefully the vines are just long enough...or just *short* enough...to bring them to a bone-jarring, shuddering halt a mere few centimetres from certain death. There have been fatal errors, and of course there is great pressure on the jumpers to be the one who skims closest to eternity. A display of extreme macho, the terrifying performance is a mix of primitive indigenous as well as Christian religious ceremonies.

Then, on the island of Tanna to the south, there is the John Frum cult whose adherents believe that a man of that name will come to deliver them from the influence of European interlopers in general and Christian missionaries in particular. The arrival of American troops in the islands during 1940 and '41, bringing with them their trucks, fridges, canned food and cigarettes, persuaded them that these goodies were freely available to everyone in the outside world and that only the presence of Europeans prevented them from being around for the Tannese too. Many of the islanders still hold to this 'cargo cult', an innocent enough belief, and though they haven't recently displayed open hostility to foreigners, their child-like, but very understandable idea, simmers away not far beneath the surface.

Also simmering away, like some constant geographical counterpoint to all this, is Tanna's active volcano, Mt Yasur. It has been quiescent enough for the past 100 years to persuade visitors that it is safe enough to climb to the rim of the crater, there to look down into the bubbling sulphuric cauldron.

North again, and a little to the west of Pentacost, on the island of Malekula are the more reticent tribes of the Little and Big Nambas, whose men wear nothing more than a G-string and a boastful penis-guard. Both of these tribes, although often at war with each other, have stayed aloof from the mainstream of modern-day life in the rest of the New Hebridean group. Surprising, really, to be still able to find tribes like these, some three and a half centuries after the first Western contact.

The first European to clap eyes on the island chain was the Spanish explorer Pedro Fernandez de Quiros. That was in 1606. He stayed for 55 days, during which time he named the largest island 'Australia del Espiritu Santo' and planned a future city called La Nueva Jerusalem. But his dream of a New Jerusalem was doomed from the start, for despite the sturdy stockade he had erected and the high masses and fireworks with which the settlement was inaugurated, he seems to have overlooked a rather basic requirement to its ongoing viability—there were no women on his expedition's ships! Perhaps his Mum had never told him, and he believed the story of the stork, whatever the reason, the idea expired from sterility and de Quiros sailed on into history.

It was a further 160 years before the French explorer Bougainville paid only a passing visit and, once again, it was left to the indefatigable Captain James Cook to chart the islands eight years later, in 1774. With a fine disregard for the disparateness of the population, who certainly didn't think of themselves as having a great deal in common with each other, Cook lumped them all together and called them the New Hebrides. Not really very original.

The great pass on and, as so often happens, it is left to smaller, meaner people to take advantage of what they've left behind. In this instance those people were *much* smaller and meaner. They were the blackbirders. Even the name is racially insulting.

By the time the first blackbirder visited the New Hebrides, half-way through the 1800s, the missionaries had come to stay and, if it hadn't been for these people of God, perhaps the depredations of the slave traders would have been even greater. As it was, they were terrible enough.

In 1847 whaling ships from Twofold Bay in New South Wales stopped off in the islands and New Hebrideans were 'recruited' to work as shepherds on Ben Boyd's properties in the Monaro district of New South Wales. The dreadful commerce in human flesh had begun.

In the next 30 years, 7200 New Hebrideans were taken to Queensland to work as labourers, 4500 went to Fiji to work in the sugar and cotton plantations and 2000 went to New Caledonia. Many died, either en route, or on foreign soil due to disease, inhuman conditions and homesickness. The comparatively few who did return often brought with them new diseases which played havoc among innocent islanders.

Aghast at this awful de-population, missionaries begged the governments of their home countries, France and Britain, to come to the islanders' aid. Their pleas were met with stone-faced indifference. The French even mooted the idea that freed convicts from New Caledonia should be re-settled in the New Hebrides. This seems to have been the thing which finally pushed for the creation of a protest movement in Australia which agitated for Britain and France to stop the slave traffic and take responsible charge of the New Hebrides.

There was much political to-ing and fro-ing, which was finally resolved in 1906, due in large part to Anglo-French fear of expanding German influence in the Pacific, when Britain and France agreed to govern the islands jointly. Neither of them wished to take sole responsibility or was willing to let the other one do so either. A childish dog-in-the-manger attitude, which we were to discover persisted through more than 70 years of joint administration.

The New Hebrides seems, in retrospect, to have fallen foul of much that is petty and cruel in our culture. It is certainly not a history of which either Europe or Australia can be proud.

That evening, on our way back to the Guest House from our talk with Chris Turner we stopped off at the little Chinese general store and bought some pork chops and vegetables to cook up on the small stove in the Guest House kitchen. Both Zara and Sean were sitting in the big communal room when we got back, engrossed in magazines. They'd hardly noticed that we'd been gone. There were piles of Australian, English, and New Zealand magazines and they were devouring them one by one.

After dinner I played a couple of games of Chinese checkers with them both and we all went to bed early. I recall thinking though, that evening, about how the patterns of one's life can change within days. In less than a week we would be back in Sydney, adjusting to new patterns and trying to fit into a city we hadn't seen for two and a half years. Simple days of doing and seeing things would become more complex. Making a living would once again take precedence over everything else. Zara and Sean would be back at school. There'd be music lessons, squash, football, ballet, homework. . . the whole pattern would be radically changed, and I must admit I had very mixed feelings about it all.

In the morning we went out to the offices of U.T.A. airlines in the town to check on flights to New Caledonia. They told us that the only plane we could take out of Vila, unless we wanted to wait more than a week, was one which left Port Vila late that same afternoon. It wasn't much of a choice really. We had wanted to spend a couple of days visiting Tanna, and possibly Santo, but eight or nine days in our present financial situation was unfortunately a little too long. We accepted the afternoon flight and firmed up the bookings.

Then we went off to meet Calcott Matas. We'd arranged an appointment at the headquarters of the Vanua'aku party, which at that stage occupied second-floor rooms in a small office building at one end of the town. The rooms were a bit of a shambles, littered with election pamphlets and posters. There were cardboard boxes full of various political advertising and promotional materials for their party, as well as dozens of other posters from various Third World countries and several revolutionary organisations.

Calcott Matas was not there when we arrived so we spoke for some minutes to Hilda Lini, a woman very prominent in the party and also the youngest sister of the prime minister elect, Father Walter Lini.

She gestured to the mess of papers and pamphlets scattered all over the floor and the desks. 'We are moving shortly,' she explained a trifle apologetically. 'That's why the place is in such a mess. We're just packing it up.'

'Moving' seemed a rather modest way of putting it. The party was in the process of taking over a country. Quite a move!

Calcott Matas arrived a few minutes later. He was a slim, dark, bearded man with glasses. He was only in his early 30s, we estimated, but he had considerable 'presence'. He sat down without any hesitation in front of a large flag of green, black, yellow and red which was hanging on one wall. . . the flag of the new nation of Vanuatu. It was almost as if *he* was the new leader.

'I am sorry our prime minister is not here,' he said. 'I am sure he would have liked to have talked with you. Unfortunately he is in Europe at the moment.'

'There is a lot of work for everyone to do, I imagine. . . before you take over the reins of government,' I said.

'Yes, that's true. It will be a difficult time, because both Britain and France will continue to compete for influence and we must try to remain friends with both of them. It will be hard because there are some steps we must take that will be unpopular.'

He seemed to speak with some authority on the party's behalf and yet we wondered what role he personally would be playing. We had heard that he had been a very effective and prominent figure in the successful election campaign waged by the Vanua'aku party and that he had played a significant part in formulating the party's platform and policies, yet he was apparently not an elected member of the new parliament.

'I had been fulfilling roles that could be described as shadow minister for information and also, at times, spokesman on areas such as land and education,' he explained when we asked about his future in the government, 'but I did not stand for election and I will not be playing any part here after the next two weeks.'

'But why not?' I asked. 'Surely, you have...'

He smiled and held up his hand. 'I am going to Papua New Guinea, to university there, for two years, to study law. It's a post-graduate course. I think it will be very helpful for me when I return.'

'To practise law?' Trish asked.

He smiled. 'Not necessarily.'

'In the government then?'

'Well, I would hope so. I think I have something to offer...but I feel a need for a greater understanding of the law, before I become too involved in politics.'

If only a few more politicians felt the same way, I thought. And were prepared to spend two years of their lives developing that understanding.

The conversation shifted on to the new government and how it would work when independence came...what changes it might institute.

'Of course, many people have suggested that we would be able to play the French off against the British and vice versa...and thereby benefit from both sides, but that is a tricky game,' Calcott said. 'I think that we'll keep good relations with them both, but at the same time adopt a slightly more independent foreign policy under which we wouldn't necessarily be identified with any major power block.'

One of the party workers from another room brought in a pot of tea and several cups, but Calcott Matas kept talking as we poured ourselves a cup each and one for him. 'As far as the economy of the place is concerned,' he said, 'most of the enterprises here are dominated by overseas interests. We want to have a bigger local share in those organisations...51 per cent is normal, I believe, in your own country and many others...and that would be all right for us...even 49 per cent in some cases. But we can't change those things overnight. That will take time. The main shock, I think, will be land.'

'Land?'

'Yes, land is the crucial issue here, between islanders and foreigners... and also between islanders and local Europeans. Some of our best land has been alienated from the people of these islands and that is not good. We will change that...' He paused for a moment. 'But we will do it carefully...so as not to disrupt the country and cause economic turmoil. Nevertheless, I think it will be an upsetting time when we begin to transfer the important pieces of land back.'

'Do you feel the islands will stay unified under the new government?' Trish asked. 'I was thinking particularly about the secessionist movement on Santo.'

'Jimmy Stevens is just a troublemaker,' Calcott Matas said. 'He is just an actor. There is nothing he can do. If he tried to take over Espiritu Santo and secede, we would just step in and take it back over. It is an integral part of Vanuatu.'

As things turned out, however, it just wasn't as simple as that. When Jimmy Stevens and his followers *did* take over on Santo in June, 1980, capturing 19 French and British police officers in the process, then disarming and expelling them from the island, it took weeks before Santo was re-taken, and then it was necessary for a detachment of troops to be sent from Papua New Guinea to do the job. Britain and France studiously avoided becoming involved in the squabble. . . a squabble which could easily re-surface again to trouble the young Vanuatu at any time.

Leaving Calcott Matas we went to see Marie Pusinelli at the Hotel Rossi where she worked, in the centre of town, to tell her we were moving on. After saying goodbye and thanking her again for the Sunday lunch, we went to Mike's office, a little farther along Rue Higginson, to repeat the process and then, collecting our gear from the Guest House, we took a cab to the airport where we were informed that the aircraft had not arrived. It had apparently developed some technical troubles in Noumea and would be delayed by about three hours.

Eventually when our plane, a Fokker Friendship, arrived to carry us to Noumea, our last stopping place between Santiago and Sydney, we were told that the technical fault in the plane had been 'a faulty horizon'—a twentieth-century malady which we hoped would not afflict Vanuatu.

164° E   165° E   166° E   167° E   168° E

*BELEP I.*

20°S

POUM

*KOUMAC*

OUAC

HEINGHENE

OUVÉA

21°S

KONÉ

HOUAILOU

LIFOU I.

THIO

BOURAIL

22°S

TONTOUTA
AIRPORT

YATÉ

MARÉ I.

*TO SYDNEY*

*NOUMEA*

CAPE QUEEN
CHARLOTTE

*Ritual
Mask*

ISLE OVEN

ISLE OF
PINES

FROM NEW HEBRIDES/VANUATU

NEW
CALEDONIA

KILOMETRES
0   10   20

164° E   165° E   166° E   167° E   168° E

# NEW CALEDONIA

## 23 NOUMEA
### A foretaste of what *could* happen

For a man who stood head and shoulders above all the other navigators of his time, who showed such skill and daring, not to mention indefatigable energy, Captain James Cook was surprisingly short on imagination when it came to the naming of the islands he 'discovered' and surveyed.

The story goes that on seeing pine trees on barren cliffs, he named the second biggest island in the Pacific (only New Zealand is larger), New Caledonia because it reminded him of Scotland. Obviously he had been at sea too long, or perhaps home-sickness prejudiced his sight.

That all happened in 1774, but New Caledonia, which consists of four island groups (the main island, at whose southern end is the capital Noumea, the Loyalty Islands, the Huon Islands and the Isle of Pines), had been inhabited by a fierce tribe of cannibal Melanesians for many hundreds of years before Europeans sailed over the horizon, faulty or otherwise.

It's been estimated that the islands supported a population of up to 70 000 resulting from migrations from Papua and Polynesia. This number dropped considerably with the arrival of Europeans and the attendant breakdown of the supportive tribal lifestyle. It has only climbed again in this century, so that the most recent figures show a population of almost 60 000 Melanesians, and 55 000 Europeans, with the overall population figure of 145 000 reached with smaller groupings of Wallis Islanders, Tahitians, Indonesians and Vietnamese.

By the middle of the nineteenth century the French and British were jockeying for control in the Pacific and New Caledonia, with its large land mass, looked very enticing indeed, though neither of them wanted to make the financial and military commitment involved in an actual land grab unless it seemed that the other was about to move in. There was talk in France about its suitability as a penal settlement. It was also pointed out that it was within striking distance of Australia, which already had a burgeoning trade with Europe. Still, it would look a little better if, at least on the surface, a charitable, rather than a purely mercantile reason could be given for the takeover.

Every now and then a French missionary, let's be blunt. . .Catholic missionary, for after all much of the power play between Catholic France and Protestant Britain was a thinly-disguised religious war...would end up in the local stew. This caused pressure from inside France for the government to annex the islands, not only to protect French missionaries, but of course to more easily bring the word of God to the heathen. The word also being that it was simply 'not on' to go around eating people, especially not French people.

The final excuse came in 1850 when a French survey ship, the *Alcmene,* was attacked and the entire crew killed and eaten. Frogs' legs! Outraged, the French reciprocated by raising the French flag and declaring the islands an overseas territory of France, which is what they still are today. They then set about turning New Caledonia into a penal settlement.

Perhaps my values are up the spout, but the idea of pinching someone else's country and then, by force of arms, using it as a prison for the overflow from your own jails, as Britain did with Australia, has always seemed the veritable peak of barbarity. It's like dumping your excrement on someone else's lounge room carpet. *Worse* than eating human flesh.

Anyway, that's what they did. During the 33 years of its abuse as a penal settlement, 40 000 prisoners of La Belle France were transported to New Caledonia. Many of these were political prisoners, victims of the wars which were sweeping back and forth across Europe at the time. They were garrisoned either at Ducos, near Noumea, the Isle of Pines, some 150 kilometres off the southern tip of the main island or, worst of all, on the infamous Île Nou, in Noumea Harbour.

None of this did much to improve the humour of the inhabitants (would it yours?) who remained so hostile to the French that there were continual confrontations, many of them with a sizeable loss of life and the last being as recently as 1917.

It's amazing that, after this mutually antagonistic start, the islanders fought for France in both World Wars. People are endlessly extraordinary!

Perhaps a major reason for this change of heart was the discovery in 1863 of nickel. By 1870 a nickel rush was on and, in the rapid changeover to a cash economy, many New Caledonians no doubt felt that, 'if you can't beat them, then you may as well join them,' and that way take advantage of what they have to offer.

And what the profits from the nickel industry had to offer becomes abundantly clear from the moment you land at New Caledonia's Tontouta International Airport. What with the delay in take-off and a flight so bumpy that, for one mad moment I thought it might have been preferable to make the 1100 kilometre crossing from Vanuatu on board the *Mataora,* by the time we landed at Tontouta, I wasn't feeling exactly in the mood to be impressed. But, almost against my will, I was. The size and style of the airport was the first thing, then the uniforms and efficiency of the officialdom, the comfort of the large air-conditioned bus, which was the only way of getting into Noumea, and of course, again the exorbitant prices which the French seem to bring to all their ex and present colonies...from Djibouti to French Polynesia...as a seemingly inescapable concommitant of French bread and Gallic manners. The bus ride was our first shock—$8 each!

It was dark, so we saw nothing of the countryside, but we were aware that the vehicle was running on the best roads we had seen in the whole Pacific. Even though we knew the island was almost 400 kilometres long and about 50 kilometres wide, we reached the end of the one-hour drive surprised to have been able to take such a long ride on a Pacific island without ending up back where we had started. We could see that we were approaching the largest and most modern city in the Pacific, with the exception of those in Hawaii and New Zealand. Tall street lights, sidewalks, kerbs, gutters and seemingly more cars than we had seen on the entire journey. At the end of a seven-kilometre stretch of American-style freeway, the town itself could have been mistaken for a town in Europe, it had so many of the trappings of twentieth-century living. In the well lit fronts of boutiques and *magazins,* chic imported fashions were displayed by fibreglass mannequins. It looked incredibly wasteful to have all that electricity blazing away. There were streets lined with restaurants, *super-marchés,* hotels, and high-rise apartments and office buildings. There were white people in smart suits and natty little 'after-five' numbers.

In my none-too-settled mind it seemed appropriate that this should be our last stop in the Pacific before home. After all the gentle low-key living we'd seen on the other islands, this looked like a grim forecast of what could happen all the way back across to Santiago if they're not careful. Though of course that can't really be. For nature has been bountiful to New Caledonia and no other place in the Pacific has her wealth of resources. Or at least if they have, then luckily it's yet to be discovered.

In the Caledonia Hotel we took a room with three beds for $20. In the morning it was already steamy hot by 8 a.m. when we smuggled some long loaves of delicious fresh-baked bread back under the patrician nose of our landlady. With her badly-dyed flame-red hair, which was pulled back tightly into a chignon, and her black dress which equally snuggly fitted all her curves, she looked like all Parisienne concierges are supposed to look!

Then I retreated to bed and oblivion. . .all the better to cosset my nervous anticipation of returning home, while Iain and the children went off to the Qantas office to arrange our tickets to Sydney. I'd never seen Zara and Sean so anxious that tickets should be bought!

When they returned, with the smile of satisfied people, the future secure, or so they imagined, in their pockets, we all went out again to take a bus a few kilometres to the beach at Anse Vata.

Before taking the bus, we had a snack in a small café of the sort which always proliferate around bus stations. We also had a *conversation!* more a monologue really, or at least a 'duo-logue'—Iain and I doing the responsible parent bit. We tried to explain how, especially for Sean, this return to Australia was a step into a new and more demanding way of life. In two weeks time he would start high school and, as all parents know, this marks a turning point in a young person's life. Sean, who has a greater capacity for enjoying life than anyone else I know, listened dutifully to us telling him that we expected him to try his very hardest at school and not to let his effervescent nature lead him into troubled waters. Yes, there would be surfboards and skateboards, barbeques, his mates and football but there would also be school and homework, trumpet and piano lessons, and the necessity to pull his weight and live up to his responsibilities (why did it all sound so clichéd!). We included Zara in all this, although she had already done her first year of high school in England, so that it wasn't quite such a traumatic step for her and, anyway, so far, she has hardly ever needed to be encouraged. In fact, it's rather the opposite. She needs more hours than there are in the day just to fit everything in.

I think that both Iain and I were also preparing *ourselves* for their entering that period of assertion of their individuality which is necessary for them to become young adults. By 'preparing' I mean as prepared as any parent can ever be, which for me is mostly a matter of gritting my teeth and for Iain of being philosophical!

'You've had a good trip,' Iain was saying, 'and the biggest thankyou we could get from you is for you both to do well at school and at home in the coming year...'

'...why's that man wearing that little hat?' Sean asked. !!?

The man behind the counter was wearing a little white cotton skull cap.

'It means he's a haji...' I began and then stopped myself. 'Now listen,' I said, turning on Sean sternly, 'did you take in any of what I was just saying...about next year?'

'Oh yes, Dad...you don't need to worry...everything'll be okay. What's a haji?'

I think I must have emitted a sigh of exasperation and sat back in my chair. Trish said nothing.

'Well?' Sean persisted.

'Well, he's an Arab...or a Muslim rather, and whenever Muslim men wear a little white hat like that, it means that at some stage in their lives they have been to Mecca on a pilgrimage. Mecca is the holiest place in the world for all Muslims...like Jerusalem is for Christians.'

'But what's an Arab doing here?' Sean asked. 'I've seen others wearing those hats.'

'It's one of those historical quirks...like the Indians in Fiji.'

'You mean they were brought here to work...like the British did with the Indians in Fiji?'

'Right. It's not *exactly* the same situation, but you see France used to have a lot of colonies too...like Britain. Several of France's colonies were the Arab countries of North Africa. They're independent now, but in France and in various other places around the world where France still has colonies or dependencies, you find Arabs who have either been brought there to work, or migrated themselves to work or start businesses. There are also quite a few Vietnamese here. Vietnam was once one of France's possessions.'

Through the window of the little café we saw our bus pull in to the stand opposite and we left to board it for the five or six kilometres run out to the beach. Sitting in the bus as it rolled along out of the city and along through the coastal suburbs, I thought about the man in the café. It had seemed perfectly natural—when I explained it all to Sean—that French-speaking Arabs should be here in French New Caledonia...after all, the Pacific was full of non-indigenous Chinese and Europeans...why not Arabs? Yet, somehow, he seemed out of place.

It was more than likely just a prejudice on my part, because my feelings had no relevance to reality. New Caledonia has an extraordinarily polyglot population of which less than half are Melanesian. The big influx of out-siders, nearly all of French nationality, from France, North Africa, the French Caribbean nations and Tahiti, began as recently as the 1960s with the planned massive expansion of the nickel industry. It changed Noumea, almost overnight, into the most urbanised, industrialised city in the South Pacific islands.

New Caledonia has become, after Canada, the second-largest producer of nickel in the world. All of its production goes to Japan. The island also possesses large deposits of chrome, iron, manganese and cobalt. The tremendous income generated by the nickel industry has been a mixed blessing. On the one hand it has pushed living standards up, at least in the urbanised areas around Noumea, but on the other, it has brought extremely high prices, which have tended to discourage tourism, an industry the country has come to rely on as its second most important income earner. New Caledonia was also significantly affected in this area (tourism) during the early 70s by boycott action against French shipping and airline companies to protest France's nuclear test programme in the eastern Pacific.

Our landlord—or owner, or manager, or whatever he was—at the hotel where we were staying didn't seem overly concerned about the issue of nuclear testing. In the small lobby of the hotel he proudly displayed two large, poster-sized colour photographs of a couple of the biggest above-ground atomic explosions on Muraroa atoll. He obviously felt the test programme in French Polynesia could not affect tourism in Noumea. And in the late 70s and early 80s, maybe he was right. The average number of tourists visiting Noumea each year had climbed back up to 40 000—many of them Australians travelling on cruise ships.

The bus ride to Anse Vata, which is a few kilometres to the south of the city, was brief but pleasant. It took us past three attractive bays; Baie de la Moselle, Baie de l'Orphelinat and Baie des Citrons, all of which were fairly urbanised or sub-urbanised, with hotels, apartments and houses dotted around yacht basins, marinas and beaches. The air was one of considerable affluence. At Anse Vata, a long, narrow beach, we swam out and played for a while on three floating platforms...rafts which were anchored to the bottom about 100 metres from the shore, then sat back on the sand sunning ourselves and watching the wind-surfers sailing higgledy-piggledy amongst the bathers. Some of the sailors were experts, but others couldn't even get started.

A man on the beach was hiring the sail-powered surfboards for 500 Francs (about $7) an hour. Doing some quick arithmetic, I concluded that what he was doing would take some beating as a means of making a relaxed living. He had 30 wind-surfers available for hire. There were never less than 20 of them out at a time. That's $140 an hour! At only five hours a day, (and he was there much longer than that) he's making $700 a day...almost $5000 a week...a quarter of a million a year. Not bad! I started having visions of sitting on the beach at Surfers, or somewhere along the N.S.W. coast, just living off wind-surfers. I'm a little prone to daydreams.

At this stage of our lives, I suppose it was excusable, at least to some degree. We had no real idea how we were going to pull ourselves out of the financial hole we were in. The trip was all but over now and the real world was charging in at us. We would have to admit that the New Hebrides (Vanuatu) and New Caledonia didn't really get the time or attention we wanted to give them...and they deserved. But that's life. A trip of this nature, of this distance and duration of time, is a complex thing, depending on a great many factors—personalities, temperaments, time available, and, of course, money. We'd spent a lot of money doing it, but then, for four people travelling for four months and covering some 20 000 kilometres of the South Pacific, you'd expect to.

It's a little difficult, though, to think of it with any degree of equanimity when the money's all gone and you're not sure where the next lot is coming from. A book like this? Sure. But it all takes time. . . something like 18 months or more, when you consider the writing and the publishing time lags. And we were facing the 'now' problems.

In any event, as we returned to the hotel that day from the beach, we were very aware of the fact that this was our last day. We bought some French bread, some beautiful Camembert cheese and some fruit. We ate in our room, washed some clothes and hung them out to dry, then lay on our beds and read. Everyone was quiet. There was an air of expectancy.

Next morning we ate our breakfast (more Camembert!) and waited for our clothes to dry properly in the morning sun, then packed up our gear and, after checking out of the hotel, carried our packs around to the airport bus depot which was nearby.

On the ride out from Noumea to Tontouta Airport we travelled in daylight this time and had a good view of the lush, green countryside and the mountains rising to the east. Looking at the map in one of the small brochures we had, we felt great regret at having to just zip into New Caledonia and zip out again. There was so much more of the island to see and, from everything we'd read, the rest of it was far better and more beautiful. Away from the urbanised and industrialised centres near Noumea, there are many Melanesian communities which still remain relatively isolated, making their livings by subsistence agriculture and fishing. We wondered for how long, though. Some of the mountains we could see through the windows of the bus showed obvious signs of having been terraced. But it was equally clear that the terraces, and their supporting irrigation systems, used for over hundreds of years to grow taro, were falling into disrepair. Again I thought it somehow symbolic that the last island we visited on our journey across the South Pacific should be the one on which traditional Pacific culture was being most quickly eroded.

The airport lounge was crowded when we arrived there and the air thick with Australian accents. I experienced a sudden mixture of depression and exhilaration at meeting Australians en masse for the first time in two and a half years. They appeared so confident and affluent. Of huge proportions. I felt shrunken and timorous.

Worse was to come. The plane turned out to be a 'Fun Jet'. Oh, dear! And all the stewards, sun-tanned and unself-consciously egalitarian, wore casual shirts in tropical designs. I felt as though I had been caught in a time-warp. . .that I came from a bygone century, or at least from a bygone culture. Which I guess is true! They were all very friendly and helpful and kept offering drinks. And I thought I might burst into tears. Stupid!

Over the intercom, once we were in the air, the captain told us that his name was Dave. Not David. Dave. And that the flight service director was Grant, but that we should call him Curly. I ventured a quick glance at Zara and Sean and was comforted to see that they too were suffering a little culture shock, feeling bombarded and set back on their heels.

But all these feelings quickly passed. Zara pored through the aircraft's stock of magazines. Sean asked for cards and games and settled back to entertain himself. Iain and I talked spasmodically, both of us with unsettled emotions.

We looked back over the South Pacific, fast finishing its final lap beneath us and agreed that, more than any other part of the world in which we have been fortunate enough to travel, it would be remembered by us for its people. Whether they were Rapa Nuian, Tahitian, Tongan, Samoan, Fijian or Cook Islander, we found that they regarded all of the islands of this great ocean as their home. And, in keeping with the enormous size of their territory, they themselves tended to be somewhat larger than life, embarrassingly hospitable and always friendly.

It had been very rewarding for us to be able to view the rest of the world from the perspective of a Pacific Islander. New York, London and Sydney quickly became rather insignificant and their values somewhat questionable, when seen from places like Mitiaro or Rangiroa. Being an independent, small nation at this end of the twentieth century has many hazards, but it was heartening to find that the peoples of the Pacific have withstood the awful shocks of their 'discovery' as well as they have. It's this display of stamina they've shown that gives me confidence that they will cope with what the next century brings, perhaps even more successfully than other parts of the world.

As far as we were concerned. . . I guess I felt reasonably sure that we would cope too. Even knowing the immediate problems that awaited us, Iain and I discussed future travel. It seems that the more we travel, the more we realise how little we have seen and how much more there is to experience. Travel is something of a drug. Sitting in one place for too long brings on severe withdrawal symptoms for us, but fortunately both Iain and I are equally addicted. Sometimes I wonder if it is a lack in us which makes us feel we must uproot ourselves yet again. Are we searching for something? Nirvana perhaps? Or maybe trying to fulfil a childhood dream of discovering lost worlds both inside and outside ourselves. More than likely it's just that we are grossly irresponsible!

Whatever the motivation was, we were pleased to find that we were still able to experience at this time that great sense of achievement and fulfilment at having completed a long journey. It had been a very different one from our other family journeys in Africa and South America in that we had made long hops by aircraft on this trip, but there had also been some rough patches. . . notably the voyage on the *Mataora*. In any event, we were certainly left with the feeling of having covered an immense distance.

For us, this long, slow travel over large areas is extremely satisfying. . . the only way to go. We've found that what is instantly achievable is also instantly forgettable. The most rewarding things in life are those which have to be laboured over.

The vastness of the Pacific Ocean—its majesty, the beauty of its islands and the complex and intriguing story of its peoples—were things that had now lodged in our consciousness. . . an experience and understanding that was there now, as a memory that could never be erased. I would like to think that it will surface frequently, not just as a reminder of happy and fascinating days, but as an inspiration to return to the islands of the South Pacific.